Augustine

CONFESSIONS

Translated, with
Introduction and Notes, by
Thomas Williams

Hackett Publishing Company, Inc.
Indianapolis/Cambridge

For further information, please address
 Hackett Publishing Company, Inc.
 P.O. Box 44937
 Indianapolis, Indiana 46244-0937

 www.hackettpublishing.com

Cover design by Brian Rak
Interior design by Elizabeth L. Wilson
Composition by Aptara, Inc.

Cataloging-in-Publication data can be accessed via the Library of Congress
Online Catalog.

ISBN-13: 978-1-62466-783-1 (cloth)
ISBN-13: 978-1-62466-782-4 (pbk)

The paper used in this publication meets the minimum requirements of American
National Standard for Information Sciences—Permanence of Paper for Printed
Library Materials, ANSI Z39.48–1984.

∞

Contents

Introduction   vii

   1. Augustine's life, thought, and influence   viii

   2. Putting together Augustine's *Confessions*   xi

   3. Intertextuality and Augustine's use of Scripture   xvii

Essential Scriptures   xxv

Notes on the Latin Text   xxviii

Notes on the Translation   xxx

Abbreviations   xxxiii

Suggestions for Further Reading   xxxiv

   Book One   1

   Book Two   19

   Book Three   29

   Book Four   43

   Book Five   61

   Book Six   78

   Book Seven   98

   Book Eight   119

   Book Nine   139

   Book Ten   163

   Book Eleven   202

   Book Twelve   224

   Book Thirteen   249

Appendix A: Psalm 4   279

Appendix B: Psalm 41   280

Appendix C: Psalm 100   281

Appendix D: *Reconsiderations*, Book 2, Chapter 6   282

Topical Index   283

Scriptural Index   289

Introduction

The *Confessions* is a prayer: a prayer of avowal, a prayer of thanksgiving and praise, and a prayer of repentance. For these are the three meanings of the Latin verb *confiteor*, of which *confessio* is the noun form.

To confess is to avow or acknowledge, as in the hymn *Te Deum laudamus*, "We praise thee, O God: we acknowledge (*confitemur*) thee to be the Lord," and the Nicene Creed, "We acknowledge (*confitemur*) one baptism for the forgiveness of sins." To confess is to offer thanks and praise, a usage very frequent in Augustine's Psalter: for example, "Give thanks (*confitemini*) to the Lord, for he is good, for his mercy endures for ever" (Psalm 117:1). And to confess is to admit to one's own sin, as in 1 John 1:9: "If we confess (*confiteamur*) our sins, God, who is faithful and just, will forgive us our sins and cleanse us from all unrighteousness."

In some ways, the last aspect of confession is the least important of the three in the *Confessions*, a disappointment for those who go to the work expecting lurid tales of past sin and find instead something rather different. And confession of sin is, in any event, not separable in Augustine's mind from avowal and thanksgiving: for to acknowledge our faults is to acknowledge the goodness of the nature that God has given us—"it is he that hath made us, and not we ourselves"[1]—and to give thanks that we are no longer what we once were; it is to acknowledge that "we have no power of ourselves to help ourselves"[2] and to give thanks that God is making us what we long to be.

Accordingly, the *Confessions* is also the history of a life: a life granted by God, desperately mismanaged by Augustine, and then brought into order by the God who was always present even as Augustine, like the prodigal son in the parable of which he is so fond, ran away from God into a "far-off country," a "land of unlikeness." It is three histories, really, because the story of Augustine's own life opens up into the story of creation, given being, form, and order by the same God who made and then remade Augustine's life, and the story of creation in turn opens up into an allegory of the life of the Church.

The complexity of these three interwoven histories requires some elucidation, and that is what I attempt to provide in this Introduction. I begin with a brief account of Augustine's life and then turn to a reading of the *Confessions* that attempts to illuminate its structure and provide a framework in which to make sense of its diverse themes. I conclude with a discussion of Augustine's use of Scripture, the most important unifying feature of the *Confessions*.

---

1. Psalm 100:2 in the Coverdale Psalter.
2. Collect for the Third Sunday in Lent, *Book of Common Prayer* (1979), 167.

1. Augustine's life, thought, and influence

By the time Augustine started writing the *Confessions* in 397 AD, he had been a priest at Hippo Regius (now Annaba in Algeria) for six years and bishop for one or two. He had not sought ordination, preferring a quiet life of ascetic discipline and philosophical contemplation; but ordination was forced on him, and he found himself not only a teacher, preacher, and minister of the sacraments, but also (especially as bishop) a judge, public figure, and controversialist. The prodigiousness of Augustine's literary output—two hundred years later, Isidore of Seville would say that anyone who claims to have read all of Augustine must be a liar—is all the more remarkable when we consider how busy he was, how many claims there were on his time.

Augustine was born on 13 November 354 in Thagaste (modern Souk Ahras), about sixty miles south of Hippo Regius. His father, Patrick,[3] was a landowner of modest means, probably of Roman descent. His mother, Monnica, may have been of Berber stock; the name, at any rate, suggests Berber heritage. (The Berbers are the indigenous people of North Africa west of the Nile.) Whatever exactly Augustine's ethnicity, his education was thoroughly Roman, though he retained a North African accent, which was a professional liability for him.[4]

The profession in question was rhetoric. All his education was meant to make him into a successful rhetorician: a "salesman of words" (9.5.13), as he describes it dismissively from the perspective of someone whose life has been radically reoriented around quite different aims. And he did succeed, accent or no, before he gave up his career and turned to the life of Christian philosophical contemplation that he was not destined to enjoy for very long. The story of Augustine's life as we have it in the *Confessions* is the story of how he pursued that career, and along the way pursued other things—sensual gratification, knowledge, influence—until at last he gave in to the God who had been pursuing him, and who became his one true and enduring love.

That part of the story I do not need to retell here, because you have it before you in the *Confessions*. But Augustine would live another thirty-three years after he began to tell that story,[5] and I do want to offer a brief overview of the rest of his life before turning to the much more important question of Augustine's enduring influence. Though there is, somewhat surprisingly, no trace of the dispute in

---

3. There is no good reason to call Augustine's father "Patricius" that is not also a good reason to call his bishop "Ambrosius," and there is no good reason to call his bishop "Ambrosius."
4. *De ordine* 2.17.45.
5. I am being careful in the way I formulate this. The date of the composition of the *Confessions* is conventionally given as 397–401, and I have seen a period as long as 397–403 suggested; but to my mind the thematic and structural unity of the work suggests a shorter and more continuously sustained period of composition, and there is nothing to prevent one from supposing that the whole work dates from 397. On the issues here, see James J. O'Donnell, *Augustine: A New Biography* (HarperCollins, 2005), 33–34, 141–142.

the *Confessions*, there were two rival Christian factions in North Africa, thanks to a controversial ordination in 311. One of the bishops participating in the consecration of Caecilianus, bishop of Carthage, had handed over sacred books to the imperial authorities when the church in North Africa was under persecution. One faction argued that no such *traditor* (from the Latin for "hand over," the root of our word "traitor") could participate in a valid consecration; the purity of the Church would be compromised. So they rejected Caecilianus and started their own rival line of episcopal succession. The purist party, known as Donatists after their second bishop, Donatus the Great, was much larger; Augustine was bishop of the smaller group, the Caecilianists, or, as he would have us call them, the catholics.[6] Much of his work as bishop involved the defense and support of his catholic flock and polemic against the Donatists. He gradually came to prominence as an able defender of the catholic position, and his arguments carried the day at a conference held in Carthage in 411 to settle the dispute (though Augustine himself did not speak much there).[7]

411 would prove to be a consequential year in other ways. The connections he made at the conference made him aware of ideas and debates that would shape much of the rest of his career. He heard from the imperial commissioner, Marcellinus, that some Roman aristocrats were blaming Christians and their God for the decline of Rome, which had been sacked by the Visigoths the year before. Augustine worked on his response for the next fifteen years. He called it *On the City of God against the Pagans*; we generally know it simply as *The City of God*. Next to the *Confessions* it is Augustine's most widely read work. There are two cities, he says, founded on two loves: the city of God, founded on love for God to the point of contempt for self, and the city of the devil, founded on love for self to the point of contempt for God. The city of God is not the Church, and the city of the devil is not the state: there are people within the visible Church who do not belong to the city of God, and the state can be an instrument of God's providential governance, though no earthly authority—not even the great and glorious Rome—is anything more than a temporary arrangement, destined, as all things this side of eternal peace are destined, to pass away.

Marcellinus also made Augustine aware of the ideas of Pelagius and his disciple Caelestius. At least as Augustine understood the matter (a qualification I introduce in order to sidestep historical arguments about the exact character of Pelagian teaching), Pelagians taught that human beings retain the free will necessary to lead a morally good life without any need for divine grace. Adam's fall damaged only himself; it was not transmitted to the rest of the human race, except insofar as Adam set a bad example. There is therefore no such thing as original sin, and infants are born in the same state Adam was in before the fall; infant baptism is accordingly unnecessary.

---

6. For the lowercase "c" in "catholic," see Notes on the Translation.
7. O'Donnell writes most engagingly about the conference in *Augustine: A New Biography*, 234–243.

Just as Adam could have done, all human beings can, by our own free choice, resist sin and live righteously. Augustine was particularly horrified to find an earlier work of his own, *On Free Choice of the Will*, quoted in support of such views; he devotes quite a bit of space in his later *Reconsiderations* to showing that *On Free Choice of the Will* was anti-Pelagian even before he knew there was such a thing as Pelagianism. The polemic against Pelagianism would occupy Augustine for the rest of his life, leading him—this much, I think, is uncontroversial—into increasingly stark portrayals of the damage of original sin and the wretchedness of the human condition apart from grace.[8] But the seeds were there long before, and we see them clearly in the *Confessions*, from the discussion of infant sinfulness in Book 1 to the pervasiveness of the idea that it was God's initiative, not Augustine's own, that won Augustine for God.

The fall of Rome, which had led to the writing of *The City of God*, was part of the broader collapse of the Roman Empire. That collapse came very close to home in 430, when the Vandals besieged Hippo Regius as Augustine lay on his deathbed. He died of natural causes on 28 August 430. The city fell to the Vandals a few months later.

Quite extravagant things are said about Augustine: that he was "the first modern man," that he invented "the inner self," that he refounded Christianity. Such things are said because they can be, not without challenge but also not without a certain plausibility, and because it is hard to do justice to Augustine's brilliance, his inventiveness, and his influence without falling into some sort of extravagance. For a thousand years and more of Western Christianity, Augustine was a theologian of unrivaled importance. To a remarkable degree, Christians even to this day—whether they realize it or not—think Augustine's thoughts and draw up battle lines around Augustine's controversies; theologians still wrestle with his understanding of the nature of God, of grace, of providence, of sin and the remedy for sin. But one need not share any of his theological beliefs to find Augustine well worth reading. Philosophers of all sorts still engage with his understanding of belief and knowledge, his analysis of human action, his accounts of will and desire and freedom, his subtle exploration of time and eternity, and his astute observation of the human condition. And any reader—Christian or not, philosopher or not—will find much in Augustine that is captivating, inspiring, and challenging. For the story of Augustine's life as he presents it in the *Confessions* is at once startlingly intimate and dizzyingly cosmic. "How can *I* make sense of *this* action?" turns effortlessly into "How can *anyone* make

---

8. O'Donnell calls the polemic against Pelagianism "Augustine's great failure," saying that "Augustine failed to see that his doctrinal positions were unsustainable as a matter of pastoral practice" (254). I think this misdiagnoses the failure, if it is a failure. It's precisely as a matter of pastoral practice that Augustine's position is strongest: ask any serious participant in a twelve-step program about the power of acknowledging that life is unmanageable without divine assistance. It's as a doctrinal or intellectual matter that I think everyone has to have a little Pelagianism somewhere; otherwise, the only difference between those who act rightly and those who do not turns out to be God's arbitrary bestowal of grace on some and withholding of grace from others.

sense of *any* action?" "Why did I keep stepping on my own feet?" leads to "Why do we all make such a mess of things?"—and, inevitably, to reflection on what exactly it means for a life, any life, to be a mess, and what it might look like for the mess to get cleaned up, for what is broken and fragmented and dispersed to get put back together.

2. Putting together Augustine's *Confessions*

I chose the heading "Putting together Augustine's *Confessions*" because I want to talk about the structure of the *Confessions*, how it's all put together. But as I suggested at the end of the first part of the Introduction, "putting things together" is also a big theme of the *Confessions*, and I want to emphasize that too: the ways in which Augustine sees human life as dispersed, disintegrated, pulled apart by sin, and how it must be collected, reintegrated, "put together" by God.[9]

We can begin to see the connection between these two things by focusing first on the autobiographical books of the *Confessions*, Books 1 through 9. Augustine likes to divide things up into halves. The midpoint of Books 1 through 9 is of course Book 5. And right in the middle of Book 5 Augustine leaves Africa for Italy. So here we have a nice dividing point: the first half of the autobiography takes place in Africa and the second in Italy. (And Book 9 ends with Augustine waiting for a ship to return to Africa.) Now one thing that one notices is how few names Augustine uses in the first half. He mentions his parents, for example, but doesn't actually name them until much later. Even his dear friend of Book 4, the one whose death throws him into such a frenzy of grief, isn't given a name.

But once the midpoint passes, the names come flooding in: Elpidius, Ambrose, Alypius, Nebridius, Romanianus, and on and on. Why? Because Augustine wants to illustrate the way in which his movement away from God, which occupies the first half of the autobiographical books, is also a movement away from community. As his soul loses its integrity and is torn apart by sin, he is also torn apart from other people. As he gets put back together inside, he also gets put back together with other people, until finally he is reunited with the whole community of the faithful through baptism. His use of proper names is meant to reinforce this connection between the disintegration and reintegration of his soul and the disintegration and reintegration of his human relationships.

---

9. I first encountered this reading of the structure of the *Confessions* with my teacher, Frederick J. Crosson, who had written about it in the essay later reprinted as "Book Five: The Disclosure of Hidden Providence" in Kim Paffenroth and Robert P. Kennedy, eds., *A Reader's Companion to Augustine's Confessions* (Westminster John Knox Press, 2003), 71–88; I found it developed persuasively by James J. O'Donnell in his three-volume work on the *Confessions*. My debt to both writers for this section of the Introduction is great and pervasive.

So that gives us an initial structure for the narrative books: a first half of progressive disintegration, a second half of progressive reintegration. The next step is to look more closely at the process of disintegration. Augustine takes his organizing principle here from 1 John 2:16: "For all that is in the world—the lust of the flesh, the lust of the eyes, and worldly ambition—is not of the Father but is of the world." These three temptations are sometimes called the three "concupiscences" after their Latin names, sometimes the three "lusts." This passage was one Augustine reflected on a great deal. They represent the progressive disintegration of the human personality. Lust of the flesh is the excessive or misdirected love of sensible things. Lust of the eyes is excessive, undisciplined curiosity. Worldly ambition is overweening self-aggrandizement. Augustine thinks of this as the Unholy Trinity. Just as the Holy Trinity was thought of as Power (Father), Wisdom (Son), and Love (Holy Spirit), this Unholy Trinity involves Perverted Power (worldly ambition), Perverted Wisdom (lust of the eyes), and Perverted Love (lust of the flesh).

This structure is pervasive, both in the fine details and in the overall architecture of the work. Book 2 emphasizes the lust of the flesh, both in the sexual sins of adolescence and in the famous pear-tree incident. Book 3 emphasizes the lust of the eyes, where Augustine falls victim to two sorts of curiosity: the spectacles in Carthage and his allegiance to the Manichees. Book 4 deals with worldly ambition, especially regarding Augustine's career, including the dedication of his philosophical work to Hierius in the hope that it would attract his attention.

Then beginning with Book 6, we get the same three temptations again. This time they're in reverse order, as Augustine is brought back to integrity. Book 6 (especially section 6) shows how Augustine's zeal for a public career fades and how his pride is broken by the realization that his attacks on Christianity were misguided and misinformed. In Book 7 he is freed from his allegiance to the Manichees, largely thanks to his discovery of Platonism, which enables him to think properly about God. In Book 8 he is freed from his enslavement to lust.

So there is a sort of mirror structure around the Book 5 midpoint. Books 2–4 are Augustine's moral descent; Books 6–8 are his moral ascent. Book 9 is his baptism, which not only is the obvious place to go after conversion but also mirrors the baptism that should have taken place in Book 1 but was postponed. Moreover, baptism is sacramental death and rebirth, so it is fitting that Book 9 reports the baptism and death of five people and the baptism and new life of three others, including Augustine himself. Of the deaths reported in Book 9, only one, Monnica's, takes place during the time in which that book takes place—a useful reminder that Augustine's principles of organization, even in the autobiographical books, are as much thematic as chronological.

The mirror structure extends even further. For example, in Book 2 we get a symbolic Fall involving a pear tree; in Book 8 we get a literal conversion involving a fig tree. In Book 3 we get a reading of philosophy (Cicero) followed by a turn to Scripture, and unanswered questions about the origin and nature of evil; in Book 7 we get a reading of philosophy (the Platonists), followed by a turn to Scripture, and answers to questions about the origin and nature of evil. In Book 4 Augustine's greatest difficulty is his intellectual arrogance—his pride in understanding Aristotle's *Categories* on his own, his certainty that he could raise his mind to God on his own without any need for faith. In Book 6 he realizes how pervasive belief is in human life; we all have to live on borrowed epistemic capital. Finally, in the first half of Book 5 he is disappointed by the empty eloquence of the Manichee bishop Faustus; in the second half he is surprised by the solid eloquence of the Christian bishop Ambrose.

The place of the remaining four books, in which the history of Augustine's life opens up into the larger histories of creation and the Church, still remains to be accounted for. But before I turn to that issue, I want to note how a proper understanding of the structure of the *Confessions* is necessary in order to interpret its philosophical message correctly. There are many possible illustrations of this point, but I'll concentrate on one episode that I think has been widely misinterpreted precisely because people have failed to appreciate the structure of the *Confessions*.

My illustration is the vision at Ostia in Book 9.[10] Augustine and Monnica are at a window overlooking a garden. We're in the last days of Monnica's life, and she is looking forward to the life of the saints in heaven. As she and Augustine are thinking about this, their minds rise from the realm of change, up through the whole hierarchy of being, until they arrive at the realm of changelessness. For just a moment they glimpse God himself, and then the moment's gone.

Now the usual interpretation of this episode is that it's pretty much the same sort of thing as the intellectual ascent that Augustine experienced in Book 7, where he reflected on the limited and imperfect things of the sensible world and raised his mind step by step to the unlimited and perfect Truth. There too he glimpsed God only for a moment, and the moment's gone.

But if you pay careful attention to the structure of the *Confessions*, you know that can't be right. The intellectual ascent of Book 7, which derives from Platonic philosophy, is just that: an *intellectual* ascent. That's what you'd expect in the book devoted to overcoming lust of the eyes. But we already know that intellectual success is not enough. In fact, intellectual success is powerless, as we discover in Book 8. Even when Augustine's intellectual difficulties are all resolved, the will still needs to be converted. That's the work of the Holy Spirit.

So by the time we get to Book 9 there's been a fundamental change. You can see the differences in many ways. For example, the imagery in the Book 7 ascent is nearly all of sight—appropriately enough, since sight is Augustine's usual metaphor for intellectual understanding. But in the Book 9 ascent the imagery is nearly all of

---

10. I draw here from "Augustine vs. Plotinus: The Uniqueness of the Vision at Ostia," in John Inglis, ed., *Medieval Philosophy and the Classical Tradition in Islam, Judaism, and Christianity* (Curzon Press, 2002), 169–179.

hearing. Why? Because "faith comes by hearing," as Paul says in Romans 10:17.[11] In Book 7 Augustine had knowledge but not faith; in Book 8 he was given faith by the working of the Holy Spirit. So now in Book 9, faith, and the imagery associated with faith, take center stage.

Here's a further point. "Faith comes by hearing, and hearing by the Word of Christ"—in other words, through Scripture. There's no Scripture to speak of in the Book 7 ascent, where Augustine is relying solely on philosophy. But in the Book 9 ascent, Scriptural language is everywhere. The whole experience, in fact, is prompted by a question that comes out of Scripture: What will the life of the saints be like, a life that "eye has not seen, nor ear heard, nor has it entered into the human heart"?

You can already begin to see that the vision at Ostia is a distinctively *Christian* experience, whereas the intellectual ascent of Book 7 was a merely *philosophical* experience. Some other points make this even clearer. One thing that's striking about the Book 7 experience is how little emotional involvement there seems to be. It's all very abstract, intellectual, a bit cold. But Monnica and Augustine are spurred on "with affections more fiercely enkindled"; they touch Wisdom "with the utmost energy of [their] hearts." Why? Because Book 8 is the Book of the Holy Spirit, and the Holy Spirit is God as Love, active through faith. So in Book 9 Monnica and Augustine go before God passionately, through faith.

And a final point about the differences: at the end of the Book 7 vision, Augustine is left dissatisfied, wistful. He feels empty. But at the end of the Book 9 vision, there is no such dissatisfaction. Why? Because now he doesn't need intellectual visions in order to have God. He has the Holy Spirit in his heart and the sacramental life of the Church to mediate God's presence. Augustine uses a particularly striking metaphor after the Book 7 experience has left him hungry for more: he had "a longing for food that [he] could smell but could not yet eat." That food is the Eucharist, in which Christ gives himself to his people. By the time of the vision at Ostia, Augustine is a baptized Christian, so he has the strength to eat that food.

The point of this extended comparison between the two episodes is that if you ignore the structure—the role of Book 7 as a merely intellectual resolution, awaiting the volitional changes of Book 8 and the work of the Holy Spirit—you get a skewed idea of what the vision at Ostia is all about. Instead of "high flattery for Platonism,"[12] as most commentators find here, there is a systematic effort to deflate the pretensions of the Platonists. The way Augustine narrates the vision at Ostia is designed to show just how great the difference is between the Platonists, who know

---

11. Here I can take the opportunity to draw attention to another structural feature. Augustine has a standard order in which he considers the five senses: sight, hearing, smell, taste, touch. Notice, for example, the sequence in 4.7.12 and 10.8.13; he sometimes reverses the order, as in his exploration of the sins of the five senses in 10.30.41–10.34.53. Whenever Augustine departs from this order and puts hearing before sight, as at 10.27.38, it is in a context in which faith, which "comes by hearing," is paramount.

12. O'Donnell, *Augustine: Confessions*, III:128.

the goal but do not know the way to reach it, and Christians, who not only know the goal but have embraced Christ, who is himself the Way, the Truth, and the Life (John 14:6).

In Books 1–9 Augustine confesses what he once was; in Book 10 he confesses what he is at the time of writing his *Confessions*. On a purely structural level, the place of Book 10 in the work as a whole is fairly clear: having been baptized, Augustine is now able to receive the Eucharist, and self-examination and repentance are necessary preparation for receiving the Eucharist. Book 10 enacts that self-examination and ends with thoroughly Eucharistic imagery. But the book also has a much more ambitious aim: developing the theme of fragmentation and reintegration that we have already seen in the narrative books. He explores this theme in the richest and most fully developed ascent in the *Confessions*.

In discussing Augustine's philosophical reflections in Book 7 and his explicitly Christian reflections in Book 9, I spoke of both of them as "ascents," and that is what they are usually called. But the word is somewhat misleading, because the common pattern is not simply movement upward: the movement is always first inward, then upward. That is, Augustine starts from the things he encounters outside himself in the material world, moves inward to the sense powers by which he perceives those external objects, and then proceeds upward through the higher powers of the soul and beyond them until he comes to the Unchangeable Truth that is above all that is within him and all that is outside him. In Book 10 the in-and-up pattern is even clearer. Augustine wants to tell us who he is at the time of writing the *Confessions*. He loves God, he says; we can't actually know that he really does love God, he reminds us, but if we are bound to him by charity, we will believe him. Very well: one cannot love what one does not know. How, then, does Augustine—how does anyone—know God?

He begins, as always, from the things outside him; they say to him, "We are not God" and "He is the one who made us" (10.6.9). Images of material things—of colors, sounds, smells, tastes, tactile qualities—enter through the senses and are stored in memory. They are compartmentalized, fragmented, but memory retrieves them and imagination combines them. Intelligible truths—not images now, but the truths themselves—are also in memory. They too are compartmentalized, fragmented, but memory retrieves them and thought combines them. By gathering up in thought what is scattered in memory, we can reflect on the happy life, which we cannot help loving and therefore must, in some sense, know. (For again, we cannot love what we do not know.) The happy life is joy in truth, and Truth is God: not truths, multiple, fragmented, partial, but Truth, one, whole, and complete.

And now, having looked for God within himself and found God as creator, as unitary and perfect truth, and as the source of all goodness and happiness, Augustine turns back to the created world so that he can see it properly as God's action. In Book 11 Augustine examines God as creator, in Book 12 as unitary and perfect Truth, and in Book 13 as the source of all goodness and happiness.

Books 11 and 12 both speak to the theme of fragmentation and reintegration. In Book 11 the central contrast is between time and eternity. As eternal, God is the One, ultimate unity. He doesn't get his experience piecemeal, as we do; instead, he has all of his life in one indivisible eternal present. By contrast, we human beings are dispersed, fragmented, scattered. We can endure through time only by being stretched out, distended. We could not tell a story, sing a song, or carry out an action if our minds could not in some sense transcend time, holding together in its attention what otherwise would slip away as soon as it arrived. Our existence in time is paradoxically both painful and glorious: painful because we cannot escape such fragmentation, glorious because the mind's power to hold passing times together gives us a taste of the divine eternity that encompasses all things, and from which nothing is ever lost.

In Book 12 the central contrast is between the one Word we will know in full in heaven (as discussed at Ostia) and the plurality of words through which it is manifested here: "The poverty of human understanding so often makes for an abundance of speech, for seeking says more than finding, asking takes longer than obtaining, and the hand that knocks has more to do than the hand that is open to receive" (12.1.1). We would like for there to be a single, correct reading of the world, a single, correct reading of the Book of Genesis. But there is no such thing; multiple interpretations are not merely possible but even desirable.

The striking humility of Augustine's admission that multiple interpretations of Scripture are permissible should not be underestimated. We learn in Book 10 that Augustine recognized (and hated) in himself the need to be praised, to be the impressive intellectual whose words were heeded precisely because they were *his* words. In Book 12 Augustine scrambles down from the pedestal on which he knows he likes to place himself and acknowledges that Truth is no private possession, that the only unambiguous and unitary act of divine self-communication to human beings is the Incarnation, that words (as distinguished from *the* Word) reveal God in multiple and, if you like, fragmented ways. In the background here, largely unnoticed by modern commentators, is Augustine's conviction that intellectual success is all too often accompanied by moral failure. Even in Book 7 Augustine tells us that God procured for him the books of the Platonists—the source of the most consequential intellectual breakthrough recorded in the *Confessions*—"because it was your will to show me how you resist the proud but give grace to the humble, and how great is your mercy, which you have shown to human beings by the way of humility, in that your Word was made flesh and dwelt among us" (7.9.13). Submission to the Humble One (to use one of the striking Christological titles Augustine scatters throughout this work) is the only safe path for the exegete.

In Book 13 Augustine turns from literal to allegorical exegesis, reading the creation story as an allegory for the work of the Holy Spirit in bringing order and goodness to human lives through Scripture, sacraments, spiritual gifts, and the Church. Augustine pursues the allegory through all six days of creation and then concludes his exegesis of Genesis with the seventh day, when "God rested from all his work"

(Genesis 2:2–3). We know why Augustine undertook his exegesis of Genesis in the first place: to return to the creation by which he came to know God and to see it now as God's work. But why end his exegesis here, on the seventh day? It is not merely because creation is now finished, but because now we have reached rest. In the very first paragraph of the *Confessions* Augustine announces the theme: God has made us for himself, and our heart is restless until it comes to rest in God (1.1.1). And now, in the last paragraphs of the *Confessions*, Augustine sees that rest. Not that he has made it his own,[13] but he sees the promise of a "peace on which no night ever falls" (13.35.50). To Augustine's mind, what more satisfying ending could there be, this side of heaven?

3. Intertextuality and Augustine's use of Scripture

Why yet another translation of the *Confessions?* There are several relatively recent translations; indeed, two more appeared in the time that I was working on this one. When I set out to work on this project, I thought the answer to that question was simple: we need a translation that is sensitive to the philosophical content. We have translations by classicists, historical theologians, experts in late antiquity, and literary translators, but (until now) none by a philosopher. And although the *Confessions* is certainly more than a philosophical work, it is not less than a philosophical work, and only a philosophically informed translation can do justice to that aspect of the text.

I still think that's right, and a perfectly compelling reason by itself to justify another translation. But in the course of the long gestation of this project I came to regard another desideratum as more compelling still, and this aim ended up being far more pervasive, and far more distinctive of my translation, than the goal of doing justice to Augustine's philosophical genius. This aim takes a bit of explaining, however, and I begin in what is perhaps a surprising place: a scene from a novel by Dorothy Sayers.

Lord Peter Wimsey's investigations have brought him to the offices of a theatrical impresario whom he interrupts in the middle of casting "a young lady in the minimum of clothing." After a brief wait in the outer room, we are told, "the inner door opened . . . and the young lady emerged, clothed and apparently very much in her right mind."[14] She is described as "clothed" so that we will know she has changed out of her skimpy chorus-girl outfit and is fit to be seen in the outer room and to head out into the streets of London looking respectable. But what is "very much in her right mind" doing? In context it points ahead to her announcing to a friend that she has been cast in a show, an announcement met with suitable congratulations. Yet it is an odd formulation, surely, since we have been given no reason to question

---

13. Philippians 3:13.
14. Dorothy L. Sayers, *Have His Carcase* (New York: HarperCollins, 1986), 319.

her sanity; and if we had, the ability to report a modest professional success in a few sensible words is not obviously decisive evidence in favor of her being *compos mentis*.

The words are (as many readers will no doubt recognize) an allusion to the story of the Gerasene (or Gadarene) demoniac as recounted in the Gospels according to Mark and Luke. To anyone who doesn't recognize the language, "clothed and in her right mind" is puzzling and incongruous; but Dorothy Sayers was writing for an audience that could be expected to recognize the source of the language—at the very least to know that it is Scriptural, even if its precise original context did not come immediately into their minds—and so the language would not be in the least jarring.

But let's take this a step further. We recognize the language—we know that it's a quotation from Scripture; perhaps we even recognize its context. What does that do for us? In this case, not much: we are not to think of the chorus girl as in any way like a demoniac, or of Lord Peter as a Christ-figure (he is responsible neither for her being clothed nor for her being in her right mind), or of anyone in the story as being like swine. The quotation adds a fillip of literary *jeu d'esprit*, and we readers who are in on what the author is doing feel a pleasant sense of innocent self-satisfaction; but there is nothing more than this. The quotation does not help the text "make meaning," as the literary folks say. It's just decorative.

Now suppose my copy of the novel put "clothed and in her right mind" in quotation marks and attached a footnote that read "Mark 5:15/Luke 8:35." What would be the point of that? Precisely because the quotation does not help the text make meaning, there's no particular reason to identify its source. The quotation marks and footnote would tell me that Sayers is quoting Scripture—a fact that, if I have to learn it by means of quotation marks and a footnote, cannot do for me what little there is to be done for me.

When one text helps another text make meaning, we call this relationship "intertextuality." My illustration from Dorothy Sayers is not a case of intertextuality, I think, but a case of merely decorative quotation. But what got me thinking about this was, of course, a very practical problem in translating Augustine's *Confessions*. How should I handle Augustine's very frequent quotations from Scripture? There are several different possibilities. Some translators put the Scriptural language in italics, others in quotation marks. Some give parenthetical citations, others use footnotes, and still others collect a list of citations by section or chapter without clearly attaching them to particular sentences. In a moment I will address the technical problems that beset these solutions, but for now, the important point is that in order to decide what to do about Augustine's quotations, one first has to decide what Augustine's quotations are doing. And that is what this section is about.   ·

*****

"Great are you, Lord, and highly to be praised." These are the words with which the *Confessions* opens: *magnus es, domine, et laudabilis valde*. They are a quotation from the Psalms. Except they aren't, exactly: Psalms 47:2, 95:4, and 144:3 all have "great is the Lord and highly to be praised" (*magnus dominus et laudabilis valde*), but Augustine has turned the third-person statements into second-person address. He is not describing God but speaking to him.

On the face of it we might think this is a merely decorative quotation, like the one from Dorothy Sayers. Augustine's use of the Psalms even has this in common with Sayers's use of the Gospels, that both quotations are casually edited to fit the literary context. Sayers changes the gender of a pronoun ("clothed and . . . in *her* right mind"—the chorus girl is a woman whereas the demoniac was a man); Augustine adds a second-person verb and changes the case of a noun. In both instances the reader who doesn't recognize the source of the quotation is no worse off, it seems to me, and the reader who does is no better off. Putting quotation marks around the Scriptural quotation and attaching a parenthetical citation or footnote to it therefore seems as needlessly intrusive, as pointless a display of editorial knowing-best, in the case of Augustine as it would be in the case of Sayers.

In one respect, in fact, the apparatus is even *more* intrusive in the Augustine case than it would be in the Sayers case. As I noted earlier, a thoughtful reader of *Have His Carcase* who didn't recognize the quotation from the Gospels might well puzzle a bit over the language; a footnote would at least explain why the language might seem a little odd ("ah," such a reader would say to himself, "she's quoting Scripture; Sayers is such a literate writer of detective fiction. That's exactly why I like her"). In Augustine's case, there's nothing odd about his starting off his *Confessions* with "Great are you, Lord, and highly to be praised." It does not clash with the context— as the opening sentence, there's no context yet for it to clash with—and it does not unsettle any of our expectations, particularly if we know what *Confessions* means. (See the beginning of this Introduction for the threefold meaning of *confessio*.) So what exactly is gained by the quotation marks and citation?

Ah, but you rightly object: the cases are not parallel. Sayers's quotation really is purely decorative, but Augustine's is substantive. He is not adorning his ordinary speech with the language of Scripture as a display of erudition: the language of Scripture *is* his ordinary speech. Now that, I think, is right. What I like to say is that in the *Confessions*—other works of his are different, but in the *Confessions*—Augustine does not quote Scripture; he speaks the language of Scripture as his own language. Now suppose that's right. Then how much sense does it make to wall off the Scriptural language from the non-Scriptural language by using quotation marks or italics or some other such device? Quotation marks reinforce the idea that Augustine is quoting Scripture in something like the way Sayers is, although no doubt to more serious purpose; but if what he's actually doing is speaking the language of Scripture as his own language, the quotation marks are out of place. And the citations are, if anything, even worse. What are we to do with them? There are two possibilities. One is that we're supposed to see them and think, "Oh, he's quoting Scripture again"— which is unedifying and distracting and serves no useful purpose—or we're actually supposed to look them up, which turns Augustine's text into a kind of crossword puzzle challenge, or perhaps something like Joyce's *Ulysses*, where the thick texture of allusion and linguistic legerdemain is a virtuoso performance that only the most initiated can hope to appreciate.

So at this point, I would argue for no quotation marks (or other typographical device) to separate Scriptural language from non-Scriptural, and no citations either. To my mind, the resulting text reads the way it ought to read, as one continuous unified voice, sometimes (as a well-instructed reader will know) in language that Augustine speaks from the sacred text, and sometimes in language that Augustine speaks from his own store of thought and reflection. There are no "special bits" that demand to be read with particular solemnity or in a different voice or with air quotes or what have you.

I noted earlier that the giving of Scriptural citations is complicated by various technical problems, and it's time to look at some of those. In fact we have already encountered one of the difficulties, though it is admittedly the least of them. I mean the fact that Augustine frequently makes small changes to the Scriptural text so that it fits seamlessly in context. If we're going to give a reference for "Great are you, Lord, and highly to be praised," what should it be? Chadwick gives us "Ps. 47: 2," which (understandably) gives no indication that the wording of the original has been slightly changed and (rather less understandably) overlooks the other two passages in Augustine's Psalter that have exactly the same wording as Psalm 47:2. Sheed cites the other two passages but not Psalm 47:2. Boulding cites all three passages and tips us off that it's not an exact quotation: "See Ps. 47:2 (48:1); 95 (96):4; 144 (145):3." If you're going to use "See" for any quotation that's not exact, you're going to be using it an awful lot—as indeed she does, with admirable consistency.

Not much hinges on getting this right, of course. Whatever translation you're reading, your understanding of the opening sentence of the *Confessions* is not affected one whit by the reference. And even if you *did* look up the reference (which I find it hard to imagine anyone would actually do), you'd find some language reasonably close to Augustine's (to which the only sensible reaction is, "huh, here's some language reasonably close to Augustine's, which is what he was quoting," which wasn't worth the trouble of looking up the reference).

Sometimes, however, the language you would find if you looked up the reference isn't in fact reasonably close to Augustine's. His text is not ours. In some cases it would be sheer scholarly overkill to note the discrepancy between Augustine's text and ours, but there are certainly passages where such information is helpful. Consider Augustine's exegesis of *In principio*, "In the beginning," the opening words of Genesis. In the course of arguing that the "beginning" of which this text speaks is in fact God the Son, we find this puzzling language: "This is your eternal Word, who is also the Beginning, because he speaks to us" (11.8.10). The language is puzzling in much the same way that Sayers's crack about "clothed and apparently very much in her right mind" is puzzling. How does the fact that the Word speaks to us establish that he is the Beginning? That's hard to make out, unless we look at Augustine's text of Scripture. Here is his version of John 8:24–25:

> [Jesus said,] "Unless you believe that I am he, you will die in your sins." So they said to him, "Who are you?" Jesus said to them, "The Beginning, because I am also speaking with you."

We may still wonder what Augustine's text of John is supposed to mean, but at least we can now understand why this language appears here.

This example—there are many others I could give—points up the way in which the kind of experience that Augustine intended for his readers is simply unrecoverable for us. Suppose I know the Fourth Gospel very well, so well that I catch every echo of John in the *Confessions* and delight in the way in which this very Johannine thinker makes the evangelist's thought and language his own. I'm still not going to get this one, because my text of the relevant passage will have Jesus saying, not "The Beginning, because I am also speaking with you," but something like "Even what I have told you from the beginning." The footnote that informs me about Augustine's peculiar text does clear up the mystery for me, but the immediacy of the experience is lost. That's not how intertextuality works its magic.

Consider a fairly mundane example of intertextuality that does work. I once asked a friend of mine, "What do you think of when you hear this: 'It is he that hath made us'?" He immediately replied, "And not we ourselves." So for him, for me, and for anyone else who is minded to complete the phrase in that way, when Augustine in Book 10 goes looking for God in creation, and creature after creature answers his inquiry, "He is the one who made us," the unspoken half of the verse still sounds. It is not only that God is their creator, but that they themselves bear the marks of their own insufficiency; they witness to their dependence, their contingency, their moment-by-moment need for God; and this is no less true of the creature Augustine, and of the memory by which and in which he seeks God. It is God who has made us, God who has remade us, and not we ourselves.

But here's the problem. My friend completed the verse in that way because, like me, he's an Anglican steeped in our historic liturgies, and that's the way the verse goes in the text of the *Jubilate* that has been a key part of Morning Prayer in our tradition since the first English Prayer Book. As it happens, that's also the way the text went in Augustine's Psalter—*ipse fecit nos, et non nos*—so my friend and I have just the right mindset to get out of this passage everything that Augustine was expecting us to get out of it, things said and left unsaid. But almost every modern translation of the Psalter says something like "He made us, and we are his" or "He made us, and we belong to him." So most people who recognize the Psalm and complete the quotation in their minds will complete it in the wrong way, and "we are his" unfortunately doesn't fill out Augustine's meaning in the same way.

My favorite example of a case in which the difference between Augustine's text and ours thwarts intertextuality comes in Book 11:

> Yours is the day, yours also the night. At your command the moments fly away. Generously make room in them for our meditations on the hidden things of your law, and do not close your law against us when we knock. For it was not in vain that you willed the writing of so many pages of dark secrets, and those woods do not lack for your stags, which shelter there and are refreshed, ranging and feeding, lying down and chewing the cud. O Lord, perfect me and reveal them to me. (11.2.3)

There is a particularly dense texture of Scriptural allusion here, and much of it will be familiar to many. "Yours is the day, yours also the night" is Psalm 73:16. "Do not close your law against us when we knock" recalls Matthew 7:7–8: "Ask, and it will be given you; seek, and you will find; knock, and it will be opened to you. For every one who asks receives, and he who seeks finds, and to him who knocks it will be opened." The Matthew text appears often in the *Confessions*, and it would be very difficult to make it all the way to Book 11 without recognizing the allusion. But then what on earth is going on with the sudden intrusion of stags in the woods? The strange imagery of these two sentences derives from Augustine's text of Psalm 28:9: "The voice of the Lord perfects the stags and has revealed the woods; and in his temple all cry, 'Glory.'" Note, then, that Augustine is asking to be one of the stags who are at home in, and nourished by, the mysterious dark woods of Scripture. That's a bit of meaning that is absolutely lost without a footnote; strangely, almost no English translations supply the text and interpretation that are needed here. This points up one of the things I find most puzzling about the standard approaches to intertextuality in translations of the *Confessions*: translators provide unnecessary help in the form of detailed references to Scriptural texts when knowing those references doesn't actually shed light on the meaning of Augustine's text, and then offer nothing in cases where readers actually need a reference, text, and explanation in order to make sense of what Augustine is doing.

For these reasons, then, my translation includes references, texts, and explanations where they're genuinely helpful; and I admit that I could not bring myself to break from the consensus of translators and offer no apparatus at all for the garden-variety quotations, semi-quotations, and allusions. For even if knowing the particular source of Augustine's language isn't always, or even usually, important to understanding the text of the *Confessions*, knowing that the source is Scriptural arguably is. Even in my by now well-worn example of the opening lines of the *Confessions*, though the particular reference carries no meaning—you could look up the passages in the Psalms, think hard about them, and be not one bit more enlightened—the fact that Augustine begins his work with the language of Scripture is surely important. It is precisely the signal that Scriptural language is his language, the Psalmist's voice his voice. And more than that, it incarnates the idea—which

Augustine is shortly to make explicit—that God is not merely the object but the source of praise: God gives the need for praise and gives also the will and the words by which that need is fulfilled. Here Augustine's own commentary on the Psalms reveals the principle at work:

> The words of the psalm that we have heard and in part sung: if we should say that they are our words, it would be altogether astonishing if what we said were true; for they are the words of the Spirit of God, and not our own. And yet if we should say that they are not our own, we are most certainly lying. (*Enarr. in Ps.* 26, *en.* 2.1)

So to let the opening words of the *Confessions* stand with no indication at all that they are both the words of the Spirit of God and Augustine's own words would surely be a mistake.

And there are other reasons for indicating when Augustine's language has a Scriptural source. Sometimes the texture of Scriptural quotation is very dense; sometimes pages go by with little or nothing from Scripture. Attention to when Scripture is present and when it's absent is often revealing, and that dimension of meaning is likely to be lost without some sort of apparatus. Further, there are patterns of use of Scripture that can also be informative. I always tell my students that you know Augustine is particularly serious when he's quoting the Psalms, the Fourth Gospel, or Romans. We've seen why the Psalms are so important and pervasive in the *Confessions*. The Gospel of John is particularly important for Augustine's Christology. Romans (Paul generally, but Romans in particular) plays a decisive role in the story of Augustine's conversion; in Book 8 Augustine carefully leads up to the conversion scene by quoting several passages from Romans in their canonical order before he gets to the decisive quotation from 13:13.

So my solution has been to put Scriptural citations in the margins next to the parts of Augustine's text in which those passages are quoted, half-quoted, or alluded to, but not to use quotation marks or italics to set off the Scriptural text from Augustine's text. That way Augustine's text can be read as the unified voice that it is, but the fact of his dependence on Scripture—the fact that his words are also the words of the Spirit of God—can be evident as well. Footnotes are used for the kinds of cases I've noted, in which Augustine relies on a text of Scripture that differs from ours in a way that impedes understanding of his text or otherwise calls for explanation.

My determination to do justice to the place of Scriptural language in the *Confessions* has been a crucial determinant of the prose style I have used for this translation, perhaps even more crucial than my desire for philosophical sensitivity. I have sought to translate in such a way that Scriptural language and Augustine's own language interpenetrate seamlessly. What this means in practice is that Augustine's language must sound like Scripture. But what does Scripture sound like? Here the variety of English translations makes it impossible to give a definitive answer. My own twice-daily encounter with Scripture in Morning and Evening Prayer is with the Revised

Standard Version and the Psalter of the *Book of Common Prayer* (1979), so Augustine's Scriptural quotations naturally assimilate themselves to those sources as far as the Latin allows (which admittedly is often not very far). The resulting style is formal without being stilted or archaic.[15] It is not colloquial, and not meant to be; it is, I hope, good liturgical prose. After all—to come full circle by returning to the point with which I began—the *Confessions* is a prayer.

---

15. One might object that "behold" as a translation for *ecce* is a bit fusty, but *ecce* is a word of solemn attestation, and in most cases "look" simply does not do the same job.

Essential Scriptures

As I discuss in section 3 of the Introduction, a reading of the *Confessions* is greatly enriched by an intimate knowledge of the text of Scripture as Augustine had it. As a help toward such a reading, I include here a translation of nine passages that Augustine frequently quotes, half-quotes, alludes to, or otherwise draws upon. They are translated from the Latin text as Augustine had it, which does not always correspond to the text from which our current (or historic) English translations are drawn: so even those who are familiar with Scripture in English translation may find it useful to acquaint themselves with the passages in the versions found here.

1. Psalm 99:3

It is he who has made us, and not we ourselves.

2. Wisdom 11:21

You have arranged all things by measure and number and weight.

3. Matthew 7:7 (paralleled at Luke 11:9)

Ask, and it will be given to you; seek, and you will find; knock, and it will be opened to you.

4. Matthew 11:28–30

Come to me, all you who labor and are burdened, and I will refresh you. Take my yoke upon you and learn from me, for I am gentle and humble in heart, and you will find rest for your souls. For my yoke is easy, and my burden is light.

5. Luke 15:11–32 (The Parable of the Prodigal Son)[1]

A certain man had two sons. And the younger of them said to the father, "Father, give me the portion of your property that belongs to me." And he divided his property between them. And after not many days, having gathered everything together, the younger son went away into a far-off land and there wasted his property in riotous living. And after he had used up everything, there was a great famine in that land, and he began to be destitute. And he went away and attached himself to one of the citizens of that land, and he sent him into his fields to feed the pigs. And he longed to fill his belly with the husks that the pigs ate, and no one gave him anything. But

---

1. Augustine focuses almost exclusively on the first paragraph, but it is still good to have the whole parable in mind; and the bit about prostitutes in the third paragraph does get used. It is also helpful to know that the word translated "property" is in each case *substantia,* "substance."

returning unto himself, he said, "My father's hired hands have plenty to eat, yet here I am perishing of hunger. I shall arise and go to my father, and say, 'Father, I have sinned against heaven and before you. And I am no longer worthy to be called your son. Make me as one of your hired hands.'"

And, arising, he went to his father. But when he was still a long way off, his father saw him; and he was moved by mercy, and, running toward him, he fell upon his neck and kissed him. And he said to his father, "Father, I have sinned against heaven and before you; I am no longer worthy to be called your son." But the father said to his servants, "Make haste: bring forth the finest robe and put it on him, and place a ring on his hand and sandals on his feet. And bring out the fatted calf and kill it, and let us eat and make merry. For this my son was dead and has come to life again; he was lost and has been found." And they began to make merry.

But his elder son was in the field. And when he drew close to the house, he heard music and dancing. And he called one of the servants and asked what these things were. And he said to him, "Your brother has come, and your father has killed the fatted calf, because he has got him back safe." And he was indignant, and would not go in. But his father went out and began to entreat him. And he answered his father, "Behold, I have served you for so many years, and I have never disobeyed any command of yours; and you have never given me a kid so that I might make merry with my friends. But now that this son of yours, who has devoured his property with prostitutes, has come back, you have killed for him the fatted calf." And he said to him, "Son, you are always with me, and everything that I have is yours. But it is right that there should be merriment and rejoicing, because your brother was dead and has come to life again; he was lost and has been found."

6. John 1:1–14 (The Prologue to John)

In the beginning was the Word, and the Word was with God, and the Word was God. He was in the beginning with God. All things were made through him, and without him nothing was made. What was made is, in him, life, and [this] life was the light of human beings. And light shines in the darkness, and the darkness has not swallowed it up.

There was a human being sent from God, whose name was John. He came as a witness, that he might bear witness to the light, that all might believe through him. He was not the light, but [came] to bear witness to the light, that all might believe through him. The true light was [the light] that enlightens every human being coming into the world. He was in the world, and the world had been made through him, and the world did not recognize him. He came to his own things, and his own people did not receive him. But to as many as received him, he gave power to become children of God, to those who believe on his name, who are born not of blood, nor of the will of the flesh, nor of the will of a man, but of God.

And the Word was made flesh and dwelt among us, and we saw his glory, glory as of the Only-begotten of the Father, full of grace and truth.

7. John 14:6

Jesus said, "I am the Way, the Truth, and the Life."

8. Romans 1:21–25

For although they knew God, they did not honor him as God or give thanks to him, but they became futile in their thinking and their senseless minds were darkened. Claiming to be wise, they became fools, and exchanged the glory of the immortal God for images resembling mortal man or birds or animals or reptiles. Therefore God gave them up in the lusts of their hearts to impurity, to the dishonoring of their bodies among themselves, because they exchanged the truth about God for a lie and worshiped and served the creature rather than the Creator, who is blessed for ever! Amen.

9. Romans 5:5

And hope does not disappoint us, because the charity of God has been poured into our hearts through the Holy Spirit who has been given to us.

Notes on the Latin Text

I have followed the edition of James J. O'Donnell in volume I of *Augustine: Confessions* (Oxford: Clarendon Press, 1992; the text is also available online at stoa.org/hippo). I have adopted only one variant reading: at 10.36.59 I read *benedicitur* for *benedicetur*. In a few places I have altered O'Donnell's punctuation; I reproduce those passages here, with the punctuation I have adopted.

3.6.10

ista quae videmus visu carneo, sive caelestia sive terrestria. cum pecudibus et volatilibus videmus haec,

5.3.4

et mirantur haec homines et stupent qui nesciunt ea, et exultant atque extolluntur qui sciunt, et per impiam superbiam recedentes et deficientes a lumine tuo tanto ante solis defectum futurum praevident, et in praesentia suum non vident. non enim religiose quaerunt unde habeant ingenium quo ista quaerunt, et invenientes quia tu fecisti eos, non ipsi se, dant tibi se ut serves quod fecisti, et quales se ipsi fecerant occidunt se tibi, et trucidant exaltationes suas sicut volatilia, et curiositates suas sicut pisces maris quibus perambulant secretas semitas abyssi, et luxurias suas sicut pecora campi, ut tu, deus, ignis edax consumas mortuas curas eorum, recreans eos immortaliter.

8.10.22

pereant a facie tua, deus, sicuti pereunt vaniloqui et mentis seductores, qui cum duas voluntates in deliberando animadverterint, duas naturas duarum mentium esse adseverant, unam bonam, alteram malam. ipsi vere mali sunt, cum ista mala sentiunt, et idem ipsi boni erunt, si vera senserint verisque consenserint, ut dicat eis apostolus tuus, 'fuistis aliquando tenebrae, nunc autem lux in domino.'

9.3.6

nam longi et multi videbantur prae amore libertatis otiosae ad cantandum de medullis omnibus, 'tibi dixit cor meum, "quaesivi vultum tuum; vultum tuum, domine, requiram."'

12.15.21

etsi non solum ante illam nec in illa invenimus tempus, quia est idonea faciem tuam semper videre nec uspiam deflectitur ab ea (quo fit ut nulla mutatione varietur), inest ei tamen ipsa mutabilitas, unde tenebresceret et frigesceret nisi amore grandi tibi cohaerens tamquam semper meredies luceret et ferveret ex te.

13.10.11

in illa vero dictum est quid esset nisi inluminaretur

13.13.14

quae est illa speciei lux, cum videbimus eum sicuti est

13.14.15

'quare tristis es, anima, et quare conturbas me? spera in domino. lucerna pedibus tuis verbum eius.'

Notes on the Translation

Three aims have determined the character of this translation. First, I have sought philosophical precision. This means, among other things, that conceptual connections are made evident by the use of more connective words (such as "for") than is usual in contemporary English, and that I keep to a consistent translation of a particular word in passages where that word, or the concept it represents, is being subjected to analysis. For example, in Augustine's analysis of the divided will in Book 8, I translate *voluntas* consistently as "will." To translate *voluntas* variously as "urge," "whim," "volition," "impulse," and "inclination," as one of the most widely used English translations does, is to obscure what Augustine is up to.

Second, as I discuss in the introductory section on intertextuality, I have sought to translate in such a way that Scriptural language and Augustine's own language interpenetrate seamlessly. See the last paragraph of the Introduction for the implications of this aim for the prose style of this translation.

Third, I wanted the language of the translation to be as musical as possible. I have taken great care over the rhythm and cadence of the language. Sentences are often long, because successions of short sentences sound choppy.[1] (My first aim likewise promotes long sentences: keeping together what is conceptually connected is an essential part of philosophical precision.) I have a strong preference for Germanic vocabulary over Latinate vocabulary: Germanic vocabulary tends to be livelier and more vivid, Latinate vocabulary stodgier and more technical-sounding. God is almighty rather than omnipotent; he enlightens rather than illuminates; Augustine marvels at God's deeply hidden oneness rather than his profound latent unity.

The translation of certain particular words calls for some comment. *Dominus* is "Lord." A recent translator argues for "Master" on the grounds that it "seems impossible that Augustine consciously and fervently prayed to a *dominus* in the symbolic form of a political ruler, instead of a householder like so many highly respected adult males he knew—and like himself."[2] On the contrary, it seems impossible to me that his thoughts about God were so narrowly anthropomorphic, that his God was the same sort of chap as Augustine himself, just with a rather larger household. Augustine's theological imagination was thoroughly informed by "the throned God of imagery starting in the Hebrew Bible,"[3] and I am convinced that when he addressed God as *dominus* he had very much the same thing in mind that present-day Christians have when they address God as "Lord."

---

1. Of course, strings of long sentences can be wearying, so I avoid those as well.
2. Ruden xxxii.
3. Ruden xxxi.

I have translated *sinus* as "bosom" only in the Scriptural expression "bosom of Abraham"; elsewhere the word obviously has incongruous overtones for a contemporary reader. One surely cannot say, for example, that the bodily creation enfolds all perceptible natures "in its huge bosom" without raising a laugh.

For *viscum* I have settled on "honey-trap." Strictly speaking, *viscum* is bird-lime, "a glutinous substance spread upon twigs, by which birds may be caught and held fast" (OED); it is made from the berries of the mistletoe, which is also called *viscum* in Latin. But "bird-lime" is an obscure word, and "honey-trap" gets the two essential elements of the image: it's a trap, and it's sticky.

Catholicus is an insuperable problem because for most of us "Catholic" means Roman Catholic (as opposed to Protestant, Orthodox, etc.) whereas Augustine uses *catholicus* to describe an adherent of authentic, non-heretical, mainstream Christianity (as opposed to Manicheanism, Donatism, etc.), and we have no straightforward way of conveying that meaning in English. So I translate *catholicus* as "catholic," with a lowercase "c," and trust the reader not to import connotations that have no place before the Great Schism of East and West and the Reformations of the sixteenth century. *Ecclesia*, when it refers to the Body of Christ (as opposed to a local assembly of that Body, or a building in which such an assembly worships), is always "Church," with a capital "C."

Despite my usual allergy toward cognates, *caritas* is always "charity"[4] and *cupiditas* often "cupidity"; *caritas* is never just "love" and *cupiditas* seldom "desire." These are both technical terms for Augustine: charity is "the motion of the soul toward enjoying God for his own sake, and oneself and one's neighbor for God's sake," and cupidity is "the motion of the soul toward enjoying oneself, one's neighbor, or any bodily thing for the sake of something other than God" (*De doctrina christiana* 3.10.16).

Vanus and *vanitas* are translated in various ways ("empty/emptiness," "trifling," "pointless," and so forth), but I have not avoided "vain" and "vanity," in order to capture the echo of the frequent complaint of the writer of Ecclesiastes: "Vanity of vanities (or, in Augustine's text, vanity of those who work vanity), all is vanity." Think "vain" as in "all my work was in vain."

I have retained the traditional "firmament" for *firmamentum*. Neither "vault" nor "dome" allows the flexibility of imagery that "firmament" (perhaps precisely because of its obscurity) allows, and Augustine is always mindful of the first syllable of the word. The firmament is firm, solid, stable; vaults and domes are just roofs of a particular kind.

I have taken some care to avoid unnecessarily gendered language regarding humanity. Wherever possible I translate *homo* as "human being" rather than "man," and I sometimes recast singulars as plurals so that I can use "they" rather than "he" (or "she," or "he or she"). The expression *filii hominum*, traditionally "sons of men," is "children of men"—admittedly a halfway measure, but "children of human beings"

---

4. With one exception: at 7.10.16 I use "love" in order to capture the elegance of "O eternal Truth and true Love (*caritas*) and beloved (*cara*) Eternity."

is simply too ungainly. *Fratres* are not just "brothers" or "brethren," but "brothers and sisters," except at 9.7.15, where I use "brethren" because men and women would not have sung together in a mixed assembly.[5]

I have, however, retained gendered language for God. Although Augustine could hardly be clearer that God has no body and is accordingly neither male nor female, his language for God is, as both Christian tradition and Latin usage made inevitable, largely masculine. Recourse to the contemporary expedients of using "God's" rather than "his" and "Godself" rather than "himself" would portray Augustine as having concerns that he simply did not have. Fortunately, there is a good deal more second-person address than third-person description of God, so the masculine language is less pervasive than one would expect. Occasionally Augustine will use feminine pronouns in referring to the Incarnate Word as Wisdom (the Latin for wisdom, *sapientia*, is feminine), and I translate accordingly; perhaps the use of feminine pronouns for Jesus (who does have a body and is unproblematically male) will go some way toward mitigating the effect of the generally masculine language for God.

I capitalize "Wisdom," "Truth," "Way," and other such words when they refer to God the Son, and "Gift" and "Charity" and other such words when they refer to God the Holy Spirit.

Scriptural references are given to Augustine's Bible. Most English translations of Scripture number the Psalms according to the Hebrew text, which has a different numbering from the one Augustine knew. For the sake of space I have not included marginal citations according to the Hebrew numbering, but I have included such citations in parentheses in the Scriptural Index. Where Augustine's text of Scripture differs from ours because he is using the Old Latin Version (an umbrella term for a number of Latin translations of Scripture before Jerome produced the Vulgate), I add VL (for *vetus Latina*, "old Latin"). Where the difference between Augustine's text and ours impedes understanding, I explain in a footnote.

I give no citations to any "books of the Platonists" (7.9.13). Any such citations must be to some degree speculative; we probably no longer even have those works in the Latin versions that Augustine knew. But there is a reason I find much more compelling than that. On nearly every page of the *Confessions*, and many times on most pages, we find the words of Scripture: quoted exactly, slightly adapted, developed, extended, the object of comment, meditation, argument, and analysis. Nowhere, not once, do we find such a treatment of the works of the Platonists; and when Augustine does tell us what he learned from the Platonists, crucially important though it was, he tells us in the words of Scripture. So I have given credit where Augustine thinks credit is due, and kept silent where Augustine thinks it best to keep silent.

---

5. Also of relevance to that passage: church music at that time, as for some centuries afterward, was monophonic (that is, sung in unison, not harmonized), so I avoid the anachronism of speaking of its "sweet harmony."

Abbreviations

1 Cor.	1 Corinthians	Heb.	Hebrews
1 Jn.	1 John	Is.	Isaiah
1 Kgs.	1 Kings	Jas.	James
1 Pet.	1 Peter	Jdt.	Judith
1 Sam.	1 Samuel	Jer.	Jeremiah
1 Thess.	1 Thessalonians	Jn.	John
1 Tim.	1 Timothy	Josh.	Joshua
2 Chron.	2 Chronicles	Lam.	Lamentations
2 Cor.	2 Corinthians	Lev.	Leviticus
2 Kgs.	2 Kings	Lk.	Luke
2 Macc.	2 Maccabees	Mal.	Malachi
2 Pet.	2 Peter	Mic.	Micah
2 Sam.	2 Samuel	Mk.	Mark
2 Thess.	2 Thessalonians	Mt.	Matthew
2 Tim.	2 Timothy	Num.	Numbers
Bar.	Baruch	Phil.	Philippians
Col.	Colossians	Prov.	Proverbs
Dan.	Daniel	Ps.	Psalms
Deut.	Deuteronomy	Rev.	Revelation
Eccl.	Ecclesiastes	Rom.	Romans
Eph.	Ephesians	Sir.	Sirach
Ex.	Exodus	Song	Song of Solomon
Ez.	Ezekiel	Tob.	Tobit
Gal.	Galatians	Tit.	Titus
Gn.	Genesis	Wisd.	Wisdom
Hab.	Habakkuk	Zech.	Zechariah

AV	Authorized (King James) Version	VL	Old Latin version (*vetus Latina*)
LXX	Septuagint		
NRSV	New Revised Standard Version		
par.	paralleled at		
RSV	Revised Standard Version		
qtd.	quoted at		
qtg.	quoting		

Suggestions for Further Reading

Michael Mendelson's entry on Augustine for the *Stanford Encyclopedia of Philosophy* (https://plato.stanford.edu/entries/augustine) is an excellent place to start for an overview of Augustine's life and work. *The Cambridge Companion to Augustine,* 2nd ed. (Cambridge University Press, 2014), edited by Eleonore Stump and David Vincent Meconi, presents accessible essays by several leading scholars on a wide range of themes in Augustine's work. Mary T. Clark's *Augustine* (Georgetown University Press, 1994; new edition, Continuum, 2005), is a very fine introduction to Augustine for general readers and students. A more advanced work (though by no means prohibitively difficult, and amply repaying any amount of effort) is John M. Rist, *Augustine: Ancient Thought Baptized* (Cambridge University Press, 1994), organized around general themes: words, signs, and things; certainty, belief, and understanding; soul, body, and personal identity; will, love, and right action; individuals, social institutions, and political life; and evil, justice, and divine omnipotence.

The classic biography of Augustine remains Peter Brown's *Augustine of Hippo: A Biography* (University of California Press, 1967; updated edition, 2000). Also noteworthy is James J. O'Donnell's *Augustine: A New Biography* (Harper, 2006).

There are two especially useful collections of essays on the *Confessions* in particular. *A Reader's Companion to Augustine's Confessions,* edited by Kim Paffenroth and Robert P. Kennedy (Westminster John Knox Press, 2003), comprises thirteen essays, one on each of the thirteen books of the *Confessions,* reading the whole in light of its parts and the parts in light of the whole. *Augustine's Confessions: Critical Essays,* edited by William E. Mann (Rowman & Littlefield, 2006), explores philosophical, theological, and psychological themes in the *Confessions* from a variety of perspectives.

Works Cited

The following translations and editions are cited by their author's last name:

Boulding, Maria. *The Confessions.* 2nd ed. Hyde Park, NY: New City Press, 2012.

Chadwick, Henry. *Saint Augustine: Confessions.* New York: Oxford University Press, 1991.

Constantine, Peter. *Confessions.* New York: Liveright Publishing Corporation, 2018.

O'Donnell, James J. *Augustine: Confessions.* Volume I: Introduction and Text. Volume II: Commentary, Books I–VII. Volume III: Commentary, Books VIII–XIII. Oxford: Clarendon Press, 1992.

Ruden, Sarah. *Confessions.* New York: The Modern Library, 2017.

Book One

The story begins with infancy and boyhood, but the telling of the story begins with praise to God. Augustine struggles to find words by which to fulfill the deep desire of the human heart to praise God, just as the infant Augustine will struggle to find words to express the desires of his body—the Latin word for infancy, *infantia*, is literally "speechlessness"—and the boy Augustine will struggle to master words in the service of ambition. Augustine acknowledges God's gifts in every aspect of his early life; he also acknowledges the misuse of those gifts, which—just like words themselves—are no less good for being misused; their misuse is lamentable precisely because they are good.

Augustine opens with praise to God and meditation on God's nature (1.1.1–1.5.6). He recalls the gifts that sustained him in his infancy and the sin that is manifest even in infants (1.6.7–1.7.12). In his boyhood (1.8.13–1.19.30) he learns to speak (1.8.13) and begins his studies (1.9.14–1.10.16, 1.13.20–1.18.29); his baptism is deferred (1.11.17–1.12.19), and he already manifests the sins of lust of the eyes, lust of the flesh, and worldly ambition (1.19.30). Nevertheless, Augustine thanks God for the gifts of his infancy and boyhood (1.20.31).

1.1   Great are you, Lord, and highly to be praised. Great is your power, and your wisdom is beyond measure. And human beings want to praise you—they who are just a portion of your creation, who carry around their mortality, who carry around the evidence of their own sin and the evidence that you resist the proud. And yet human beings, this portion of your creation, want to praise you. You rouse them to take delight in praising you: for you have made us for yourself, and our heart is restless until it comes to rest in you. *Ps. 47:2, 95:4, 144:3; Ps. 146:5; Prov. 3:34; Jas. 4:6; 1 Pet. 5:5*

Grant to me, Lord, that I may know and understand whether we must call upon you before we praise you, and know you before we call upon you. But who calls upon you without knowing you? One who calls upon you without knowing you is apt to call upon something altogether different. Or do we instead call upon you in order that we may know you? Yet how will they call upon one in whom they have not believed? And how will they believe without a preacher? And those who seek the Lord will praise him, for those who seek him find him, and those who find him will praise him. Let me seek you, Lord, by calling upon you; let me call upon you by believing in you; for you have been preached to us. It is my faith, Lord, that calls upon you: the faith *Ps. 104:1; Rom. 10:13–14; Ps. 21:27 / Mt. 7:7 par. Lk. 11:9*

1

that you have given me, that you inspired in me through the humanity
of your Son, through the ministry of your Preacher.[1]

2.2   And how will I call upon my God, my God and my Lord? For
surely I call him into myself when I call upon him.[2] And what place is
there in me for my God to come into me? Where shall God come into
me, God who made heaven and earth? Is it truly so, Lord my God?   *Gn. 1:1*
Is there something in me that can contain you? Do even heaven and
earth, which you made, and in which you made me, contain you? Or
does it turn out that whatever is contains you, because without you
whatever is would not be? And so because I too am, why am I asking
you to come into me, who would not be unless you were in me? I am
not hell, after all; and yet even in hell, you are present; for if I descend
into hell, you are there. I would not be, my God, I would not be at all   *Ps. 138:8*
if you were not in me. Or is it rather that I would not be if I were not
in you, from whom, through whom, and in whom are all things? This   *Rom. 11:36; 1*
too, Lord; this too. What place do I call you into, when I am in you?   *Cor. 8:6*
From what place do you come into me? To what place beyond heaven
and earth may I retreat so that my God can come into me there, my
God who said, "I fill heaven and earth"?   *Jer. 23:24*

3.3   Then do heaven and earth contain you, because you fill them? Or
do you fill them and something remains, because they do not contain
you? And into what do you pour out what remains of you after heaven   *Acts 2:17, 2:18; Joel*
and earth have been filled? Or have you, who contain all things, no   *2:28–29; Is. 44:3*
need to be contained in any place, because it is by containing them
that you fill the things you fill? They are not vessels that are full of you
and thereby give you shape and solidity; if they are shattered, you are
not poured out. And when you are poured out over us, you do not
run down to the lowest level, but instead you lift us up to the heights;   *Ps. 145:8*
you are not dispersed, but instead you gather us into one. But you,
the whole of you, fill all the things you fill, and you fill all things. Or,
because all things cannot contain the whole of you, do they contain
some part of you, and all things contain the same part of you at the
same time? Or does each thing contain a different part, bigger things
containing bigger parts and smaller things smaller parts? So then is one

---

1. Who is "your Preacher"? Some say Ambrose, but how would Augustine expect his readers to
recognize an allusion to someone he has not even mentioned yet? (Chadwick cites Letter 147.23.52,
but Augustine does not in fact call Ambrose "Preacher" there.) The most natural reading in context
is that "the ministry of your Preacher" is parallel to "the humanity of your Son." Augustine is saying
that the Incarnation is God's "fundamental act of revelation" (O'Donnell I:17), and the Preacher is
the Incarnate Word.
2. "Call upon" is *invocare*; "call . . . into" is *vocare in.*

part of you bigger than another? Or are you everywhere as a whole, and no thing contains the whole of you?

4.4   What are you, then, my God? What are you, I ask, if not the Lord God? For who is the Lord besides the Lord? Who is God besides our God? O highest, best, most powerful, most all-powerful, most merciful and most just, most hidden and most present, most beautiful and most steadfast, unwavering and incomprehensible, unchangeable but changing all things, never new, never old, making all things new and bringing old age upon the proud, though they know it not: you are always at work, always at rest, gathering, but not from any need, upholding and filling and protecting, creating and nourishing and bringing to maturity, going forth to seek even though you lack nothing. You love and do not burn with passion; you are jealous and free from anxiety; you repent and do not sorrow; you are angry and undisturbed. You change your works and do not change your plan. You take back what you find and have never lost. Though never in need, you are glad of gain; though never greedy, you demand interest. People offer you more than is required so that they will make a debtor of you, and yet who has anything that is not already yours? You repay debts, though you owe no one anything; you cancel debts but lose nothing. And what have we said, my God, my life, my holy sweetness? What does anyone say when speaking of you? But woe to those who keep silent about you, for though they prattle on and on, they are mute in all that matters.[3]

Ps. 17:32

*Jer. 32:19; Rom.
11:33 / Wisd.
7:27*
Job 9:5

*Ex. 20:5, 34:14; Joel
2:18; Zech. 1:14,
8:2 / Gn. 6:6–7;
1 Kgs. 15:35 / Ex.
4:14; Deut. 9:20*

Mt. 25:27

Lk. 10:35

1 Cor. 4:7

Jn. 11:25, 14:6

Ps. 31:3

5.5   Who will grant me rest in you? To whom shall I appeal for you to come into my heart and so intoxicate it that I forget what is bad in myself and embrace you, my one good? What are you for me? Have mercy, that I may speak. What am I to you that you command me to love you, and if I do not, you are angry with me and threaten me with overwhelming misery? Is not my very failure to love you great misery in itself? Woe is me! Tell me, Lord, through your acts of mercy, what

*Ps. 106:8, 106:15,
106:21, 106:31*

---

3. Literally: "for the talkative are mute" (*quoniam loquaces muti sunt*). My translation follows the interpretation given by O'Donnell (and borrows some of his language). Augustine frequently describes the Manichees (though not only them) as talkative, a fault he associates with curiosity and vanity. The point here is that those who say nothing about God—they may use the word "God," but they never succeed in saying anything true about the real God—spout a lot of words about other things but are hopelessly tongue-tied about the one crucial subject ("human beings want to praise you"). An alternative interpretation, frequently adopted, is that "those who say most say nothing," that is, nothing genuinely worthy of God, who is beyond our capacity to describe. But in that case it is hard to see how the second part of the sentence provides a reason for the first part, as the conjunction "for" (*quoniam*) requires. How is the impossibility of speaking worthily about God a reason to condemn those who keep silent? Shouldn't it be just the opposite?

you are to me. Say to my soul, "I am your salvation." Speak these words   *Ps. 34:3*
in such a way that I can hear them. Even now the ears of my heart are
before you, Lord. Open them, and say to my soul, "I am your salvation";
I will chase after the sound until I have you in my grasp. Do not hide
your face from me. Let me die, lest I die,[4] that I might see your face.   *Deut. 31:17, 32:20*
                                                                                  I Ex. 33:23
5.6   The house of my soul is too small for you to enter: make it spa-   *Is. 49:20*
cious. It is in shambles: restore it. There are things in it that you grieve   *Ez. 36:10, 36:33*
to look upon: I acknowledge and know this. But who will make it
clean? It is to you, and to no other, that I cry out, "Cleanse me, O Lord,
from the hidden faults that come from within me, and spare your ser-
vant from those that come from without."[5] I believe, and because I   *Ps. 18:13–14*
believe, I speak, Lord: this you know. In your presence, my God, I have   *Ps. 115:10; 2 Cor.*
spoken judgment against myself for my sins, and you have forgiven   *4:13*
the ungodliness of my heart. I do not contend in judgment with you,   *Ps. 31:5 / Jer. 2:29*
who are Truth itself; nor would I deceive myself, lest my iniquity lie   *Jn. 14:6*
to itself. So I do not contend in judgment with you: for if you, Lord,   *Ps. 26:12*
should make note of iniquities, O Lord, who will endure it?   *Ps. 129:3*

6.7   Yet even so, allow me to speak in the presence of your mercy; dust
and ashes though I am, allow me to speak. For truly it is to your mercy   *Gn. 18:27; Job*
that I am speaking, and not to human beings who mock me. Perhaps   *42:6 VL*
you, too, mock me; but you will turn and have mercy on me. For   *Ps. 70:20; Jer.*
what do I want to say, Lord, except that I do not know from where I   *12:15*
came here, into this—what shall I call it?—this life that dies, this death
that lives? I do not know. The comforts of your acts of mercy upheld
me, as I have heard from the parents of my flesh, from whom and in
whom[6] you formed me in time; for I do not remember. The comforts
of human milk welcomed me; neither my mother nor my nurses filled
their own breasts, but you, through them, provided the nourishment
of my infancy in the way that you have appointed, through the riches
that you have provided even for the lowest of things. It was your gift as
well that I did not want more than you gave, your gift that those who

---

4. Sermon 213.3.3: "Now someone who has not yet died or been resurrected is still living badly;
and if he is living badly, he is not alive. Let him die, lest he die. What does this mean, 'Let him die,
lest he die'? Let him be changed, lest he be damned. . . . 'For you are dead, and your life is hidden
with Christ in God' (Col. 3:3)."
5. Augustine interprets "the hidden faults that come from within" as sins that arise in the natural
course of our own thinking (*spontanea cogitatione*) and "those that come from without" as those
we commit at the suggestion or persuasion of someone else (*persuasione alterius*). See *De lib. arb.*
3.10.29, *Enarr. in Ps. en.* 1.14 and *en.* 2.13.
6. The first "whom" is masculine, referring to Augustine's father; the second is feminine, referring
to his mother.

nourished me wanted to give me what you had given them—for so well-ordered was their affection that they wanted to give to me out of the abundance they had received from you. It was good for them that I should have from them what was good for me, a good that came not from them, but through them. Indeed all good things come from you, God, and from my God comes all my salvation. It was only later that I came to know all this, when you cried out to me through these very things that you bestow both within and without. But in those early days all I knew was how to suck, to be content with bodily pleasures, and to cry over bodily pain: nothing more.

6.8   Later I also began to smile, first when I was asleep but then when I was awake. For so I have been told about myself, and I believe it, since we see other infants do so; of course I do not remember these things about myself. Little by little I became aware of where I was, and I wanted to make my desires apparent to those who could satisfy them, but I could not: for my desires were inside me, whereas they were outside, and no sense of theirs could give them entry into my soul. And so I tossed out gestures and noises, signs like my desires—such small and weak signs as I was able to make—and indeed they were not really like my desires. And when my elders did not do as I demanded, either because they did not understand me or because it would not have been good for me, I was furious that my betters were not under my control, that free people were not my servants, and I took my revenge on them by crying. The infants whom I have had the opportunity to observe have taught me that infants are like this. Unaware of it as they are, they are the ones who have informed me that I too was like this, more than my nurses, who knew me.

6.9   And now my infancy is long dead, but I am alive. But you, Lord, who are always alive, in whom nothing dies—because before the beginning of the ages, before anything that can be called "before," you are, and you are the God and Lord of all you have created, and in you the causes of all feeble things stand firm, the sources of all changeable things abide unchangeably, and the reasons of all reasonless and temporal things live eternally—answer my prayer, O God, and in your pity tell me, pitiable as I am, whether there was an earlier age of mine that died and gave way to infancy. Was it the age that I spent in my mother's womb? I have been told something about that age as well, and I have seen pregnant women myself. And what about the time before that, my sweetness, my God? Was I somewhere? Was I someone? I have no one who can tell me about such things: neither my father nor my mother could, nor yet the experience of others or my own memory. Or do you

laugh at me for asking these questions and command me instead to   *Ps. 36:13*
praise you and give thanks to you for what I do know?

6.10   I give thanks to you, Lord of heaven and earth, praising you for   *Mt. 11:25 par. Lk.*
my earliest days and my infancy, which I do not remember. You have   *10:21*
left it to human beings to infer these things about themselves from
what they see of others, and to believe many things about themselves
on the authority even of lowly women. Even then I was and I lived,
and already as my infancy was coming to a close I was looking for
signs by which to make my ideas known to others. From where could
such an animal come if not from you, Lord? Can anyone be the artisan
who fashions himself? Or is there any other spring from which being
and living flow into us besides your making us, Lord? For you, being
and living are not two different things, because supremely being and
supremely living are the Selfsame.[7] You are supreme being and you   *Ps. 4:9*
do not change. In you there is no "today" that runs its full length and
comes to an end—and yet today does run its full length and come to an
end in you, because all these things, too, are in you; and there would be   *Rom. 11:36*
no paths by which they could pass away if you did not contain them.
And because your years do not fail, your years are a "today." How many   *Ps. 101:28*
days—our own days and those of our ancestors—have already passed
through your today! From your today they received their boundaries
and existed in the way that you prescribed; still other days will succeed
them, and they too will receive their boundaries from your today and
exist as you prescribe. But you are the Selfsame, and it is today that you   *Ps. 101:28*
will accomplish, today that you have accomplished, all that is yet to
come tomorrow in the ages beyond, and all that belonged to yesterday
and to the yet more distant past. What is it to me if someone fails to
understand this? May even those who ask "What is this?" rejoice. May   *Ex. 13:14; Sir.*
they rejoice even in their perplexity; may they be glad that in failing   *39:26*
to find their answers they have found you, rather than finding answers
but missing you.

7.11   Hear my prayer, O God. Alas for human sins! And a human   *Ps. 54:2 / Is. 1:4*
being says these things, and you have mercy on him, because you made
him and did not make sin in him. Who will recount for me the sin
of my infancy? For in your eyes no one is free from sin, not even the
infant who has lived but one day on the earth. Who will recount them   *Job 14:4–5*

---

7. Augustine takes "the Selfsame" to be a name for God as immutable Being itself, in line with the
divine self-revelation of Exodus 3:14, "I am who I am." The word also occurs in the *Confessions*
at 7.9.14 in emphatic affirmation of the divinity of Christ ("since he is by nature the very same as
God," *quia naturaliter idipsum est*) as well as at 9.4.11, 9.10.24, and 12.7.7.

for me? Surely all babies recount them for me now, because in them I see what I do not remember about myself. So what was my sin in those days? Was it that I cried in my eager desire for the breast? If I were to behave this way now (not desiring the breast, of course, but the food suitable for my age), I would be quite justly scorned and rebuked. So what I did then deserved rebuke; but custom and reason alike forbade any rebuke because I would not be able to understand it. We root out such behavior and get rid of it as people grow up, and I have never seen anyone knowingly throw away something good when clearing his ground. Or were those things indeed good—for that time? Crying for what I wanted, even if getting it would be harmful? Growing bitterly angry when free people—my elders, even my parents, people who were far wiser than I—did not serve me, did not obey every whim of mine? Striking out, doing my best to hurt them, because they did not yield to my demands, when their yielding would only have harmed me? It is the bodily weakness of infants that is innocent, not their minds. I have seen and experienced an infant who was jealous: he could not yet speak, but he grew pale and gave a nasty look to another infant who was sharing his milk. Everyone knows about this sort of thing. Mothers and nurses say they have ways of correcting such behavior, though I do not know what they are. But we can hardly call it "innocence" when a baby cannot bear that someone else in direst need should have a share in this life-giving nourishment, even though the fountain of milk pours forth its riches unstintingly and in great abundance. We gently tolerate such behavior, not because it is trivial or inconsequential, but because it will be left behind as the child grows up—as is proved by the fact that we will not put up with such things in someone who is older.

7.12   And so, O Lord my God, who gave an infant life and a body that, as we see, you have furnished with senses, fashioned limb by limb, adorned with due proportion, and infused with all the vital forces needed to keep it whole and sound: you command me to praise you for all these things, to give thanks to you and sing praises to your Name, O Most High, for you are God, almighty and good, even if you had *Ps. 91:2* made only these things, which no one could make but you, O One and Only, from whom is all measure, O Most Beautiful, who give beautiful form to all things and set all things in order by your law.[8] I do not

---

8. The triad *measure/form/order* is frequent in the *Confessions*. Augustine understands measure as a thing's mode of being, form as its distinctive character as a certain kind of thing, and order as the dynamic interrelationship of things. He associates measure with God the Father, form with God the Son, and order with God the Holy Spirit. This triad gives shape to the last three books of the *Confessions*, with Book 11 devoted to measure, emphasizing the initial creation of formed matter, Book 12

remember living through this time—I believe what others have told me, and I infer from what I observe of other infants what I must have done, though these inferences are quite reliable—and so I hesitate to consider it part of the life that I am living in this present day. It is hidden in a darkness beyond the reach of my memory, every bit as much as my life in my mother's womb. If indeed I was conceived in iniquity, and in sins my mother nourished me in her womb, where, I beseech you, my God, where or when, O Lord, was I, your servant, innocent? But look: I will say no more about that time. What is it to me now? I cannot remember even a trace of it.

Tit. 2:12

Ps. 50:7

Ps. 115:16

8.13   And thus I moved on from infancy and entered boyhood. Or is it rather that boyhood entered me and displaced infancy? Infancy did not depart from me—for where would it go?—and yet it was no more. I was no longer a speechless infant; now I was a boy who could talk. I remember this, and later I came to understand how I learned to talk. My elders did not teach me by putting words in front of me according to some settled method of instruction, as a little later they taught me to read. No, I myself, using the mind that you, my God, had given me, tried with groans and various noises and gestures to convey the thoughts of my heart, so that my desires would be known; but when I could not express everything I wanted or make myself understood by everyone, I grasped with my memory: when my elders called something by its name and responded to that same sound by moving toward the thing, I took note of this and remembered that the sound they made when they wanted to indicate the thing was their name for it. That this is what they intended was evident from the movements of their bodies, which are like a natural, universal language: the expression of the face, the movement of the eyes, the gestures of the limbs, and the tone of the voice all expressing the disposition of the mind concerning the things that it seeks, possesses, spurns, or flees. And in this way, by hearing these words again and again in their proper context in various sentences, I gradually learned which things they were the signs of; and once my mouth had acquired facility with these signs, I was able to use them to express my desires. Thus I came to share with those among whom I lived in the use of signs for expressing desires, and I was drawn more fully into the tempestuous fellowship of human life, though I was still subject to the authority of my parents and the will of my elders.

---

devoted to form, emphasizing the forming of unformed matter into distinct kinds of things, and Book 13 devoted to order, emphasizing the work of the Holy Spirit in orienting believers to God.

9.14   O God, my God, what miseries I endured,[9] and for such trivialities! I was told that it was right for me as a young boy to submit to
those who were advising me about how to make my way in the world
and excel in the rhetorical skills by which I could gain a reputation and
earn deceitful riches. So I was sent to school to learn letters,[10] though,
wretch that I was, I had no idea of what was genuinely useful in this
study. And yet if I slacked off in my work, I was beaten—which drew
praise from my elders. And indeed many who came before us in this
life had laid down the paths of suffering on which we were compelled
to go, as labor and sorrow were multiplied upon the sons of Adam.[11]   *Gn. 3:16; Sir. 40:1*

   We did encounter people who prayed to you, Lord, and we learned
from them, thinking of you (so far as we could) as someone great who,
though not manifest to our senses, could hear us and come to our help.
For as a boy I began to pray to you, my help and my refuge. I untied   *Ps. 93:22*
my tongue to call upon you; small as I was, it was with no small eagerness that I prayed to you that I would not be beaten at school. And
when you did not heed me and thereby give me over to my foolishness,
my beatings were most amusing to my elders—even to my parents,
who did not want any evil to befall me. But the beatings were a great
and serious evil to me in those days.

9.15   O Lord, is there anyone so courageous, so powerfully and
eagerly devoted to you, that he disdains the rack and hooks and other
such tortures from which people throughout the world beg you, with
great terror, to deliver them? Is there such a one, I ask, who is so high-
minded because of his fervent devotion to you (for stupidity can produce the same attitude) that he regards these torments as trivial, even
though he loves those who fear them so bitterly, as our parents made
fun of the sufferings that our teachers inflicted on us boys? For we were
no less afraid of them, no less earnest in our prayers to be delivered
from them. And yet we sinned by not doing as much writing or reading or studying as was demanded of us. For it was not that we lacked

---

9. Terence, *Adelphoe* 867.

10. *Litteras* is hard to translate. It is sometimes "letters"—either in the sense of the symbols that are
combined to produce written words or in the sense that survives in English largely in the name "Col-
lege of Arts and Letters"—sometimes "literature" or even "literary culture." Here Augustine intends
the full range of meaning but particularly emphasizes reading, writing, and the study of literature.

11. "You come of the Lord Adam and the Lady Eve," said Aslan. "And that is both honour enough
to erect the head of the poorest beggar, and shame enough to bow the shoulders of the greatest
emperor in earth. Be content" (C. S. Lewis, *Prince Caspian* [New York: Macmillan, 1970], 211–
212). In Lewis, the expression "Son of Adam" is variously an endearment, a rebuke, and a badge
of honor; but in Augustine, the emphasis is always on the shame, not the honor. See also 8.9.21,
8.10.22, 13.21.30.

the capacity[12] or the talent, Lord—by your will you had given us those things, enough for our age—but that we enjoyed playing, and we were punished for it by people who, of course, behaved in exactly the same way themselves. But when adults waste their time, they call it "business," whereas when children do such things, they are punished. And no one feels sorry for the children or the adults. In fact, a fine judge of the matter would no doubt approve of my being beaten because my ball-playing as a boy interfered with my learning letters, which I would use as an adult to play a much more depraved game. And did the teacher who beat me act any differently? If he had been bested by a fellow teacher in some trivial dispute, he would have been racked with greater bitterness and envy than I felt when a playmate of mine outscored me in a ball game.

10.16   And yet I sinned, Lord God, ruler and creator of all natural things, though of sins only the ruler: O Lord my God, I sinned by disobeying the commands of my parents and teachers. Whatever they might have had in mind for me, I would be able afterward to make good use of the letters that they wanted me to learn. I was not disobedient because I was choosing better things; I simply loved playing. I loved the glory of victory in our games. I loved having my ears tickled by false tales that made them itch all the more insistently, and that same curi-   *2 Tim. 4:3–4* osity drew my eager eyes to the spectacular shows that are games for adults. Those who put on these spectacles enjoy such esteem and status that nearly all parents would be happy for their children to attain it; and yet they gladly allow their children to be beaten if such spectacles get in the way of the studies that they hope will someday enable their children to put on exactly those sorts of shows. Look mercifully on these things, O Lord, and deliver us who call upon you now; deliver,   *Ps. 24:16–18, 78:9* too, those who do not yet call upon you, so that they may call upon you and you may deliver them.

11.17   For even as a boy I had heard about the eternal life promised to us through the humility of the Lord our God in stooping to encoun-   *Phil. 2:8* ter our pride, and I was signed with the sign of his cross and salted with his salt[13] even from the time I came forth from the womb of my mother, who trusted firmly in you. You saw, Lord, when I was still a

---

12. *Memoria* here (as often in Augustine) means not merely memory but the total capacity of the mind for learning and retention. "Talent" translates *ingenium*, which can mean someone's "cast of mind"—the quality or distinctive character of someone's thinking—or, as here, brilliance, intellectual talent.
13. These practices marked Augustine as a catechumen, a status in the Church short of full membership, which came with baptism.

boy, how one day I suddenly fell ill with a stomach ailment and burned with fever and was on the verge of death. You saw, my God—for even then you watched over me—with what agitation of mind, with what faith, I begged for the baptism of your Christ, my God and my Lord, throwing myself on the mercy of my mother and of the mother of us all, your Church. And the mother of my flesh was greatly troubled, for in her heart, made chaste by her faith in you, she was more lovingly bringing my everlasting salvation to birth. She would have seen to it that I was hurriedly initiated and washed clean in your health-giving sacraments, confessing you, Lord Jesus, for the forgiveness of sins, had I not recovered right away. And so my cleansing was deferred, on the grounds that if I lived, I would inevitably become still more defiled, because the guilt incurred in the defilement of sins would be greater and more dangerous after that washing than before. I was already a believer, as were my mother and the whole household, except for my father alone. Yet though he did not yet believe in Christ, he did not keep me from believing; my mother's devotion had a grip on me, and he did not break it. For she did everything in her power to see to it that you, my God, would be my father more truly than he was, and you so helped her in this that she had the victory over her husband, whom she served—though she was the better of the two—because in doing so she was also serving you, who gave her this command.

Jn. 20:28

Gal. 4:26

Lev. 16:30

Tit. 3:5

11.18 I ask you, God: I would like to know—if only you were willing for me to know— for what purpose my baptism was delayed. Was it for my good that the reins of sin were in a manner loosened for me? Or were they indeed loosened? How is it that even now we hear voices from all sides, saying of all kinds of people, "Leave them alone; let them do as they please. They have not yet been baptized." Yet when it comes to the health of the body, we do not say, "Let them be wounded more severely. They have not yet been healed." How much better it would have been if I had been healed right away and then looked after by my own care and that of my family, so that you, having restored the health of my soul, would also preserve it in your safekeeping. Truly it would have been better. But waves of temptation, many and great, could be seen approaching on the far side of my boyhood. My mother knew them, and she preferred to let them break on the earth from which I would afterward be formed, rather than on the new image itself.

Ps. 34:3

12.19 Yet even in that very boyhood, about which there was so much less anxiety than there was about my adolescence, I did not like to study and hated being forced to; but I was forced to study, and it was a good thing for me that I was. I was not acting well, for I studied only

because I was compelled, and no one acts well unwillingly, even if what
he does is good. Nor did those who forced me act well; it was you, my
God, who acted well toward me. They did not see the use to which I
would put the things they were compelling me to learn, beyond satisfying the insatiable cravings of a wealth that was really poverty and
a glory that was really disgrace. But you, by whom our very hairs are
numbered, used for my benefit the error of those who were insisting   *Mt. 10:30*
that I learn; and my own error, my unwillingness to learn, you used for
my punishment. So small a boy, so great a sinner: I did indeed deserve
the beatings I received. Thus you acted well toward me through those
who were not acting well, and you justly punished me through my own
sin. For you have commanded—and so it comes to pass—that every
disordered mind is its own punishment.

13.20   But why was it that I hated learning the Greek I had to study
as a boy? To this day I do not quite understand it. I loved Latin—not
the elementary grammar but the literature.[14] For I found those earliest lessons, in which I learned to read and write and do arithmetic, as
much of a chore and a punishment as all my instruction in Greek. But
that, too, came from sin, from the vanity of the life by which I was flesh
and a breath going forth and not returning. For those first lessons were   *Ps. 77:39*
of course better than the later ones, because they were more depend-
able. I was being given the capacity, which I acquired and still have,
to read any writing that I come across and to write things myself, if I
choose. How much better than those later lessons in which I was forced
to memorize the wanderings of Aeneas, whoever that was, forgetting
my own wanderings, and to weep over dead Dido, who killed herself
for love, when all the while I had no tear to shed for myself, wretch
that I was, dying in the midst of these things, far away from you, O
God my life.

13.21   For what is more wretched than a wretch who feels no sorrow for himself but mourns the death of Dido, caused by her love for
Aeneas, yet does not mourn his own death, caused by a lack of love for
you, O God, light of my heart, bread of the inward mouth of my soul,   *Jn. 1:9, 3:19–21; 1*
power that marries my mind to the storehouse of my thought? I did   *Jn. 1:5 / Jn. 6:35*
not love you, and I was unfaithful to you, and from all around I heard   *Ps. 72:27–8*

---

14. Literally, "I loved Latin *litteras*, not [the *litteras*] that the first masters [teach] but [the *litteras*]
that those who are called *grammatici* teach." By "the first masters" he means those who taught reading, writing, and grammar (as well as arithmetic); the *grammatici* taught literature, especially poetry.
See fn. 10 for the range of meaning of *litteras*. In the present context, we lack a single expression in
English that will cover the whole ground from basic reading to literary criticism, so I have left the
word out altogether.

shouts of encouragement for my unfaithfulness. For friendship with
this world is unfaithfulness to you, and those shouts of encouragement
make one ashamed not to be that kind of person. For these things I
shed no tear, but I wept for Dido, "slain by the sword, chasing after an
end to her woe,"[15] while I had left you behind to chase after the lowest
of your creatures, dust returning to dust. And if I were forbidden to
read them, I would be sad because I was not reading something that
would make me sad. It is by such madness as this that the study of
literature is regarded as more prestigious and more fruitful than the
lessons in which I learned to read and write.

13.22   But now let my God cry out in my soul, and let your Truth say
to me, "It is not so; it is not so. That earlier teaching is better by far." I
would certainly rather forget the wanderings of Aeneas and all that sort
of thing than how to read and write. To be sure, curtains hang before
the doorways of the schools of literature—not, however, to give honor
to what they conceal, but to keep its errors out of sight. Let those buy-
ers and sellers of literary study not cry out against me—I am no longer
afraid of them—as I confess to you, my God, what my soul wishes to
confess; let them not cry out against me as I come to rest in denounc-
ing my evil ways so that I may love your good ways. Suppose I were to
ask these teachers whether it is true, as the poet says, that Aeneas once
went to Carthage. The more ignorant among them would not know
how to reply, but the well-instructed would say no, it is not true. But
if I were to ask how the name "Aeneas" is spelled, everyone who has
learned this would give the correct answer according to the convention
and custom that human beings have established for the use of these
signs. And if I were to ask which would be a greater hindrance in life,
to forget how to read and write or to forget these poetic fancies, anyone not utterly out of his senses would know precisely how to answer.
So I was sinning as a boy when I loved those worthless studies more
than the quite useful ones—or rather hated the useful ones and loved
the worthless. But "One plus one is two, two plus two is four" was
an annoying singsong to me in those days, whereas the showcasing of
vanity—a wooden ship full of soldiers and Troy ablaze and "the very
shade of dead Croesus"[16]—was sweet to me above all else.

14.23   Why, then, did I hate Greek literature, which is also full of
such stories? For Homer too was adept at weaving such fictions, and
there is great sweetness in his vanity, but to me as a boy he was bitter. I

Ps. 39:16

Jas. 4:4

Gn. 3:19

*Ps. 118:101; Jer.
18:11*

---

15. Virgil, *Aeneid* 6.457.
16. Virgil, *Aeneid* 2.772.

believe Virgil seems this way to Greek children when they are forced to learn him as I was forced to learn Homer. It must be the difficulty, the very great difficulty, of learning a foreign language that sprinkled gall over all the sweetness of marvelous tales told in Greek. I knew none of the words, and I was sternly threatened with savage terrors and punishment to get me to learn them. Of course, there had been a time as an infant when I knew no Latin words either, and yet I learned, simply by paying attention, without any fear or struggle, amidst the endearments of my nurses and the jests and laughter and banter of those around me. I needed no threat of punishment to impel me to learn them, because my own heart impelled me to bring forth its thoughts, and there was no way to do so without learning some words, from people who were not teaching but simply talking, and in their hearing I brought forth whatever I was thinking. This shows clearly enough that unrestrained curiosity is a greater force for learning these things than is fearful constraint. But such constraint keeps curiosity in bounds according to your laws, O God—your laws, which from the schoolteacher's cane to the martyrs' trials can mix up the bitter medicine that calls us back to you from the destructive delight that is the path along which we run away from you.

15.24   Hear my cry, O Lord, lest my soul grow faint under your discipline, lest I grow faint in confessing to you your acts of mercy, by which you delivered me from all my very evil ways, so that you may become sweeter to me than all the allurements that I once followed, and I may love you with all my strength and take hold of your hand with the deepest affection, and you will deliver me from all temptation even to the end. For truly, O Lord, my King and my God, I want everything useful I learned as a boy to be of service to you; let my speaking and writing and reading and counting be of service to you. For when I was learning empty trifles, you gave me your discipline; you have forgiven me the sins of my delights in such vanity. I did, after all, learn many useful words in the course of my studies; but those words could have been taught apart from all that foolishness, and that is the safe path in which children ought to walk.[17]

Ps. 54:2 / Ps. 83:3

2 Kgs. 17:13; 2 Chron. 7:14; Jer. 36:3, 36:7

Ps. 17:30; Mt. 6:13 / Ps. 15:10, 37:7, 67:17; 1 Cor. 1:8 / Ps. 5:3, 43:5

16.25   But woe to you, torrent of human custom! Who will withstand you? How long will it be until you are at last dried up? For how long will you toss the children of Eve into that great and fearsome sea which even those who have come on board the wooden vessel are scarcely

Ps. 75:8

Gn. 3:20

---

17. "empty trifles," "vanity," and "foolishness" all translate forms of *vanus;* the variety of translations is intended to convey the many nuances of that word.

able to cross in safety?[18] Did I not read in you that Jupiter was both the Thunderer and an adulterer? Of course he could not be both: but the story is told in this way so that the false thunderbolt will accredit his genuine adultery as worthy of imitation. Is anyone among these gowned masters content to listen to one of their own, a combatant in the same arena, who cries out and says, "Homer invented these tales, ascribing human qualities to the gods; but how much better to ascribe divine qualities to us"?[19] Yes, Homer invented these tales: but it would be truer to say that he ascribed divine qualities to human depravity, so that shameful acts would no longer be accounted shameful, and those who indulge in them would think that they are emulating the very gods of heaven instead of corrupt human beings.

16.26   And yet, you hellish torrent, the children of men are cast into you, fees in hand, so that they can learn these things. There is great interest when this is offered openly in the marketplace, in view of the law that appoints a public salary over and above the private fees. And you break upon the rocks and make your noise: "This is the place to learn words! This is the place to acquire the eloquence that is so essential for persuasion and argument!" So then do you mean that we would not know the words "golden rain," "lap," "trick," and "heavenly temples," and the other words that appear in that passage, if Terence had not used them to tell of a wicked young man who took Jupiter as a model for his own fornication? He looks at a wall painting that shows how Jupiter tricked a woman by sending a shower of golden rain into Danae's lap. Look how he incites his own lust under this heavenly tutelage: "Oh, what a god," he says, "who shakes the temples of heaven with his mighty thunder! Mortal that I am, I cannot call down thunder; but his other act I have indeed accomplished, and with pleasure!"[20] Such filth does not make these words at all easier to learn, but such words embolden those who would perpetrate this filth. I do not blame the words, which are chosen and precious vessels. I blame the wine of error that was poured into them by drunken teachers who would beat us if we did not drink what they set before us and would not permit any appeal to a sober judge. And yet, my God, in whose sight I can now remember this without anxiety, I took pleasure in learning these things. Wretch that I was, I enjoyed them, and thus I acquired a reputation as a promising young man.

---

18. "the wooden vessel": literally, "the wood" (*lignum*). The metaphor, of course, requires a ship; but the language makes it clear that the wooden vessel that allows safe passage is the Cross of Christ.
19. The quotation is from Cicero, *Tusculan Disputations* 1.26.65.
20. Augustine takes the story, and much of his language in recounting it, from Terence, *Eun.* 583–591.

17.27 Permit me, my God, to say something of my intelligence, which was your gift, and of the acts of madness by which it was squandered. I was given an assignment that greatly unsettled me: for my reward would be either praise or disgrace and, I feared, a beating. I was to declaim a speech that Juno made when she was angry and grieved because she could not repel the Trojan king from Italy.[21] Juno had never made such a speech, I was told; but we were forced to follow the wandering footprints of poetic fictions and express in prose what the poet had expressed in verse. And the speaker who would gain the most applause would be the one who, without compromising the dignity of the person being portrayed, most effectively conveyed the emotions of anger and grief and found suitable words to express his meaning. And what good did it do me, O true life, my God, that I received greater acclaim for my speech than my many fellow students of my own age? Are not all those things smoke and wind? Was there no other subject in which I could have put my intelligence and my tongue to work? Yes: your praises, O Lord; your praises, given in your Scriptures, could have propped up the branch of my heart so that it would not be carried off by these empty trifles, a prey to the birds of the air. For there is more than one way to sacrifice to fallen angels.

18.28 But it was hardly surprising that I was carried away from you, my God, and into vanities, considering the people who were held up as examples for me to emulate. If, in recounting some acts of theirs that were not at all bad, they had fallen into some error of pronunciation or grammar,[22] they would have been mortified and held in contempt; but if they told the story of their lusts in well-chosen words and with style and elegance, they would be proud of themselves and win praise from others. You see all this, Lord, and you keep silent; you are long-suffering and rich in mercy and truth. Will you always keep silent? Even now you deliver from this monstrous pit the soul that seeks you and thirsts for your delights, whose heart says, "I have sought your face. Your face, O Lord, will I seek": for I was far from your face in the darkness of my affection. It is not by walking, not by spatial distance, that we journey away from you and return to you. That younger son of yours[23] did not look for horses or chariots or ships, or fly away on visible wings or make his journey by any movement of his limbs, to go live in that far country where he would waste in riotous living what

Ps. 85:15, 102:8

Ps. 85:13

Ps. 41:3–4, 62:2

Ps. 26:8

---

21. Virgil, *Aeneid* 1.38.
22. Augustine gives an example of mispronunciation (*barbarismus*) in the second sentence of 18.29 and an example of a grammatical mistake (*solecismus*) in the last sentence of that paragraph.
23. "That younger son of yours"—that is, the prodigal son in the parable found in Luke 15.

you had given him on his departure. You were a loving father in giving to him, and still more loving when he returned empty-handed. So it is by the lustfulness, the darkness, of our affections that we are far away from your face.

18.29 Look down, Lord God; look down, as you always do, with forbearance. See how carefully the children of men observe the conventions about letters and syllables that they have received from previous speakers but give no heed to the eternal covenant of everlasting salvation that they have received from you—so much so that those who uphold and teach the standard pronunciation would give greater offense by saying "'uman being," without the aspirate, in violation of the orthodoxies of literate culture, than they would by hating a fellow human being, in violation of your commandments. As if there were any greater danger from a human enemy than from the very hatred that one feels toward him! As if one did more serious harm to someone else by persecuting him than to one's own heart by stoking one's hostility! And certainly no knowledge of literature lies as deep within us as what is written on our conscience, that we are doing to another what *Rom. 2:15* we would not want done to ourselves. How hidden you are, dwelling *Tob. 4:16; Mt.* on high in silence, O God, who alone are great! In accordance with *7:12; Lk. 6:31 /* your never-failing law, you scatter the punishment of blindness over *Is. 33:5* unlawful cravings. Someone who is seeking a reputation for eloquence will take the greatest care not to make a grammatical error[24] when excoriating his enemy with the most savage hatred before a human judge and with a crowd standing around; but against the prospect that his fury will cut off a human being from human society he will take no precaution at all.

19.30 I lingered on the threshold of this kind of life throughout my boyhood, wretch that I was. This was my training ground, one where I was more fearful of mispronouncing a word than I was concerned, if I made such an error, not to envy those who did not. I say these things and confess to you, my God, the things for which I was praised by those whose good opinion meant to me that I was living a worthy life. For I was blind to the abyss of wickedness into which I had been cast, far from your eyes. What indeed could have been more dis- *Ps. 30:23* gusting in your eyes than I was? Even my fellows were put off by the countless lies I told to deceive the servant who accompanied me to

---

24. Augustine actually gives a specific example of a grammatical error, but because it involves using the ablative case with a preposition that requires the accusative (*inter hominibus* instead of *inter homines*), it obviously would not survive translation into English.

school, my teachers, and my parents, and all because I loved to play and was absurdly eager to watch worthless shows and imitate them. I stole things from my parents' cellar and from the table, driven by gluttony or in order to have things to give to the other boys as payment for playing with me; for they would not play unless I gave them something, even though they enjoyed our games as much as I did. In our play I cheated in order to win, overcome by my pointless craving for superiority. But I could not bear it if others did to me as I was doing to them: if I caught someone else cheating, I denounced him ferociously. And if someone else caught me and denounced me, I preferred to lash out rather than to give way. Is this the innocence of boyhood? It is not, O Lord; it is not. I beseech you, my God. As the years go by, these sins concerning servants and teachers, marbles, balls, and pet sparrows, yield to sins concerning magistrates and kings, gold, estates, and slaves; and the master's cane likewise yields to more severe punishment. So, our King, when you said that "of such is the kingdom of heaven," it *Mt. 19:14* was only the small stature of children that you commended as a sign of humility.

20.31   Yet even if it had been your will, O Lord, that I should not live past boyhood, I would have owed thanks to you, our God, most excellent and supremely good Creator and Governor of the universe. For even then I had being, I lived, and I had sensation; I looked after my own health and wholeness, a trace of that deeply hidden Oneness from which I had my being; by an inner sense I guarded the integrity of my outer senses; and in my small thoughts about small things I delighted in truth. I hated to be deceived, I had an excellent memory, I was well furnished with speech, I was touched by friendship. I avoided pain, humiliation, and ignorance. In such a living creature how astonishing, how worthy of praise, were all these things! But they were all gifts from my God. I did not give them to myself; they are good, and all of them together make me who I am. Therefore, the one who made me is good, and he is himself my good, and in him I rejoice for all the good things *Ps. 2:11* that made me who I was even as a boy. For this was my sin: I sought pleasures, exaltations, and truths not in him, but in his creatures—in myself and in the rest of them—and so I rushed into pains, embarrassments, and errors. I give thanks to you, my sweetness, my honor, and my assurance; my God, I thank you for your gifts. Preserve them for *2 Cor. 9:15* me, I pray. For so you will preserve me, and your gifts to me will be enlarged and brought to completion; and I myself will be with you, for my very being is also your gift.

Book Two

Lust of the flesh—excessive or misdirected love of sensible things—had been present from the beginning, but in adolescence it takes on a powerful new form: sexual desire. No one in Augustine's life, least of all Augustine himself, is willing to impose restraint on his desire. He "did not keep the measure of mind to mind: friendship, its boundaries set off with dazzling light" (2.2.2). The perversion of friendship also plays a key role in Augustine's theft of a neighbor's pears, a misdeed that receives sustained attention not because it is particularly wicked, but because it is particularly puzzling. It seems unintelligible that anyone could do wrong simply for the sake of doing something wrong, as Augustine did; but even such an apparently inexplicable act makes sense when seen as a perverse imitation of God, the source of all good.

Augustine recounts his sexual awakening in adolescence (2.1.1–2.3.8), which his father notices with pride (2.3.6) and his mother does too little to restrain (2.3.7–8). With a group of companions Augustine steals some pears from a neighbor's tree (2.4.9–2.10.18). All people act for the sake of obtaining something they regard as good (2.5.10–11), but there seems to have been nothing good to motivate the theft (2.6.12). Augustine reflects that all goodness, real or apparent, has its source in God (2.6.13), and his theft can be understood as a perverse imitation of God (2.6.14), though he would not have done it if he had been alone (2.8.16–2.9.17).

1.1   I want to call to mind the ugly deeds I carried out and the carnal corruptions of my soul, not because I love them, but in order that I might love you, my God. It is for the love of your love that I do this, that I revisit the memory of my utterly depraved way of life. How bitter it is to think over it all again! Yet I do this so that I might receive your sweetness, O sweetness that cannot deceive, sweetness that is blissful and secure. It is for the love of your love that I gather together the scattered fragments into which I was torn while I wandered away from you, who are One, and lost myself among the Many. For in the days of my adolescence I was on fire to take my fill of hell, and I had the effrontery to make a savage of myself in various shadowy loves. My beauty wasted away, and in your sight I was wholly putrid; yet in my own eyes I was an appealing sight, and I wanted very much for others to find me appealing too.   *Ps. 78:10*

2.2   And what was it that gave me pleasure? Only to love, and to be loved. But I did not keep the measure of mind to mind: friendship, its boundaries set off with dazzling light. No, I was caught in the vapors

19

of murky lust of the flesh, of the bubbling sores of puberty, which so   *1 Jn. 2:16*
clouded and darkened my heart that I could not distinguish the clear
brightness of love from the fog of lust. A disorderly mixture of the
two tossed me about like a storm, ravaging me in the weakness of my
youth, casting me over the cliffs of desire and plunging me into the
raging abyss of vice. Your wrath against me had grown strong, and I
knew it not. I had been deafened by the clanking of the chains of my
mortality, the punishment for my soul's pride, and I was going further
and further away from you—and you allowed it. I was tossed around,
poured out; I was melting away, boiling over in my fornications; and
you kept silent. O my joy, so late in coming! You kept silent then, and
I went ever further from you, into more and more sterile seeds, seeds
that brought forth only sorrows, proud in my humiliation and restless
in my weariness.

2.3   Who might have set a measure to my turmoil and turned the
fleeting beauties of these newest temptations to some good use, fixing
a boundary for their sweetness, so that the roiling waves of my youth
would break upon the shore of marriage? If I could not have found
tranquility in the end of begetting children—as your law prescribes,[1]
O Lord who form even the offspring of our mortality and can impose
a gentle hand to soften the thorns that were excluded from your paradise; for your omnipotence is not far from us even when we are far   *Gn. 3:17–18*
from you—this, at any rate, is certain: I could have heeded the voice
from your clouds: "Those who marry will have tribulation in the flesh,
but I would spare you this," and "It is good for a man not to touch a   *1 Cor. 7:28*
woman," and "He who has no wife thinks on the things of God, how   *1 Cor. 7:1*
he might please God; but he who is joined in marriage thinks on the
things of the world, how he might please his wife." I should have lis-   *1 Cor. 7:32–33*
tened more carefully to these words; cut off for the sake of the kingdom
of heaven, I would have awaited your embrace with still greater joy.   *Mt. 19:12*

2.4   Instead, wretch that I was, I boiled over, following the violent
impulse of my own debauchery and leaving you behind. I transgressed
all your laws but did not escape your chastisements—for what mortal
can? You were always present, raging against me in your mercy and
scattering the most bitter vexations over all my illicit joys so that I
would look for a joy that had no vexation and find that I could have
none outside of you, O Lord: outside of you, who make suffering into
a teacher, and strike in order to heal, and kill us lest we die apart from   *Ps. 93:20 / Deut.*
you. Where was I? How distant was my exile from the delights of your   *32:39*

---

1. Genesis 1:28, "Be fruitful and multiply and fill the earth."

house in that sixteenth year of the age of my flesh, when the madness of   *Mic. 2:9*
lust wielded its scepter in me—and I surrendered to it completely—a
lust that is given free rein by human shamelessness but is forbidden by
your laws? And no one in my family tried to save me from falling by
getting me married; they cared only that I learned how to speak as well
and as persuasively as possible.

3.5   My studies had been interrupted in that year. I had been brought
back from Madaura, the nearby town where I was staying in order to
begin to learn literature and rhetoric, and my father, who was only a
poor citizen of Thagaste, was getting the money together to send me
farther afield, to Carthage—he was not wealthy, but he had great ambitions for me.

To whom am I telling this story? Not to you, my God; no, it is in
your presence that I tell this story to my own race, the human race, to
however small a part of it may chance across these words. And to what
purpose am I doing this? So that I, and anyone else who reads this, may
think from how great a depth we must call upon you. And what comes   *Ps. 129:1*
closer to your ears than a heart that confesses, a life that is lived by faith?   *Hab. 2:4; Rom.*
1:17; Gal. 3:11;
Heb. 10:38

Everyone was full of praise for that man, my father, who spent
beyond his means to provide his son with whatever was needed for a
long stay in a distant city so that I could continue my studies. Many
much richer citizens took no such trouble for their sons, much as my
own father gave no heed to how I was growing up in you or how chaste
I was, as long as I was cultured—though this culture was a lack of cul-
tivation from you, O God, who are the one true and good master of
this field of yours, my heart.[2]

3.6   But in that sixteenth year, when our household's straitened circumstances kept me from my studies, I went back to live with my
parents and was freed from all schoolwork. The brambles of lust grew
over my head, and no one lifted a hand to clear them away. Indeed,
when my father saw in the baths that I was growing into manhood
and was endowed with the arousal of adolescence, he boasted of it to
my mother, as though he were already expecting grandchildren. He
rejoiced in the sort of drunkenness by which this world forgets its creator and loves your creature rather than you, drunk on the invisible   *Rom. 1:25*
wine of a perverse self-will that is bent upon the very lowest things. But

---

2. See 1 Corinthians 3:9, "You are God's field," and the parable of the wheat and the tares in
Matthew 13:24–30, in which the landowner whose field has been sown with weeds (darnel), and
who instructs his servants to wait for the harvest to separate the wheat from the weeds, is addressed
as "master" (*dominus*).

you had already begun to build your temple in my mother's heart and   *1 Cor. 3:16–17*
laid the foundation of your holy dwelling place; but my father was a   *Sir. 24:14*
catechumen, and a recent one at that. And so she was seized with holy
fear and trembling, and although I was not yet a believer, she feared the
misshapen paths followed by those who turn their back to you rather
than their face.   *Jer. 2:27*

3.7   Alas for me! And do I dare to say that you, my God, were silent
as I went further and further away from you? Did you really say nothing to me in those days? The winsome words that you spoke into my
ears through your faithful servant, my mother: whose words were
they, if not yours? But they did not make their way from my ears into
my heart, so that I might act as they urged me to do. For it was her
desire—and I remember how she admonished me privately and with
great anxiety—that I should avoid fornication and, above all, that I
should not commit adultery with another man's wife. Womanly admo-
nitions, I thought them; I would have been embarrassed to obey them.
But no: they were yours, and I knew it not. I thought you were keeping
silent and she was the one speaking; but you were not silent; you were
speaking through her, and in scorning her I was scorning you—I, her
son, the son of your handmaid, I, your servant. But I knew it not. I   *Ps. 115:16*
rushed ahead, so blind that among those of my own age I was ashamed
of being less vicious than they were. For I would hear them boasting
of their crimes: the more disgraceful the act, the more they boasted. So
I had pleasure not only in doing what I wanted to do but also in the
praise I received for having done it.

What deserves reproach, if not vice? But I became more vicious in
order to escape reproach, and when I had nothing to admit that would
have put me on the same level as those who were lost, I would pretend
to have done what I had not done, lest I should appear contemptible
because I was more innocent and be looked down upon because I was
more chaste.

3.8   What companions I had as I walked the streets of Babylon and   *Rev. 17:5*
wallowed in its filth as if it were spices and precious ointments! And as I   *Jer. 38:22 / Song*
4:14
clung more and more tenaciously to its very center, the invisible enemy
trampled me underfoot and seduced me—for I was ripe for seduction.
And the mother of my flesh, though she had fled from the center of
Babylon, lingered still in its outskirts. Though she admonished me to   *Jer. 51:6*
be chaste, she was not concerned about what she heard about me from
her husband. She thought it would be burdensome for the present and
dangerous for the future if I were restrained within the limits of marital
affection (assuming my lust could not be cut down to the quick). She

made no effort to get me married because she was afraid that being shackled to a wife would interfere with my hopes: not the hope that my mother had of life with you in the age to come, but hopes for my literary career. I could not tell which of my parents was more determined that I should have such a career: my father, who thought hardly at all about you and thought trivialities about me, or my mother, who thought that the usual course of study in that field would not merely do no harm but would actually help me appreciably in coming to you. At any rate, so I conjecture from what I remember of my parents' characters. And the reins were slackened to let me dissipate myself amidst various affections, with no stern hand to put me in check. All these things were a dense fog cutting me off from the brightness of your truth, O my God, and my iniquity burst out as from fatness.

Ps. 72:7

4.9   Certainly, O Lord, your law punishes theft; and it is a law written upon human hearts, a law that not even iniquity itself erases. After all, what thief will tolerate another thief? Even a rich thief will not put up with someone who steals out of need. And yet I willed to steal, and I carried out the theft, driven by no neediness except that I was bereft of justice—which I loathed—and crammed full of iniquity. For I stole something of which I already had plenty, and much better than what I stole. Nor did I want to enjoy the thing that I desired to steal; what I wanted to enjoy was the theft itself, the sin.

Ex. 20:15; Deut. 5:19 / Rom. 2:14–15

There was a pear tree near our vineyard, laden with fruit that was not enticing in either appearance or taste. One wretched night—it was our unhealthy custom to keep up our games in the streets well into the night, and we had done so then—a band of altogether worthless young men set out to shake that tree and run off with its fruit. We took away an enormous haul, not for our own food but to throw to the pigs. Perhaps we ate something, but even if we did, it was for the fun of doing what was not allowed that we took the pears. Behold my heart, O God; behold my heart, on which you had mercy in the depths of that abyss. Behold, let my heart tell you now what it was seeking there: seeking in such a way that I would be wicked for no reason, so that there would be no cause for my wickedness but wickedness itself. It was foul, this wickedness, and yet I loved it. I loved perishing. I loved my own falling away: I did not love the thing into which I fell, but the fall itself. In my very soul I was vile, and I leapt down from your stronghold into destruction, not striving for something disgraceful, but seeking disgrace.

Gn. 3:6

Mt. 7:6; Lk. 15:15

Ps. 70:3

5.10   Truly there is a loveliness in beautiful bodies, in gold and silver and all the rest; in fleshly touch there is great power in harmony;

and each of the other senses has a bodily quality accommodated to it. Honor in this age and the power to command and subdue have their splendor; from them arises the eagerness to exact vengeance. And yet in striving after all these things we must not depart from you, O Lord, or stray from your law. The life that we live here has an attractiveness all its own because of the due measure of its beauty and its fitting relation to all these things that are the lowest of beautiful objects. Human friendship, too, is sweet in its precious bond because it makes many souls one. On account of all these things, and others like them, we make room for sin: because of our ungoverned inclination toward these things—for though they are goods, they are the lowest goods— we abandon the better and the highest goods; we abandon you, O Lord our God, and your truth and your law. For even those lowest things have their delights, but not like my God, who created all things; for the righteous delight in God, and he is the delight of those who are upright in heart.

Gn. 1:1

Ps. 63:11

5.11 When a question arises about why some criminal act was done, people do not typically accept any explanation until it appears that there was a desire to attain, or a fear of losing, one of those goods that we have called the lowest goods. These are beautiful and becoming, though they are abject and contemptible in comparison with the higher goods that bring true happiness. Someone has committed murder. Why did he do it? He loved his victim's wife or estate, or he wanted to steal enough to live on, or he was afraid of losing something to his victim, or he was burning to revenge himself on someone who had injured him. Surely no one has ever committed murder simply because he delighted in murder itself! Who would believe such a thing? Even for that savage and most cruel man of whom it was said that he was wicked and cruel for no reason, a cause is nonetheless stated: "lest through idleness," it says, "his hand or spirit should become useless."[3] And ask again: "Why did he do this?" It was so that once he seized the city through the practice of his crimes, he might obtain honors, powers, and riches, and he would be free from the law and "from the burden of the poverty of his estate—and his own consciousness of the guilt of his crimes."[4] So not even Catiline loved his crimes; he loved something else that was the cause of his committing those crimes.

6.12 What did I—wretch that I was—love in you, my theft, my crime by night in my sixteenth year? You were not beautiful, for you

---

3. Sallust, *Catil.* 16.3.
4. Sallust, *Catil.* 5.7.

were a theft. Or are you indeed anything at all, so that I might speak to you?

Those pears that we stole were beautiful, for they were created by you, O most beautiful of all, Creator of all, good God, God my supreme good and my true good. Those pears were beautiful, but they were not what my wretched soul lusted after. After all, I had plenty of better pears; I picked those merely in order to steal. The pears that I had plucked I threw away. The only thing I tasted from them was iniquity; enjoying that was what made me happy. For even if something from those pears did enter my mouth, it was the crime that gave it savor. And now, O Lord my God, I am asking what delighted me in that theft, and behold! there is no beauty there. I do not merely mean such beauty as is found in equity and practical wisdom, or in the human mind and memory and the senses and the life of the body; not even as the stars are beautiful and adorn their proper places, as the earth and the sea are beautiful, teeming with new lives that are born to take the place of things that are passing away—it lacked even the abortive and shadowy beauty of deceptive vices.

6.13   For pride mimics loftiness, when in fact you are the one God, Most High above all things. What does ambition seek but honors and glory, when in fact you are the one who is to be honored before all things and are glorious unto eternity? The cruelty of the powerful is meant to inspire fear, but who is to be feared except the one God? And in what respect can his power be curtailed or lessened, when or where or how or by whom? The enticements of the lustful are meant to arouse love, but nothing is more enticing than your charity, and no love is more wholesome than the love of your Truth, which surpasses all things in beauty and splendor. Curiosity makes a show of zeal for knowledge, when in fact it is you who supremely know all things. Even ignorance and stupidity are concealed under the name of simplicity and harmlessness. For nothing simpler than you can be found; and what is more harmless than you, since it is their own works that are the enemies of the wicked? Idleness desires rest, but what rest is there apart from the Lord? Luxury would like to be called repletion and wealth, but you are fullness and the never-failing abundance of incorruptible sweetness. Extravagance masquerades as generosity, but you are the supremely bountiful giver of all good things. Avarice wants to possess many things, but you possess everything. Envy struggles for preeminence. What is more preeminent than you? Anger seeks vengeance. Who exacts vengeance more justly than you? Fear shrinks from unexpected and sudden threats to things it loves, while it takes precautions

Rom. 12:19

to keep them secure. What is unexpected to you? What is sudden? Or
who will separate you from what you love? Or where, except in you,   *Rom. 8:35*
is unfaltering security? Sadness pines for things it has lost, things that
cupidity had delighted in. It would wish to lose nothing, as nothing
can be taken away from you.

6.14   Thus the soul commits fornication when it turns away from   *Ps. 72:27*
you and seeks outside you those things that it cannot find pure and
unadulterated unless it returns to you. All those who place themselves
far from you and exalt themselves against you are perversely imitating
you. But even in this way, by imitating you they declare that you are
the Creator of all of nature, and so there is nowhere they can flee from
you altogether.

What, then, did I love in that theft of mine, and in what way was I
viciously, perversely, imitating my Lord? Did it please me to act against
your law, at least by deceit—since I could not do so by force—and
thus mimic the curtailed freedom of a prisoner by getting away with
doing what was not permitted, in a shadowy likeness of omnipotence?
Look at that slave, fleeing his master and chasing after a shadow. What   *Job 7:2*
rottenness! What a monstrous life, and what an abyss of death! Could
he do, freely, what was not permitted, for no other reason than that it
was not permitted?

7.15   What shall I offer to the Lord in thanksgiving for recalling these   *Ps. 115:12*
things to my memory in such a way that my soul is not made fearful
thereby? I will love you, Lord, and give thanks to you and confess to
your Name, because you have forgiven me for such wicked and abomi-   *Ps. 53:8*
nable deeds. I owe it to your grace and to your mercy that you have
melted my sins like ice. To your grace I owe also whatever evil things I   *Sir. 3:17*
did not do: for what was I not capable of doing, I who loved even crime
for no reason at all? And I acknowledge that I have been forgiven for all
these things, both those I did of my own accord and those I refrained
from doing because you were guiding me.

Who among human beings, seeing how feeble they are, would dare
to ascribe their chastity or innocence to their own powers and so love
you less, as though they had less need of your mercy, by which you
forgive the sins of those who turn to you? As for those who have been   *Ps. 50:15*
called by you and have followed your voice and have avoided the things
they have read about me, the things that I have recorded and acknowledged about myself, let them not mock me because I have been healed
by the same physician who was present with them so that they did not
fall ill—or rather, so that they were less gravely ill. And let them therefore love you as much—no, let them love you even more—because

they see that he who has rescued me from the great infirmities of my sins has kept them from being ensnared by such great infirmities of sin.

8.16   What fruit had I then, wretch that I was, in these things that I now blush to recall, and especially in that theft in which I loved the *Rom. 6:21* theft itself, and nothing else, when indeed the theft was nothing and I was all the more wretched on account of it? And yet I would not have done it by myself—this is how I remember my state of mind—I would certainly not have done it by myself. So I also loved the companionship of those with whom I did it. So is it true after all that I loved nothing other than the theft? To be sure, I loved nothing else, since that companionship too is nothing. What is it, really? (Who is it that teaches me, but the one who enlightens my heart and pierces its shadows?) *Sir. 2:10; Eph. 1:18* What is it? I am impelled to ask this question and discuss it and ponder it, because if I had loved the fruit that I stole and wanted to enjoy it, I could have done that even if I had been by myself; if I had been after only the thrill of committing the evil act, I would not have inflamed the itch of my cupidity by rubbing up against souls who shared my guilt. But since there was no pleasure for me in the pears, the pleasure was in the crime itself, and it was my companionship with fellow sinners that created this pleasure.

9.17   What was that disposition of mind? It was most assuredly very base, and plainly so; and woe is me that I had it. But what was it? Who *Job 10:15 VL* understands sins? It was a joke; our hearts were tickled that we were *Ps. 18:13* deceiving people who did not expect us to do such things and fervently wanted us not to. Why, then, did it please me that I was not doing it by myself? Is it that no one is easily moved to laughter when alone? Not easily, perhaps, but still, a laugh will sometimes get the better of people when they are quite alone and no one else is around, if something quite ridiculous strikes their senses or their mind. But I would not have done it by myself. I would certainly not have done it by myself. Behold before you, my God, this living recollection of my soul. If I had been by *Num 10:9* myself, I would not have done that theft in which what pleased me was not what I stole, but that I stole; it would not have pleased me to do it alone, and I would not have done it. O you too unfriendly friendship, unsearchable seduction of the mind! Out of playing and joking came a passion to do harm and a desire to damage someone else without any gain for myself, without any lust for revenge! But when someone says, "Let's go, let's do it," we are ashamed not to be shameless.

10.18   Who will unloose this most twisted, this most tangled intricacy? It is foul: I shrink from considering it; I do not want to look upon

it. I want to look upon you, beautiful and seemly justice and innocence, with honorable eyes and with a desire that is always satisfied but
never sated. In your presence there is rest indeed, and a life that knows
no disturbance. Those who enter into you enter into the joy of their
Lord; they will not be afraid, and all will be supremely well with them   *Mt. 25:21*
as they dwell in the one who is supremely good. I deserted you and
wandered away, my God, very much astray from your steadfastness in   *Ps. 118:176*
my youth; and I became for myself a land of destitution.   *Lk. 15:13–14*

Book Three

Lust of the flesh continues, and worldly ambition is always in the background, but lust of the eyes—excessive and undisciplined curiosity—takes center stage. Both the eyes of Augustine's flesh and the eye of his mind are misdirected. He is entranced by shows in the theater that awaken a sham pity, a perverted imitation of friendship. (Perverse friendship is treated in Books 2, 3, and 4, perhaps a structural clue that Augustine regards true friendship as an imitation of the inner life of the Trinity.) In the course of his studies he comes across Cicero's *Hortensius* and is inspired by its encouragement to seek wisdom, but his search goes wrong almost immediately when he turns to Scripture and finds it unworthy of comparison to Cicero. He falls in with the Manichees, who jeer at catholic Christianity and raise objections that Augustine finds appealing. Augustine's mother grieves over his heresies, but she is reassured by a vision and by the words of a bishop.

Augustine goes to Carthage to continue his studies in rhetoric (3.1.1–3.6.6). His sexual sins continue (3.1.1, 3.3.5), and he indulges in the illusory pity of theatrical shows (3.2.2–3.2.4). He encounters Cicero's *Hortensius* and is set on fire to seek wisdom (3.4.7–8), which he is too arrogant to find in Scripture (3.5.9). He joins the Manichees (3.6.10–3.10.18), who offer an illusory picture of God and creation (3.6.10–11) and raise questions about the origin of evil, the claim that human beings are in the image of God (does God have a bodily form and hair and nails?), and the polygamy, killings, and animal sacrifices of the Old Testament patriarchs (3.7.12). Answering the last of these objections, Augustine reflects on the differences between temporal and eternal law (3.7.13–3.9.17). Augustine's mother receives reassurance that he will eventually become a catholic Christian (3.11.19–3.12.21).

1.1   I came to Carthage, and all around me was the noisy bubbling and sizzling of disgraceful loves. I was not in love, but I was in love with love, and in my innermost emptiness I hated myself because I was not emptier still. I was searching for something to love, in love with love itself, and I hated serenity and the path without pitfalls. For I was famished within for want of the inner food that is you, my God; and yet, famished though I was, I felt no hunger. No, I had no desire for incorruptible food, not because I had had my fill of it, but because the emptier I was, the more loathsome I found it. And so my soul was sick; all covered in sores, it rushed outside itself, eager to scratch its miserable itch with the touch of sensible things. But if those things had no soul, they could not truly be loved. To love and to be loved were sweet

Lk. 16:20

29

to me, and all the more if I could enjoy the lover's body. So I polluted the clear stream of friendship with the filth of concupiscence and clouded its brightness with the hell of lust. And yet, foul and dishonorable though I was, I carried myself—such overwhelming vanity!—like an elegant and courtly fellow. I longed to be captured by love, and so I plunged headlong into it. My God, my mercy, how good you were in sprinkling gall over what was sweet to me. For I was loved, and I reached the bondage of enjoying her (though in secret). I was happy to be bound together with wretched chains, to be scalded with the iron rods of jealousy and suspicions, of fears and angers and quarrels.

Ps. 58:18

Ps. 2:9

2.2   I was entranced by spectacles in the theaters that were full of images of my own miseries and kindled the fire within me. Why is it that in the theater someone wants to feel sorrow when he sees lamentable and tragic events that he would by no means want to suffer himself? Yet the spectators do want to suffer sorrow from these things, and their sorrow is their pleasure. What is this but an astonishing madness? For the more someone is afflicted by such feelings in his real life, the more he is moved by them when he sees them on stage. We ordinarily call it misery when someone suffers himself, and mercy when he suffers out of compassion with others: and yet what sort of mercy is there in the make-believe of the stage? The audience is not instigated to provide help, but simply enticed to feel sorrow; the greater their sorrow, the greater their applause for the actor who portrays these images. And if those human tragedies, whether historical or fictional, are so portrayed that the audience feels no sorrow, they leave the theater complaining and finding fault; whereas if they do feel sorrow, they remain, rapt in attention and enjoying their tears.

2.3   So then even sorrows are loved. Surely all human beings want to be joyful. Yet although no one wants to be miserable, still, there is something gratifying about being merciful, and there can be no mercy apart from sorrow. Is it for this reason, this reason alone, that sorrows are loved? And this too flows from the stream of friendship. But where does this go? To where is it flowing? To what end does it run into a bubbling whirlpool of pitch, a monstrous cauldron of foul lusts, its course changed and its path diverted, twisted and cast down from heavenly serenity by its own impetus?

Is. 34:9

Should we therefore renounce mercy? By no means. Sometimes, then, sorrows are rightly loved: but beware uncleanness, O my soul, under God, my Guardian and Teacher, the God of our fathers, praiseworthy and exalted above all for ever. Beware uncleanness. It is not that I no longer feel pity, but in those days in the theater I shared the

Dan. 3:52

happiness of lovers in their wicked enjoyment of each other, though what they did was only make-believe, images made into a spectacle for the stage. But when the lovers lost each other, I grieved with them; it was a feeling akin to mercy. Yet both my happiness and my grief were a delight to me. Now, however, I pity someone who is happy in his wickedness more than someone who suffers great hardships from missing out on some destructive pleasure or losing some happiness that is really misery. Surely this is more truly mercy: but the sorrow in such mercy gives no pleasure. One who is sorrowful for the wretched is rightly praised, for charity is at work in him; but of course someone who is genuinely merciful would prefer that there be no cause for sorrow. If it were possible—as it is not—for benevolence to will evil, someone who truly and sincerely feels pity could desire that people be miserable just so he can pity them.

And so some sorrows merit our approval, but no sorrow is to be loved. For your pity, O God, lover of souls, is far and away more pure and more indestructible than ours, because no sorrow torments you. And who is sufficient for these things?   *2 Cor. 2:16*

2.4   But I in those days, wretch that I was, loved sorrow, and I went looking for things to be sorrowful about. I delighted then in an actor's portrayal of someone else's miseries, false and theatrical as they were, and the more tears they wrung from me, the more powerfully they enticed me. And it was no wonder that an unhappy sheep,[1] wandering away from your flock and impatient of your care, should become infected with a festering wound. Thus it came about that I loved sorrows, not those that reached deep within me—for I did not love suffering the things that I loved to see on stage—but the imaginary sorrows I witnessed that touched me only on the surface. They were like nails scratching the skin, causing feverish swelling and decay and a terrible poisoning of the blood. Such was my life: was it even really a life, O my God?

3.5   And above me hovered your mercy, faithful from afar. I spent myself in great sins and followed a sacrilegious curiosity that led me to abandon you for the abyss of unbelief and the deceitful service of demons, to whom I offered my evil deeds. And in all these deeds you whipped me with the rod of your chastisement. I even dared, during the celebration of your solemnities and within the walls of the church,

---

1. The words "unhappy sheep" (*infelix pecus*) are from Virgil, *Eclogue* 3.3, but the image of the sheep that wanders away from the flock is Scriptural. See especially the Parable of the Lost Sheep in Luke 15 (the same chapter that contains the Parable of the Prodigal Son), Isaiah 53:6, and 1 Peter 2:25.

to lust after a deed that would procure for me the fruit of death, and
yes, even to bring it to completion. For this you beat me soundly,
inflicting punishments that were heavy and yet were as nothing com-
pared with my sin, O my God, who are boundlessly merciful to me,   *Ps. 58:18, 143:2*
my refuge from the terrifying harms among which I wandered with a
stiff neck, withdrawing further and further from you, loving my own
paths and not yours, loving the freedom of a runaway.

3.6   My studies—regarded as honorable ones—were meant to prepare me for success in court: the more of a fraud I should become, the
more praise I would earn. So great is the blindness of those who glory
even in their blindness! And I was already at the top of the School of
Rhetoric; I preened myself, swollen with pride. Still, I was exceedingly
restrained (as you know, O Lord) and had nothing whatever to do with
the destructive acts of the "Destroyers"[2]—a perverse and devilish name
that somehow marked them out as an elite. I lived among them, feeling
a shameless shame because I was not like them. And I was with them
and sometimes enjoyed their friendship, though I always loathed their
behavior, the acts of destruction by which they wantonly persecuted
nervous freshmen just for the fun of it and thereby gorged themselves
on their malicious enjoyment. What could be more like the behavior
of demons? "Destroyers" was surely just the right name for them, for
clearly they had first been destroyed and perverted themselves: deceitful spirits hidden within them were mocking them and leading them
astray so that they would enjoy mocking and deceiving others.

4.7   Among them, at that feeble age, I was studying the books of
eloquence. I longed to make a name for myself as a rhetorician, to
gratify my damnable and arrogant love of human vanity. In the normal course of study I came across a book by an author named Cicero,
whose tongue nearly everyone admires, though not so much his heart.[3]
This book of his, called *Hortensius*, contains an exhortation to philosophy. That book changed my way of feeling; it changed my prayers
to you, O Lord; it created new resolves and new desires in me. In an
instant all vain hope became repugnant to me, and my heart was on
fire with an incredible longing for the immortality of wisdom. I began

---

2. "Destroyers": *eversores*, from the verb *everso*, meaning "to overturn, dispossess, subvert, destroy."
It is "evidently a vivid expression, whether it is merely A.'s term of abuse or an authentic piece of
local slang" (O'Donnell II:161).
3. "heart": *pectus*, the inner source of the words that fall from the tongue, and particularly the
feelings from which they spring. To say that people do not admire Cicero's *pectus* is to suggest that
people suspect his eloquent words reflected his ambition and self-importance rather than his genuine thoughts and feelings.

to arise and return to you. I did not put this book to use in order to
sharpen my tongue, which was what I was meant to be doing with my
mother's money in this, the nineteenth year of my age (my father having died two years before). No, I did not put this book to use in order
to sharpen my tongue: what had won me over was not the style, but
the substance.

Lk. 15:18–20

4.8   With what passion, my God, with what great passion I longed
to fly away from earthly things to you, and I did not know what you
would make of me. For with you is wisdom. Now the love of wisdom
has in Greek the name "philosophy," and it was this love that those
writings set aflame in me. There are those who lead others astray
through philosophy, using that great and alluring and honorable name
to whitewash their errors and wrap them in a false beauty; and nearly all
such people, both in those days and earlier, are identified and exposed
in that book. The healthful admonition of your Spirit through your
good and dutiful servant is also made manifest there: "See to it that no
one deceive you through philosophy and empty seduction, according
to human tradition, according to the elements of this world, and not
according to Christ. For in Christ dwells all the fullness of Godhead
bodily." In those days, as you know, O Light of my heart, these words
of the Apostle were unknown to me. No, what delighted me in that
exhortation was just this: it encouraged me not to follow this or that
sect but instead to love wisdom itself, whatever it should turn out to
be, and to love it and seek after it and pursue it and hold on to it and
embrace it with all my strength. And the book stirred me and set me
aflame, and I was filled with passionate longing. But in my great ardor
there was just one thing that held me back: the name of Christ was
not there. For by your mercy, O Lord, my tender heart had drunk that
name, the name of my Savior, your Son, with my mother's milk; and
still it retained that name deep within. Whatever lacked that name,
however literate and polished and truthful it might have been, could
not capture me altogether.

Job 12:13, 12:16

Col. 2:8–9

Ps. 24:7

5.9   And so I made up my mind to look into the Holy Scriptures
and to see what they might be like. And what I see there is something
not disclosed to the proud or laid bare to children; one must stoop
to enter, but it is lofty within, and veiled in mysteries. Such was my
character at that time that I could not enter; I could not bend my neck
to follow its path. For what I say now is not what I thought then when
I gave my attention to Scripture. Quite the contrary: I found it unworthy of comparison with the great dignity of Cicero. My swollen pride
disdained its restraint, and my gaze did not penetrate its innermost

mysteries. It was the very Scripture that would grow with little children as they grew, but I refused to be a little child; in my arrogance and self-importance I was, in my own eyes, a grown-up.

6.10 And so I fell among people who were deranged in their pride, thoroughly carnal people who prattled on and on.[4] Their words were snares of the devil, a honey-trap concocted of the syllables of your Name and the names of the Lord Jesus Christ and of the Holy Spirit, our Advocate and Comforter. These names were constantly on their lips, but it was only noise and a wagging of the tongue; their hearts were empty of the truth. They kept calling out "truth, truth," and they said many things to me, and yet there was never any truth in them. They spoke falsehoods, not only about you, who are truly the Truth, but also about the elements of this world, your creation. For love of you, my Father, Highest Good, the Beauty of all beautiful things, I ought to have passed beyond even what the philosophers say—and say truly—about such things.

O Truth, Truth, how deeply I longed for you in the very marrow of my mind while they were holding forth about you to me many times and in many ways, in speech (though their words were mere noise) and in their many and massive books. Their teachings were like platters from which they served not you—the one for whom I hungered—but the sun and moon, beautiful works of yours, but still, only your works, not you yourself, not even the first of your works. For your spiritual works come before these bodily works, however heavenly and full of light they are. And I was hungry and thirsty not even for those higher, spiritual works, but for you yourself, the Truth in whom there is no variation, no flickering shadow of change. And from those platters they kept serving me glittering phantasms, and it would have been better for me to love the sun itself, which is at least a true object for the eyes, than to love those false phantasms with a mind deceived by the eyes. And yet, because I thought they were you, I ate them, though not with any great eagerness, for they did not taste to me of you (for you were not those empty fictions) and they gave me no nourishment; instead they depleted me. What we eat in our dreams is very much like what we eat when we are awake, but sleepers receive no nourishment from their food, since they are asleep. But those fictions were not like you in any way at all (as you have now told me) because they were bodily phantasms, false bodies, less certain than the true bodies, whether heavenly or earthly, that we see with the vision of our flesh. Just like cattle and

1 Tim. 3:7; 2 Tim. 2:26

Jn. 14:26

Josh. 1:8

Jn. 14:6

Jas. 1:17

---

4. "who prattled on and on": *loquaces*. See 1.4.4, fn. 3.

birds we see these things, and they are more certain when we see them than when we imagine them; and they are in turn more certain when we imagine them than when we use their images to build castles in the air, things that do not exist at all. I was being fed on such emptiness, and so I was not being fed.

But you, my Love, in whom I am weak so that I may be strong, you are not those bodies we see, though they are in heaven; neither are you the things we do not see in heaven, for you created them and you do not regard them as the highest of your creations. How distant, then, you are from those phantasms of mine, phantasms of bodies that do not exist at all! They were less certain than phantasms of bodies that do exist, which are in turn less certain than bodies, and yet even bodies are still not you. Nor are you the soul, which is the life of bodies (for of course the life of bodies is better and more certain than bodies). No, you are the life of souls, the life of lives, yourself alive with your own life, and you do not change, O Life of my soul. *2 Cor. 12:10*

6.11 So where were you then in relation to me? How far away? I was journeying far away from you, shut out even from the husks that I *2 Cor. 5:6* fed to the pigs. How much better were the fables of the grammarians *Lk. 15:16* and poets than those snares! For verse and song and flying Medea are certainly more useful than the five elements, variously embellished to correspond to the five Dens of Darkness, which are nothing at all and bring death to those who believe in them. Verse and song I can use for genuine nourishment, and though I may have sung about flying Medea, I gave no assent, and if I heard someone else singing about her, I did not believe it. But those fictions I did believe. I was being led step by step—how horrible to recall this!—into the depths of hell. *Prov. 9:18* Bereft of truth, I worked away feverishly, because I was seeking you, my God (for it is to you that I make my confession, you, who had mercy on me even when I had not yet made my confession to you), through the senses of the flesh and not through the understanding of the mind, which you had given me that I might be superior to beasts. But you were more deeply within me than the innermost part of my being, higher than what was highest in me. I had encountered that bold woman, bereft of prudence, in Solomon's allegory, sitting outside her doorway and calling out, "Eat hidden breads with plea-sure, and drink stolen waters that are sweet."[5] She led me astray, for she found me dwelling outside in the eye of my flesh and chewing

---

5. Proverbs 9:13–17 (VL): "A foolish and bold woman, made bereft of bread . . . sits outside the doorway of her house on a chair in the highest place of the city. . . . 'Let him who is stupid turn aside to me. . . . Eat hidden breads with pleasure, and drink stolen waters that are sweet.'"

over and over again the things that I had greedily devoured through that eye.

7.12   For I did not know that other reality which truly is. I was being prodded somewhat sharply to agree with those foolish deceivers when they asked me where evil comes from, and whether God is hemmed in by a bodily form and has hair and fingernails, and whether we should esteem as righteous those who had many wives at the same time and killed other human beings and made animal sacrifices. Being ignorant of such matters, I was greatly unsettled by these questions. It seemed to me that I was going toward the truth, though in fact I was drawing away from it; for I had not yet learned that evil is nothing but a privation of good: so much so that it is nothing at all. How could I have seen this when the eyes of my flesh were fixed on bodies and the eyes of my mind on phantasms? And I had not yet learned that God is a spirit, that he has no parts spread out with length and breadth, that he   *Jn. 4:24* has no bulk—for what has bulk has parts smaller than the whole, and if it is infinite, it is smaller in any determinate region of space than it is in its infinity, and so it does not exist as a whole everywhere, as a spirit does, as God does. And I was utterly ignorant of what there is in us by which we are, and are rightly said in Scripture to be, in the image of God.   *Gn. 1:26; Sir. 17:1*

7.13   And I had not yet learned of that true inward righteousness, which does not judge according to custom but according to the supremely upright law of Almighty God. The norms of behavior in different places and at different times are formed according to that law as befits those places and times, but that law itself does not vary from one place or time to another. It was in accordance with this law that Abraham and Isaac and Jacob and Moses and David and all those men who received praise from the mouth of God were indeed righteous. Yet people unaccustomed to serious thinking—people who judge according to standards of their own time and treat their own behavior as   *1 Cor. 4:3* the standard for the whole human race—judge that these men were wicked. It is as if someone who knew nothing about armor and about which piece is designed for which part of the body should try to cover his head with a shin guard and wear a helmet as a shoe, and then complain that nothing fits; or as if someone should complain on a public holiday that he is not allowed to transact business in the afternoon as he was permitted to do in the morning; or if one should observe in a certain house that one servant handles something that the one who carries the cup would not be allowed to handle; or that something is done behind the stables that is forbidden at the dinner table, and someone is indignant that the same rules do not hold for every person and every place, even though it is a single dwelling and a single family. Such are the people who are indignant when they hear that in that age the righteous were allowed to do things that the righteous are not allowed to do in this present age, and that God gave different commands to different people as were appropriate for the times in which they lived; yet both were servants of one and the same righteousness. And yet they see that one thing is permitted for a certain person on a certain day and in a certain household, but something else for another; that what was allowed up to a certain time of day is no longer allowed afterward; that something is permitted, or even required, in one part of the house that is forbidden and punished in another part right next to it. Is righteousness, then, variable and changeable? Not at all. But the times over which it presides are not uniform as they pass by: for they are times. Yet human beings, whose life is brief upon the earth, *Wisd. 15:9* cannot by their senses trace the causes that apply to bygone ages and other peoples, of which they have no experience; but they do have the experience to see quite readily how this applies to one body, one day, or one house and to recognize what is suited to a given part of the body, or time, or parts or persons in the household. They take offense at the idea of different rules for different ages or peoples, but they are slaves to the customs they know well.

7.14 I did not know those things then, and I paid no attention to them. From every direction they came before my eyes, but I did not see them. I wrote poetry, and I was not allowed to place just any foot wherever I pleased; in different meters there were different places in which each foot belonged, and in a single line the same foot could not go just anywhere. But the art of writing did not vary from one poem to another; the same art embraced them all at once. Yet I did not recognize that the righteousness that good and holy people obeyed encompasses all at once in a far more excellent and exalted way all the things that it commands. It does not vary in the slightest respect, and yet it makes provision and lays down commands for varying times: not the same commands for all times, but for each time the commands that are suitable for it. In my blindness I reproached the holy fathers who not only made a right use of things present, as God commanded and inspired them, but also foretold things yet to come, as God revealed.

8.15 Is it wrong at any time or in any place to love God with your whole heart and your whole soul and your whole mind, and to love

your neighbor as yourself? And so sins of passion⁶ that are against   *Mt. 22:37–40; Mk. 12:33; Lk. 10:27 / Rom. 1:26 / Gn. 19:5ff.*
nature, as the sins of the Sodomites were, are to be detested and pun-
ished always and everywhere. If all peoples did such things, they would
be accounted equally guilty before the law of God, which did not make
human beings so that they should use each other in this way. The fellowship that we should have with God is broken when the very nature
of which he is the Author is polluted by the perversity of lust.

As for sins of passion that are against human customs, they should
be avoided as the diversity of customs requires, so that the agreement
within a city or people, founded on custom or law, should not be broken because of the intemperate desire of a citizen or a stranger. For any
part that does not fit properly into its whole is disgraceful.

But if God commands something contrary to the custom or agreement of any people, it must be done, even if it has never been done
before. If it has fallen into disuse, it must be brought back; and if it
had never been required before, it must be required now. A king, after
all, may command something in the city he rules that neither anyone
else nor he himself had ever commanded before, and yet obedience to
this command is not contrary to the unity and common life of the city.
Quite the opposite: disobeying the command would be contrary to the
unity and common life of the city, since our common life as human
beings is governed by a general agreement that we will obey our rulers.
All the more, then, must God the Ruler be obeyed without hesitation
by all his creatures in whatever he commands. For as in the governance
of human society a greater power is entitled to the obedience of a lesser
power, so in the governance of the universe God is entitled to the obe-   *Rom. 13:1*
dience of all.

8.16 Consider also crimes of violence, in which there is a desire to
hurt someone by insulting or injuring him. The motive in either case
may be revenge, as when one enemy acts against another; or gaining
some benefit, as when a robber sets upon a traveler; or avoiding some
evil, as when we attack someone we fear; or envy, as when someone

---

6. "sins of passion": *flagitia*, contrasted with the more serious "crimes of violence" (*facinora*), which
Augustine discusses in 3.8.16. (He develops the distinction further in 4.15.25.) There is no fully sat-
isfactory translation for *facinora* in Augustine's usage; he calls his theft of the pears a *facinus*—that's
the singular form—but it would be a stretch to call it a crime of violence. "Crimes against the person" (Boulding) and "injurious acts" (Chadwick) are wrong, because *flagitia* are also injurious and
are crimes against the person, as Augustine is in the process of explaining. Ruden and Constantine
do better with "crimes" (though some *flagitia* are illegal, which makes them crimes too), but they
miss the mark with "shameful acts" (Ruden) and "sinful acts" (Constantine) for *flagitia: facinora*,
too, are shameful and sinful.

less fortunate hates someone who is happier, or someone who has prospered in some respect fears that someone else will equal him—or laments that someone already has. Or it can be sheer pleasure in someone else's suffering, as spectators enjoy the suffering of gladiators, and those who mock and ridicule others enjoy their suffering.

These are the chief sins that spring forth from the lust for dominance, the lust for vision, and the lust for sensation:[7] from one of them or two or all three at once. Thus people lead lives opposed to the three plus seven, your ten-stringed lute, your Decalogue,[8] O God Most High and Most Sweet. *Ps. 32:2, 143:9*

But how can our sins of passion do anything to you, who cannot be corrupted? How can our crimes of violence be against you, who cannot be harmed? But you punish what human beings do within and against themselves, for even when they sin against you, they act wickedly against their own souls. Their iniquity speaks falsehoods to them, *Ps. 26:12* whether by corrupting or perverting their own nature, which you created and ordained, or by making immoderate use of licit things, or by so burning with desire for illicit things that they use them contrary to nature. They are held guilty either for the savagery of their mind and their words against you, for kicking against the goads, or for taking *Acts 26:14* pleasure in the breakdown of human society and presumptuously setting up their own private factions based on nothing more than their personal likes and dislikes.

All these things come about when people abandon you, O Fount of Life, the One and true Creator and Ruler of the whole universe, and love instead, with self-regarding pride, a false One in a part of that whole. And so it is by reverent humility that we return to you, and you purify us from our evil habits and are merciful toward the sins of those *Ps. 77:39, 78:9;* who make their confession to you. You hear the cry of the captives and *Lk. 18:13 / Ps.* set us free from the chains we make for ourselves, so long as we do not *101:21* raise up against you the horn of a false freedom, greedy to have more *Ps. 74:5* and punished with the loss of everything, loving our own good more than you, the Good of all things.

9.17   But among these sins of passion and crimes of violence and so many iniquities are the sins of those who are making progress. Those who judge rightly both condemn those sins as deviations from the rule of perfection and praise them as promising a good harvest to come,

---

7. These are otherwise known as worldly ambition, the lust of the eyes, and the lust of the flesh, respectively.

8. *en. Ps.* 32 *en.* 2 s 1.36: "There are ten commandments in the law; there you have the ten-stringed lute. . . . In three you have love of God, and in seven love of neighbor."

like the first green blades of growing grain. And there are some acts that are like sins of passion and crimes of violence but are not sins because they are not offenses either against you, O Lord our God, or against human society. For example, someone might procure goods to use in his daily life at an opportune time, and it is not clear whether he does so from a lust for possession; or the appropriate authorities might inflict punishment for something if they are eager to set things right, and yet it is not clear whether they acted out of a desire to do harm. Your testimony gives approval to many deeds that human beings think deserve reproach, and your witness condemns many deeds that receive human praise. For it often happens that the appearance of an act belies what the agent has in mind, and it can be difficult to judge what the circumstances of a given era require.

But suppose you suddenly command something unaccustomed and unforeseen—something, even, that you had once forbidden. Would anyone doubt that we should act as you have commanded, even if for the time being you hide the reason for your command, even if it is contrary to the settled agreement of some human society? For a just society is one that serves you. Blessed are they who know that you have given commands! For all your commands are carried out by those who serve you either to demonstrate what is needed in the present or to foretell things that are yet to come.

10.18 But I did not know all this, and so I mocked your holy servants and prophets. And what was I doing when I mocked them but earning mockery from you? For little by little I was being led astray into such frivolous beliefs: that a fig weeps when it is plucked and its mother-tree sheds milky tears—but if one of their saints ate a fig that had been plucked by someone else's misdeed and not his own, he would transform it within his stomach and breathe out angels; indeed, in his prayers he would sigh out particles of God and belch them forth. These particles of the supreme and true God would have remained trapped in that fruit if the elect saints had not set them free by their teeth and their stomachs. Wretch that I was, I came to believe that greater mercy should be shown to the fruits of the earth than to human beings, for whose sake those fruits grow. If anyone who was not a Manichee were hungry and begged for some fruit, you would be imposing a sentence of death on any bit you gave him; that is what they thought.

11.19 And you sent forth your hand from on high and rescued my soul from this foggy abyss. For my mother, your faithful one, wept over me in your presence, more than mothers weep over the bodies of their dead children. For through the faith and the Spirit she had

Ps. 143:7

Ps. 85:13

Gal. 5:5

from you, she saw that I was dying; and you hearkened to her prayer, Lord God. You hearkened to her prayer and did not scorn her tears. In every place in which she prayed she watered the earth beneath her eyes, and you hearkened to her, O Lord. What else would explain that dream by which you gave her comfort, so that she agreed to live with me and share meals at home with me? (She had initially resisted doing so because she rejected and detested the blasphemies of my error.) In this dream she saw herself standing on a wooden rule. Coming toward her was a young man in bright clothes, cheerful and smiling at her, though she was sad and overcome with sorrow. He asked her why she was sad and why she wept day after day—asking, as so often happens in dreams, not in order to find out but in order to teach. She replied that she was lamenting my destruction. So that she might be able to rest secure, he instructed and encouraged her to pay attention and see that where she was, there I would also be. And when she looked, she saw me standing next to her on that same rule. How else did this dream come about, except that your ears were up against her heart, O Almighty Good, who care for each of us as if we were your only concern and for all of us just as you care for each of us?

11.20   And how else did it come about that when she told me about this vision, and I tried to twist it into saying that she must hope someday to be where I was, she replied immediately and without hesitation, "He did not say, 'Where he is, there you will also be,' but 'Where you are, there he will also be'"? I confess to you, Lord, that as far as I can remember—and I have spoken of this often—I was more moved by the response you gave through my mother's alertness than I was by the dream itself. For she was not disturbed at all by the interpretation I offered, so smooth and yet so false; she saw immediately just what she ought to see, which I certainly had not seen until she said it. Through this dream you gave this devout woman comfort in her present distress and assured her of the joy to come, long before it actually happened. For it was nearly nine years that I wallowed in the mire of deep and shadowy falsehood; and though I tried again and again to lift myself out, I would only sink further. But that chaste widow, devout and sober, such as you love, though she was now upheld by a livelier hope, did not grow slack in her tears and groanings to you. Hour by hour she did not cease to pour forth her prayers for me to you, and her prayers entered into your presence. And yet you left me to myself, to wallow in the mire and be engulfed in it.

Ps. 68:3

Ps. 87:3

12.21   And in the meantime you gave her another response that I remember. (For I am leaving out many things and hastening on to

those that I most long to confess to you; and there are many things
I do not remember.) You gave this other response through a priest of
yours, a bishop nourished in your Church and well trained in your
Scriptures. My mother entreated him to speak with me and refute my
errors, to unteach me what was bad and teach me what was good; for
he often did this when he happened to find suitable people to instruct.
But when she asked this of him, he refused—quite sensibly, as I realized later. He answered that I was unteachable because I was so puffed
up with the novelty of that heresy and had already disturbed many
unlearned people with my frivolous questions, as she had already told
him. "Let him be where he is," he said. "Just pray to the Lord for him.
He will discover in his reading what his error is and how great is his
impiety." At the same time he told her the story of how his own mother
had been led astray by the Manichees and given him over to them, and
that he had not only read nearly all of their writings but had even written some Manichee books himself.[9] But even without anyone to argue
with him or convince him, it had become clear to him that that sect
was to be shunned, and so he left it. When he said all this, she refused
to give in; instead she insisted all the more, imploring him with copious
tears to see me and engage me in discussion. By now he was a bit angry
and fed up. "Leave me," he said. "As sure as you live, it cannot be that
the son of tears like these will perish." And she took this answer, as she
often recalled to me in our conversations, as though it had been a voice
from heaven.

---

9. Many interpreters and translators interpret this as meaning that the bishop had *copied* (rather
than composed) Manichee books; I do not see how the Latin can be made to bear this meaning.

Book Four

Now a teacher of rhetoric, Augustine is chasing "after the emptiness of popular acclaim" (4.1.1). He is intrigued by astrology, which (like Manicheanism) offers an explanation for human action that would relieve Augustine of responsibility for his misdeeds. The death of a close friend sends Augustine into a frenzy of grief; looking back on his grief, Augustine reflects on the right way to love other human beings, and all transient goods, and on the true joys of friendship. We must look for the happy life in God, who has brought it to us through the humility of the Incarnation: a rebuke to the pride that keeps us from God. Augustine writes a philosophical work, *On the Beautiful and the Fitting*, and dedicates it to the orator Hierius in the hope of further-ing his own ambitions by bringing himself to the great man's attention. He also reads Aristotle's *Categories* on his own and takes great pride in his ability to understand the work without a teacher.

Augustine teaches rhetoric in Carthage (4.1.1–4.3.6), seeking money and acclaim from his work (4.1.1–4.2.2) as well as self-exculpation from astrology (4.3.4–6). The death of his unnamed friend (4.4.7–4.12.19) devastates him (4.4.9–4.6.11) because he had not loved his friend as transient things should be loved (4.7.12–4.12.19). He writes a philosophical work on beauty (4.13.20–4.15.27), hoping to attract attention by dedicating it to a famous orator (4.14.21–23), but failing both in his ambition and in his attempt to reach an understanding of God by his own efforts (4.15.24–27). He succeeds in understanding Aristotle's *Categories* and various books of the lib-eral arts on his own (4.16.28–31), but fails by trying to fit God into the categories (4.16.29) and taking pride in his intelligence (4.16.30–31).

1.1   In that same period of nine years, from the nineteenth year of my age up to the twenty-eighth, we were led astray and led others astray, deceived and deceivers in various passions: openly so through the teachings that are called the liberal arts, secretly so under a false guise of religion, proud in one domain, superstitious in the other, and worthless everywhere. In one we chased after the emptiness of popular acclaim—applause in the theaters, poetry competitions, contests for quickly fading crowns, frivolous spectacles, uncontrolled lusts—and in another we endeavored to purge ourselves from all such filth by offer-ing food to those who were called the elect and saints, whose stomachs were the factories in which they would make the angels and gods by whom we would be set free.

Let the arrogant mock me, those who have not yet, for their own
salvation, been cast down and broken in pieces by you, my God. Yet for
your praise I will confess to you my disgraceful acts. Grant this to me,
I beseech you; let me encircle with my present memory the circuitous
errors of my past, that I may offer you the sacrifice of rejoicing. For   *Ps. 26:6*
without you, what am I to myself but a guide to my own downfall? And
when all is well with me, what am I but an infant at your breast, or one
who feeds on you, the food that is not corrupted?[1] What sort of human
being is anyone who is merely human? Let the strong and mighty laugh
at us: let us who are weak and destitute make our confession to you.

2.2   I was teaching the art of rhetoric in those days. Myself a victim
of greed and ambition, I sold victory in speech. Yet you know, O Lord,
that I preferred to have good students, as students are accounted good,
and without deceit I taught them deceit, not to use against the life of
the innocent but sometimes to secure the acquittal of the guilty. And
you saw me, O God; from afar you saw me stumbling along that slippery path; you saw the spark of honor, shimmering in the midst of a
great cloud of smoke, that I showed to those who loved vanity and
sought after lies; and I was their companion.   *Ps. 4:3*

In those days I had one woman. We were not married in the eyes
of the law; my errant passion, bereft of serious thought, had sought
her out. But still, I had only her, and I was faithful to her. I discovered
by my own experience how great a difference there is between the due
measure of lawful marriage, which is a covenant for the sake of pro-
creation, and an agreement between lustful lovers who mean to avoid
having children—though once children are born, we cannot help loving them.

2.3   I also recall that once, when I had decided to enter a poetry com-
petition in one of the theaters, some magician or other sent a mes-
senger to ask me what I would be willing to give him to be assured of
victory. But I replied that I loathed and detested those vile mysteries

---

1. "an infant at your breast": literally, "one sucking your milk." O'Donnell (II:206) suggests that
we should think here of 1 Corinthians 3:1–2: "And I could not speak to you, brothers and sisters,
as to those who are spiritual, but as to those who are carnal, as little ones in Christ. I gave you milk,
not solid food, for you were not yet able [to eat solid food]. Nor indeed can you even now, for you
are still carnal." (Cf. Hebrews 5:12–14.) But although the image of the infant at its mother's breast
would by itself suggest immaturity (especially since it recalls the language of 1.6.7), the remainder
of the sentence cancels any such implication; and so we are reminded that although babies outgrow
their need for milk, human beings never outgrow their need for the good that comes from God. See
7.10.16: "I am food for those who are full-grown; grow, and you will feed on me. And you will not
change me into you, as you change the food of your flesh, but instead you will be changed into me."

and that I would not let even a fly be killed for me to win the prize, even if it were an immortal crown of gold. For he was going to kill living creatures in his sacrifices, and it seemed to me that he would be paying homage to demons in order to win me their favor. But even this evil I did not reject out of the chastity that belongs to you, O God of my heart. For I had not yet learned to love you, whom I had not yet learned to think of except as flashes of bodily light. Does not a soul that sighs after such fictions commit fornication against you, trusting in falsehoods and feeding the winds? So indeed I refused to have any-one sacrifice to demons on my behalf, when I myself was sacrificing to them by my superstition. For what does it mean to feed the winds but to feed demons? And this we do when our errors make us a delight to them and an object of their scorn.

Ps. 72:26

Ps. 72:27

Prov. 10:4

3.4   And so I saw no reason at all to stop consulting those frauds known as astrologers, for it was as if they made no sacrifices and addressed no prayers to any spirit for the purposes of divination. But true Christian piety necessarily rejects and condemns them: for it is good to confess to you, O Lord, and to say, "Have mercy on me; heal my soul, because I have sinned against you"—not to misuse your mercy as license for sinning, but to keep in mind the words of the Lord: "Behold, you have been healed. Now sin no more, lest something worse happen to you." The astrologers try to destroy these healing words when they say, "The stars make your sin inevitable" or "Venus did this, or Saturn, or Mars," meaning that human beings—flesh and blood and rotten pride—are without fault, and instead the creator and ruler of the heavens and the stars is to blame. And who is this but you, our God, our sweetness, the fount of justice, who repay everyone according to his deeds and do not despise a contrite and humble heart?

Ps. 91:2

Ps. 40:5

Jn. 5:14

Ps. 61:3; Mt. 16:17; Rom. 2:6 / Ps. 50:19

3.5   At that time there was a wise man, highly skilled in the art of medicine and greatly renowned for his skill. He was the proconsul who placed the crown of victory upon my unhealthy head, though he did not do so as a doctor. For you are the Healer of that disease, you who resist the proud but give grace to the humble. And yet surely you were present to me, bringing healing to my soul, even through that old man. For once I had become more familiar with him and with the way he spoke—he was not a polished speaker, but his words were appealing and carried weight because of the liveliness of his thoughts—I devoted myself eagerly and attentively to his company. In the course of my conversation with him he discovered that I was devoted to the books of those who cast horoscopes; he admonished me, in a gentle and fatherly way, to throw those books away and not to waste on such nonsense the

Jas. 4:6; 1 Pet. 5:5

effort and attention needed for things that are actually useful. He said that he had studied astrology when he was first starting out, intending to make it the profession by which he would earn his living; and if he had understood Hippocrates, he certainly was capable of understanding the writings of the astrologers. But having read them, he abandoned them to pursue medicine, precisely because he had discovered that they were full of utter falsehoods, and as a man of serious purpose he was not willing to make a living by deceiving people. "But you," he said, "have rhetoric as a profession. You do not need astrology to put food on the table; you are pursuing that fraudulent subject solely as a pastime. All the more reason for you to listen to me, because I put in the effort to make a thorough study of it, since I intended to make it my only source of income."

I asked him how it was, then, that so many of the astrologers' predictions came true. He gave the best answer he could: that it was because of the power of chance, which is dispersed throughout the universe. For example, someone might consult the work of a poet who was writing and thinking about something else altogether, yet he happens to find a passage that is astonishingly relevant to some matter of concern to him. It is no surprise, he said, when some line chimes in with the things or deeds one is asking about; it happens, not by skill, but by chance, through some higher instinct in the human soul that is not even aware of what it is doing.

3.6 It was of course you who provided this for me from him, or through him, and sketched in my memory the questions that I would later investigate for myself. At the time, however, neither he nor my dear friend Nebridius—a very good and very chaste young man, who used to laugh at the whole business of divination—could persuade me to abandon astrology. For the authority of the astrologers had greater weight for me, and I had not yet found the sort of decisive proof I was looking for: proof that would convince me, without any room for doubt, that the true predictions they made for those who consulted them were the result of luck or chance, not of skill in observing the stars.

4.7 In the years in which I first began to teach in the town in which I had been born, I had made a very dear friend who was following the same course of study. He was my age, in the prime of his youth, as I was.[2] He had grown up with me since boyhood; we were companions

---

2. *Conflorentem flore adulescentiae: adulescentia* was commonly reckoned to be the period between fifteen and thirty years of age. Augustine taught at Thagaste in 375/376; he turned twenty-one on 13 November 375.

at school and companions in play. But he had never been—nor was he even in those days—a friend in the true sense of the word. For there is true friendship only when you bind together those who cling to you through the charity that has been poured into our hearts through the Holy Spirit who has been given to us. Still, it was very precious to us, *Rom. 5:5* and it had grown into something solid thanks to our enthusiasm for the studies we shared. For I had also turned him away from the true faith (which, being young, he did not embrace faithfully or whole-heartedly) to the superstitious and dangerous fables that so grieved my mother. So his mind joined me in my wanderings, and my soul could not do without him. But you were there, as you are always close upon the heels of those who flee from you, O God of vengeance and yet *Ps. 93:1* also fount of mercy, who turn us back to yourself in wondrous ways. Behold, you took that man from this present life when I had spent hardly a year in my friendship with him, a friendship that was sweet to me beyond all other sweetnesses of this life.

4.8   How can anyone recount your praiseworthy deeds, even those *Ps. 105:2* which he alone has experienced? What did you do then, O my God? How unsearchable was the abyss of your judgments! For when he was *Ps. 35:7; Sir. 42:18;* suffering from a high fever, for a long time he lay unconscious, sweat- *Rom. 11:33* ing as one who would die, and they lost hope. He was baptized— knowing nothing of it. I was not bothered at all; I assumed he would hold on to the way of thinking he had received from me and pay no heed to what had been done to his body when he was unaware of it. But things turned out quite differently. He rallied and the fever abated, and as soon as I could speak with him (which was as soon as he could speak to me, since I never left his side and we were very depen- dent on each other) I tried to make jokes with him, assuming that he would join me in mocking the baptism that he had received when he could not at all understand or feel what was being done to him, though at this point he had been told he had received it. But instead he recoiled from me as if I were an enemy. He told me, with a sudden self-assurance that took me aback, that if I wanted to be his friend I would stop saying such things to him. I was dumbfounded and greatly disturbed, so I decided I would hold off on my efforts until he had recovered his full strength; then I could do as I pleased with him. But he was snatched away from my madness and brought to safety in your presence, for my consolation. After a few days the fever returned, and he died. I was not there.

4.9   My heart was clouded over with such grief, and I saw death *Lam. 5:17* wherever I looked. My hometown was a torment, my father's house unfathomable misery. Whatever I had shared with my friend turned into savage affliction without him. My eyes looked for him everywhere, but he was nowhere to be found. All things were hateful to me because they did not contain him, and they could no longer say to me, "Look, he is coming," as they had when he was alive and we were apart. I had become a great question to myself, and I asked my soul why it was sad and why it was so disquieted within me, and I had no answer to give myself. If I said, "Put your hope in God," I quite rightly did not obey, for that most precious friend whom I had lost was truer and better than the phantasm in which I was commanded to put my hope. Nothing was sweet to me but my own tears, and they took the place of my friend among the delights of my mind.

Ps. 41:6, 41:12, 42:5

Ps. 138:11

5.10   And now, O Lord, these things have long since passed away, and time has softened my grief. Can I hear from you, who are the Truth, and bring the ear of my heart to your mouth so that you might explain to me why tears are sweet to those who are unhappy? Is it because, even though you are everywhere, you cast our unhappiness far away from you, and you abide in yourself while we endure the turmoil of one experience after another? And yet, unless we brought our cries before your ears, there would be no hope left for us. How is it, then, that from the bitterness of life we can pluck the sweet fruit of mourning, weeping, sighing, and lamentation? Are these things sweet to us because we hope that you are listening? Certainly that is true of our prayers, because when we pray, we want our prayers to come before you. But surely it was not true of the grief and mourning over my loss that overwhelmed me in those days. For I had no hope that he would be restored to life, and I did not beg for that in the midst of my tears. I merely grieved and wept. For I was wretched; I had lost my joy. Is it, then, that weeping is a bitter thing, and yet it also gives pleasure because we now loathe the things that we had once enjoyed but now regard with disgust?

Jn. 14:6

Wisd. 7:27

6.11   But why am I saying these things? For now is not a time for asking questions; it is a time for confessing to you. I was wretched: every mind is wretched that is vanquished by friendship for mortal things and is torn apart when it loses them, feeling then for the first time the wretchedness that was already there even before it lost them. That was how I was in those days, and I wept bitterly and found rest in bitterness. So wretched was I that my own wretched life was more precious to me than my friend. Yes, I would have gladly changed my life, but I would not have wanted to lose my life rather than to lose my friend, and I am not sure whether I would have given up my life even for his sake. It is told of Orestes and Pylades (if that is not merely a story) that they wanted to die each for the other, or at least at the same time, because not to be alive at the same time was to them worse than death. But quite the opposite feeling had somehow sprung up in me: I was heartily sick of living but afraid of dying. I think that the more I loved him, the more I hated and feared death as the dreadful enemy who had taken him from me. I thought that death would suddenly swallow up everyone as it had been able to do to him. I remember that this is exactly how I was.

Look upon my heart, O my God; look within me. Observe, because I remember, you who cleanse me from the uncleanness of such affections, directing my eyes to you and rescuing my feet from the snare. *Ps. 24:15* For I marveled that other mortals were alive when he, whom I had loved as though he would never die, was dead; I marveled even more that I, who was his other self, was alive though he was dead. Someone once said that his friend was half of his soul,³ and truly he spoke well. For I felt that my soul and his were one soul in two bodies, and so life was a terror to me, because I did not want to live on as one half; and perhaps I feared death because I did not want the one whom I had loved so much to die altogether.⁴

7.12   What madness it is not to know how to love human beings as human beings ought to be loved! How foolish is someone who cannot keep within due bounds in bearing up under the difficulties of the human condition! And so I raged and sighed and wept and was in turmoil; I could not be at peace, could not think clearly. I carried my wounded and bleeding soul around with me; it could not bear to be carried around, but I could find nowhere to set it down. Not in pleasant groves, not in games and songs, not in sweet-smelling places, not in well-prepared banquets, not in the pleasures of the bedroom, not even in books or poetry: nowhere could it find rest. Everything was a horror to me, even the very light itself. Everything that was not what he had been was vile and hateful to me—everything but my groans and tears, for in them alone I did find a little peace, and when my soul was distracted from them, it weighed me down with a great burden of unhappiness. I knew, O Lord, that you were the one who must lift my burden and heal my soul, but I did not want you to, and I lacked the strength to ask you, all the more so because when I thought of you, I did not regard you as something solid and firm. It was not you who

---

3. Horace, *Carmina* 1.3.5–8.
4. Augustine criticizes this sentence in *Reconsiderations* 2.6.2 (see Appendix D).

were my God, but an empty phantasm, my own error. If I tried to set down my burden there so that it might come to rest, it would slip through the void and fall heavily upon me once again. I had become, and I remained, a place of desperation for myself; I could not bear to stay there, and I had no power to leave. For where could my heart go to flee from my heart? Where could I go to flee from myself? Where could I go that I would not follow?

But I did at least flee from my hometown. For my eyes would not be seeking him out so much where I was not accustomed to seeing him. So I left the town of Thagaste and came to Carthage.

8.13   Times are not idle, nor do they roll along through our senses in vain; they do astonishing works in the mind. They came and went from day to day, and in coming and going they brought me other hopes and other memories; it was not long before they restored to me the kinds of pleasures I had once known, the pleasures that had given way to my great sorrow, which yielded its place not indeed to other sorrows, but to causes of other sorrows. How was it, after all, that this sorrow had pierced me so easily, so deeply, if not because I had poured out my soul upon the sand[5] by loving someone who was going to die as if he were immortal? And indeed what restored and renewed me above all else were the comforts of other friends. With them I loved what I loved instead of you: an uncouth myth, a great lie, and by our adulterous affair with that falsehood our minds, with itching ears, were corrupted. But for me that myth would live on even if one of my friends died. What captivated me in my friends were other things: talking together, laughing together, gladly serving each other, reading sweetly phrased books together, sharing in conversations both trivial and earnest, disagreeing from time to time without rancor, as a man might debate within himself, such rare disagreements making our usual agreement all the sweeter, teaching each other or learning from each other, missing those who are absent and greeting with joy those who return. These and others like them are the signs, given by the mouth, the tongue, the eyes, and a thousand tender gestures, from the hearts of those who love and who return love, the signs that enkindle souls and make of many one.

2 Tim. 3:3–4

---

5. O'Donnell (II:231) finds an echo of Ovid here (*Tristia* 5.6.43–44: "He who is not content with these things would pour sand upon the beach, wheat upon the fields, waters into the sea"); but the connection, both topical and verbal, is tenuous. Much more likely is an oblique reference to Matthew 7:26–27: "And every one who hears these words of mine and does not do them will be like a foolish man who built his house upon the sand; and the rain fell, and the floods came, and the winds blew and beat against that house, and it fell; and great was the fall of it" (RSV).

9.14   This is what we love in friends—love in such a way that our conscience is ill at ease if we do not love those who love us in return or return the love of those who love us, seeking nothing from their bodies but these marks of goodwill. Hence our grief if someone dies; hence the darkness of sorrow, a heart drenched in tears, its sweetness turned to bitterness: the death of those who lose their lives becomes a death for those who live on. Blessed are those who love you, and their friend in you, and their enemy for your sake. For they alone lose no one dear to them to whom all are dear in him who is not lost. And who is this but our God, who made heaven and earth and fills them, because by filling them he made them? No one loses you but those who send you away—and in sending you away, where do they go? To where do they flee? Only from you and to you: from your good pleasure to your wrath. For where in their punishment do they not encounter your law? And your law is truth, and truth is you.

Gn. 1:1; Ps. 145:6 / Jer. 23:24

Ps. 138:7

Ps. 118:142 / Jn. 14:6

10.15   God of hosts, turn us and show your face, and we shall be saved. For wherever the human soul turns, it is fixed upon sorrows unless it turns to you—even if it is fixed upon beautiful things outside you and outside itself, beautiful things that would be nothing at all if they were not from you. They rise and fall: in rising they begin to be, and they grow so that they might become fully mature, and once they have matured they grow old and perish. Not all things grow old, but all things perish. So when they rise and bend their course toward being, the more quickly they grow into being, the more they hasten toward non-being. Such is their condition. Only this much have you granted to them, because they are parts of things that do not exist all at once; instead, as one thing passes away and another takes its place, they all together constitute a whole. So indeed it is when we express something through audible signs: there will be no complete utterance unless one word passes away so that another can take its place.

Ps. 79:8

For all these things let my soul praise you, O God, Creator of all things,[6] but let it not be fixed upon them by the glue of love through the senses of the body. For they go where they will go, so that they exist no more, and they tear the soul apart through its unhealthy desires; for the soul wants to exist, and it loves to rest in the things it loves. But there is no place to rest in them, for they do not stay put: and who can chase after them through the sense of the body? Who indeed can grasp them fully even when they are present? The bodily sense is

Ps. 145:2

---

6. "O God, Creator of all things": *Deus, creator omnium,* the first line of a hymn by Ambrose, which is quoted at 2.6.12, 6.4.5, 9.6.14, 9.12.32, 10.34.52, and 11.27.35.

sluggish, simply because it is the bodily sense: such is its condition. It is sufficient for the purpose for which it was created, but it is not sufficient to hold steady the things that are hastening from their appointed beginning to their appointed end. For in your Word, by whom they are created, they hear you say, "From here, to there, and no farther." *Job 38:11*

11.16   Do not be empty, my soul, and let not the ear of your heart be deafened by the uproar of your emptiness. Listen: the Word himself cries out for you to return, and there, in him, is a place of quiet rest that cannot be disturbed, a place where love is not forsaken unless love itself forsakes you. Those things pass away so that others might take their place, and all its parts together make up this lowly universe: but the Word of God says, "Will I ever depart and go elsewhere?" Fix your dwelling place in him, O my soul; entrust to him whatever you have from this world. If *Jn. 14:23* only because you are weary of falsehoods, entrust to the Truth whatever of truth you have, and you will not lose anything. What is rotten in you will begin to flourish again, and all your diseases will be healed. All the *Ps. 102:3; Mt. 4:23* things that are wavering and unsteady in you will be given form again and made anew and bound firmly to you; they will not cast you down to the places where they go, but instead they will stand firm with you and abide with God, who stands firm and abides for ever. *Ps. 101:13; Heb. 1:11; 1 Pet. 1:23–25*

11.17   Why do you turn aside to perversity and follow your flesh? Turn instead to God, and let your flesh follow you. Whatever you perceive through your flesh is only a part, and you pay no heed to the whole of which these things are parts, and yet they give you pleasure. If the sense of your flesh were fit to grasp the whole and were not justly constrained, for your own punishment, to accept its place as a part of the whole, you would want whatever exists in the present to pass away, so that all things might please you even more. After all, through that same bodily sense you hear what we say, and you do not want the syllables to stay put; no, you want them to pass away so that others may come and you can hear the whole. Such is always the case when one thing composes a whole, and the things of which the whole is composed do not all exist at once: if all the things that compose the whole can be sensed, they all together give greater pleasure than any one of them by itself. But better by far than all these things is the one who made all things, and this is our God; and he does not pass away, for nothing else takes his place.

12.18   If bodies please you, praise God for them, and turn your love back to their Maker, lest you displease him amidst the things that please you. If souls please you, love them in God, for they are changeable in themselves but in him are made steadfast and firm—otherwise they would depart and perish. So love them in God. Seize as many souls as you can and bring them with you before God, and say to them:

"It is he whom we must love. He made these things, and he is not far from us. For he did not make them and then depart: they are from him and in him. This, then, is where he is, wherever there is the savor and fragrance of Truth. He is deep within the heart, but our heart has wandered far from him. Return, sinners, to your heart, and cling to the one who made you. Abide with him, and you will abide; rest in him, and you will have rest. Where are you going along these thorny paths? Where are you going? The good that you love is from him, and insofar as it is for him, it is good and sweet; but if you abandon him, whatever is from him will rightly become bitter as it is wrongly loved. Why do you go on and on walking along difficult and wearisome paths? There is no rest where you are seeking rest. Seek what you are seeking, but it is not where you are seeking it. You are seeking the happy life in the land of death: it is not there. How indeed can there be a happy life where there is no life at all?

12.19 "And our very Life came down here and bore our death and killed it by the abundance of his life. And he thundered forth, crying out that we should depart from here and return to him, to that most hidden place from which he first came forth to us into the Virgin's womb, where he married himself to created human nature, to our mortal flesh, so that it might be no longer mortal. And from there he came forth like a bridegroom out of his chamber and rejoiced like a champion to run his course. For he did not tarry: he ran, crying out by his words, his deeds, his death, his life, his descending and his ascension—crying out for us to return to him. And he vanished from our sight, so that we might return to our hearts and encounter him there. For he departed: and lo, he is here. He would not be among us any longer, and he did not abandon us. For he departed for a place he had never left, because the world was made through him, and he was in this world and came into this world to save sinners. My soul makes its confession to him, and he heals my soul, because it has sinned against him. O mortals, how long will your hearts be weighed down? Now that your Life has come down to you, do you not long to ascend and be fully alive? But to where will you ascend? For you are haughty, and you have set your mouth against the heavens. Come down, then, that you may ascend, and ascend to God. For you have fallen by rising up against God."

Say these things to them, so that they might weep in the valley of weeping, and in this way seize them and bring them with you before

Ps. 99:3

Acts 17:27

Rom. 11:36;
1 Cor. 8:6

Is. 46:8

Wisd. 5:7

Is. 9:2 qtd.
Mt. 4:16

Jn. 14:6; Col. 3:4 /
Jn. 3:13, 6:33;
Eph. 4:9–10 / 2
Tim. 1:10 / Jn.
10:10

Ps. 18:6–7 / Ps.
39:18; Hab. 2:3;
Heb. 10:38 /
Eph. 4:8–9 / Lk.
24:52; Acts 1:9

Jn. 1:10–11

1 Tim. 1:15

Ps. 40:5

Ps. 4:3

Ps. 72:8–9

Ps. 83:7

God. For it is by God's Spirit that you say these things to them, if when you speak you are aglow with the fire of charity.

13.20   In those days I did not yet know all this. I loved lower beauties, and I sank into the depths. I said to my friends, "Surely we love nothing but what is beautiful. So what then is beautiful? And what is beauty? What is it that draws us to the things we love and unites us with them? If there were no splendor in them, no comeliness, they would in no way move us toward themselves." And I looked around and saw in bodily things that some are beautiful because of what they are as a whole, while others are suitable because they are fittingly accommodated to something else, as a part of the body is suited to the whole body, a shoe is suited to the foot, and so on. And this line of thought welled up in my mind from my inmost heart, and I wrote books *On the Beautiful and the Fitting*—two or three books, I think. You know, God, for I have forgotten. I no longer have them; somehow or other I lost track of them.

14.21   But what was it, O Lord my God, that impelled me to dedicate those books to Hierius, the orator of the city of Rome? I had never met him, but I loved the man for the splendid reputation he had earned from his teaching, and I had heard some of his words and found them pleasing—though what pleased me most was that others found them pleasing and lavished praises on him. They marveled that a man of Syria, educated originally in Greek eloquence, had later become an astonishing speaker in Latin and was exceedingly knowledgeable about matters pertaining to the study of wisdom; all this was pleasing to me. A man who is not even present is praised and loved. Does that love go forth from the mouth of the one who offers praise and enter into the heart of the one who hears it? May it never be! But one person's love is enkindled by another's, and so when we believe that the one who is proclaiming his praise has no deception in his heart—when, that is, he genuinely loves the person he is praising—we love the one who is praised.

14.22   That indeed was how I loved people in those days, relying on other people's judgment and not on yours, my God, in which no one is deceived. But then why was my love for Hierius not like what one might feel for a famous charioteer or a fighter adored by the crowds? It was far different, far more serious: I praised him in the very way in which I wanted to be praised myself. I did not want to be praised and loved as actors are, though I myself praised and loved actors; indeed, I would rather have been unknown than to be famous in that way, rather have been hated than to be loved in that way. Where are these various and divergent weights of love apportioned within a single soul?[7] How is it that I love in someone else what I also hate—for I would loathe and reject it in myself—even though both of us are human beings? A good horse is loved by someone who would not wish to be a horse, even if that were possible. But that is not what we should say of an actor, who shares our nature. Do I then love in a human being what I should hate to be, even though I too am a human being? We human beings are a great mystery, though you, O Lord, have numbered the very hairs of our head, and in you they are not diminished: and yet the hairs of our *Mt. 10:30* head are easier to number than our affections and the movements of our heart.

14.23   But that rhetorician was the kind of man whom I loved in such a way that I wanted to be like him. I was going astray in my pride, carried about by every wind, yet in a most hidden way you were at the *Eph. 4:14* helm, steering me. How is it that I know, how is it that I confess to you with such certainty, that I loved him more because of the love of those who praised him than because of the things for which he was praised? If people had said the very same things about him, but with scorn and contempt, no love for him, no enthusiasm, would have been enkindled in me. Yet everything else would have been exactly the same, and the man himself would have been no different; only the attitudes of those who told me about him would have been different. Look upon this frail soul, not yet grasping the solidity of truth. Whichever way the winds blow from the hearts of those who give their opinions, the soul is carried about by them, turned this way and that, its course directed now one way, now the opposite. Its light is hidden by the clouds, and it cannot discern the truth: though look! the truth is right before us.

It was a matter of great importance to me that my writing and my efforts should come to that man's attention. If he were to approve of them, the fire of my love would grow all the more; but if he were to disapprove, my vain heart, empty of your solidity, would have been gravely hurt. And yet I was glad to bring the beautiful and the fitting (the subject of the books I had dedicated to him) again and again before the mouth of my contemplation, and I was enraptured, no matter whether anyone else shared my appreciation.[8]

---

7. For the image of love as the weight of the soul, see 13.9.10.

8. "I was enraptured, no matter whether anyone else shared my appreciation": *nullo conlaudatore mirabar*, literally, "I admired, with no co-praiser." My own translation is meant to convey that Augustine was excited by the *topic* (not that he admired his own book, as most translators have it; the phrasing of the sentence does not suggest that reading to me) and enjoyed thinking about it

15.24   But I did not yet see in your art the pivot on which so great a thing turns, O Almighty, who alone do wondrous things. It was through corporeal forms that my mind defined and distinguished the beautiful, which was such through itself, from the fitting, which was suitable because it was accommodated to something else; and it was from corporeal things that I collected my examples. And I turned my attention to the nature of the mind, and the false opinion that I had about spiritual things prevented me from discerning the truth. The very might of truth itself fell upon my eyes, but I turned my struggling mind away from incorporeal things to shapes and colors and swelling magnitudes, and because I could not see them in the mind, I concluded that I could not see the mind.

Ps. 71:18, 135:4

Now since in virtue I loved peace, whereas in vice I hated discord, I observed that in virtue there is unity and in vice, division. And it seemed to me that the rational mind and the nature of the truth and of the supreme good consisted in that unity, whereas the division of irrational life constituted—in some way I could not understand—the substance and nature of the supreme evil. This supreme evil was not merely a substance; it was altogether a living thing. And yet it was not from you, my God, from whom are all things. Such was my wretched opinion. I called that unity "the Monad," as a mind without sex, and the division I called "the Dyad," which was wrath in crimes of violence, lust in sins of passion—I had no idea what I was saying. I did not know, I had not learned, that evil is not a substance, or that our own mind is not the supreme and unchangeable good.

Rom. 11:36; 1 Cor. 8:6

Lk. 9:33

15.25   For as there are crimes of violence when a vicious movement of the mind that provides the impulse to act breaks out with insolence and violence, and as there are sins of passion when the soul's affection casts off its restraint and drinks deeply from carnal pleasures, so too the rational mind itself is vicious when errors and false opinions contaminate its life.[9] And so it was for me in those days: I did not know that there was another light that should have been enlightening my own mind to make it partake of truth. For my mind is not the very nature

---

whether or not anyone else found the topic worthwhile. It would press the text too far to represent Augustine as saying that in fact no one else liked his book, though perhaps that is true. O'Donnell (II:254) comments astutely: "The phrase evokes a sense of intellectual isolation, of a time when A. had outstripped his colleagues and contemporaries and was pursuing lines of thought that he could not share with others."

9. Here Augustine extends his distinction between crimes of violence and sins of passion (first seen in 3.8.16) by adding errors of the rational mind and making the Trinitarian structure (worldly ambition, lust of the flesh, and lust of the eyes) clear.

of truth. For it is you who light my lamp, O Lord; O God, you make my darkness bright; and from your fullness we have all received. For you are the true light that enlightens every human being who comes into the world, and in you there is no variation, no flickering shadow of change.

Ps. 17:29 / Jn. 1:16

Jn. 1:9

Jas. 1:17

15.26 Yet I was grasping toward you, and I was cast off from you so that I might have a taste of death: for you resist the proud. What indeed could show greater pride than asserting in my own astonishing madness that I was naturally what you are? For I was changeable—as was evident to me from the very fact that I truly wanted to become wise and thus change from worse to better—yet I preferred to think that you too were changeable, rather than that I was not what you are. And so I was cast off; you resisted my bluster and my stubbornness. I went on imagining corporeal forms. Flesh that I was, I accused the flesh, and my wandering spirit had not yet returned to you; I wandered off into things that are not, neither in you nor in me nor in a body: things that were created for me not by your truth but by my own vanity, which fashioned them out of bodies. And I said to your faithful little ones, my fellow citizens,[10] from whom I was living in exile, though I did not know it—I said to them, rambling on in my impertinent way, "Why then does the soul, which God made, fall into error?" But I would not allow anyone to ask me, "Why then does God fall into error?" So I preferred to argue that your unchangeable substance was coerced into error rather than confessing that my own changeable substance had gone astray of its own accord and fallen into error for its own punishment.

Ps. 42:2

Jas. 4:6

Ps. 77:39

Mt. 11:25 par.
Lk. 10:21; 1
Cor. 3:1

15.27 I was perhaps twenty-six or twenty-seven years old when I wrote those volumes, pondering within myself the bodily fictions that clamored in the ears of my heart. In my thinking about the beautiful and the fitting, my ears were attentively listening for your inner melody, O sweet Truth; I was eager to be still and hear you and to rejoice with joy at the voice of the bridegroom—but I could not, because I was dragged away into external things by the voices of my own errors and sank to the depths in the weight of my pride. For you did not make

Jn. 3:29

---

10. I seem to be alone in hearing here an echo of Ephesians 2:19, "You are no longer strangers and sojourners, but fellow citizens with the saints and members of the household of God," but that echo for me is decisive for the interpretation of "fellow citizens" as fellow citizens in the city of God, not (as some have suggested) fellow citizens of Thagaste—an improbable interpretation in any case, since Augustine would, of course, know whether he was in Thagaste or not, and the language about "faithful little ones" implies Christians generally.

me hear of joy and gladness, nor did my bones exult, for they had not
yet been humbled.

Ps. 50:10

16.28   When I was about twenty years old, I got hold of a certain
work of Aristotle called *The Ten Categories*. My teacher, the rhetor of
Carthage, and others with reputations as learned men would puff out
their cheeks with pride when they mentioned this book; and I had
somehow conceived the idea that it was a great and divine work, and
so I was desperately eager to read it. I read it—by myself—and understood it.

And what good did that do me? When I discussed the work with
people who said they had barely been able to understand it with the
help of the most learned teachers, who not only spoke about it but
made many diagrams in the sand, they could tell me nothing about
the work that I had not come to know just from reading it by myself.
I thought in fact that the book dealt quite straightforwardly with substances, such as human beings; and the characteristics of substances,
such as the shape of a human being, what he is like; his size, how many
feet tall he is; relation, whose brother he is; or where he is; or when he
was born; or whether he is standing or sitting; or whether he is wearing
shoes or armor; or whether he is doing or undergoing something; and
all of the innumerable things that fall into the nine categories of which
I have given examples, or into the category of substance itself.

16.29   What good did this do me? It in fact did me harm, because
I thought that everything whatsoever was entirely contained within
those ten categories, and so I tried to understand you, my God, who
are wondrously simple and unchangeable, as if you were the subject of
your own greatness and beauty, so that they were in you as a subject in
the way that greatness and beauty are in a body. But no: you yourself
are your own greatness, your own beauty, whereas a body is not great
and beautiful simply by virtue of being a body—for if it were less great
and less beautiful, would it be any less a body? What I thought about
you was falsehood, not truth, the fictions of my own wretchedness,
not the firmament of your happiness. For you had commanded—and
so it was done in me—that the earth should bring forth thorns and
thistles for me, and with difficulty would I attain bread.

Gn. 3:18–19

16.30   And what good did it do me—desperately wicked slave of evil
desires that I was—that I read and understood on my own all the books
of the liberal arts that I could get my hands on? I rejoiced in them,
but I did not know the source of everything that was true and certain
in them. For I had my back to the light and my face to the things on

which it shone; I saw the things on which the light was shining, but on the face that I had turned to look at them, no light shone. With no great difficulty, and with no need for human instruction, I understood whatever I read about the art of speaking and reasoning, about the dimensions of shapes, about music and numbers. This you know, O Lord my God, because the quickness of my understanding and the keenness of my discernment are your gift. But I offered no sacrifice to you for these things, and so they worked more to my detriment than to my benefit. For I worked tirelessly to keep this very good part of my substance[11] under my own control, and I did not give over my strength to you for safekeeping. Instead, I journeyed away from you to a far country and wasted my substance on whorish desires.

Ps. 53:8

Ps. 58:10

Lk. 15:12–13, 15:30

What good did this good thing do for me? For I was not putting it to good use. Indeed, I did not realize that even dedicated and talented students found the liberal arts extremely difficult to understand until I tried to teach them, and it was a most exceptional student who could follow my explanation without falling far behind me.

16.31   But what good did this do for me, who thought that you, O Lord God, O Truth, were an immense shining body and that I was a fragment of that body? Such incredible perversity! But that is how I was, and I do not blush, my God, to confess to you and to give thanks for your mercies toward me and to call upon you—I who in those days did not blush to profess my blasphemies before others and to bark against you like a dog. What good did it do me in those days to have a mind adept for the teachings of the liberal arts, unraveling the most intricate complexities of those books with no need for the assistance of any human instruction, when in my deformity and sacrilegious wickedness I was wandering away from the teaching of true piety? What harm did their much more sluggish minds do to your little ones, since they had not gone far from you, but were fledglings safe in the nest of your Church, taking nourishment for their wings of charity through the food of a sound faith? O Lord our God, may we place our hope beneath the covering of your wings; protect us and carry us. You will carry your little ones, carry them even to grey hairs, for when you are our strength, there is strength indeed; but when the strength is ours alone, then it is weakness. Our good is always alive in you, and because

Ps. 106:8

Ps. 83:4

Job 39:26

Ps. 16:8, 35:8, 56:2, 60:5, 62:8, 90:4 / Is. 46:4; Sir. 6:18

---

11. *Substantia:* the word looks both back to the discussion of Aristotle's *Categories*, in which substance is the fundamental category (notice that Augustine's substance, unlike God's, can rightly be said to have a part), and ahead to the allusion to the story of the prodigal son in the next sentence (since the word for "property" in such phrases as "Give me my portion of the property" and "He wasted his property (AV: substance) in riotous living" is *substantia*.

we have turned away from our good, we have turned to perversity. Turn us back now, O Lord, so that we might not turn our backs on you, for our good is alive in you, a good from which nothing is lacking: for this good is you yourself. Though we have fallen away from it, we have no fear that there is nowhere for us to return to: for though we may be absent, our true home, your eternity, does not fall.

Book Five

Augustine is restless in heart and mind, moving from one teaching post to the next in search of prestige, money, and better working conditions, moving from one philosophy and one teacher to the next in search of a solid foundation of truth, which continues to elude him—guided all along, though he does not know it, by the hand of divine providence. The Manichees teach falsehoods about the natural world; the philosophers find the truth but fail to seek the Author of truth. Augustine looks to the Manichee bishop Faustus to answer his questions but is disappointed to find that Faustus's words are long on style but short on substance; turning to the Christian bishop Ambrose solely to admire his style, he begins to appreciate the substance of what he has to say. But Augustine despairs of finding truth in either Manicheanism or Christianity, and he toys with the skeptical idea that human beings are incapable of achieving certainty.

After a prologue (5.1.1–5.2.2) that reflects again on the nature of confession and looks ahead to the themes of divine initiative and the search for God that dominate Book 5, Augustine tells the story of his twenty-ninth year. While teaching in Carthage, he encounters Faustus (5.3.3–5.7.13); his hopes that Faustus will answer his questions (5.3.3–5.5.9) prove groundless (5.6.10–5.7.13). He leaves Carthage for Rome to advance his career (5.8.14–5.11.21), abandoning his mother (5.8.15), only to fall gravely ill once he arrives (5.9.16–5.10.18). He loses hope of finding truth (5.10.19–5.11.21). Finding the students in Rome dishonest, he applies for a teaching post in Milan, which he receives (5.12.22). In Milan he encounters Ambrose, from whom he learns how to interpret troublesome Old Testament passages figuratively (5.13.23–5.14.25).

1.1   Accept the sacrifice of my confessions from the hand of my tongue, which you formed, which you have roused to give thanks to your Name.[1] Heal all my bones, and let them say, "Lord, who is like you?" Those who make their confession to you do not teach you what is going on within them, for a closed heart is not hidden from your eye and no human hardness can rebuff the touch of your hand. No, you melt it whenever you please, whether by showing mercy or

Mal. 1:10

Prov. 18:21

Ps. 53:8 / Ps. 6:3

Ps. 34:10

---

1. Recall that the words translated "confessions" and "give thanks" (*confessionum* and *confiteatur*) are from the same stem. Note also the parallel with 1.1.1, "You rouse [human beings] to take delight in praising (*laudare*) you," where *laudare* is a synonym for *confiteor*. The effect of this echo and of the thick texture of Psalm citations at the beginning of this book, like that at the beginning of Book 1, is to mark Book 5 as the beginning of a new structural unit.

by exacting punishment, and there is no one who can hide from your burning heat. But let my soul praise you that it might love you; let it give thanks to you for your acts of mercy that it might praise you. The whole of your creation never ceases to praise you, never grows silent in singing your praises: every spirit whose mouth is turned toward you speaks your praises, every animal and every bodily thing speaks your praises through the mouths of those who pay them heed, so that our soul might shake off its weariness, leaning upon the things you have made and passing over from them to you, who made these things in a most wonderful way, and find in you refreshment and true strength.

Ps. 18:7 / Ps. 145:2

Ps. 106:8

Ps. 71:18, 135:4

2.2   Let the wicked who are restless depart from you and flee. You see them and mark out their shadows, and behold! the totality of things that includes them is beautiful, though they themselves are unsightly. What harm have they done to you? In what way have they marred the beauty of your dominions, which are just and flawless from the heavens even to the lowliest places? Where indeed did they flee when they fled from your face? Where do you fail to find them? Yet they have fled so that they might not see you who see them, and, in their blindness, stumble into you—for you abandon nothing you have made—that the unjust might stumble into you and be justly tormented; they draw back from your gentleness only to stumble over your righteousness and fall into your severity. They know not that you are everywhere; no place confines you, and you alone are present even to those who take themselves far away from you. Let them turn, therefore, and seek you; for you have not abandoned your creatures as they have abandoned their Creator. Let them turn to you. And behold, you are in their hearts, in the hearts of those who confess to you and throw themselves into your arms and weep upon your breast when they have come to the end of their difficult paths. You are gentle to them and wipe their tears; they cry all the more and rejoice in their weeping, for it is you, O Lord—not any human being, flesh and blood, but you, O Lord—who make them anew and give them comfort. And where was I when I was seeking you? You were right in front of me, but I had departed from myself; I could not find even myself, let alone you.

Ps. 138:7–8

Rom. 11:7–11 / Wisd. 11:25

Ps. 72:27

Wisd. 5:7 / Is. 25:8; Rev. 7:17, 21:4

3.3   In the sight of my God I shall tell the story of my twenty-ninth year. A certain Manichee bishop, Faustus by name, had just come to Carthage. He was a great snare of the devil; his smooth and winning speech enticed many and entrapped them. I was a great admirer of eloquence, of course, but I knew the difference between eloquence and the truth regarding the matters that I was eager to learn about. What I

1 Tim. 3:7, 6:9; 2 Tim. 2:26

cared about was the banquet of knowledge that this celebrated Faustus of theirs would set before me, not the style of language in which he would serve it. For I had already been told about his reputation: he was, they said, extraordinarily well versed in all fields of genuine value and particularly learned in the liberal arts. And because I had read and memorized many sayings of the philosophers and still remembered them, I compared them to those interminable fables of the Manichees, and it seemed to me that what the philosophers had to say was more probable, though their ability stretched only far enough that they could appraise this present world; they could in no way discover its Lord. For great are you, Lord, and you look with favor on what is lowly but perceive from afar what is highly exalted. Only to those whose hearts are contrite do you draw near; the proud do not find you, not even those who in their meddlesome expertise number the stars and the sand and measure the domains of the heavens and follow the paths of the constellations.

Wisd. 13:8–9 / Ps. 47:2, 95:4, 144:3 / Ps. 137:6 / Ps. 33:19

3.4   For with their minds they seek out these things, and with the brilliance that you gave them they made many discoveries; many years ago they predicted eclipses of the sun and the moon—on what day and at what hour they would take place; how much would be eclipsed— and their calculations did not deceive them. Everything happened just as they predicted it would, and they wrote down the rules that their investigations had revealed. Those writings are read to this day, and based on them predictions are made about the year, the month, the day of the month, the hour of the day, and how great a part of the light of the sun or the moon will be eclipsed; and it will happen exactly as predicted. People are in awe of these things: those who have no knowledge of them are stunned, and those who do have knowledge boast of it and gain great renown. By their irreligious pride they draw back from your light and eclipse it. They foresee the eclipse of the sun long before it happens, but they do not see their own eclipse even as it is taking place. For they have not the humility and piety to seek the source of the brilliance by which they seek these things, and, discovering that it is you who made them, and not they themselves, to give themselves to you that you might safeguard what you have made, and to kill, for your sake, what they have made of themselves, slaughtering their self-exaltations like birds of the air, their inquisitiveness like the fish of the sea with which they walk the secret paths of the deep, and their lusts like the beasts of the field, so that you, O God, might be a devouring fire, consuming the preoccupations that bring them death and creating them anew for everlasting life.

Ps. 99:3

Ps. 8:8–9

Deut. 4:24, 9:3; Heb. 12:29

3.5 But they do not know the Way, your Word, through whom you *Jn. 14:6* made the things they number and those who number them and the sense *Jn. 1:1–3* by which they perceive the things they number and the mind by which they number them: but for your wisdom there is no number.[2] Instead *Ps. 146:5* your Only-begotten has become for us wisdom and righteousness and sanctification; he has been numbered among us and paid tribute to *1 Cor. 1:30* Caesar. They do not know this Way, by which they might descend from *Mt. 17:24–27* themselves to him and, by him, ascend to him. They do not know this Way, and they suppose that they are lofty, among the stars and the heavenly lights; but in truth they have fallen heavily to earth, and their foolish *Is. 14:12–13* hearts are darkened. They say many true things about creation, but they *Rom. 1:21* do not search piously for the Truth, the Maker of creation, and so they *Jn. 14:6* do not find him: or if they do find him, then although they know God, they do not honor him as God or give him thanks, but they become futile in their thinking. They call themselves wise by attributing to them- *Rom. 1:21* selves what belongs to you, and then go on from there—so extraordinarily perverse is their blindness—to attribute to you what belongs to them, joining their lies to you, who are Truth, and changing the glory of the uncorrupted God into the likeness of an image of corruptible human beings and birds and beasts and reptiles. They change your truth into a lie, and worship and serve the creature rather than the Creator.[3]

3.6 Nevertheless, I kept in mind the many true conclusions they had reached from creation itself, and there I found a rational explanation based on numbers and the order of times and the visible manifestations of the stars. I compared this with the sayings of Mani, who in his madness wrote quite prolifically about such matters, and I found no such rational explanation of solstices and equinoxes, or of eclipses, or of any similar phenomenon that I had learned about in the books of secular wisdom. Among the Manichees I was simply told that I must believe: the rational explanations confirmed through numbers and by my own eyes were nowhere to be found, and what I was told instead was far different.

4.7 Lord God of truth, are those who know these things pleasing to *Ps. 30:6* you simply because they know them? Surely not. Miserable indeed are those who know all these things but do not know you; but happy are they who know you, even if they do not know these things. And those

---

2. "but for your wisdom there is no number": *et sapientiae tuae non est numerus*, the same verse quoted in the second sentence of 1.1.1, there translated as "and your wisdom is beyond measure."
3. The end of this paragraph quotes and expands upon Romans 1:21–25. For the text, see Essential Scriptures, text 8.

who know both you and them are not happier because of them. No: they are happy only because of you, if knowing you as you are they glorify you and give you thanks and do not become futile in their thinking. Someone who owns a tree and gives thanks to you for the benefit *Rom. 1:21* he has from it, even though he does not know how many feet tall it is or how broad is its canopy, is better off than someone who measures the tree and numbers all its branches but does not own it or know and love its Creator. And so it is with faithful human beings, whose wealth encompasses the whole world,[4] and who, as having nothing, yet possess all things by clinging to you, whom all things serve. They may not *Prov. 17:6 VL* *2 Cor. 6:10* know even the paths of Ursa Major, yet it would be foolish to doubt that they are better off than someone who measures the heavens and numbers the stars and weighs the elements but pays no heed to you, who have arranged all things by measure and number and weight. *Wisd. 11:21*

5.8   And besides, who asked this Mani fellow to write all these things? No one needs expertise in them in order to learn piety. For you have said to humankind, "Behold, piety is wisdom." Even if Mani had under- *Job 28:28 VL* stood these things perfectly well, he could still have been ignorant of piety: but he knew nothing of them, and so it was extraordinarily presumptuous of him to teach them, and he therefore could also not know piety. To profess these things—even when one knows them—is vanity; to confess to you is piety. He, straying from the path of piety, spoke at length about these things, thereby exposing himself as a charlatan to everyone who had learned the truth about them; he made it quite clear just what his opinion would be worth in more obscure matters. He was certainly not content to be held in low esteem: he sought, in fact, to persuade people that the Holy Spirit, the Comforter and Enricher of your *Jn. 14:16* faithful ones, was in him, personally and with full authority. So when he was caught out speaking falsehoods about the sky and the stars and the movements of the sun and moon, his shameless ramblings were revealed as the height of sacrilege: not because these matters are part of religious doctrine (for they are not), but because he spoke of things he did not know—he even spoke falsehoods—with such an insanely deceptive pride that he sought to attribute them to himself as a divine person.[5]

5.9   For when I hear fellow Christians speaking ignorantly and mistakenly about such things, I bear with them patiently as they express

---

4. Proverbs 17:6 in the Old Latin version: "The whole world is the wealth of the faithful human being." Augustine's use of the verse has additional resonance because "faithful" (*fidelis*) so often carries for him the meaning, or at least the connotation, "baptized Christian."
5. The language here echoes that of the next-to-last sentence of 5.3.5.

their opinions. I do not even think it does them any harm to be ignorant of the structure and arrangement of the material creation, as long
as they do not believe anything unworthy of you, O Lord, Creator of
all things. It does, however, do them harm if they suppose that these
matters are an essential part of the teachings of the faith and have the
effrontery to make obstinate assertions on topics they know nothing
about. Yet even so, charity, our mother, offers support and strength for
such weakness in those who are still in the infancy of their faith, until
the new man rises up and becomes a mature man who can no longer   *Eph. 4:24*
be carried about by every wind of doctrine.   *Eph. 4:13–14*

Yet this man—who set himself up as teacher, as authority, as guide
and leader of those whom he had won over to his side—dared to present himself in such a way that his disciples believed they were following,
not just a human being, but your Holy Spirit. Who, then, on discovering that he had spoken falsehoods, would not judge that such utter
madness must be held in contempt and entirely rejected? But I had not
yet worked out with certainty whether there was some way of explaining why days and nights become longer or shorter, and why there is day
and night at all, why there are eclipses, and other such things that I had
read in other books, in a way consistent with what he had written. If I
could perhaps manage to do that, it would remain an open question for
me whether Mani was right or the astronomers were right; and then I
would favor Mani because of his reputation for holiness.

6.10   For almost the whole nine years in which I was a hearer among
the Manichees as my mind went astray, I was awaiting the arrival
of Faustus with intense longing. Any other Manichees I might have
encountered who failed to answer the questions I posed about such
things promised me that when Faustus came, and I had the opportunity
to confer and speak with him, he would answer those questions with
the utmost ease—and if I happened to have other, even more difficult,
questions for him, his explanations would resolve all my doubts. So
he came: and I found him a charming man with a delightful way of
speaking; but he said the very same things the rest of them always say,
just more smoothly and fluently. But I was thirsty, so what good did
it do me to have a well-dressed waiter bringing me expensive drinking
vessels? My ears had already had their fill of such things, which did not
seem better to me just because they were well said, or true because they
were eloquently expressed; nor did I think his soul wise just because
his features were agreeable and his speech was elegant. Those who had
made such promises to me about him were poor judges of how things
really were: they thought him intelligent and wise because his way of

speaking gave them so much pleasure. Yet I have also had experience of a quite different group of people, who hold truth itself in suspicion and refuse to accede to it if it is presented in rich and well-adorned language.

But you, my God, had by then taught me in marvelous and hidden ways, and therefore I had learned from you, that I should not think something is true just because it is said with style or false just because the words that express it fall awkwardly from someone's lips; nor, conversely, is something true just because it is expressed in an ungainly way or false just because the language is beautiful. (And why do I believe that it was you who taught me this? Because it is true, and there is no teacher of truth besides you, wherever and however that truth may have become clear.) Instead, wisdom and folly are like wholesome and unwholesome foods, and elegant and plain words are like silver platters and rough earthenware:[6] either kind of food can be served on either kind of plate.

6.11   So the eagerness with which I had awaited this man for such a long time was certainly gratified by how he carried himself in discussion and the spirit in which he engaged in it, and by the apt words and well-turned sentences that came so easily to him. I was delighted, and along with many others—even more, in fact, than many others—I praised him and spoke glowingly of him. But I was annoyed that I was not allowed to address him in the presence of an audience and share with him the questions that concerned me, so that we could debate as equals and enjoy the give and take of discussion. I finally did have the opportunity to speak with him, in the company of some friends, at a time that was appropriate for genuine discussion, and I put forward some of the questions that had been troubling me. And what I found was a man whose knowledge of the liberal arts extended only as far as literature, and even that in the most ordinary and conventional way. He had read some of Cicero's speeches, a few books of Seneca, and some of the poets, along with any writings of his own sect that were in Latin and well written; and he used these, along with his daily opportunities to engage in public speaking, to fill out his eloquence, which was made all the more gratifying—and seductive—by his judicious use of his intellectual gifts and by a certain natural charm.

Was this all just as I remember it, O Lord my God, judge of my conscience? My heart and my memory are open to you, who even then were at work in me by your hidden and secret providence, setting my

---

6. "silver platters and rough earthenware": *vasis urbanis et rusticanis*, (very) literally, "city and country vessels," with "vessels" *(vasis)* picking up on the description of words as "chosen and precious vessels" in 1.16.26.

dishonorable errors before my eyes so that I might see them and hate them.

7.12   For once it became clear to me that he lacked expertise in the very arts in which I had thought he would excel, I began to lose hope that he would be able to shed light on the matters that troubled me and to resolve my difficulties. Of course, he could have been ignorant of these matters and still have upheld genuine piety, if only he had not been a Manichee. Their books are full of the most interminable fables about the heavens and the stars, the sun and the moon, and I very much wanted to set before him the calculations I had read elsewhere and then ask whether the accounts found in the books of the Manichees were true instead, or at least whether some equally compelling explanation could be drawn from their works. But I no longer had any confidence that he could give a sophisticated answer. Still, I did present the topic as something to be considered and discussed; he quite modestly declined to take up the challenge. For he knew that he had no knowledge of such things, and he was not ashamed to admit it. He was not one of those talkative[7] people—I have endured so many of them—who try to teach me without managing to say anything. No, he had a heart, and though it was not right toward you, it was also not unguarded toward himself. He was by no means ignorant of his own ignorance, and he did not wish to entrap himself by recklessly engaging in discussions in which he could not acquit himself with success and from which he could not retire gracefully: and for this, too, I admired him all the more. For the modesty of a mind that acknowledges its limitations is more beautiful than the things that I desired to know. And I found such modesty in him concerning all questions of great difficulty and subtlety.

7.13   And so I broke off my planned study of Manichee writings: once that renowned Faustus[8] had appeared and proved ignorant on the questions that most concerned me, I lost any hope that other Manichee teachers could do any better. I began to spend a great deal of time with him because of his eager interest in the literary studies that I was at that time teaching to adolescents in my capacity as orator of Carthage; together we read books that he was interested in reading or that I thought were appropriate for his cast of mind. But that was all:

---

7. For the significance of "talkative" (*loquaces*), see 1.5.4 (with fn. 3).

8. "that renowned Faustus": *ille nominatus* (not actually calling Faustus by name). "The one with the remarkable name" would perhaps convey in English both senses of the Latin: he had a remarkable name in the sense of a great reputation as well as in the sense that Faustus (which means "lucky") was a striking name (not in use among Christians because of its pagan overtones).

my acquaintance with him had killed any further efforts on my part
to advance in that sect, though I did not break with them completely.
Instead, since I had not yet found anything better, I decided to make
do in the meantime with the company I had rather thoughtlessly fallen
into, until perhaps a better choice might become clear. In this way
Faustus, who was a deadly snare for many, had begun to loosen the
hold of the snare that had entrapped me, though he neither desired
this nor knew it. For in the hidden workings of your providence, O
my God, your hands did not abandon my soul, and by the blood of
my mother's heart a sacrifice of tears was being offered up to you for my
sake day and night; and you were at work in me in wondrous ways, for
our steps are directed by the Lord, and it is he who chooses our paths.
And what is there to bring health and salvation? Only your hand,
which makes anew the things you have made.

Ps. 17:6

Ps. 36:23

8.14   It was, therefore, by your work in me that I was persuaded to
go to Rome and to teach there what I was teaching in Carthage. And I
shall not omit to confess to you the reasons by which I was persuaded
to do so, because even for them the remoteness of your infinite loftiness, and the intimate presence of your mercy in us, are worthy to be
pondered and proclaimed. The friends who persuaded me promised
me a larger income and greater dignity, but it was not for those reasons
that I decided to go to Rome (though they did have their appeal for me
at the time). No, the main reason—practically the only reason—was
that I heard the students in Rome were better behaved and were kept
under control by stricter discipline: they did not shamelessly burst in
on lessons offered by a teacher who was not their own, and in fact they
were not allowed entry at all unless the teacher gave permission.

At Carthage, by contrast, students enjoy a disgusting, unrestricted
freedom. They burst in impudently, with almost crazed looks on their
faces, and throw into chaos the orderly instruction that the teacher
has set up to ensure that his students make progress. With astonishing
crassness they do great damage: they ought to be punished according
to the laws, but custom gives its approval. They show themselves to
be all the more wretched by doing, as though it were permitted, what
your eternal law will never permit. They think they are acting with
impunity when in fact the very blindness by which they do these things
is their punishment, and what they suffer is incomparably worse than
what they do. So I was forced as a teacher to put up with behavior on
the part of others that I had refused to engage in myself when I was a
student. And so I was of a mind to go to a place where, as everyone who
was well informed told me, such things were not done.

But it was you, my hope and my portion in the land of the living, *Ps. 141:6* who for the salvation of my soul induced me to move from one land to another: it was you who applied the goads by which I was driven away from Carthage, you who put before me the attractions by which I was drawn to Rome. All this you did through people who love this deadly life, some doing works of madness, others promising trifles and vanity; and to correct my steps you were secretly using both their perversity and my own. For those who were destroying my peace were blind in their disgusting madness, and those who were promising me peace elsewhere had their minds set on earthly things.[9] But though I detested *Phil. 3:18–19* the genuine misery I suffered in Carthage, I still desired the false happiness I was promised in Rome.

8.15   But you knew, God, why I left Carthage and went to Rome. You did not reveal the reason to me or to my mother, who wailed ferociously about my departure and followed me all the way to the sea. She clung to me with all her strength, pleading for me to stay or to allow her to go with me. But I deceived her. I pretended that I had a friend whom I did not want to leave until the wind changed and he could set sail: I lied to my mother, and to such a mother! And I escaped, because in your mercy you have forgiven me even this, saving me from the waters of the sea, full though I was of detestable stains.[10] You kept me safe until I could reach the water of your grace, and once I had been washed clean, the streams of tears that my mother poured out to you for my sake every day, watering the earth beneath her face, would be dried.

But at the time she refused to go home without me, and I just barely managed to persuade her to stay that night at a memorial of Saint Cyprian, which was very near our ship. During the night I departed in secret—without her. Instead she remained where she was, praying and weeping. And what was she asking of you, my God, with so many tears? Just this: that you would not allow me to sail. But you were listening attentively to what was really foremost in her desire, and in your

---

9. Boulding (123) follows O'Donnell (II:307) in suggesting that "their minds [were] set on earthly things" (more literally, "they were wise with respect to earth") is particularly appropriate as a description of the Manichees who were encouraging Augustine to move to Rome, because the Manichees believed that Christ was not genuinely crucified (5.9.6) and that their elect converted food into particles of God (3.10.18, 4.1.1). The connection is tenuous. Augustine tells us here what the earthly things were on which his friends' minds were set, and they were by no means so theologically inflected: more tranquil circumstances in which to pursue his career, a better income, and greater prestige.

10. "detestable stains": *sordes*. As also at 1.1.17, the stains to be removed in baptism, which Augustine refers to in the next sentence as "the water of your grace."

deep wisdom you did not grant what she was asking of you just then, so that you might make of me what she was always asking for. The wind blew and filled our sails, and the shore receded from our sight, and on that morning she was out of her mind with grief; she filled your ears with her reproaches and lamentations. But you had no regard for them, for you were dragging me away by my own disordered desires in order to put an end to those very desires, and you were justly punishing her with the whip of sorrow for her too-worldly affection. For like all mothers, but much more than many, she loved my presence with her, and she did not know what joys you were going to bring her through my absence. She did not know, and so she wept and wailed. Her agony bore witness to the remnants of Eve that remained in her: she sought in sorrow what she had borne in sorrow. And yet when she had finished crying out against my deceptions and my cruelty, she turned again to her prayers to you for my sake; she went back to her normal life, and I went to Rome.

Gn. 3:16

9.16   Once there, I too was lashed with the whip of bodily sickness, and I was on my way to hell, carrying with me all the wrongs I had committed against you and against myself and against others, many and serious wrongs over and above the bondage of original sin by which we all die in Adam. For you had not yet pardoned me in Christ for any of my sins, and he had not yet by his Cross broken down the enmity with you that I had caused through my sins. For how could he break down that enmity on the cross of a phantasm, which is what I believed about him in those days? The death of my soul was real, just as much real as I supposed the death of his body was false; and as real as the death of his body was, so false was the life of my soul, which did not believe it. My fever grew worse and worse, and I was on the point of departing and dying. And where would I have gone if I had gone from here? Where else but into the fire, into the torments that in the truth of your governance were fitting for my deeds?

1 Cor. 15:22

Eph. 2:14–16

Mt. 25:41

My mother knew nothing of this, yet she was praying for me in my absence; and you, who are present everywhere, heard her where she was, and had mercy on me where I was, so that I recovered the health of my body, though I remained sick in my sacrilegious heart. For even in such great danger I did not desire your baptism: I was better as a boy, when I appealed to my mother's piety and begged for baptism, as I have already remembered and confessed.[11] No, I had grown up into my disgrace, and in my madness I mocked the remedy that you prescribed.

---

11. See 1.11.17.

But you did not permit me to die the second death in such a state; it   *Rev. 2:11, 20:6,*
would have so wounded my mother's heart that she would never have   *20:14, 21:8*
recovered. For I cannot adequately express the depth of her love for me,
and with how much greater care she labored to give birth to me in the
spirit than she had in the flesh.   *Gal. 4:19*

9.17   And so I do not see how she could have recovered if my death in
such a state had stabbed her in her very heart.[12] And where would her
earnest prayers have been, the prayers she poured forth abundantly and
without ceasing? With you, and nowhere else. Would you, the God of   *1 Thess. 5:17*
mercies, despise the humble and contrite heart of a chaste and sober   *2 Cor. 1:3 / Ps.*
widow who was generous in giving to the poor, who was gracious to   *50:19 / 1 Tim.*
                                                                            5:10
your saints and served them, who did not let a day pass without making her offering at your altar, and twice a day, morning and evening,
went without fail to your church, not to listen to empty gossip and idle
chit-chat, but so that she might hear your words to her and you might
hear her prayers to you? Her tears were not asking you for silver and
gold, or for any feeble or swiftly fleeing good, but for the salvation of
her son; and it was by your gift that she was so. Would you then despise
her tears and deny her your help? On the contrary, you were present
to her and heard her prayers and did everything in the order in which
you had predestined it to be done. Far be it from you to deceive her in
the visions and answers you gave her—those I have already set down
in writing[13] and those I have not—which she treasured in her faithful
heart and always urged upon you in her prayers as promises given in
your own handwriting. For your mercy endures for ever, and so by   *Col. 2:14 / Ps.*
your promises you graciously make yourself a debtor to those whose   *117:1*
debts you wholly forgive.   *Mt. 6:12, 18:32*

10.18   You therefore healed me from that sickness and saved the son
of your handmaid: saved me, for the time being, in my body, to pre-   *Ps. 85:16, 115:16*
serve me for the better and truer salvation that you would give me. At
that time in Rome I associated with those false and deceptive saints,
not merely with their hearers (one of whom was the man in whose
house I had been ill and recovered), but also with those whom they call

---

12. "stabbed her in her very heart": *transverberasset viscera dilectionis eius,* literally, "pierced the
bowels of her love." "Bowels" no longer has in English the sense of "the seat of the tender and sym-
pathetic emotions" (OED), though it once had: see Colossians 3:12 (AV), "bowels of mercies" (now
generally translated "compassion"); Philippians 2:11 (AV), "bowels and mercies" (often "compassion
and sympathy"); and Luke 1:78, where the Vulgate "through the bowels of the mercy of our God"
generally makes it into English as "through the tender mercy of our God." Augustine probably has
this Biblical usage of the word in mind without intending an allusion to any particular passage.
13. The vision of the wooden rule (3.11.19–20) and the response of the bishop (3.12.21).

the elect. For I still thought that it is not we who sin, but rather that some alien nature, I knew not what, sins in us. It gratified my pride to be without fault and, when I did something bad, not to confess that I had done it, so that you might heal my soul, because I had sinned against you; instead I loved to excuse myself and accuse something *Ps. 40:5* else, I knew not what, that was with me but was not me. But in fact it was me, wholly me, and my impiety had divided me against myself. *Mt. 12:26* My judgment that I was not a sinner was itself an even more incurable sin, a detestable iniquity: I would rather believe that you—you, Almighty God—were overcome within me to my detriment than be overcome by you for my salvation. You had not yet set a watch before my mouth or guarded the door of my lips, so that my heart would not incline to evil words, to make excuses for sins in the company of those who work iniquity; and for this reason I was still a companion of their elect. But by then I had given up any hope that I could advance in *Ps. 140:3–4* that false teaching;[14] still, I had decided to make do with it if I found nothing better, though I held on to it more and more reluctantly and half-heartedly.

10.19   Indeed I began to think that the philosophers who are called Academics were more sensible than the rest. They held that all things should be doubted, and taught that human beings cannot know any truth with certainty. For it seemed clear to me, just as popular opinion held, that this was their teaching; I had not yet come to understand what they really meant. Nor did I neglect to curb the excessive enthusiasm that I realized my host had for the wild tales that fill the books of the Manichees. Yet I enjoyed closer friendships among them than I did with others who did not belong to that heresy. I no longer defended it with the combative spirit I had shown at first, but my comfortable relationship with them—and there are many of them hidden away in Rome—made me rather sluggish in looking for something else, especially since I had no hope at all that I could find the truth in your Church, O Lord of heaven and earth, Creator of all things visible and *Mt. 11:25 par.* invisible.[15] For they had turned me against your Church. It seemed *Lk. 10:21 / Col.* altogether contemptible to me to believe that you have the nature of *1:16* human flesh and are bounded as we are by the shape of a body. And when I tried to think of my God, I did not know how to think of anything but a bodily mass, for I did not think anything existed that was

---

14. "advance in that false teaching": this means both "make intellectual progress by way of that false doctrine" and "rise in the hierarchy of that false sect."
15. The Nicene Creed as Augustine knew it begins, "We believe in one God, the Father Almighty, maker of all things visible and invisible."

not bodily: and this was the chief, and indeed almost the only, cause of my unavoidable error.

10.20   It was for this reason that I believed that evil too was a bodily substance, with a foul and ugly mass of its own: either dense, which they called earth, or rarefied and fine, as is the body of air, which they imagined as a malignant mind creeping through the earth. And because my piety (such as it was) compelled me to believe that a good God created no bad nature, I set up two masses in opposition to each other; both were unbounded, but the evil mass was more contracted and the good mass more expansive. And from this unwholesome starting point other sacrileges came chasing after me. For when my mind tried to return to the catholic faith, I was rebuffed, because the catholic faith was not what I thought it was. And it seemed to me more pious to believe that you, my God, whose acts of mercy toward me I am now confessing, were altogether unbounded—with one exception: the fact that there was a mass of evil opposed to you meant that I had to acknowledge you were bounded in one respect—than to hold that you were wholly bounded within the form of a human body. And it seemed better to me to believe that you had created nothing evil than to believe that the evil nature as I conceived it was from you. For it was not merely that I did not know that evil was not a substance: I actually thought it was a bodily substance; I did not even know how to think about mind except as a fine body that was somehow diffused throughout space.

Ps. 106:8

As for our Savior himself, your Only-begotten, I thought of him as a piece of your brightly shining mass, broken off for our salvation; I could believe about him only what I could picture in my empty imagination. I concluded that such a nature could not be born of the Virgin Mary without becoming intermingled with the flesh, and I could see no way that he (or rather, what I imagined him to be) could become intermingled with the flesh without being contaminated by it. And so I was afraid of believing that he was born in the flesh, lest I be compelled to believe that he was contaminated by the flesh. Now your servants who are spiritually mature[16] will laugh at me, gently and lovingly, if they have read these confessions of mine: but that is how I was.

11.21   I also thought there was no way to defend your Scriptures against the Manichees' criticisms, though I did sometimes wish to

---

16. "your servants who are spiritually mature": *spiritales tui*, more literally, "your spiritual ones." The mature *spiritales* are contrasted with the immature *carnales* (carnal ones) in the passage from 1 Corinthians 3 cited at 4.1.1 fn. 1.

discuss the particular passages they criticized with someone exceptionally well versed in Scripture and discover at first hand what his views were on this subject. Even when I was still in Carthage I had begun to be troubled by the speeches and disputations of a man named Elpidius, who spoke openly against the Manichees and expounded the Scriptures in ways that could not easily be withstood. And I found the Manichees' response—which they were reluctant to put forward in public, but imparted to us privately—quite weak. They said that the New Testament scriptures had been falsified by people (I have no idea who they supposedly were) who sought to insert the Jewish law into the Christian faith; but they could not produce any uncorrupted copies. Still, more than anything else, it was bodily things that held me captive, as though they were pressing down on me and suffocating me; I was gasping for breath under the weight of the masses that were the objects of my thought, and I could not breathe the clean and pure air of your truth.

12.22   So I threw myself into the work that I had come to Rome to do: teaching the art of rhetoric. First I gathered a few students in my home, and I began to make a name for myself with them and through them. But I soon learned that things went on in Rome that I had not had to put up with in Africa. Granted, I saw clearly that the destructive acts[17] of lost adolescents were not done in Rome; but, I was told, "in order to avoid paying their teacher, groups of youth will collude in transferring to another teacher. They go back on their word and hold justice cheap in comparison with their great love for money." My heart hated them, though not with a perfect hatred. For I hated what I was going to suffer from their behavior more, perhaps, than I hated the fact that they were doing wrong to someone. No doubt such people are detestable: they commit fornication against you by loving their acts of derision, which pass away in a moment, and filthy money that stains their hands as soon as they take hold of it, and by embracing this fleeting world and scorning you, who abide for ever and call them back to yourself and forgive a human soul that has consorted with prostitutes but is now returning to you.[18] Even now I hate such depraved and twisted people, although I love them as people who can be set right, so that they have less regard for money than for the teaching they receive, and less regard in turn for that teaching than for you, O God, purest truth, purest abundance of unshakable good, purest peace. But in those

Ps. 138:22

Ps. 72:27
Tit. 1:7; 1 Pet. 5:2

---

17. "destructive acts": *eversiones*. See 3.3.6, and especially fn. 2, for the behavior of these *eversores*.
18. The language here recalls the story of the prodigal son. See Essential Scriptures, text 5.

days it was for my own sake—so that I would not have to suffer at their hands—that I wanted them not to be bad, rather than, for your sake, wanting them to be good.

13.23   Some time later a message was sent from Milan to Rome, asking the prefect of the city to arrange for a professor of rhetoric in Milan; it even offered the right to travel at public expense. And so I put myself forward for the job through my connections with people drunk on Manichee nonsense. (I was leaving in order to get away from them, though neither they nor I knew it.) I gave a trial speech on a set subject; Symmachus, the prefect at that time, gave his approval and sent me on to Milan.

And in Milan I encountered Bishop Ambrose, who was known throughout the world as a most excellent man. He was a devout worshiper of yours, and in those days his powerful preaching set before your people your finest wheat, the gladness of oil, and the sober intoxication of your wine.[19] I was being led unknowingly by you to him, so that by him I would be led knowingly to you. That man of God received me in a fatherly way and watched over my journey in a manner fully befitting a bishop.[20] And I began to love him—not at first as a teacher of the truth, because I had no hope at all of finding truth in your Church, but simply as a man who was kind to me. I listened attentively to his public disputations, not with the intention I should have had, but testing his eloquence, to see whether it lived up to its reputation or was more or less fluent than everyone said. I hung on his words with full attention, but I had no interest at all in the substance of what he was saying—only contempt. I was delighted by the sweetness of his speech, which was more learned than that of Faustus, though it lacked his sparkle and lightness of touch. That is a matter of style. As to substance, there was no comparison: for Faustus was wandering off among the deceptions of the Manichees, whereas Ambrose was most healthfully teaching salvation. But salvation is far from sinners such as I was in those days: and yet I was drawing near to it little by little, though I did not know it.

14.24   For although I was making no effort to learn the things he said, but only to hear how he said them (that empty concern was all that was left for me, now that I had given up hope that human beings could find their way to you), the substance, to which I was paying

Ps. 80:17, 147:14 /
Ps. 4:7–8

Deut. 33:1; 1 Sam.
9:7; 1 Kgs. 13:4;
2 Kgs. 1:9; 2
Chron. 8:14

Ps. 118:155

---

19. An echo of a hymn written by Ambrose himself: "Let Christ be our food, and faith our drink; gladly let us imbibe the sober intoxication of the Spirit" (*hymn.* 1.7.23–26).
20. 1 Timothy 3:2: "A bishop should therefore be beyond reproach . . . hospitable, learned."

no attention, began to make its way into my mind along with the style, which I cared about very much; in fact, I could not separate the two. And as I opened my heart to acknowledge how beautifully he spoke, I was likewise struck by how truly he spoke, though this happened only gradually. At first I began to think that what he said could be defended after all; until then I had supposed that there was nothing to be said in answer to the criticisms of the Manichees, but now I no longer thought it rash to affirm the catholic faith, especially once I had heard one Old Testament passage after another, indeed a great many of them, explained allegorically—passages that had been deadly to me when I understood them literally.[21] And so, after many places in those books had been expounded to me spiritually in this way, I found my despair—my loss of hope that there could be any way at all to withstand those who detest and mock the law and the prophets—reprehensible. But the fact that the catholic way, too, could have learned defenders, who refuted objections at length and without absurdity, was not enough to convince me that one had to accept it, or that the way I followed had to be condemned: for the defenses on each side were evenly matched. Thus the catholic faith was, I thought, not vanquished; but it was not yet obviously victorious.

14.25 At that point I firmly directed my thoughts toward seeing whether there were any irrefutable proofs by which I could somehow convict the Manichees of error. If I had been able to conceive of a spiritual substance, all their deceptions would have been unmasked and cast out of my mind: but I could not. Nevertheless, as I gave more and more thought to the views of the philosophers and compared them with those of the Manichees, I concluded that the views generally held by philosophers concerning the body of this world, and every nature that the senses of the flesh can perceive, were more probable. And so, like the Academics (as they are generally understood), I was in doubt about all things, uncertain about everything. I did at least decide that I should leave the Manichees: in that time of doubt I did not think it was right for me to remain with them, now that I held some of the philosophers in higher esteem. Yet I refused altogether to entrust the healing of my soul's disease to those philosophers, for they lacked the saving *Mt. 9:35* name of Christ. So I decided, for the time being, to be a catechumen in the catholic Church (the Church into whose care my parents had committed me) until some light of certainty dawned by which I might direct my steps.

---

21. See 2 Corinthians 3:6, quoted explicitly at 6.4.6: "the letter kills, but the spirit gives life."

Book Six

As worldly ambition begins to lose its grip on Augustine and his pride is rebuffed, the narrative brings others—Monnica, Ambrose, and Alypius—into the spotlight for the first time. Monnica joins Augustine in Milan, and we read about her piety and her devotion to Ambrose, who himself confounds Augustine's pride by not making himself available for questioning and by showing that Manichee attacks on Christianity were ill founded. An encounter with a drunken beggar brings home to Augustine the emptiness of his worldly ambition, but he cannot bring himself to renounce his career; and his common-law wife, an obstacle to the society marriage that will help him advance in the world, is "torn from [his] side" (6.15.25).

Monnica follows Augustine to Milan; she comes to revere Ambrose, who in turn honors her for her piety (6.1.1–6.2.2). Augustine has no sustained opportunity to question Ambrose privately (6.3.3), but he learns from Ambrose's public preaching that catholic Christians do not conceive of God as bodily (6.3.4–6.4.5) and interpret the Old Testament in ways that destroy the force of Manichee objections (6.4.6–6.5.8). An encounter with a drunken beggar (6.6.9–10) makes Augustine realize that his search for happiness is going badly wrong. Augustine's friends, Alypius and Nebridius, share his longing for wisdom, as well as his frustrations (6.7.11–6.10.17). Augustine recounts his uneasy state of mind (6.11.18–20) and his inability to face the prospect of sexual abstinence (6.12.21–6.16.26). Monnica tries to secure him a socially advantageous marriage (6.13.23); marriage plans thwart Augustine's hope of founding a community devoted to philosophical contemplation (6.14.24) and require the dismissal of his common-law wife (6.15.25).

1.1   My hope since the days of my youth, where were you, and why had you gone so far from me? Had you not created me and set me apart from the beasts and made me wiser than the birds of the air? And I was walking in dark and slippery paths: I sought you outside myself, and I did not find the God of my heart. I had plunged into the depths of the sea, and I was distrustful and without hope of finding truth.

Ps. 70:5
Ps. 9:22
Job 35:11 VL
Is. 50:10; Ps. 34:6
Ps. 72:26
Ps. 67:23

By then my mother, steadfast in her piety, had come to me, following me over land and sea,[1] confident in you in the face of every danger. Ordinarily it is the sailors who reassure frightened passengers who are unaccustomed to sea travel, but in this case it was my mother who reassured the sailors when danger threatened: she promised them that they

---

1. Cf. Virgil, *Aeneid* 9.492.

would arrive safely, for you had promised her this in a vision. And she found me in grave peril, in despair of finding the truth. Nonetheless, when I told her that I was no longer a Manichee, though neither was I a catholic Christian, she rejoiced, but not as though this news were unexpected: for she was already confident that I would be rid of that part of my wretchedness, over which she wept for me as one who was dead but would be restored to life by you. She brought me before you on the bier of her thought, that you might say to the widow's son, "Young man, I say to you, arise," and he would come to life again and begin to speak, and you would entrust him to his mother. So there was no turmoil in her heart, no frenzy of jubilation, when she heard that I had already become in part what she was daily pleading with you to make of me: that though I had not yet embraced the truth, I had been rescued from falsehood. Quite the contrary: she was certain that you would grant her what remained, for you had promised her all of it. So with perfect calm and a heart full of faith, she replied to me that she believed she would see me a faithful catholic before she departed this life.

Lk. 7:12–15

This indeed is what she said to me. But to you, fount of mercies, she prayed all the more fervently, with tears flowing more copiously, that you would make haste to help me and make my darkness bright. She went even more eagerly to church and hung upon the words of Ambrose, finding in his preaching a spring of water welling up to eternal life. Oh, she loved that man like an angel of God, for she knew that it was through him that I had been brought to the wavering and doubt through which I would pass from sickness to health. She had unshakable confidence that I would be healed, though first there would be what physicians call a "crisis," in which my sickness would grow more acute and I would be in graver danger.

Ps. 30:3, 37:23, 69:2 / Ps. 17:29

Jn. 4:14

2.2   And so when she brought cakes, bread, and wine to the memorials of the saints, as was the custom in Africa, and the doorkeeper turned her away, as soon as she discovered that the bishop had forbidden this, she accepted his determination so piously and obediently that I marveled at how much readier she was to condemn her own former practice than to sit in judgment on his prohibition.[2] For drunkenness

---

2. The only surviving comment from Ambrose on this practice, made in passing in *De Helia et ieiunio* 17.62, suggests that he regarded it as superstitious: "and they believe that these offerings come before God, like those who bring chalices to the tombs of the martyrs and drink from them into the night: they believe that otherwise they cannot be heard." The rest of the paragraph adds a second reason for the prohibition: it placed temptation in the way of those who were inclined to excessive drinking.

had not taken possession of her spirit, and love of wine had not incited hatred of truth, as it has in so many men and women who are made as queasy by the praise of sobriety as a drunkard is by watered-down wine. No, when she had brought the basket filled with the solemn foods that she would first taste and then share, she would take no more than a small cup, measured out to suit her very sober palate, and take a small sip for courtesy's sake. And if there were many of the departed who were to be honored in this way, she would take that same cup around with her—she carried it everywhere—and by the time she was finished the wine was thoroughly diluted and tepid; she would share tiny sips with others who were there with her. For it was piety, not pleasure, that she was seeking there. And so when she learned that this dazzling preacher, this high priest of piety, had commanded that these things not be done, even by those who did them soberly, so that no stumbling block should be placed in the way of those overmuch given to drink, and because these behaviors were very much like the superstitious Parentalia of the Gentiles,[3] she was quite happy to give them up. Instead of her basket full of the fruits of the earth, she learned to bring a heart full of prayers to the memorials of the martyrs, both so that she could give to those who were in need[4] and so that the communion of the Lord's Body could be celebrated there:[5] for it was in imitation of his Passion that the martyrs were sacrificed and received their crowns.

And yet it seems to me, Lord my God (and so my soul attests to this matter in your sight), that my mother would perhaps not have been so easily persuaded to curtail her customary practice if it had been prohibited by someone she did not love as she loved Ambrose. She loved him for the sake of my salvation, whereas he loved her for her supremely religious way of life: so fervent in spirit, she abounded in good works and went regularly to church—so much so that when he saw me, he would break out in praise of her, congratulating me for having such a mother, little realizing what sort of son she had in me. For I was still in doubt about all things and believed it impossible to find the way of life.

Acts 18:25; Rom. 12:11 / 1 Tim. 5:9–10, 6:18

Ps. 15:11 qtd. Acts 2:28; Prov. 6:23, 10:17, 15:10

3.3   I had not yet begun to beg you in prayer that you would help me. Instead my restless mind was intent on asking questions and engaging

---

3. "The authentic Parentalia were celebrated on 13–21 February, with offerings to the shades of ancestors" (O'Donnell II:338). By "the Gentiles" Augustine means pagan non-Christians.

4. Not merely give them prayers but give them the money she would formerly have spent on the offerings to the saints.

5. Fasting was required before the Eucharist, so someone engaged in drinking at the martyrs' shrines would be unable to participate in the Sacrament.

in disputation. I thought Ambrose himself was a happy man in the eyes of the world, since so many powerful people esteemed him; only his celibacy struck me as a heavy burden to bear. But I could not conjecture, and I had no firsthand experience, of what his hopes were, what struggles he had against the temptations to which his prominence exposed him, what solace he had in adversities, or how sweet were the joys that his hidden mouth, the mouth of his heart, tasted in chewing on your bread. Nor did he know my irresolution or the pit I was in danger of falling into. For I could not ask him what I wanted, in the way that I wanted, since the crowds of people who had business with him, whose troubles he sought to alleviate, kept me from his ear and his mouth. When he was not with them—a very small portion of his time—he would be restoring his body with the nourishment he needed or restoring his mind by reading. But when he read, his eyes moved along the pages and his heart looked deeply into their meaning, but his voice and his tongue were still. Whenever we were there—which was often, for anyone was allowed to enter, and it was not the custom to announce visitors—we would see him reading in this way; it was never otherwise. We would sit in prolonged silence (for who would dare to interrupt someone so intent on his work?) and then leave. We came to the conclusion that in the very short time he had for renewing his mind, when he had a break from the commotion of other people's business, he did not wish to be distracted by anything else; and perhaps he was taking care that if he came across something rather obscure in his reading, he would not have to explain it or answer difficult questions about it for a perplexed listener who was paying careful attention, and by devoting his time to such work he would make less progress in the book than he wanted. But another possibility was that by reading silently he could more appropriately save his voice, which very easily grew hoarse. Still, for whatever reason he did this, it was undoubtedly a good one.

Ps. 56:7; Mt. 15:14

3.4   But certainly I was not given the opportunity to pose the ample questions I wanted to ask of your holy oracle, his understanding; I was only allowed questions that could be answered in a few words. I needed him to be very much at leisure to respond to my ardent inquiries, but I never found him so. Still, I heard him every Sunday in public, rightly handling the word of truth, and more and more it was confirmed for me that the whole net of cunning attacks woven by our deceivers against the divine writings could be unraveled. But when I discovered that your spiritual children, those who through grace have been reborn from our mother, the catholic Church, did not understand the claim

2 Tim. 2:15

that human beings were created in the image of God to mean that you *Gn. 1:26, 9:6;*
are bounded within the shape of a human body—that was not what *Sir. 17:1*
they believed, not how they thought of you—I rejoiced in my embar-
rassment that what I had been railing against all those years was not
the catholic faith, but fictions concocted by carnal thoughts. (But I
still had no inkling, not even a meager and dim idea, of what a spiri- *1 Cor. 13:12*
tual substance might be like.) I had indeed been rash and irreligious:
instead of learning about these things by asking questions, as I should
have done, I had gone ahead and spoken out against them. But you,
Most High and Most Near, most hidden and most present, do not have
bodily parts, some bigger and some smaller; you are everywhere as a
whole, and nowhere are you in a place. You are not after all this bodily
form, and yet you made human beings in your image, and behold! they
are in a place from their head to their toes.

4.5   Therefore, since I did not know how this image of yours sub-
sisted, I should have knocked, asking what one ought to believe, not *Mt. 7:7 par. Lk.*
insulting and contending against what I had supposed they believed. *11:9*
But the more ashamed I was that I had been so taken in and deceived
by the childish errors and combative spirit put forward by certain men
that I prattled on and on about uncertain matters as though they were
certain, the more sharply did the desire to possess something certain
gnaw at my inmost self. That they were in fact false became clear to me
only later; but it was certain that they were uncertain and that I had
for a while held them as certain, when I cast my blind accusations at
your catholic Church. Even if I had not yet discovered that the Church
teaches what is true, I knew at least that it did not teach the things I
had so bitterly criticized.

And so I was thrown into confusion and was turned; and I rejoiced, *Ps. 6:11*
my God, that your only Church, the Body of your only Son, in which *Col. 1:18, 1:24*
the name of Christ had been marked on me in my infancy, did not
teach childish nonsense. Its sound teaching did not hold that you, the
Creator of all things, are confined within a spatial location, lofty and
vast though it might be, yet still bounded on all sides by the shape of
a human body.

4.6   I rejoiced also that the Old Testament, the law and the prophets, were no longer brought before my eyes to be read in the ways
that had formerly seemed absurd, back when I was arguing as if your
saints believed those absurdities, though in fact they did not. And I was
delighted to hear Ambrose in his popular sermons often commending
this passage, most insistently, as a rule to be followed: "The letter kills,
but the spirit gives life." When the Old Testament scriptures taken *2 Cor. 3:6*

literally seemed to teach perversity, he would lift the mystical veil and uncover their spiritual sense; and what he said did not displease me, though I did not know whether what he said was true. For my heart hung back from all assent: I was afraid of committing myself too hastily, but I was being killed by hanging. For I wanted to be made as certain of the things I could not see as I was certain that seven plus three is ten. I was of course not so insane as to think that not even this could be comprehended, but I wanted other things to be just like this: whether bodily things that were not present to my senses, or spiritual things, which I did not know how to think of except as bodily. I could have been healed by believing, so that the gaze of my mind, purified by faith, might somehow be directed to your truth, which abides for ever *Ps. 116:2* and never fails, even in the smallest respect. But as often happens with someone who has experienced a bad doctor and is afraid to entrust himself even to a good doctor, so was the sickness of my soul: it could not be healed except by believing, but, for fear of believing something false, it refused to be cured, resisting your hands, which have fash- *Ps. 16:8; Dan. 4:32* ioned the medicines of faith and sprinkled them over the diseases of the world and endowed them with such great authority.

5.7   From then on I preferred catholic teaching. I realized that among the catholics I was bidden to believe what was not demonstrated (whether it was demonstrable but, as it happened, a particular believer was not capable of grasping the demonstration, or just not demonstrable at all), and they made no extravagant demands and were quite honest about what they were asking; whereas the Manichees rashly promised knowledge and ridiculed belief but then commanded one to believe so many extraordinarily absurd and fanciful tales, on the grounds that they could not be demonstrated.

And then, little by little, you, O Lord, touched my heart and calmed it with your most gentle, your most merciful hand. I considered how many things there were—more than I could count—that I believed even though I had not seen them or been present when they came to pass: so many events in the history of the nations, so many truths about places and cities I had never seen, so many things told me by friends, by doctors, by this person and that. If we did not believe all these things, we could get absolutely nothing done in this life. And finally I considered how firmly and unshakably I believed who my parents were, something I could not know except by believing what I had heard.

And as I considered these things, you persuaded me that it was not those who believe your Scriptures, which you have established with such great authority among almost all the peoples of the world, but

rather those who do not believe them, who deserve reproach. And I
should pay no attention to them if they should ask me, "How do you
know that those books were given to the human race by the Spirit of
the one true and perfectly truthful God?" For precisely that is what is
worthy of belief above all else. For among all the conflicting sayings of
the philosophers that I had read, there was no attack, no onslaught of
cunning questions, that could ever wrench me away from my belief
that you existed (whatever exactly you were, for I did not yet know)
and that the governance of human affairs belonged to you.

5.8   But I believed this sometimes more firmly, sometimes more fee-
bly: yet I always believed that you exist and that you care for the human
race, even though I did not know how to think properly about what
you are, and I did not know what way would lead, or lead back, to
you. And so because we were too weak to discover the truth by clear   *Rom. 5:6*
and convincing reason and therefore needed the authority of the Holy
Scriptures, I began to believe that you would by no means have granted
the Scriptures such outstanding authority throughout all the world if
you had not wanted us to believe in you through them and seek you
through them. Now that I had heard many passages of Scripture plau-
sibly explained, I saw that what I used to find absurd and offensive
in fact contributed to the lofty mystery of Scripture, whose authority
seemed to me all the more venerable, and worthier of inviolable faith,
precisely because it could be easily read by all and yet preserved the
dignity of its hidden meaning for those of deeper understanding. By
its simple words and humble style it offers itself to everyone, and yet
it challenges the ingenuity of those who are not light of heart.[6] Thus it   *Sir. 19:4*
welcomes all people into its very center, and through the narrow pas-
sage of the needle's eye it brings a few to you, though many more than   *Mt. 7:13, 19:24*
it would if its authority were not at such a peak of eminence, drawing
the throngs into the embrace of its holy humility.[7]

I thought upon these things and you were with me; I sighed and
you heard me; I wavered and you guided me; I walked along the broad
path of this world and you did not abandon me.   *Mt. 7:13–14*

6.9   I longed for honors, money, and marriage, and you mocked
me. The distress that I suffered on account of those desires was bitter

---

6. Sirach 19:4: "Those who are quick to believe are light of heart."
7. The words here translated "very center" and "embrace" are *sinu* and *gremio*, respectively. Both
mean "bosom" or "lap": Lazarus in the parable in Luke 16 is carried *in sinum Abrahae*, "to Abraham's
bosom," and the Prologue to John says that the only Son is *in sinu Patris*, "in the bosom of the
Father" (cf. NRSV, "close to the Father's heart").

indeed, and the less you permitted me to find sweetness in anything that was not you, the kinder you were toward me. Look upon my heart, O Lord, whose will it is that I call this to mind and confess it to you. Let my soul cling to you now: my soul, once stuck fast in the honey-trap of death, from which you have set it free. How wretched it was! And you pierced me and made me feel how sorely I was wounded, so that it might leave all things behind and turn to you, who are above all things, and without whom all those things would be nothing: that it might turn to you and be healed.

I was wretched, and you worked in me so that I might feel and know my wretchedness. One day I was preparing to give a speech in praise of the emperor—the speech would be full of lies, and well received by people who knew I was lying—and my heart was suffocated with these cares and burning with the fever of the thoughts that consumed me. I was passing through a certain section of Milan and came across a poor beggar, already drunk, I believe; he was laughing and joyful. I groaned, and I spoke to the friends who were with me of the many sorrows that our madness had brought upon us. For in all our great efforts—as in the work I had before me just then, goaded by my desires to drag behind me the burden of my own unhappiness, a burden made all the heavier by dragging it—all we wanted was to attain a joy that was free from care. The beggar had got there before us: he had already attained such joy, and we, perhaps, might never reach it. A few small coins, the proceeds of his begging, had bought for him what I was pursuing along such circuitous paths, so full of distress: the joy of some momentary happiness.

What he had was of course not true joy, but it was far more genuine than the joy I was seeking through my ambitions. He at least was cheerful; I was distressed. He was free from care; I was desperately worried. If anyone had asked me whether I would rather be joyful or fearful, I would have replied, "Joyful." Yet if he had gone on to ask me whether I would rather be as I was than as the beggar was, I would have chosen to be as I was, with all my troubles and fears—a perverse preference, surely, and not in accordance with truth. For I ought not to have thought myself better than he was simply because I was more learned, because my learning brought me no joy; I merely used it as a way to please other people—not for the sake of teaching them something, but simply in order to please them. And for this reason you were breaking my bones with the rod of your discipline.

6.10   Let them therefore depart from my soul, those who say to her, "It makes a difference why someone is happy. That beggar was happy

Ps. 72:28

Lk. 5:11, 5:28 / Ps. 21:28, 50:15 / Rom. 9:5 Is. 6:10 qtd. Mt. 13:15

Ps. 41:11 / Ps. 22:4

in his drunkenness, but you were longing for happiness in glory." But what glory, O Lord? A glory that is not in you.[8] His was no true joy, but mine was likewise no true glory, and it captured my mind all the more completely. He would sleep off his drunkenness that very night, but I had fallen asleep with mine and awakened with it, and I would yet again fall asleep with it and awaken with it, day after day! Yes, it does make a difference why someone is happy; I know that: the joy of a trustworthy hope is far different, incomparably different, from that vanity. But even then there was a difference between me and the beggar: for he was far happier, not only because he was filled to overflowing with enjoyment while I was being hollowed out by anxieties, but also because he had obtained his wine by wishing good luck to the passers-by whereas I was seeking self-importance through lying.

I said much in this vein to my dear friends, and on such occasions I often turned my thoughts to how I was faring. Badly, I found: and by lamenting my sorry state I made it even worse. And if fortune ever did smile on me, I could not be bothered to seize the opportunity, for it would fly away almost before I could catch hold of it.

7.11   Those of us who were living together as friends all had our share in these sorrows, but it was with Alypius and Nebridius that I had my most extensive and intimate conversations about such things. Alypius had been born in the same town in which I was born; his parents were important people there. He was younger than I. He had studied under me when I first began to teach in our town, as well as afterward in Carthage. He was very fond of me because he thought I was good and learned, and I was very fond of him because of his natural aptitude for virtue, which even at such a young age was quite striking. But the maelstrom of Carthaginian customs—the feverish love of worthless spectacles—had swallowed him up, and he was engrossed in the madness of the circuses. At the time that he was spinning about aimlessly in this wretched way, I was teaching the art of rhetoric there in a school that was open to the public. He was not a student of mine, because of a quarrel that had arisen between his father and me. When I learned that he had this destructive passion for the circus, I was grieved to think that such a promising young man was going to be lost, or indeed was already lost. But I had no resources to advise him or to recall him to sanity by imposing some restraint on him: neither the goodwill of a friend nor the authority of a teacher. For I thought he had the same

---

8. There is perhaps an echo here of 1 Corinthians 1:31 and 2 Corinthians 10:17, "Let the one who boasts (*gloriatur*) boast (*glorietur*) in the Lord."

opinion of me that his father had, though in fact he did not. And so he disregarded his father's wishes in this dispute and began to greet me when he saw me; he would come to my lectures, listen for a while, and then go away.

7.12 I meant to try to persuade him not to destroy so fine an intelligence by his blind and reckless enthusiasm for meaningless games, but I failed to keep this in mind. But you, O Lord, who govern all things you have created, did not forget this man, who was to be among your sons and daughters as a high priest of your Sacrament. And in order that his chastisement should be manifestly attributed to you, you brought it about through me without my knowing it. For one day, when I was sitting in my usual place and my students were with me, he came in, greeted me, and sat down, and he paid close attention to what was being discussed. As it happened, I was expounding the reading we had before us, and it occurred to me that I could use the circuses as an illustration that would help me make my point more humorously and effectively by sarcastically mocking those who were prisoners of such madness. You know, our God, that I was not thinking then about curing Alypius of that sickness. But he immediately took it to heart and thought I had said this entirely on his account. Someone else would have taken this as reason to be angry with me, but that worthy young man took it as reason to be angry with himself and to love me more fervently. For you had said long ago, and you wove it into your Scriptures, "Chastise a wise man, and he will love you." But I was not the one who chastised him: it was you. You make use of all things, both knowing and unknowing, according to the order that you already knew—and that order is just—and you were at work making my heart and my tongue blazing coals by which you would burn away the ruins of his ailing mind, so full of good promise, and heal it.[9] Let anyone who does not regard your mercies keep silent and withhold your praise: your mercies confess to you from the very marrow of my bones. For after those words he sprang forth out of the deep pit into which he had willingly fallen, in which he had taken astonishing pleasure in his blindness. With powerful temperance he shook his mind, and all the filth of the circuses flew away from it; he never went back.

Prov. 9:8 VL

Ps. 139:11

---

9. "burn away the ruins of his ailing mind . . . and heal it": *mentem . . . adureres tabescentem ac sanares*, more literally, "burn his decaying mind . . . and heal it." Some translators render *adureres* as "cauterize," but that is a mistake. The image is not of cauterizing a wound (for cauterizing does not merely heal, it deadens: see 1 Timothy 4:12) but of burning off what is bad, so that "in the purity of that place God might construct a building of his own" (*en Ps.* 119:5).

Eventually he prevailed upon his reluctant father to let him have me as his teacher; his father yielded and allowed it. And when he resumed his studies with me, he became entangled along with me in that superstition. What he loved in the Manichees was their vain display of continence, which he thought was true and genuine. On the contrary: it was senseless and seductive, luring precious souls who did not yet know *Prov. 6:26* how to reach the depths of virtue and were easily deceived by what was on the surface, the outward appearance of what was in fact a feigned and counterfeit virtue.

8.13　His parents had bewitched him with visions of an earthly path that he was not willing to abandon, and so he went ahead of me to Rome in order to study law. And there, in an extraordinary way, he was seized by an extraordinary passion for gladiatorial shows. He hated and detested such spectacles, but when some of his friends and fellow students were coming back from the midday meal, and the stadium happened to be open, they forced him to go in, using the kind of pressure we use on those with whom we are on familiar terms, though he protested vehemently and tried to resist. It was one of the days for cruel and deadly games. He said, "You can drag my body into that place and keep me there, but you certainly cannot force my mind and my eyes to pay attention to the shows. I will be present and yet absent, and in that way I will overcome both you and them."

When they heard this, they were no less determined to bring him with them; perhaps they were eager to find out whether he could do as he said. When they had gone in and taken whatever seats they could find, all the spectators were on fire with the most savage pleasures: but he shut his eyes and forbade his mind to attend to such evils. If only he had been able to close his ears! For in the course of the fight a man went down, and a huge roar from the whole crowd struck Alypius with tremendous force. He was overcome by curiosity, and he opened his eyes, as though resolved to scorn the sight and overcome it, whatever it might be. He received a more grievous wound in his soul than the man he was eager to see had received in his body; he fell more wretchedly than the man whose fall had caused the crowd to roar. That clamor entered through his ears and unclosed his eyes, so that they might be the instruments by which his mind would be beaten up and cast down: a mind more reckless than it was strong, and all the weaker because it trusted in itself when it should have relied on you. He saw the blood *Jdt. 6:15* and drank in the savagery all at once, and he did not turn away: he fixed his gaze and soaked up the madness and did not know what he was doing; he delighted in the wickedness of the contest and was drunk with the lust for blood. He was no longer the one who had come; he was one of the crowd to which he had come, a true companion of those who had brought him there.

What more is there to say? He watched, he shouted, he burned with passion; he took away with him a madness that goaded him to return, not merely with those who had first dragged him there, but even before them, and dragging others with him. And yet you rescued him from all this by your most powerful, your most merciful hand, and you taught him to trust not in himself but in you. But that was much later. *Prov. 3:5; Is. 57:13*

9.14 For now, however, this was being stored in his memory as a remedy for his future healing. So too was this: while he was still my student in Carthage, he was in the forum in the middle of the day, thinking over what he was going to recite—practicing, as students do. You allowed him to be arrested by the temple guards as a thief. And I believe you permitted it, our God, for no other reason than this: that a man who would one day be so great should begin to learn that in hearing cases one person should not rush to judgment in condemning another. He was walking in front of the law court by himself, notebooks and pen in his hands. He was completely unaware that another young man—the real thief, one of the students—was secretly carrying an axe, gained access to the lead gratings over the silversmiths' shops, and began to hack away the lead. The silversmiths who were below heard the sound of the axe and began to whisper among themselves; they sent people to catch whomever they might find. When he heard the commotion, the thief dropped his axe and left, afraid of being caught with it. But Alypius, who had not seen the thief enter, did notice him leave; he saw that he was running off in a hurry, and, wanting to know the reason for this, he went inside. He found the axe and stood there, wondering what was going on, when those who had been sent found him, alone, holding the very axe whose sound had alerted them to come. They seized him and dragged him off, boasting to a crowd of bystanders in the forum that they had caught a manifest thief;[10] from there they led him away to be presented before the judges.

9.15 But that was as far as the lesson needed to go. For immediately, O Lord, you came to the help of his innocence, of which you alone were witness. As he was being led away to face either imprisonment or *Wisd. 1:6; Jer. 29:23*

---

10. "manifest thief": *furem manifestum*, a legal term for a thief either caught in the act or (as here) caught in the place where the theft was committed: see Justinian's *Institutes* 4.1.3. *Digest* 47.2.3 gives a somewhat different definition, but in either case the notion is broader than our "thief caught red-handed," as many translators render the phrase here.

a beating, they met a certain architect who was in charge of the public buildings. They were delighted to have encountered him in particular, because he had frequently had suspicions that they were the ones who had taken away items that went missing from the forum; now, they thought, he would finally realize who was really responsible for those thefts. But this man had frequently seen Alypius in the home of a certain senator whom he often visited to pay his respects.[11] He recognized Alypius immediately, took him by the hand, and led him away from the crowd. He asked him what the cause of the trouble was, and when he heard what had happened, he commanded all those who were present, making an uproar and shouting menacingly, to come with him.

They arrived at the home of the young man who had committed the theft. Now there was a boy at the door who was too young to fear he might implicate his master and so was likely to tell the whole story—for he had been his master's attendant in the forum. Alypius recognized him and pointed him out to the architect, who showed the axe to the boy and asked him whose it was. "Ours," he said, without hesitation; and on being questioned he told all the rest of what had happened. Thus the case was brought instead against that house, and the crowd, which had already begun to crow over Alypius, was thrown into turmoil. And Alypius, who would one day be a steward of your word and judge many cases in your Church, went away a more experienced and a better-informed man. *Tit. 1:7*

10.16 So I found him at Rome, and he became deeply attached to me and went on with me to Milan so as not to lose my company—and also to put to work some of the legal knowledge he had acquired, although that was more in accordance with his parents' wishes than his own. He had already sat three times as an assessor and showed an integrity that astonished others, while he was more astonished by those who valued money more than innocence. His natural honesty was put to the test not only by the enticements of greed but also by the prick of fear. At Rome he was assessor to the Chancellor of the Italian Treasury. At that time there was a very powerful senator who had bought off many with favors and kept others in line through intimidation. He wanted permission to do something that was not permitted by the laws. Ordinarily his influence enabled him to get away with such things, but Alypius opposed him. A bribe was offered; Alypius laughed wholeheartedly. Threats were made; he scorned them. Everyone was amazed at this

---

11. O'Donnell comments, cynically and quite correctly, "Alypius' innocence does not get him a hearing; his social connections save him" (II:367).

exceptional soul that neither wanted this man as a friend nor feared him as an enemy, great though he was, and widely known for the countless ways he had of helping or hurting others. Now the judge whom Alypius served as counsel did not want to grant the petition, but he was not willing to refuse openly; so he laid the responsibility on Alypius, claiming that Alypius prevented him from doing as he pleased: for if the judge had granted the petition, Alypius would have left the court.

He was, however, almost enticed by his love for literature to order books made for him at the court's expense.[12] But he gave heed to justice and steered his thinking toward a better course, judging that equity, which forbade this, was of greater value than power, which allowed it. This is a very little thing, but one who is faithful in a very little is faithful also in much, and these words that proceeded from the mouth *Lk. 16:10* of your Truth will never be in vain: "If you have not been faithful in dishonest wealth,[13] who will give you the true riches? And if you have not been faithful in that which is another's, who will give you that which is your own?" *Lk. 16:11–12*

Such a man as this was my close friend in those days, and with me he wavered as we sought to determine what way of life we ought to follow.

10.17   Nebridius, too, had left everything behind—his hometown near Carthage, and Carthage itself, where he had spent a great deal of time; his father's fine country estate;[14] his home; his mother, who was not to follow him—and come to Milan for no other reason than to live as my companion in a passionate search for truth and wisdom. He had the same longings, the same uncertainties; he was a fervent seeker for the happy life and an extraordinarily acute investigator of the most difficult questions.

There were three mouths gaping open in their need, breathing out their poverty each upon the other, and looking to you to give them their food in due season. And in all the bitterness that, by your mercy, *Ps. 103:27, 144:15* attended our worldly acts, we tried to glimpse the reason why we were

---

12. "at the court's expense": *pretiis praetorianis*, "at praetorian prices." The meaning of the Latin is uncertain. One possibility, reflected in my translation, is that Alypius was tempted to have books copied for him by the official scribes and charge the court's expense fund (so that the books would cost him nothing). Another is that he was tempted to buy books at special prices reserved for palace officials.

13. "in dishonest wealth": *in iniusto mammona*. See KJV, RSV: "in the unrighteous mammon."

14. "his father's . . . country estate": *paterno rure*, an echo of *paterna rura* in Horace, *epod.* 2.3, though the sentence as a whole owes much more to Matthew 19:29: "And everyone who has left homes or brothers or sisters or father or mother or children or lands for my name's sake will receive a hundredfold and will possess eternal life."

suffering, but we found only darkness. We turned away, groaning, and asked, "How long must we endure this?" Again and again we asked: but though we asked, we did not leave our worldly cares behind, because there was no gleam of anything certain that we could hold on to if we left them behind.

11.18   What struck me most of all in the midst of my troubles, when I looked back on how much time had passed since my nineteenth year, was how passionate I had been when I began to seek after wisdom, resolving that once I had found it I would leave behind all the empty hopes and mad lies of my vain desires. And yet now I was in my thirti- *Ps. 39:5* eth year, still stuck in the same mud[15] by my eagerness to enjoy present things that fled swiftly away and wasted me—all the while saying,

"Tomorrow I will find it. It will become clear, and then I will take hold of it.

"Behold, Faustus will come and explain everything.

"Oh, what great men the Academics are! Nothing certain can be comprehended by which we can guide our lives.

"No—let us instead inquire more diligently and not lose hope.

"Look, the things that seemed absurd in the Church's Scriptures are not absurd after all; they can be understood differently, creditably.

"I will plant my feet on the step on which my parents placed me as a boy, until I find some unmistakable truth. But where will I seek it? When will I seek it? Ambrose has no time for me. I have no time for reading. Where will we even find books? When and from where will we procure them? Can we borrow them from someone? Let us set aside times and dedicate certain hours to the health of our souls.

"A great hope has arisen: the catholic faith does not teach what we thought, what we in our vanity accused it of teaching. The learned among them think it is impious to believe that God is bounded by the form of a human body. And will we hesitate to knock, so that the rest may be opened to us?   *Mt. 7:7 par.*
                                                                                        Lk. 11:9
"Students take up the morning hours: what shall we do with the rest of the day? Why not do this? But when will we pay our respects to the important friends on whose patronage we depend? When will we prepare the lessons our students buy? When will we refresh ourselves by putting these cares out of our minds?

11.19   "Forget all these things! Let us say goodbye to all these empty and trifling concerns and devote all our energy to one thing: the search for truth. Life is wretched, death is uncertain. Suppose it comes upon

---

15. Terence, *Phormio* 780.

us suddenly: in what condition will we depart from here? And where will we learn the things we failed to learn here? Or will we not instead pay for our failure with punishment?

"What if death cuts off all our care as it cuts off sensation and puts an end to it? We must seek an answer to this question as well. But no: it cannot, must not, be so. It is no accident, no empty coincidence, that the Christian faith has spread throughout the world with such preeminent authority. And God would never have done such great and remarkable things for us if the life of the soul were going to be destroyed with the death of the body. So why should we hesitate to leave behind our worldly hopes and devote our whole selves to seeking God and the happy life?

"But wait. These things too are delightful; they have a sweetness of their own, a sweetness that is by no means inconsiderable. We should not lightly cut ourselves off from them, because it would be shameful to return to them. Consider what a great thing it is to be granted some high office: what more could one desire? We have an abundance of influential friends; without demanding too much, too fast, we could at least be given a governorship. And then one could take a wife who has some money, so as not to burden us with expenses, and that will be as much as anyone could want. Many great men, well worth imitating, have devoted themselves to the pursuit of wisdom even though they were married."[16]

11.20　While I was saying these things, and these winds were shifting, driving my heart this way and that, times were passing, and I delayed turning to the Lord. From day to day I put off living in you, and I did not put off dying every day in myself. I loved the happy life, but I feared it in your dwelling place, and I sought it by fleeing from it. For I thought that I would be utterly wretched if I were deprived of a woman's embraces, and I did not consider taking the medicine of your mercy to heal that infirmity, for I had no knowledge of it. I believed that continence was a matter of one's own strength, which I knew I lacked. For I was so foolish that I did not know that, as it is written, no one can be continent unless you grant it: and you would indeed grant it if I knocked at your ears with my inward groaning and cast my burden upon you with unshakable faith.

Sir. 5:8

Ps. 102:3; Mt. 4:23

Wisd. 8:21

Mt. 7:7 par. Lk. 11:9 / Ps. 37:9 / Ps. 54:23

12.21　To be sure, Alypius prevented me from taking a wife. Again and again he reminded me that we could not enjoy the settled leisure

---

16. "even though they were married": *cum coniugibus*, literally, "with spouses." As far as the syntax goes, this could equally well mean "in companionship with their wives," but it is clear that Augustine is not thinking here of a wife as a potential partner in the search for wisdom.

to live together in the love of wisdom, as we had long desired, if I did that. He was indeed already perfectly chaste in that matter, so much so that it was astonishing, since he had begun to experience intercourse early in his adolescence but did not become attached to it. Instead he regretted it and spurned it, and from then on he lived in perfect continence. I, however, countered him with examples of married people who had cultivated wisdom, lived worthily before God, and were faithful and loving to their friends—but I was far away from their greatness of mind. I was shackled by a sickness of the flesh, and with a deadly sweetness I dragged my chain, fearing to be set free; his words of well-meaning persuasion were as the hand that would set me free, and I fought against it as if it were meant to strike me and wound me. Even more, the serpent was speaking through me to Alypius; he was weaving enticing snares through my tongue and scattering them in his path, to entangle his honorable and unfettered feet.

Heb. 13:16

Gn. 3:1

12.22   For he was quite astonished that I, for whom he had such great respect, was so stuck in the morass of that pleasure that every time we talked about it, I would swear I could never lead a celibate life. He found this assertion quite remarkable. I defended myself by saying that there was a great difference between his quick and furtive experience, which he hardly remembered and so found no difficulty in rejecting, and my own habitual pleasures. If my pleasures received in addition the honorable name of marriage, there would be no reason for him to find it surprising that I was unable to give up such a life. As a result, he began to desire marriage himself, overcome not at all by the lust for such pleasure but instead by curiosity. For he said he was eager to know what this thing could be, without which my life—which to him seemed so pleasant—would in my eyes be no life at all, but punishment. His mind was free from that bondage, and so he was bewildered by my enslavement; in his bewilderment he began to long to experience it for himself. And he was determined to go ahead and have such experience, and he would perhaps have fallen thereby into the very enslavement that so bewildered him, for he desired to marry death, and one who is in love with danger will fall into it. There is beauty in married life, in carrying out the duties of marriage and having children, but neither of us had more than the most tenuous idea of that. For me what mattered most, and what violently tormented me and held me captive, was the habit of satisfying my insatiable lust; whereas for him it was his wondering curiosity that dragged him there. This is how we were, until you, O Most High, had mercy upon us in our misery;

Wisd. 1:16

Sir. 3:27

Ps. 91:2

you did not abandon our dust, but came to our help in marvelous and *Heb. 13:5* hidden ways.

13.23 Every effort was being made to get me married. I was already asking for it and being promised it; my mother in particular was hard at work, thinking that once I was married, I would be washed in the baptism that heals and saves. She rejoiced in those days that I was being made ready for it, and she saw that her prayers and your promises concerning my faith were on the point of being fulfilled. Indeed, at my insistence and by her own desire she besought you every day with a powerful cry of heart that you show her something in a vision about my future marriage, but it was never your will to do so. She did see certain things—empty and fantastical—the sort of dreams driven by the preoccupations of the human spirit. She told me of them, but not with the confidence that she customarily showed when you were revealing something to her; instead she made light of them. She said there was a certain flavor—she could not put it into words—by which she could tell the difference between your revelation and the dreams of her own soul. Even so, efforts were made, and the girl was asked; she was two years too young to get married, and since she met with approval, the waiting began.[17]

14.24 Several of us friends had turned things over in our minds, discussing how much we hated the tempestuous ills of human life, and we had nearly resolved to live at leisure, apart from the teeming crowds. We would endeavor to arrange our leisure in such a way that if we could have any possessions, we would commit them to the good of all, uniting them all into a single household treasury. Thus, in the purity of our friendship there would be no "mine" or "yours," but instead one common good for all; the whole of our goods would belong to each of us, and everything would belong to us all. We saw that we could have about ten of us in the same fellowship, and there would be some quite wealthy people among us—especially Romanianus, who was from our hometown and had at that time been impelled to attend upon the court because of serious difficulties concerning his property. He had been an intimate friend of mine since my earliest days. He was especially keen on this project, and his persuasion was very powerful because he had much greater resources than the rest of us. Our idea was that two of us at a time would serve as magistrates for a year and

---

17. O'Donnell notes the prominence of passive-voice verbs in this paragraph and comments, "control is slipping out of A.'s hands" (II:377).

look after all the business of the community, leaving the others free from concern.

But then we began to wonder whether the women would allow it—some of us already had wives, and others wanted to be married—and the whole arrangement, which we had thought through so carefully, fell apart in our hands, shattered, and was thrown away. We returned to our sighs and groanings, and set our feet again on the broad and well-worn paths of this world: for there were many plans in our hearts, but your purpose abides for ever, and by it you mocked our purposes and made ready for us your own, to give us food in due season and open your hand and fill our souls with blessing.

Mt. 7:13–14

Ps. 32:11; Prov. 19:21

Ps. 144:15–16

15.25　In the meantime my sins were being multiplied. The woman with whom I had been accustomed to sleep was torn from my side as a hindrance to my marriage, and my heart, which was deeply attached to her, was cut into pieces, wounded and dripping blood. She returned to Africa, vowing never to take up with another man, leaving behind the illegitimate son I had had by her. But I was wretched and could not even live up to a woman's example: I could not bear the delay of two years before I could marry the girl to whom I was engaged, and because I was not a lover of marriage but a slave of lust, I found another woman, not of course as a wife. Her companionship would keep alive the habit by which the disease of my soul would be sustained and prolonged, at full strength or even increased, until I entered the domain of marriage. And the wound that had been made by the earlier cut was not healed; after the searing heat and agony it grew rotten, and it throbbed with colder but more desperate pain.

Sir. 23:3

16.26　To you be praise, to you be glory, O fount of mercies! I was growing more and more wretched, and you were drawing nearer. Moment by moment your right hand was present, ready to draw me out of the mire and wash me clean, but I knew it not. And there was only one thing that prevented me from falling into an even deeper abyss of carnal pleasures: the fear of death and of your future judgment, which never left my mind even amidst all my other unstable opinions. With my friends Alypius and Nebridius I engaged in discussion of the ends of good and evil things.[18] I said that Epicurus would be awarded

---

18. "of the ends of good and evil things": *de finibus bonorum et malorum*, the title of a philosophical dialogue by Cicero that canvasses the views of several different schools of thought. Augustine may indeed mean that they were discussing this work, which includes an exposition of the Epicurean doctrine Augustine goes on to expound, though he may also mean simply that they were discussing the subject matter.

the victory in my mind if I did not believe that after death the soul continued to live and received its just reward, which Epicurus denied. And I asked, "If we were immortal and enjoyed lives of continuous bodily pleasure, with no fear of losing it, why would we not be happy? What more could we ask for?" I did not realize that it was in fact a matter of great unhappiness that I should be so sunk in the abyss, so blind, that I could not see the light of integrity and of a beauty I should have embraced for its own sake, a beauty that the eye of the flesh does not discern, a beauty that is seen from within. Nor, wretch that I was, did I pay heed to the spring that gushed forth into such sweet conversations with my friends (though on such ignoble matters), or to the fact that I could not be happy without friends, even as my mind was occupied with so great an extravagance of carnal pleasures. These friends I loved for their own sake, and I knew that they in turn loved me for my own sake.

How crooked were my paths! Woe to the foolhardy soul that hopes to have something better by departing from you. It tosses and turns, on its back, its sides, its belly, and nothing is comfortable; you alone are rest. And behold, you are close at hand, and you set us free from our wretched wanderings and plant our feet on your path and comfort us and say, "Run! I will carry you, and I will lead you all the way to the end, and there I will carry you."

Ps. 138:8

Ps. 31:8, 85:11

1 Cor. 9:24

Is. 46:4

Book Seven

Augustine is convinced that God is "incorruptible and inviolable and unchangeable" (7.1.1), but he is unable to conceive of God properly because he cannot grasp the notion of an immaterial substance; nor can he understand the origin of evil. The answers to his intellectual difficulties—though not the healing of his will—come when he reads some books of the Platonists, finding there some light on the divine nature, though nothing about the appearance of God in the world in the Incarnation. He discovers the Truth above his mind, not a physical object yet undeniably real; he discovers also that everything is good insofar as it exists, and evil is not a substance in its own right but merely an absence of goodness. But Augustine lacks the strength to fix his gaze on the Truth that he has discovered, and he would "not find it until [he] embraced the Mediator between God and human beings" (7.18.24).

Augustine is still unable to free himself from conceiving of God as a material object (7.1.1–2) and to account for the origin of evil (7.2.3–7.5.7, 7.7.11–7.8.12), but he has made progress by rejecting astrology (7.6.8–10). In the books of the Platonists (7.9.13–15) he encounters the help he needs to conceive of an immaterial substance (7.10.16) and to understand the goodness of all that exists and the nature of evil as privation and perversity (7.11.17–7.16.22). By ascending from material things through the powers of the soul, he comes to a momentary glimpse of That Which Is (7.17.23), but he lacks knowledge of the Way to God (7.18.24–7.20.26) until he begins to read Paul (7.21.17).

1.1   By now my wicked and abominable adolescence was dead, and I was heading into the prime of life,[1] and the older I grew, the lower I fell into baseness and emptiness: I was unable to conceive of any substance other than the sort that can be seen by the eyes of the flesh. I did not conceive of you, O God, in the shape of a human body; no, as soon as I had begun to hear something of wisdom, I utterly spurned such a thought and rejoiced to find that the faith of our spiritual mother, your catholic Church, agreed with me in this. But I was at a loss as to how else I might conceive of you; human being as I was—and such a human being!—I tried to conceive of you, the supreme and only and true God. And I believed in the very marrow of my bones that you   *Jn. 17:3* were incorruptible and inviolable and unchangeable, for although I did

---

1. "prime of life": *iuventus*, more literally "youth," but meaning roughly the period from thirty to forty-five years of age. Writing the *Confessions* in his early forties, Augustine remains in his *iuventus.*

not know on what basis or in what way I knew this, I did nevertheless see quite clearly and was certain that what can be corrupted is lower than what cannot, and that I unhesitatingly preferred what could not be violated to what was violable, and that what undergoes no change is better than what is subject to change. My heart cried out with fervor against all my phantasms, and I tried to drive away the whirling cloud of uncleanness² from the gaze of my mind with a single blow; but no sooner had I dispersed it than it returned, in the twinkling³ of an eye, once again heaped together so that it pressed upon my sight and clouded it over, so that although I did not imagine you in the form of a human body, I was compelled to conceive of you as something bodily, extended in space—perhaps infused in the world or perhaps also diffused through infinite space beyond the world—but also incorruptible and inviolable and unchangeable, which I ranked higher than what was corruptible and violable and changeable. For whatever I thought of as lacking all such spatial location seemed to me to be nothing, absolutely nothing, not even a kind of void left if body was removed from a place and the place remained, emptied of all body—earthly, wet, airy, and heavenly—and yet still an empty place, a nothingness that yet was somehow space-like.

Lam. 2:18

1 Cor. 15:52

1.2   And so my heart had grown dull, and I was not present even to my own sight; I thought that whatever was not stretched out or spread forth or heaped together or swollen up in some sort of space, or whatever did not or could not contain such a thing, was absolutely nothing. For my heart went looking for images of the kinds of forms that my eyes were accustomed to seeing, and I did not see that the very attention by which I formed those images was not spatial—yet my attention could not have formed such images unless it were something great indeed.

Mt. 13:15; Acts 28:27

In the same way I also thought of you, O Life of my life, as something immense, occupying infinite spaces in every direction, penetrating the whole mass of the world and the vast, boundless spaces beyond it, so that the earth contained you, the heavens contained you, all things contained you and were bounded within you, whereas you were in no way bounded. For just as the body of the air (I mean the air that is above the earth)⁴ is no obstacle to the light of the sun, which passes

---

2. Virgil, *Aeneid* 3.233.
3. "twinkling": *ictus*, the same word translated "blow" earlier in the sentence, but here translated "twinkling" in order to capture the echo of 1 Corinthians 15:52. It will be "flash" in 7.17.23, "in the flash of a trembling glance."
4. As opposed to the "unbegotten air" of the Manichees.

through it and penetrates it, not shattering it or cutting it but filling all of it, so I thought that you pervaded not only the heavens and the air and the sea but also the body of the earth, which were permeable and open to receiving your presence in every part, from the smallest to the largest, and that from both within and without, you breathed through them in a hidden way and so governed all the things you created.

Such was my opinion, for I could not conceive of anything else. But it was false. For if it had been true, a larger part of the earth would have held a larger part of you, and a smaller part a smaller, and all things would have been full of you in such a way that an elephant would contain more of you than a sparrow exactly in proportion as the elephant is larger than the sparrow and occupies a larger space, and thus you would be present piecemeal in the parts of the world, small parts of you in small places, large parts in large places. But this is not the case. You had not yet lightened my darkness.   *Ps. 17:29*

2.3   I had at my disposal, O Lord, a sufficient refutation for those deceived deceivers, those prattlers who yet said nothing[5]—for it was not your word that fell from their lips. For the argument that Nebridius had so often given long ago in Carthage, an argument that rattled all of us who heard it, was all that I needed. What (he asked) was that darkness, whatever exactly it was, going to do to you—the darkness that according to them was a mass opposed to you—if you had been unwilling to fight against it? If the answer was that it would have done something to harm you, you would be violable and corruptible. But if they said that it could do you no harm, then they could offer no reason why you would fight against it, and indeed fight in such a way that some portion or part of you, or some offspring of your own substance, would become intermingled with hostile powers, natures not created by you, and would be so corrupted and degraded by them that it would fall from happiness into misery and would need help to be extricated and purified: and that this is the soul, enslaved, contaminated, and corrupted, which is helped by your word, free, pure, and sound. Yet your word would itself also be corruptible, since it comes from one and the same substance. And so if they said that you, whatever you are—that is, the substance by which you exist—are incorruptible, all these things would be false and detestable. If, however, they said that you are corruptible, that very claim is itself false; it should be rejected the very moment it is uttered. This argument, then, was enough for me to spew them out altogether with a violent heaving of the gut, for they had no

---

5. "prattlers who yet said nothing": *loquaces mutos.* See 1.4.4, fn. 3.

way of escaping it without terrible sacrilege of heart and tongue, believing and saying such things about you.

3.4 And yet even so—even though I said and firmly believed that our God, the true God, you who made not only our souls but also our bodies, and not just our souls and bodies but all souls and bodies, could not be contaminated or altered or in any way changed—I still lacked a clear explanation of the cause of evil. Yet whatever that cause might be, I did realize that I would have to look for it as something that would not compel me to believe that the unchangeable God was changeable, lest I myself become the very thing I was seeking. And so I sought it without anxiety, convinced that what was said by those whom I wholeheartedly repudiated was false; for I saw that in their search for the cause of evil they were themselves filled with evil: the evil of believing that your substance undergoes evil rather than that their own substance does evil.

Rom. 1:29

3.5 And I paid close attention so that I might understand what I was hearing:[6] that the free choice of the will is the cause of our doing evil, and your upright judgment is the cause of our suffering evil. But I could not get a clear grasp of it. And so I tried to draw the gaze of my mind up from the abyss, but I sank back into it; again and again I tried, and again and again I sank. What I was hearing had raised me far enough into your light that I knew I had a will every bit as well as I knew that I was alive. And so I was utterly certain that when I willed something, or willed against something, it was I, and no one else, who willed it or willed against it; and again and again I perceived that the will's free choice was the cause of my sin. But it seemed to me that what I did unwillingly was something that happened to me, rather than something I did, and I determined that it was not a fault but a punishment; and since I believed you to be just, I was easily brought to acknowledge that it was not unjust that you should inflict such punishment on me. But then I would ask, "Who made me? Was it not my God, who is not merely a great good but the Good itself? How, then, does it come about that I will evil and will against good? Is it so that I can justly suffer punishments? Who placed this in me? Who planted in me this seed of bitterness, when all that I am was made by my God, who is of surpassing sweetness? Suppose the devil was responsible. Then where did the devil come from? If it was by the perversity of his will that a good angel became the devil, where did the evil will by which he became the devil come from, since the

Ps. 118:137

Heb. 12:15

---

6. Hearing, presumably, in Ambrose's sermons.

whole angel was made by the best possible Creator?" Again and again I was oppressed and strangled by these thoughts—but I was never led astray into that hell of error where no one acknowledges you, the hell of believing that you suffer evils rather than that human beings commit evils.

Ps. 6:6

4.6   For I was trying to discover other truths, as I had already discovered that the incorruptible is better than the corruptible; and therefore I confessed that you, whatever you might be, are incorruptible. For no soul ever has been or ever will be able to conceive anything that is better than you, who are the supreme and best good—whereas if the incorruptible most truly and assuredly ranks higher than the corruptible, as I had come to realize it did, then if you were not incorruptible, I would have been able to conceive of something that would be better than my God. I should have looked for you, then, in the same place where I saw that the incorruptible is to be preferred to the corruptible; it was there that I should have looked for the source of evil, that is, the source of that corruption by which your substance can in no way be violated. For there is no way that corruption can do violence to our God—not by any will, not by any necessity, not by any unforeseen chance. For he is God, and what he wills for himself is good, and he is the Good itself; but to be corrupted is not good. And you cannot be forced into anything against your will, for your will is not greater than your power. It would in fact be greater if you were greater than yourself: for the will of God and the power of God are God himself. And what is unforeseen by you, who know all things? No nature exists except because you know it. Indeed, to what purpose do we offer many arguments to show that the substance that is God is not corruptible? For if it were, he would not be God.

5.7   I looked for the source of evil, but I looked for it in an evil way, and I did not see the evil in that search of mine. With the gaze of my mind I surveyed the whole of creation: everything we can perceive in it, such as the earth and sea and air and stars and trees and mortal animals, along with whatever we cannot see, such as the firmament of the heavens above and all angels and all the spiritual beings of creation. But my imagination provided places even for these spiritual beings, as though they were bodies. And I made your creation a single great mass, articulated into kinds of bodies, whether they were genuinely bodies or the sorts of creatures I imagined as bodies. I did not make it as great as it was, for I could not know how great it was, but I made it as great as I pleased, bounded of course on all sides, but with you, Lord, encompassing it and penetrating every part, yet infinite in every direction, as if there were a sea everywhere, a single infinite sea stretching out through immeasurable space, and it had a great, yet finite, sponge in it: every part of the sponge would of course be filled with the immeasurable sea. This is the way in which I thought your finite creation was filled with you, the infinite God. And I said,

"Here is God, and here is what God created. God is good, vastly and incomparably more excellent than creatures. But this good God created good things, and see how he encompasses and fills them. Where then did evil come from? From where and by what path did it invade creation? What is its root and seed?

"Or does evil not exist at all? Why then do we fear and avoid what does not exist? Or if our fear is in vain, that fear is surely itself an evil by which the heart is disturbed and tormented for no reason. And the more we fear this non-existent evil, the greater the evil is—and we do fear it. So either there is evil that we fear, or the very fact that we fear is itself an evil.

"How, then, is there evil, given that God is good and made all these things good? A greater—indeed the greatest—Good made these lesser goods, and yet both the Creator and all created things are good. So where does evil come from? Did he perhaps make them from some matter that was evil, which he formed and ordered, yet left something in it that he did not turn to good? Why would that be? Did he lack the power to turn and transform the whole of matter so that no evil remained? But he is all-powerful.

"Finally, why did he will to make something from matter rather than using his omnipotence to bring it about that there was no matter at all? Or indeed how could matter exist contrary to his will? Or if it was eternal, why did he allow it to exist through the infinite reaches of time past, and only much later decide to make something from it? Or if he for the first time willed to act, why would the Almighty not instead bring it about that matter did not exist, and he alone existed: the whole, true, supreme, and infinite Good?

"Or if, because he is good, it was not good for him not to fashion and create something good, why would he not bring into being good matter from which he would create all things, and destroy and annihilate the matter that was evil? For he would not be all-powerful if he could not create anything good without the help of matter that he had not himself created."

I turned such questions over and over in my wretched mind, weighed down by sharply stinging cares, afraid of dying before I had found the truth. And yet the faith of your catholic Church in your Christ, our Lord and Savior, had a firm place in my heart. True, in

2 Pet. 2:20

many ways I was still unformed, still at sea beyond the bounds of right doctrine; yet my mind never let go of that faith. Indeed, day by day it drank it in more and more.

6.8   By then I had also repudiated the deceitful predictions and irreligious delusions of the astrologers. Even for this, O my God, let your mercies make their confession to you from the inmost reaches of my   *Ps. 106:8* soul. For it was you and only you—for who else but the Life that knows no death calls us back from the death of every error? who else but the Wisdom that needs no light and enlightens needy minds, the Wisdom by which the world is governed down to the rustling leaves of the trees?—who provided for me the remedy for the stubbornness by which I had resisted Vindicianus, that intelligent old man, and Nebridius, that youth of marvelous spirit. Vindicianus argued emphatically, and Nebridius with a certain tentativeness and yet repeatedly, that astrology was not an art of foreseeing the future, but instead that human conjectures often have the power of chance. The astrologers say so much that many things they say do in fact come to pass, not because those who make these predictions know anything, but because by not keeping silent they stumble upon things that will actually take place.

To this end you provided a friend for me, a man who was keen to consult astrologers, though he was not well versed in their writings. Still, as I have said, he consulted them out of curiosity, knowing something about them that he said he had learned from his father—not realizing how powerful that knowledge would be in subverting my opinion of that art. This man was named Firminus. He was well instructed in the liberal arts and trained in eloquence. When he consulted me as a dear friend about certain affairs of his in which he had come to place a rather inflated amount of worldly hope, he asked me how his constellations (as the astrologers call them) looked to me.[7] But by that time I had begun to come around to Nebridius's view of the matter; I did not refuse to make a prediction and tell him what occurred to my wavering mind, but I did add that I was almost convinced that the whole business was ridiculous and pointless. That was when he told me that his father had been exceptionally curious about such books and had a friend who was equally interested and followed astrology along with him. In studying and discussing together they stoked the fires of their hearts for those trivialities, so much so that when either of them had an animal who gave birth, they would mark down the moment of the birth and note the position of the heavens, so that they could gather evidence for their art.

---

7. Recall that Augustine, unlike Firminus, had made a careful study of astrology. See 4.3.4–5.

And so Firminus told me that when his mother was pregnant with him, a slave girl in the household of his father's friend was exactly as far along in her pregnancy. The master of the house could hardly be unaware of this: he took care to know in the minutest detail when even his dogs gave birth. And it so happened that as they were making the most careful note of the day, the hour, and the smallest fractions of an hour—the one for his wife, the other for his slave girl—both women gave birth at the same time, so that the men were forced to make the same charts, down to the very minute, for both of the newborns, the one for his son and the other for his little slave. For when the women went into labor, the two men kept each other informed about what was going on in each household; they had messengers ready to send to each other to bring the news of the birth as soon as it happened. It was easy for each man on his own estate to arrange for the news to be delivered immediately. And he said that the messengers each man sent met each other exactly halfway between the two houses, so that neither man could record any difference in the position of the stars or any other details of the moments of birth. And yet Firminus, born into a wealthy family, enjoyed a comparatively brilliant worldly career, grew in wealth, and was showered with honors, whereas the slave went on to serve his masters, and the burden of his condition was in no way lightened, as Firminus, who knew him, told me.

6.9   As soon as I heard this story, I believed it—such was the character of the man who told it to me—and all my wavering was put to an end; it simply collapsed. I first tried to dissuade Firminus from that same curiosity. I said that if I were going to make a true prediction by observing his constellations, I would have had to observe in them that his parents were distinguished people, a noble family in their hometown, and freeborn, and that he had been well brought up and trained in the liberal arts. But if that slave had come to me for a horoscope on the basis of those same constellations—for they were his as well—in order to make a true prediction for him I would have had to observe in them his family's lowly status and his own condition as a slave, and many other facts that were quite different from those I observed in Firminus's case. It followed, therefore, that in order to make true predictions, I would have to say different things on the basis of the same information; if instead I said the same things, my prediction would be false. From this I concluded with absolute certainty that people who made true predictions by observing the constellations did so by chance, not skill; those who made false predictions were not unskilled, just unlucky.

6.10   Having heard this story and accepted its truth, I began to reflect on how I might reply if one of those madmen who are devoted to such inquiry—whom I was already eager to confront and rebut with ridicule—should object that either Firminus had lied to me or his father to him. I considered those who are born as twins. Often one emerges from the womb only a short time after the other. The astrologers contend that this interval has a potent effect on the way things turn out, and yet it cannot be captured by human observation and recorded on the charts that an astrologer will consult in order to make a true prediction. And their predictions will not be true. They would observe the same charts for Esau and Jacob, but they did not have the same experiences.[8] Therefore, either their predictions would be false, or, if they were true, they would not be the same: yet they would be looking at the same information. It follows that they make true predictions not by skill, but by chance. For you, Lord, most just Ruler of the universe, act by a hidden inspiration on both those who consult astrologers and those who are consulted, though they do not know it, so that from the depths of your righteous judgment they hear what it is fitting for them *Ps. 35:7* to hear in light of the merits of their souls. Let no human being say to you, "What is this? Why is this?" No, let no one say this, let no one say *Wisd. 39:26* this: for they are only human.

7.11   And so you, my helper, had already set me free from those *Ps. 17:3, 18:15,* chains. And I looked for the source of evil, but my search went *29:11, 58:18,* nowhere. Still, you did not allow any turbulent thought to carry me off *62:8* from my faith that you exist, that your substance is unchangeable, that you exercise care and judgment concerning human beings, and that in Christ, your Son, our Lord, and in the Holy Scriptures commended by the authority of your catholic Church, you have set forth a path for human salvation for the life that is to come after death. Even as all these things were secure and unshakably firm in my mind, I was in turmoil in my search for the source of evil.

Such agonizing labor pains in my heart, such groaning, my God! And you heard me, though I did not know it. And although my vigorous questioning was silent, the unspoken griefs of my heart were loud voices crying out to your mercy. You knew what I was suffering; no one else did. There was so little I could put into words, even to my closest friends. Could they have heard all the tumult of my soul, which I had neither time nor tongue to express? I was wailing in the groaning of

---

8. See Genesis 25–27. According to Genesis 25:26, Jacob emerged from the womb grasping his brother Esau's heel.

my heart, and my longing was before you, and the light of my eyes was
not with me. For that light was within, but I was outside. Nor was that *Ps. 37:9–11*
light in a place, but I turned my attention to things that are contained
in places, and I found there no place to rest; they did not welcome me
in and let me say, "This is enough; all is well"; nor did they let me go
so that I could return where all would indeed be well. For I was higher
than these places, but lower than you. And you were my true joy, so
long as I was subject to you; and you had subjected to me the creatures
you had set below. This was the proper balance, the middle realm of
my salvation, that I might remain in your image, and in service to you
take charge of the body.[9] But because in my pride I rose up against
you and charged against the Lord with my head held high and all my
defenses at the ready, even those lowest things were set above me and *Job 15:26 VL*
oppressed me, and I could not rest, could not breathe. From every
side they pressed upon me wherever I looked, heaped up and massed
together; and when I tried to think, the very images of those bodies
stood in my way and would not let me return. It was as if they were
saying to me, "Where are you going, you worthless and sordid fellow?"
All these things had grown out of my wound, for you had humbled this
proud man with a wound. My swollen self-importance kept me from *Ps. 88:11*
you, and my face was so puffed up that it kept my eyes closed.

8.12   But you, O Lord, abide for ever, and you will not be angry with *Ps. 101:13*
us for ever, for you have had mercy upon earth and ashes. And it was *Ps. 84:6, 102:9 /*
pleasing in your sight to take my deformity and give it form again, and *Job 42:6; Sir.*
17:31 / Ps.
by your inward goads you spurred me on[10] so that I would be impa- *18:15*
tient until my inward gaze beheld you with certainty. Through the hidden hand of your medicine, my swelling subsided, and the turbulent
and clouded gaze of my mind was being healed, and day by day you
applied the salve of health-giving pains to the vision of my troubled
and clouded mind.[11]

---

9. "the body": not just Augustine's own body, as most translators have it, but the whole bodily
creation, "the creatures [God] had set below" and made subject to humanity.

10. Virgil, *Aeneid* 11:336–337, though in the *Aeneid* the goads spur one on to evil. Better, perhaps,
to hear an echo of Ecclesiastes 12:11, "The words of the wise are as goads."

11. "salve" is *collyrium*, "eye-salve," a medical term Augustine often uses for Christ: for example,
Tractates on the Gospel of John tr. 2.16: "Because the Word was made flesh and dwelt among us, by
his very nativity he made a salve by which the eyes of our hearts would be washed clean and we could
behold his majesty through his humility. This is why the Word was made flesh and dwelt among
us. . . . For all salves and medicines are nothing but earth. You were blinded by dust; you are healed
by dust. Therefore, flesh blinded you, and flesh heals you. . . . The Word was made flesh: this medicine was made a salve for you." That the salve is "of health-giving pains" may simply mean that the

9.13   And first, because it was your will to show me how you resist
the proud but give grace to the humble, and how great is your mercy,   *Jas. 4:6; 1 Pet. 5:5*
which you have shown to human beings by the way of humility, in that
your Word was made flesh and dwelt among us, you obtained for me,   *Jn. 1:14*
through a certain fellow who was puffed up with the most monstrous
arrogance, certain books of the Platonists translated from Greek into
Latin. And in them I read—not indeed in these words, but exactly the
same teaching, presented persuasively with many arguments of many
different kinds—that in the beginning was the Word, and the Word
was with God, and the Word was God. He was in the beginning with
God. All things were made through him, and without him nothing was
made. What was made is, in him, life;[12] and the life was the light of
human beings. And the light shines in the darkness, and the darkness
has not engulfed it. I read also that the human soul, although it bears   *Jn. 1:1–5*
witness to the light, is nevertheless not itself that light; rather, God the   *Jn. 1:8*
Word is the true light that enlightens every human being who comes
into this world. I read also that he was in the world, and the world was   *Jn. 1:9*
made through him, and the world did not recognize him. But that he   *Jn. 1:10*
came to his own things, and his own people did not receive him; but
to as many as received him, to those who believed in his name, he gave
power to become children of God: those things I did not read in them.   *Jn. 1:11–12*

9.14   I likewise read in those books that God the Word was born, not
of blood, nor of the will of a man, nor of the will of the flesh, but of
God. But that the Word was made flesh and dwelt among us: that I   *Jn. 1:13 / Jn. 1:14*
did not read in them. And indeed I discovered in those writings, stated
in many and various ways, that the Son was in the form of the Father
but did not regard equality with God as robbery, since he is by nature
the very same as God. But that he emptied himself, taking the form of
a slave; and being made into the likeness of human beings and found
in human form, he humbled himself, becoming obedient to the point
of death, even death on a cross; therefore God has raised him from the
dead and given him a name that is above every name, so that at the
name of Jesus every knee will bend, of things in heaven and things on
earth and things under the earth, and every tongue confess that Jesus
is Lord, to the glory of God the Father: those books did not contain   *Phil. 2:6–11*
these things.

One finds in them that before all times and beyond all times your
only-begotten Son, who is coeternal with you, abides unchangeably,

---

healing of Augustine's blindness was painful, but it may well be a reference to the Passion of Christ,
as at *Sermon* 136.4, "From his blood he made a salve for the blind."
12. For this punctuation of John 1:4, see Augustine's *Tractates on the Gospel of John*, tr. 1.17.

and that from his fullness souls receive blessedness, and that by shar- *Jn. 1:16*
ing in the Wisdom who abides in himself souls are renewed so that *Wisd. 7:27*
they become wise. But one does not find that at the right time he died
for the ungodly, and that you did not spare your only Son, but gave *Rom. 5:6*
him up for us all. For you have hidden these things from the wise and *Rom. 8:32*
revealed them to little children, so that those who labor and are bur- *Mt. 11:25*
dened will come to him, and he will refresh them; for he is meek and
humble of heart. And he will guide the meek in judgment and teach *Mt. 11:28–29*
the gentle his ways, looking upon our humility and our labor and for- *Ps. 24:9*
giving all our sins. But as for those who are lofty, as though placed on *Ps. 24:18*
the pedestal of a more sublime teaching, and so do not hear him saying
"Learn from me, for I am meek and humble of heart, and you will find
rest for your souls," even if they know God, they do not glorify him as *Mt. 11:29*
God or give him thanks; but their thoughts become barren and their
foolish hearts are darkened. Though they profess themselves wise, they
have become fools. *Rom. 1:21–22*

9.15   And for this reason I also read in those books that they exchanged
the glory of your incorruption for idols and various phantoms, for the
likeness of an image of corruptible human beings and birds and four-
footed creatures and serpents, that Egyptian food for the sake of which *Rom. 1:23*
Esau gave up his rights as firstborn. For the hearts of your firstborn *Gn. 25:33–34*
people were turned back to Egypt, and they worshiped the head of
a four-footed beast instead of you. They bowed your image—their *Ex. 32:1–6; Acts*
souls—before the image of a calf that eats hay. *7:39 / Ps. 105:20*
    These things I found there, but I did not partake of them. For it
pleased you, Lord, to remove from Jacob the reproach of his inferiority,
so that the elder would serve the younger; and you called the nations *Gn. 25:33; Rom.*
into your inheritance. And I had come to you from the nations; I had *9:12 / Ps. 78:1*
devoted myself to the gold that your people had, by your will, carried
off from the land of Egypt—for that gold was yours, no matter where *Ex. 3:22*
it was. And through your Apostle you said to the Athenians that in you
we live and move and have our being, as some of their authorities had
said. Those books were indeed from there. But I did not devote myself *Acts 17:28*
to the idols of the Egyptians, which they served with your gold, they
who transformed the truth of God into a lie and worshiped and served
the creature rather than the Creator. *Rom. 1:25*

10.16   Admonished by these books to return to myself, I entered into
my inmost self with you as my guide; and I was able to do this because
you had become my helper. I entered, and by some sort of eye of my *Ps. 17:3, 18:15,*
soul I saw—above that eye of my soul, above my mind—unchangeable *29:11, 58:18,*
Light. It was not the light that is common and visible to all flesh; nor *62:8*

was it a light of the same sort, only nobler, as if the common light had grown clearer and brighter and become so great that it filled all things. No, the Light was not that; it was something altogether different from all these things. And it was not above my mind in the way that oil is over water or the sky is above the earth; it was superior, for that Light made me, and I was inferior, for I was made by it. One who knows the Truth knows this Light, and one who knows this Light knows eternity. Love knows this Light. *Ps. 99:3* *Jn. 14:7*

O eternal Truth and true Love and beloved Eternity, you are my God; I sigh for you day and night! And when I first came to know you, you lifted me up so that I could see that what I saw has being, but that I who saw it did not yet have being. And you repelled the weakness of my gaze, beaming upon me with great force, and I trembled with love and with terror. I found that I was far away from you in a land of unlikeness, as though I heard your voice from on high: "I am food for those who are full-grown; grow, and you will feed on me. And you will not change me into you, as you change the food of your flesh, but instead you will be changed into me." And I recognized that you have chastened human beings because of their sin and caused my soul to melt away like a spider's web; and I said, "Then is truth nothing, because it is not spread out across any finite or infinite expanse of places?" And you called from afar, "No indeed; truly, I am who I am." And I heard, as one hears in the heart; and I no longer had any room to doubt. I would more easily have doubted that I was alive than I could have doubted the existence of the Truth that is perceived through the things that have been made. *Ps. 26:10* *Jer. 31:15* *Ps. 38:12* *Ex. 3:14* *Rom. 1:20*

11.17   I examined the other things that are below you, and I saw that they neither wholly have being nor wholly lack being: they do indeed have being because they exist from you, but they lack being because they are not what you are. For what truly has being is what abides unchangeably. My good, however, is to cling to God; if I do not abide in him, neither can I abide in myself. But he, abiding in himself, makes all things new; and you are my Lord, because you have no need of the goods that are mine. *Ps. 72:28* *Wisd. 7:27* *Ps. 15:2*

12.18   And it was made plain to me that things that are corrupted are good. For they could not be corrupted if they were the highest goods, but neither could they be corrupted if they were not good at all. If they were the highest goods, they would be incorruptible; but if they were not good at all, there would be nothing in them to be corrupted. Corruption, after all, harms something; and unless it diminished some good, it would not do harm. So either corruption harms nothing, which is impossible, or else—what is most certainly the case—everything that is corrupted is deprived of some good. Now if things are deprived of *all* good, they will not exist at all. For if they still exist and can no longer be corrupted, they will be better, because they will persist incorruptibly: and what could be more monstrous than to say that things become better by being deprived of all good? Therefore, if they are deprived of all good, they will not exist at all. So as long as things exist, they are good.

Therefore, all things that have being are good, and that evil whose origin I was inquiring about is not a substance. For if it were a substance, it would be good, since it would be either an incorruptible substance, and thus of course a great good, or a corruptible substance, which would not be corruptible unless it were good. And so I saw, and it was made plain to me, that you made all things good and that there are no substances that you did not make. And it is because you did not make all things equal that all things exist: for individually they are good, and taken together they are very good, because our God made all things very good.

Gn. 1:31; Sir. 39:21

13.19   For you evil does not exist at all—and not only for you, but for your whole creation, since there is nothing outside it that breaks in and corrupts the order you have imposed upon it. To be sure, certain parts of it are regarded as bad because they do not fit harmoniously with other parts; but even they fit with still other parts and thus are good, and they are also good in themselves. And all these things that do not fit harmoniously with each other are well suited to the inferior portion of things, which we call earth, which has a cloudy and windy sky suited to it. Far be it from me to say, "These things ought not to be": for even if I could see nothing but them and indeed longed for better things, I would still owe you thanks for these things by themselves. For the things of the earth—dragons and all the deeps, fire and hail, snow and ice, the stormy winds that do your word, mountains and all hills, fruit trees and all cedars, wild beasts and all cattle, creeping things and winged birds—reveal that you are worthy of praise. Kings of the earth and all peoples, princes and all judges of the earth, young men and maidens, old and young together: let them praise your Name. Let them also praise you from the heavens; let them praise you, our Lord. All your angels in the heights, all your powers, the sun and moon, all the stars and the light, the heavens of heavens and the waters that are above the heavens: let them praise your Name. I no longer desired better things, because I held all things in my thought; and with a sounder judgment I regarded the higher things as being of course better than

Ps. 148:7–10

Ps. 148:11–12

Ps. 148:1–5

the lower, but all things together as being better than the higher things by themselves.

14.20   There is no soundness in those who are displeased by any crea-   *Ps. 37:4*
ture of yours, just as there was no soundness in me when I was displeased with many things that you made. And because my soul did not
have the effrontery to be displeased with my God, it did not want anything that displeased it to be yours. And from that starting point it had
proceeded to the view that there are two substances; but it did not find
rest there, and it gave voice to opinions that were not really its own. And
returning from there it had made for itself a god extended through the
infinite expanse of all places; and it thought that this god was you. It set
up this god in its heart and again became a temple for its own idol, an   *Ez. 14:7 / 2 Cor.*
abomination before you. Yet afterward you laid my head upon your lap,   *6:16*
though I did not know it, and you closed my eyes so that I would not
look upon worthlessness. For a little while I rested from myself, and my   *Ps. 118:37*
frenzy was lulled to sleep; and I woke up and saw that you are infinite,
but in a different way. And that vision did not derive from the flesh.

15.21   And I turned my attention to other things, and I saw that
they owe their existence to you, and that all finite things exist in you,
though in a different way. They do not exist in you as though in a
place, but in the sense that you hold all things in your hand, the Truth,
and they are all true insofar as they have being. Nor is falsity anything,
except when one thinks that something is what it is not. I saw also that
all things fit harmoniously not only with their places but also with their
times, and that you, who alone are eternal, did not begin to act after
countless intervals of times; for all intervals of times, those that have
passed away and those that will pass away, would neither go away nor
come to be apart from your acting and abiding.

16.22   I had learned by experience that it is no surprise when bread
that tastes sweet to a healthy palate is repugnant to one that is unhealthy,
and when light that is pleasant to untainted eyes is hateful to eyes that
are diseased. Even your righteousness displeases the wicked, let alone
vipers and worms, which you created good and well suited to the lower
parts of your creation—to which the wicked themselves are well suited,
the more unlike you they are; but they are well suited for the higher
parts, the more they become like you. And I asked what wickedness
was, and what I found was not a substance, but rather the perversity
of a will that is turned away from the supreme substance—from you,
O God—a will that casts away what lies within itself and is swollen   *Sir. 10:10*
with what is found outside.

17.23   And I marveled that it was you I loved, not some phantasm in place of you. And I did not stand still in enjoying my God; no, I was seized by your beauty; but no sooner was I drawn to you than I was torn away by my own weight, and I fell into the depths with a sigh. This weight was the habit of the flesh. But a memory of you remained with me, and I had no doubt that it was truly you to whom I ought to cling, but I was no longer capable of clinging to you, because the body that is corrupted weighs down the soul,[13] and its earthly dwelling *Wisd. 9:15* place crushes its perception with thoughts of many things. And I was altogether certain that your invisible attributes have been seen from the foundation of the world, understood through the things that have been made, and that your power and Godhead are eternal. For I asked *Rom. 1:20* myself how it was that I approved the beauty of bodies, whether earthly or heavenly, and what this was that was so wholly present to me that I could pass judgment on changeable things and say, "This is just as it should be; that is not." And so asking what the source of my judgment was when I made such judgments, I discovered the unchangeable and true eternity of truth above my changeable mind.

And thus I ascended, step by step, from bodily things to the soul that senses through the body, and from there to that inner power by which the sense of the body gives notice of external things[14]—this is as far as the animals can go—and then further to the power of reasoning before which I bring for judgment the things I draw from the senses of the body. But this power in me took stock of itself, and finding that it too was changeable, it raised itself to its intelligence; it withdrew its thought from habit and tore itself away from the contradictory hosts of phantasms so that it might discover the source of the light that was sprinkled over it when it cried out without any doubt that the unchangeable is to be preferred to the changeable, that it might discover how it knew the unchangeable (for unless it in some way knew the unchangeable, it could by no means have been so certain in preferring it to the changeable): and I arrived at That Which Is in the flash of a trembling glance. Then indeed I beheld your invisible attributes, understood through the things that have been made, but I was not *Rom. 1:20* able to keep my vision fixed there: beaten back by my own weakness, I returned to my accustomed places, taking nothing with me but a

---

13. In explicit rejection of the Platonic view of the body, Augustine holds that the body's drag on the soul is a punishment for sin and not its cause: *City of God* 14.3.
14. The inner sense, discussed in *On Free Choice of the Will* 2.3.7–2.4.10 and alluded to at *Confessions* 1.20.31.

loving memory and a longing for a food that I could smell but could not yet eat.

18.24   And I looked for a way to muster the strength that would fit me to enjoy you, and I did not find it until I embraced the Mediator between God and human beings, the human being Christ Jesus, who is God above all things, blessed for ever, calling out and saying, "I am the way, and the truth, and the life," the food I was not yet strong enough to receive, mixing with the flesh, because the Word was made flesh, so that your Wisdom, by whom you created all things, might provide milk for our infancy. For I was not yet holding on to Jesus as my God, a humble man embracing the Humble One, and I had not yet learned what his weakness had to teach me. For your Word, the eternal Truth, greatly exalted above the highest parts of your creation, lifts up to himself those who are his subjects; but in the lowest parts he has built for himself a humble home from our very dust,[15] through which he casts down those who need to be subject to him and draws them to himself. He heals their swollen pride and nourishes their love, so that their self-reliance will not take them even further from him, but instead they will become weaker as they see before their steps the weakness that his Godhead has assumed by sharing in the garments of our flesh,[16] and in their weariness cast themselves upon him, so that he might arise and lift them up.

1 Tim. 2:5

Rom. 9:5

Jn. 14:6

Jn. 1:3; Col. 1:16

Prov. 9:1 / Gn. 2:7

1 Cor. 1:25

Gn. 3:21

19.25   But that was not at all how I thought at the time. I regarded my Lord Christ as a man of outstanding wisdom whom no one could rival, especially because he was miraculously born of a virgin and gave us an example of scorning temporal things in order to attain immortality. And so it seemed to me that in God's care for us Christ had earned great authority as a teacher. But as to the mystery of the Word

---

15. "dust": *limo*, literally "clay." But whenever Augustine quotes Genesis 2:7, he uses *limus*, so I have thought it best to use the word that appears in almost all our English translations so that the echo sounds properly.

16. "the garments of our flesh": *tunicae pelliciae nostrae*, literally, "our garments of skins." According to Genesis 3:21, once Adam and Eve had sinned and become conscious of their nakedness, and God had judged them for their sin, "the Lord God made for Adam and for his wife garments of skins, and clothed them." Despite the verbal echo, Augustine cannot mean that Christ shares in the outward covering that marks us as sinners. My translation therefore emphasizes the fleshliness of Christ's incarnation: the central theme of this paragraph. Augustine frequently uses the expression to indicate the mortality that is the evidence of sin, but this reading too is impossible here; for Augustine clearly teaches that Christ, though obviously capable of death, was not required to die, precisely because he was sinless. As Jesus says of himself in the Fourth Gospel, "I lay down my life, that I may take it up again. No one takes it from me, but I lay it down of my own accord. I have power to lay it down, and I have power to take it up again" (John 10:17b–18a).

made flesh, I had not the slightest idea of it. All I knew from what was written about him was that he ate and drank, slept, walked, rejoiced, grieved, and conversed, and that he had not joined his flesh to your Word except by a human soul and mind. Everyone knows this who knows the immutability of your Word, which I already knew as well as I could, and there was no reason to make me doubt it. For it is a mark of the mutability of a body and mind that someone now moves his limbs by his will and then moves them no longer, is now struck by some emotion and then is not, now puts forward signs expressing wise sentiments and then falls silent. If these things that were written about him were false, everything would be under suspicion as a lie and no saving faith in the Scriptures would be left for the human race. And so because those writings are true, I acknowledged in Christ a full human being, not merely a human body, or a body with a spirit but no mind, but a true human being. Yet I held that this human being was to be esteemed more highly than others, not as the Person of Truth, but because of the great excellence of his human nature and his more perfect participation in wisdom.

Alypius, however, thought that catholics believed God had been clothed in flesh in such a way that there was nothing but God and flesh in Christ; he did not know that they preached that Christ had a human spirit and mind. And since he was fully persuaded that the actions recorded of Christ could only have been done by a creature endowed with life and reason, he was in no great hurry to join the Christian faith. But afterward he learned that this view was that of the Apollinarian heretics,[17] and he was overjoyed to discover what the catholic faith truly taught and to give his allegiance to it. As for me, I must acknowledge that it was some time later that I learned how the catholic truth is distinguished from Photinian[18] falsehood: the Word was made flesh. Indeed the refutation of heretics makes it all the more evident what your Church teaches and what sound doctrine it has. For it was necessary that heresies exist, so that among the weak those who are tried and found acceptable may be made manifest.[19]

1 Tim. 1:10; 2 Tim. 4:3; Tit. 1:9, 2:1
1 Cor. 11:19

---

17. Apollinaris of Laodicea (d. 390) held that there was no human soul in Christ; its functions were supplied by the divine Word. His views were condemned as heretical in 381 by the First Council of Constantinople.

18. Photinus of Sirmium (d. 376) denied the divinity and the pre-existence of Jesus.

19. It is characteristic of Augustine to interpret all heresies as Christological heresies. See *Sermon* 183.9.13, "And if we discuss all heresies, we find that they deny that Christ has come in the flesh." His language here derives from 1 John 4:2–3a: "By this you know the Spirit of God: every spirit which confesses that Jesus Christ has come in the flesh is of God, and every spirit which does not confess Jesus is not of God."

20.26   But at that time, having read those books of the Platonists and heeded their admonition to seek incorporeal truth, I beheld your invisible attributes, understood through the things that have been made; *Rom. 1:20* but I felt a darkness in my soul that would not allow me to contemplate them. I was certain that you existed and were infinite—and not by being spread out through places, whether finite or infinite—and that you who were always the same exist most truly, not changing in *Ps. 101:28 qtd.* any part or altering by any motion, whereas all other things existed *Heb. 1:12* from you, as their very existence gives the most unmistakable proof. *Rom. 11:36;* Of all these things I was indeed certain, yet I was too weak to enjoy *1 Cor. 8:6* you. I rambled on and on as though I were an expert: and yet unless I sought your way in Christ our Savior I would be no expert; I would *Tit. 1:4* be headed for destruction.[20] For I had already begun to wish to appear wise, though I was full of my punishment and yet did not weep; no, I was puffed up with knowledge. Where, then, was the charity that builds upon the foundation of humility, which is Christ Jesus? And *1 Cor. 8:1, 13:4 /* when would those books have taught it to me? Before I turned my *1 Cor. 3:11* attention to your Scriptures, it was, as I believe, your will to impress upon my memory how I was affected by those books, so that afterward, when I had grown gentle in your Scriptures and my wounds had been probed by your healing touch, I would recognize and distinguish how great a difference there is between presumption and confession, between those who see the goal but do not see the way, and those who do not merely see the way that leads to our blessed homeland but dwell in it. For if I had been molded by your Scriptures from the beginning and you had bestowed on me the sweetness that comes from knowing them intimately, and only later had run across those books, perhaps they would have wrenched me away from the solid foundation of piety, or else, if I had remained steadfast in the devotion that I had drunk in from your life-giving fountain, I might have thought that the same devotion could also be drawn from those books if everyone learned from them, and them alone.

21.27   And so with the greatest eagerness I seized upon the noble writing of your Spirit, and especially the Apostle Paul. I had once thought that he contradicted himself and that the drift of his writing was at odds with the witness of the law and the prophets; but now *Mt. 5:17, 7:12; Lk.* all my quibbles fell to pieces, and those pure words came together in *16:16 / Ps. 11:7*

---

20. "I would be no expert; I would be headed for destruction": *non peritus sed periturus essem*, a bit of wordplay that does not survive translation into English. Boulding has "I would more probably have been killed than skilled"; Chadwick, "I would not have been expert but expunged"; Ruden, "I would have been not done but done for."

my sight as a single, consistent picture, and I learned to rejoice with trembling.

Ps. 2:11

So I set forth, and I discovered that everything true I had read in those other books was said there as well, but always with acknowledgment of your grace, so that those who see will not boast as if they had not received not only what they see but even the power to see at all—for what do they have that they have not received?—and that they might be admonished not only to look upon you, who are always the same, but to be healed so that they might hold fast to you. As for those who cannot see you from afar, let them nevertheless walk in the Way by which they will come to you and see you and hold fast to you. For even if human beings delight in the law of God in their inmost selves, what will they do about the other law in their members which is at war with the law of their minds and makes them captive to the law of sin that is in their members? Because you are righteous, O Lord, whereas we have sinned and committed iniquity and acted with impiety, your hand is heavy upon us; you have justly delivered us into the power of the ancient sinner, the ruler of the kingdom of death, because he persuaded our will to be like his own will, which did not abide in your truth.

1 Cor. 4:7

Ps. 101:28; Heb. 1:12

Rom. 7:22–23 / Tob. 3:2; Jer. 12:1; Dan. 3:27; Ps. 118:137 / 1 Kgs. 8:47; Dan. 3:29 / Ps. 31:4 / Heb. 2:14 / Jn. 8:44

What are wretched human beings to do? Who will deliver us from the body of this death? Only your grace through Jesus Christ our Lord, whom you begot coeternal with yourself and created in the beginning of your ways,[21] in whom the ruler of this world found nothing worthy of death, yet he killed him. And the handwriting of the decree that was against us was nullified.

Rom. 7:24

Prov. 8:22 / Jn. 14:30

Col. 2:14–15

Those writings have none of this. Nowhere in those pages do we find the face of true piety, the tears of confession, the sacrifice to you of a troubled spirit, a broken and contrite heart, salvation for the people, the city arrayed as a bride, the guarantee[22] of the Holy Spirit, the cup of the price that has been paid for us.[23] No one in those books sings, "Will not my soul be subject to God? For from him comes my salvation: for

Ps. 50:19

Rev. 21:2

2 Cor. 1:22, 5:5

---

21. In Proverbs 8:22 it is Wisdom who says, "the Lord created me in the beginning of his ways." Augustine accepts the by-then traditional identification of Christ with Wisdom. But by stating first that the Son is begotten by and coeternal with the Father, he avoids any suspicion of the Arian heresy, which held that the Word was created. He understands the Proverbs passage as speaking of Christ's *human* nature. See, for example, *De fide et symbolo* 4.6: "The beginning of his ways is the Head of the Church, which is Christ clothed with humanity, through whom we would be given an example of how to live, that is, a secure way by which we might come to God."

22. "guarantee": *arra*. The word means a down payment, part of the purchase price.

23. "the cup of the price that has been paid for us": *poculum pretii nostri*, more literally, "the cup of our price." The price paid for us is the shed blood of Christ, so Augustine must mean the Eucharistic chalice.

he himself is my God and my salvation, my deliverer, and I shall not be
shaken." No one in those books hears him saying, "Come to me, you *Ps. 61:2–3*
who labor." They are too arrogant to learn from him, for he is meek *Mt. 11:28*
and humble of heart. For he has hidden these things from the learned *Mt. 11:29*
and wise and revealed them to little children. *Mt. 11:25 par. Lk. 10:21*

It is one thing to see our homeland of peace from a peak in the
woods and not find the way there, and struggle hopelessly over impass-
able terrain while beset by fugitive deserters, who besiege us and lie in
wait to ambush us, doing the bidding of their master, the lion and the
dragon.[24] It is quite another to hold fast to the Way that leads there, a *Ps. 90:13*
Way fortified by the care of the heavenly king, where those who have
deserted the heavenly hosts commit no robbery, for that Way is for
them such a torment that they keep clear of it. All these things penetrated my inmost parts in wondrous ways as I read the least of your
apostles and looked upon your works with holy fear. *1 Cor. 15:9 / Hab. 3:2*

---

24. *en. Ps.* 90 s 2.9: "The lion does violence openly, the dragon ambushes secretly. The devil has
both powers."

Book Eight

One conversion story after another kindles Augustine's desire to devote himself wholeheartedly to God, but the chains of sexual desire, made stronger by habit long indulged, hold him back. He both wills and does not will to cast aside his chains, both wills and does not will to serve God. Torn between these two wills—his own wills, as he now realizes, and not external forces at war within him, as the Manichees would say—he hears a child's voice saying, "Pick up and read." He picks up the Letter to the Romans, reads the passage that first catches his eye, and "the light of assurance was poured into [his] heart and all the clouds of doubt melted away" (8.12.29).

Still wavering, Augustine goes to Simplicianus to seek his counsel (8.1.1–2). Simplicianus tells him the story of the conversion of Marius Victorinus, and Augustine reflects on why notable converts occasion greater joy than less-well-known converts and those who have never been out of the fold (8.2.3–8.5.12). Ponticianus tells Augustine and Alypius about Antony of Egypt (8.6.14) and the conversions of two imperial court officials (8.6.15–8.7.16). Augustine berates himself for his sluggishness and irresolution about turning to God (8.7.17–18). In the garden of their lodgings in Milan (8.8.19–8.12.29), Augustine struggles in agony (8.8.19–8.12.28) until a voice from a nearby house prompts him to read the Apostle Paul, and he finds resolution (8.12.29). Alypius likewise turns to God, and Monnica receives the news with joy (8.12.30).

1.1 My God, with thanksgiving to you I would call to mind and confess your mercies toward me. Let my bones be filled to overflowing with your love, and let them say, "O Lord, who is like you? You have broken my chains: I shall offer to you a sacrifice of praise." I shall tell the story of how you broke them: let all those who worship you say, when they hear these things, "Blessed is the Lord in heaven and on earth; great and wonderful is his Name." Your words had become fixed in the deepest places of my heart, and I was walled about by you on every side. Of your eternal life I was certain, though I had seen it only dimly, as if in a mirror; but I had been relieved of all my uncertainty about incorruptible substance: I was certain that from it all substance has its being. What I wanted was not to be more certain about you, but to be more firmly grounded in you. Instead, everything in my temporal life was tottering, and my heart needed to be cleansed of the old leaven. I was at once pleased by the Way, the Savior himself, and yet ashamed to enter through the narrow gate.

Ps. 32:22, 85:13; Is. 63:7 / Ps. 34:10
Ps. 115:17

2 Chron. 2:12; Ps. 8:2, 8:10, 71:18–19, 75:2, 88:53, 134:6
1 Cor. 13:12

1 Cor. 5:8 / Jn. 14:6
Mt. 7:14

And you put it in my mind, and it seemed good in my eyes, to go *Ps. 15:8 qtd. Acts* to Simplicianus: for it was evident to me that he was a good servant of *2:25* yours, and resplendent with your grace. I had also heard that he had lived with the greatest devotion toward you ever since his youth; now that he was an old man and had spent many years giving such great energy to following the way of life in you, he must, I thought, be well versed in many matters and learned about many things. And so in fact he was. Hence I wanted to confer with him about my anxieties so that he might suggest a suitable manner in which someone in such a condition as I was in could walk in your Way. *Ps. 127:1*

1.2   I saw the church full, but one person lived in one way and another in a different way.[1] But my own life in the world was hateful to me, and a great burden, because I was no longer on fire with the passions—the hope for honor and money—that used to make such great slavery bearable. Because of your sweetness and the beauty of your house, which I loved, those passions no longer gave me any plea-   *Ps. 25:8* sure; but I was still deeply in thrall to a woman. And the Apostle did not forbid me to marry, though he encouraged me to follow a better course, wishing most of all that everyone might be as he was. But I was   *1 Cor. 7:7* too weak and chose a more indulgent life. And for this reason alone I vacillated, sluggish in other matters and wasting away with concerns that had lost their strength: because the married life to which I had committed myself compelled me to put up with other things for which I had no desire at all. I had heard from the mouth of Truth that there are eunuchs who have cut themselves off[2] for the sake of the king- dom of heaven, but, he says, "let the one who can receive this teaching receive it." Certainly all who lack the knowledge of God are empty, and   *Mt. 19:12* they could not discover Him Who Is by looking among the things that seemed good to them. And I was no longer in such emptiness. I had   *Wisd. 13:1* passed beyond it, and by asking my questions of the whole of creation   *Rom. 1:20* I had discovered you, our Creator, and your Word, who with you is God, and one and the same God as you, through whom you created   *Jn. 1:1* all things.   *Jn. 1:3*

And there are impious people of another kind: those who, though they know God, have not glorified him as God or given thanks. I had   *Rom. 1:21* fallen into this error as well, and your right hand had rescued me from

---

1. See 1 Corinthians 7:7. By echoing the last words of the verse, Augustine is indicating that he means that some embraced continence and others, marriage.

2. "have cut themselves off": a quite literal translation of *se ipsos absciderunt,* meaning that they have cut themselves off from typical married life. The Vulgate says, more frankly, "have castrated themselves," which is not what Augustine has in mind here.

it and placed me where I could recover my health, for he said to human beings, "Behold, piety is wisdom," and "Do not desire to appear wise, for those who call themselves wise have been made fools." I had already found the good pearl: I should have sold all that I had and bought it, but I hesitated.

Job 28:28 VL

Prov. 3:7; Sir. 7:5 / Rom. 1:22

Mt. 13:45–46

2.3   So I went to Simplicianus, who was the father of Ambrose, then the bishop,[3] in receiving grace, and whom Ambrose truly loved as a father. I told him the circuitous story of my wanderings. Now when I told him that I had read certain books of the Platonists, which had been translated into Latin by Victorinus, formerly orator of the city of Rome, who I had heard had died a Christian, he congratulated me that I had not stumbled upon the writings of other philosophers, for they were full of fallacies and deceptions according to the elements of this world, whereas in the books of the Platonists God and his Word are made known in every possible way. Then, in order to urge upon me the humility of Christ, which is hidden from the wise but revealed to little children, he recalled Victorinus himself, with whom he had been on very friendly terms in Rome; he told me a story about him that I shall not fail to recount myself: for it is a story that redounds to the praise of your grace and should be confessed before you.

Col. 2:8

Mt. 11:25 par. Lk. 10:21

Eph. 1:6

That exceptionally learned old man was a master of all the liberal arts. He had read many works of the philosophers and had come to his own conclusions about them. He had been the teacher of many noble senators, and because of his extraordinary teaching he earned and received a statue in the Roman forum, something that the citizens of this world regarded as a very great honor. Up to his old age he had been a worshiper of idols and a participant in the ritual sacrileges that almost all of the self-satisfied Roman nobility in those days favored, firing the people's enthusiasm for Osiris[4] and "the monstrous shapeshifting god and barking Anubis, who once made war against Neptune, Venus, and Minerva"[5]—and now Rome was bowing in worship before the gods whom Rome had conquered. These rites the elderly Victorinus had defended again and again with his terrible, thundering

---

3. Simplicianus would succeed Ambrose as bishop of Milan after Ambrose died in 397.

4. The text here is corrupt, and various emendations have been suggested. Another suggestion, frequently adopted, would change "firing the people's enthusiasm for Osiris" to "enthusiastic for Pelusium." The context does seem to require some connection with Egypt (Osiris was an Egyptian god, Pelusium a city in Egypt), but beyond that it is impossible to say with certainty what the text should really be.

5. The quotation is adapted from Virgil, *Aeneid* 8:698–700.

words, yet he was not ashamed to become a child of your Christ and a
speechless babe at your font, his neck bent to the yoke of humility, his
forehead vanquished by the shame of the Cross.

Ps. 35:10; Jn. 4:14; Rev. 21:6 / Sir. 51:34; Jer. 27:12; Mt. 11:29–30

2.4   O Lord, Lord, who bowed the heavens and came down, you
have touched the mountains and they smoked. By what means did
you make your way into his innermost being? He read Holy Scripture,
Simplicianus said; he searched and examined all the Christian writings with the utmost attentiveness. And he said to Simplicianus—not
openly, but privately, in intimate conversation—"You must know that
I am already a Christian." Simplicianus replied, "I will not believe you,
nor will I reckon you among Christians, unless I see you in Christ's
church." Victorinus just laughed and said, "So the walls are what make
Christians?" Again and again he said that he was already a Christian;
again and again Simplicianus gave the same reply, and Victorinus made
the same joke about the walls. For he was afraid of giving offense to his
proud, devil-worshiping friends: he thought their enmity would crash
down upon him from the height of Babylonian greatness like cedars
of Lebanon that the Lord had not yet brought low. But eventually he
drew in strength through his eager reading, and he was afraid lest he
be denied by Christ before the holy angels if he was afraid to confess
Christ before human beings; it seemed to him that he was guilty of
grave sin by being ashamed of the sacraments of the humility of your
Word when he had not been ashamed of the sacrilegious rites of proud
demons in which he had once participated, mimicking their pride. He
was embarrassed by his emptiness and abashed before the truth.[6] Suddenly and unexpectedly he said to Simplicianus, who told me the story,
"Let us go into the church; I want to become a Christian." Unable to
contain his joy, Simplicianus went with him. He received the first sacraments of instruction,[7] and it was not long afterward that he gave in
his name to be reborn in baptism.[8] Rome was astounded; the Church
rejoiced. The proud saw it and grew angry; they gnashed their teeth

Ps. 143:5

Is. 14:4, 14:12, 14:13; Rev. 17:5, 18:2 / Ps. 28:5

Mk. 8:38 par. Lk. 12:8

---

6. "was embarrassed": *depuduit*, which irritatingly enough can also mean "ceased to be embarrassed." O'Donnell (III:22–23) prefers the latter meaning and suggests that the sentence means
"he was no longer embarrassed when his deeds ran counter to his *vanitas* [emptiness], and was now
embarrassed when they ran counter to *veritas* [truth]." I think it is much more natural to go with the
former (and much more common) meaning and read the sentence as saying that he grew ashamed
of his former emptiness (the vain service of proud demons) and was abashed before the truth as he
now understood it.

7. That is, the exorcism, signing with the cross, and giving of salt that marked the beginning of the
catechumenate.

8. Giving in one's name marked the transition to the second stage of the catechumenate, in which
one was taught the Lord's Prayer and the Creed and was examined for worthiness of life.

and pined away. But your servant's hope was in the Lord God, and he   *Ps. 111:10*
had no regard for vanities and mad falsehoods.   *Ps. 39:5*

2.5   At last the time came for him to profess his faith. The custom was
that those who were to approach your grace would profess their faith
in a set form of words that they had memorized,[9] speaking from an
elevated place in the sight of the baptized people of Rome. Simplicianus said that the presbyters offered Victorinus the opportunity to make
his profession privately, as was often done for those who seemed likely
to be unnerved by their bashfulness; but he chose instead to profess his
salvation in the sight of the holy company. What he taught in rhetoric
was not salvation, and yet he professed it publicly. He had not been
afraid to profess his own words before crowds of madmen: how much
less, then, should he have been afraid to profess your Word before your
gentle flock!

So when he went up to make his profession, everyone who knew
him—and who among those present did not?—broke out into loud
shouts of thanksgiving. Then, more quietly, the sound of his name
was on the lips of all those who were rejoicing together: "Victorinus,
Victorinus." They quickly burst into shouts of joy because they saw
him; they quickly fell silent and grew attentive so that they could hear
him. He declared the true faith with outstanding confidence, and
everyone wanted to take hold of him inwardly, in their hearts; their
love and their joy were the hands with which they held him.

3.6   O God of great goodness, what goes on in human beings so that
we rejoice more over the salvation of a soul for which we had no hope,
a soul set free from a greater danger, than we do if there had always
been hope for it and the danger had been less? And indeed you too,
merciful Father, rejoice more over one who repents than over ninety-
nine righteous people who need no repentance. We hear with great joy   *Lk. 15:7*
the story of the shepherd who carries the lost sheep on his rejoicing
shoulders, of the coin restored to your treasury as the neighbors rejoice   *Lk. 15:4–6*

---

9. The set form of words was the baptismal creed, known to us as the Apostles' Creed; it was forbidden to write the creed down, so it was "handed over" (taught by rote) to baptismal candidates, who
"gave it back" (recited it) at their baptisms. The text of the creed as known in Rome at this time can
be reconstructed from allusions and commentaries: "I believe in God the Father Almighty, and in
Christ Jesus, his only Son, our Lord, who was born of the Holy Spirit and the Virgin Mary, who
was crucified under Pontius Pilate and was buried. On the third day he rose again from the dead.
He ascended into heaven. He is seated at the right hand of the Father. From there he will come
to judge the living and the dead. And [I believe] in the Holy Spirit, the holy catholic Church, the
forgiveness of sins, the resurrection of the body." (J. N. D. Kelly, *Early Christian Creeds*, cited in
O'Donnell, III:24.)

with the woman who found it. And the joy of the solemnity of your   *Lk. 15:8–10*
house brings us to tears when the story of your younger son is read in
your house, for he was dead and has come to life again; he was lost and
now is found. You rejoice in us and in your angels who are made holy   *Lk. 15:24, 15:32*
by holy charity. For you are always the same, and your unchanging   *Ps. 101:28; Heb.*
knowledge always encompasses all things that do not always exist and   *1:12*
are not always the same.

3.7   What, then, goes on in the soul when it takes greater pleasure
in finding or getting back the things it loves than it would if it had
always had them? For other instances attest to this, and all our experience cries out clearly, "Yes, it is so." An emperor glories in his victory.
He would not have been victorious if he had not gone to war, and the
more dangerous the battle, the more joy he has in his triumph. A storm
arises and the sailors are in danger of shipwreck; everyone blanches at
the prospect of death.[10] The sky and the sea grow calm, and the sailors
rejoice exceedingly because they had been exceedingly afraid. A loved
one is sick, and his pulse reveals how ill he is; everyone who wants him
healthy grows sick in mind along with him. If he recovers, even if he
no longer goes about with the strength he once had, there is now joy
of a sort that no one felt before, when he was healthy and going about
in full strength.

Human beings derive such pleasures in life not only from unforeseen and undesired events but also from troubles that are part of the
expected course of events and those that are undertaken voluntarily.
There is no pleasure in eating and drinking unless one has first experienced the discomfort of hunger and thirst, and drunkards eat salty
foods to induce the discomfort of a furious thirst so that they will have
pleasure when their drinking relieves it. And it is part of the expected
course of events that engaged couples do not get married right away, so
that the bridegroom will long for his bride and not disdain the wife for
whom he did not have to wait.

3.8   This is true in disgraceful and abominable gladness; it is true in
gladness that is permitted and lawful; it is true even in the most genuine and honorable friendship; it is true of the one who died and came
to life again, who was lost and now is found: in every case, greater joy   *Lk. 15:24, 15:32*
comes after greater distress. Why is this, O Lord my God, when you,
you yourself, are your own eternal joy, and those creatures who are
closest to you rejoice in you always? Why is it that this part of creation
goes back and forth between decay and improvement, between strife

---

10. Virgil, *Aeneid* 4.644.

and reconciliation? Is this perhaps their proper mode of being, as much
as you have bestowed on them, so that from the heights of the heavens   *Mt. 24:31*
to the depths of the earth, from the beginning to the end of the ages,
from angels to worms, from the first motion to the very last, you set
all kinds of goods and all your righteous works in their proper places
and accomplish them at their proper times? Oh, how exalted you are in
your heights, how profound in your depths! And you never draw back
from us, yet we can scarcely return to you.

4.9   Come, Lord: rouse us and call us back, kindle us and seize us,
blaze forth, grow sweet, that we might love you, that we might run
the race. Have not many people returned to you from a deeper hell of
blindness than Victorinus? Have they not drawn near to you and been
enlightened, receiving your light? And if they receive you, they obtain   *Ps. 33:6*
from you the power to become your sons and daughters.   *Jn. 1:9, 1:12*

But if they are less widely known, even people who do know them
rejoice less over them. For when many share in rejoicing, each person's
joy is increased, because they all fire each other's enthusiasm. Moreover,
the fact that they are known to many means that they will serve for
many as an impressive example leading to salvation; they go first, and
many others will follow. And so those who have gone before rejoice
greatly over them, because they are not rejoicing over them alone. For   *Deut. 1:17, 16.19;*
may it never be that there should be partiality in your temple—that the   *Sir. 42:1; Acts*
rich should be welcomed in preference to the poor or the well-born in   *10:34; Rom.*
preference to the lowly—when you have chosen the weak things of the   *2:11; Gal. 2:6;*
world to confound the strong, and you have chosen the lowly and con-   *Eph. 6:9; Col.*
3:25; Jas. 2:1,
temptible things of this world, and the things that are not, as though   *2:9; 1 Pet. 1.17*
they were, to bring to nothing the things that are.   *1 Cor. 1:27–28*

And yet the least of your apostles, the very one by whose tongue   *1 Cor. 15:9*
you made these words ring out, loved to be called Paul rather than
his former name, Saul, to commemorate his great victory when he
defeated in combat the pride[11] of the proconsul Paul, brought his neck
under the easy yoke of your Christ, and made him a citizen of the great   *Mt. 11:29–30*
King. For the enemy's defeat is greater when he is defeated in someone
over whom he has a more powerful hold or through whom he holds
many in his power: and he has a more powerful hold on those who
are proud because they claim noble birth, and he holds many in his
power through the authority they claim. So your children were right
to rejoice all the more exuberantly because they valued so highly the
mind of Victorinus, which the devil had captured as an impregnable

---

11. Virgil, *Aeneid* 6.833.

fortress, and the tongue of Victorinus, that great, sharp sword by which the devil had brought many to destruction. For our King had bound the strong man, and your children had seen his vessels snatched away   *Mt. 12:29* and made clean, fitted for your honor and made useful to the Lord for every good work.   *2 Tim. 2:21*

5.10   As soon as I had heard this story, I was on fire to imitate Victorinus; indeed, it was for that very purpose that your servant Simplicianus told it to me. But afterward he told me something more. In the time of Emperor Julian, a law was passed prohibiting Christians from teaching literature and rhetoric. Victorinus complied: he would rather abandon the prattle of the classroom than your Word, by whom you make the tongues of babes speak clearly. He seemed to me as happy as he was   *Wisd. 10:21, cf.* bold, for he found an opportunity to be at leisure in you; this was the   *Ps. 8:3 qtd. Mt. 21:16* very thing I longed for, but I was chained up, not by anything outside myself, but by the iron fetters of my own will. The enemy held my will in his power and fashioned from it the chains that held me fast. Indeed, a perverse will gives birth to inordinate desire,[12] and when the will serves inordinate desire, a habit is formed; and when the habit is not resisted, it becomes compulsion. By these small hooks, each joined to the one before (this is why I have called them a chain), a brutal enslavement held me in its grip.

And yet a new will had begun to arise in me, a will to worship you without desire of reward and to enjoy you, O God, our only sure joy.   *Job 1:9 VL* But this new will was not yet capable of overthrowing my prior will, which had grown stronger and stronger the longer it endured. Thus my two wills, one old and one new, one carnal and the other spiritual,   *Eph. 4:22, 4:24;* were at war with one another, and by their conflict they laid waste to   *Col. 3:9–10 /* my soul.   *Rom. 7:14*

5.11   Thus I understood by my own experience what I had read: that the flesh lusts against the spirit and the spirit against the flesh. I was   *Gal. 5:17* indeed in both, but I was more in the one of which I approved in myself than I was in the one of which I disapproved in myself. For the latter was no longer so much myself, since to a great degree it was something happening to me against my will rather than something I was doing willingly; yet it was my own doing that habit had become a more powerful adversary against me, for I had willed to come where I did not now will to be. And who could rightly complain when just

---

12. "inordinate desire": *libido*, not limited (as in contemporary English) to sexual desire (though it is in fact sexual desire that has enslaved Augustine in this case), but rather "a desire on the part of the soul by which it puts certain temporal things ahead of eternal goods" (*De mendacio* 7.10).

punishment besets a sinner? I had formerly thought that I had an excuse for not rejecting the world and serving you: my grasp of the truth was uncertain. But this excuse could no longer serve, for I was certain of your truth. Yet I was still bound to earth and refused to enlist in your service; I was as afraid of having all obstacles removed as I ought to have been afraid of the obstacles themselves.

5.12 So I was oppressed by the burden of the world, but the oppression was sweet, as it so often is in sleep. The thoughts in which I would meditate on you were like the efforts of those who try to awaken but are overcome and sink back into the depths of sleep. No one would want to be asleep all the time, and everyone of sound judgment agrees that it is better to be awake; yet people will often put off getting up, for their bodies are very sluggish, and even though the time to awaken has come, the more pleasant alternative takes hold of them, though they do not approve of it. In the same way I was certain that it was better for me to surrender myself to your charity than to yield to my own cupidity. Surrender to you was what I approved, and it was the better course; but yielding to my own cupidity was pleasant, and it held me in chains. I had no answer to give when you said to me, "Awake, you sleeper, and arise from the dead, and Christ will give you light," and everything around me made it plain that you were speaking the truth. I was convinced by the truth, and I had no answer at all to give but sluggish and sleepy words: "in a little while"; "really, in a little while"; "give me just a moment longer." But "in a little while" never came, and "give me just a moment longer" went on and on.

Ps. 62:7

Eph. 5:14

In vain did I delight in your law in my inmost self, because another law in my members was at war against the law of my mind and made me captive to the law of sin that was in my members. For the law of sin is the fierce strength of habit by which the mind is carried away and held even against its will, and deservedly so, because it willingly fell into that habit. Wretched man that I was! Who would deliver me from the body of this death? Only your grace, through Jesus Christ our Lord.

Rom. 7:22–23

Rom. 7:24–25

6.13 O Lord, my helper and my redeemer, I shall now tell and confess to your Name how you released me from the chains of the desire for sex, which bound me so tightly, and from my enslavement to worldly business. I went about my usual affairs with increasing anxiety, and every day I sighed for you. I was often in your church—whenever there was leisure from the work that weighed me down and made me groan. Alypius was with me; he had finished his third session as assessor and had no legal work to do. He was waiting for people to whom he could

Ps. 18:15

Ps. 53:8

sell his advice, just as I sold facility in speech (supposing it can even be taught). Nebridius, however, had yielded to the claims of friendship and was assisting Verecundus, a very dear companion of all of us. He was a citizen of Milan and a teacher of grammar there, who very much needed reliable help and claimed it by right of friendship from among our company. And so it was not greed for gain that attracted Nebridius—he could have had a better position teaching literature if he had wanted it; no, it was a matter of goodwill on his part that he was unwilling to refuse our request, so sweet and so easy-going a friend as he was. But he carried out his work with exceptional judgment, taking care not to become known to people who are great in the eyes of the world, because he was avoiding the disturbance of mind that they would cause: he wanted to have his mind free, and as many hours as possible at his disposal, to seek out something to read or to hear about wisdom.

Eph. 2:2

6.14   So one day—Nebridius was away, I do not remember why—a man named Ponticianus came to visit me and Alypius at our home. He was a fellow citizen of ours as an African and held high office at court; he wanted something or other from us. We sat down and talked together. He happened to notice a book on top of the gaming table that was in front of us. He picked it up, opened it, and found the Apostle Paul—certainly not what he was expecting, since he had thought it would be one of the books that were wearing me down in the course of my profession. But then he smiled, looked at me, and with congratulations expressed his surprise on learning that those writings, and those alone, were before my eyes. He was in fact a baptized Christian, and he often prostrated himself in your church before you, our God, in his frequent and prolonged prayers. When I had told him that I was devoting my most careful attention to those Scriptures, he began to tell the story of the monk Antony of Egypt—a name of great renown among your servants, but unknown to us until that moment. When he learned that fact, he drew out his story, making the great man known to us who were ignorant of him, and marveling at our ignorance. But we were stunned when we heard of such wondrous deeds, definitively attested by recent memory and in nearly our own day, accomplished in the true faith and in the catholic Church. We were all astonished: Alypius and I because the deeds were so great, Ponticianus because we had never heard about them before.

6.15   From there his talk turned to the crowds of monasteries, to ways of life that send up a sweet fragrance before you, and to the fertile wastelands of the desert. We knew nothing of these things. There was a monastery in Milan outside the city walls, full of good brothers, under Ambrose's care, but we did not know about it.

He continued and went on speaking, and we kept silent and gave him our attention. And so he came to speak of a time when he and three companions of his (no doubt at Trier)[13] had gone out for a walk in the gardens adjacent to the walls while the emperor was occupied with the morning show at the circus. It so happened that as they walked along, they split into pairs; one of them stayed with Ponticianus while the other two went on together. The two wanderers happened upon a house where certain servants of yours lived, men poor in spirit, to whom belongs the kingdom of heaven, and they found there a book *Mt. 5:3* containing the *Life* of your servant Antony.[14] One of them began to read it. He was on fire with admiration, and as he read he began to contemplate taking hold of such a life for himself, leaving his worldly career behind to serve you. (They were among those known as *agentes in rebus.*)[15] Then, suddenly filled with holy love and right-minded shame, he was angry with himself; and he turned his eyes upon his friend and said to him, "Tell me, I beg of you: in all these labors of ours, what are we hoping to achieve? What are we seeking? For what are we fighting? Could we have any higher hope in palace life than being Friends of the Emperor? And what is there in such a position that is not tenuous and fraught with danger? How many dangers must we face in order to arrive at that even greater danger? And how long will it take us to attain it? But mark it well: I can become a friend of God *Jdt. 8:22; Jas. 2:23* right now if I simply will it."

He said this, and, in turmoil with the birth pangs of a new life, he turned his eyes back to the pages of the book. He read on, and he was changed within, where you saw it; his mind was being stripped of the world, as would shortly become evident. For as he read, and the tempest swirled in his heart, he groaned suddenly; he discerned the better course and chose it. Already yours, he said to his friend, "I have already torn myself away from that hope of ours and resolved to serve God, and indeed I am undertaking it from this very hour, in this very place.

---

13. Trier had been the site of the imperial court until it moved to Milan in 381. Recall that Ponticianus was described as holding high office at court. It is striking that the stories of leaving behind worldly life for the service of God—stories meant to inspire Augustine to do the same thing—are told by someone enjoying a conspicuously successful worldly career.

14. *The Life of Antony (Vita Antonii)*, attributed to Saint Athanasius and translated into Latin by Evagrius.

15. *Agentes in rebus* had a variety of functions in the imperial bureaucracy, including communications, secret service, and the supervision of public works; they also served as customs officers and inspectors.

If you are ashamed to follow my example, do not stand in my way."
His friend replied that he would be his steadfast companion for so
great a reward in so great a service. Both of them were already building
a tower for you at a fitting cost: leaving behind all that was theirs and
following you.

Lk. 14:28–33

*Mt. 19:27; Lk.
5:11, 5:28*

Ponticianus and the friend who was walking with him through
other parts of the garden went looking for them. They arrived at the
same place and, finding their two friends, encouraged them to return,
because it was getting late in the day. But their friends told them about
their decision and resolution, explaining how such a will had arisen in
them and become firmly fixed. They asked them at least not to stand in
their way if they were unwilling to join them. Ponticianus and his companion were in no way changed from their prior state, but nonetheless
they wept for their friends, as he told us, and offered them devout
congratulations, commending themselves to their prayers. Ponticianus
and his companion returned to the palace, dragging their hearts in the
earth; their two friends remained in the house, their hearts attached to
heaven. Both of them were engaged, and when their fiancées heard all
this, they likewise devoted their virginity to you.

Lk. 9:12, 24:29

7.16   Ponticianus went on telling his story. But as he spoke, you,
O Lord, were wrenching me toward myself. All the time that I had
refused to look honestly at myself, I had turned my back upon myself;
but you wrested me away from that position and set me before my
own face, so that I would see how wicked I was, how misshapen and
filthy, covered with spots and sores. I saw it, and I recoiled in horror,
and there was nowhere I could flee from myself. But if I tried to avert
my gaze from myself, he went on telling his story, and you once again
resisted me and forced me to look at myself so that I would find out
my iniquity and hate it. I had known it all along, but I disguised it,
repressed it, and put it out of my mind.

Jer. 2:27

Ps. 49:21

Ps. 35:3

7.17   But now the more ardently I loved those whose wholesome
resolutions I was hearing about, who had given themselves entirely to
you to be healed, the more I came to hate and loathe myself in comparison with them. For so many years of my life had slipped away
from me—twelve years, perhaps—since I had read Cicero's *Hortensius*
in my nineteenth year and was roused to devote myself to wisdom,
and I delayed scorning earthly happiness to be at leisure to search out
wisdom. The mere search for wisdom, let alone the actual finding of
it, was worth more than finding all the treasures of the kings of the
nations and having my fill of the pleasures of the body. But wretched
as I was in my youth—wretched at the very outset of my youth—I had

nonetheless asked you for chastity. I said, "Give me chastity and conti-nence: but not yet." For I was afraid that you would heed my prayer in that very moment, and in that very moment heal me from the sickness of concupiscence, which I wanted to be satisfied, not snuffed out. I continued to walk in the depraved paths of superstitious sacrilege, not indeed because I was certain in them but merely because I preferred them to other paths. Those other paths I did not seek out piously; no, I set myself up as their enemy and contended against them.

Sir. 2:16

7.18 I had thought that I was putting off, day after day, scorning the hope of this present world and following you alone because I had not found anything certain by which I could direct my course. Now the day had come on which I was stripped naked before myself, and my conscience spoke plainly to me: "What, nothing more to say? You always said you were unwilling to cast aside the burden of your emp-tiness because you were not certain of the truth. But look now: you are certain, and still your burden presses upon you, while people not wearied by the search, who have not been contemplating these things for ten years and more, have received wings on freer shoulders." All this gnawed away at my innermost self, and I was violently distressed with fearsome shame, while Ponticianus went on speaking of such things. But when he had finished talking and accomplished the business on which he had come, he went away, and I was left by myself.

Sir. 5:8

Ps. 54:7

Was there anything I had not said to myself? Were there any words left that I had not used to whip my soul into following me as I tried to go after you? It fought back, it resisted, but it found no excuse for itself. All its arguments were used up and defeated. What was left was a speechless dread: my soul feared being restrained from the easy flow of habit, feared this as if it were death itself, though by its habit it was wasting away unto death.

8.19 I had powerfully awakened great strife in our chamber, my heart; and in the midst of this contention in my inner dwelling place the turmoil in my mind showed in my face, and I accosted Alypius and exclaimed, "What is wrong with us? What is this? The unlearned are rising up and taking hold of heaven, and we, with all our learning: look at us, wallowing in flesh and blood! Are we ashamed to follow them because they went first, and not ashamed to refuse to follow them at all?" I said something or other like this, and then my vexation tore me away from him as he looked at me in silent astonishment—for I no longer sounded like my usual self. My brow, my cheeks, my eyes, my color, the tone of my voice all expressed my mind more eloquently than did the words that I uttered.

Mt. 6:6

1 Cor. 15:50

There was a small garden at our host's house, and we had the use of it along with the whole house, for our host, the master of the house, did not live there. The tumult of my feelings drove me out there, where no one would intervene in the fiery attack that I had launched against myself, until it was finished. What the outcome would be, you knew, but I did not. I was going mad in recovering my sanity, dying unto life, well aware of what evil was in me and unaware of what goodness would come to be in me in just a little while. So I went out into the garden, and Alypius followed close behind me. His presence with me did not intrude upon my privacy, and how could he have left me alone in such a state?

So we sat down as far from the house as we could. I was groaning in spirit, grievously distressed and greatly indignant that I would not *Jn. 11:33* enter into the bond and covenant with you, my God, though all my bones cried out for this very thing and praised it to the heavens. The *Ps. 34:10* way there was not by ship or carriage or on foot; it did not even require me to go from the house to the place where we had sat down. To go there—even, indeed, to arrive there—required only that I will to go there, but that I will it forcefully and with my whole self, not with a half-wounded will turning and twisting this way and that, struggling between a part that would rise upward and a part that was falling.

8.20 At length in the upheavals of my indecision I was making the kinds of bodily gestures that people sometimes want to make but cannot because their limbs are missing or they are bound by chains or undone by fatigue or in some way prevented. If I tore out my hair, if I beat my brow, if I clasped my hands and hugged my knee, I did it because I willed it. But it was possible for me to will these things and yet not do them, if the movement of my limbs were not under my control. So I did all these things, when the will to do them was not the same as the power to do them; and yet I was not doing what I had incomparably greater desire to do, what pleased me far more, even though I had the power to do it as soon as I willed it: for as soon as I would will it, I would will it. The ability, the will, was there, and to will it was already to do it; and yet it was not done, and my body obeyed the most trifling will of my soul and moved its limbs at the will's command more readily than my soul would obey itself and bring to completion this momentous will in the will alone.

9.21 What was the source of this remarkable conflict? How did things come to this pass? Let your mercy shine upon me, and let me inquire; perhaps I will find an answer in the secret hiding places of the punishments that beset human beings, in the darkest shadows of the griefs of the children of Adam. What was the source of this remarkable conflict? How did things come to this pass? The mind commands the body, and immediately it is obeyed; the mind commands itself, and it is resisted. The mind commands the hand to move, and so great is its control that one can scarcely distinguish the command from the obedience—and the mind is mind, whereas the hand is body. The mind commands the mind to will, and the mind is nothing other than itself, and yet it does not obey. What is the source of this remarkable conflict? How do things come to this pass, so that the mind wills what it would not command unless it willed it, and yet it does not do what it commands?

But it does not will it wholeheartedly, so it does not command wholeheartedly. So far as it wills, it commands; so far as it does not will, the command is not carried out. For what the will is commanding is that a certain will should exist: not some other will, but that very will itself. And so it is not the whole will that commands, and for this reason what it commands does not come to be. For if it were the whole will, it would not command such a will to exist, since it would already exist. So it is not remarkable after all when someone is partly willing and partly unwilling: it is an illness of the mind, because it is so weighed down by habit that it cannot wholly rise up in the truth. And the reason that there are two wills is that neither of them is the whole, and something is present in one that is lacking in the other.

10.22   There are those who observe these two wills in deliberation and conclude that there are two natures, of two minds: one good, one evil. Let them perish at your presence, O God, as empty talkers and seducers of the mind perish. It is they who are truly evil, because they hold these evil views; and they themselves will be good if they hold true views and consent to what is true, so that your Apostle may say to them, "Once you were darkness, but now you are light in the Lord." For so long as they will to be light, not in the Lord, but in themselves, by supposing that the nature of the soul is what God is, they have become a deeper darkness; for in their appalling arrogance they have drawn further away from you, the true Light who enlighten every human being who comes into this world. To them I say this: give heed to what you are saying and be ashamed; go to him and you will receive his light, and your face will not be ashamed.

When I was deliberating about whether I would now serve the Lord my God as I had long intended, it was I who willed it, I who failed to will it; it was I. I did not wholly will it; I did not wholly fail to will it. For this reason I was struggling against myself, tearing myself into

Ps. 67:3

Tit. 1:10

Eph. 5:8

Jn. 1:9

Ps. 33:6

Deut. 6:13; Jer. 30:9; Mt. 4:10

fragments, and that fragmentation was happening against my will: yet what it revealed was not the nature of a mind other than my own, but rather the punishment of my own nature. And so this fragmentation was not after all my own doing; it was the work of the sin that dwelt within me as punishment for the sin of one who had been freer than I was: for I was a son of Adam.

Rom. 7:17, 7:20

10.23   For if there are as many contrary natures as there are conflicting wills, there will not be just two, but many. Suppose someone is deliberating whether to go to a Manichee assembly or to the theater. The Manichees will cry out, "Look: two natures, a good nature that is leading him to us, and a bad nature that is leading him elsewhere. What else could be the source of this wavering between opposing wills?" But I say both wills are bad, both the one that leads him to the Manichees and the one that leads him back to the theater, whereas they believe that the one that sends him to them can only be good. What, then, if someone of our fellowship is deliberating and vacillates within himself between two wills that are opposed: will he go to the theater or to our church? Will not the Manichees vacillate about how to answer? Either they will admit what they want to deny—that his will to go to our church is good, just as good as the will of those who have been initiated into the sacraments of the Manichees and trapped there—or they will conclude that two bad natures and two bad minds are in conflict in a single person. And then either their customary answer, that there is one good nature and one bad nature, will not be true, or else they will be turned toward the truth and not deny that when someone deliberates, there is one soul, thrown into turmoil by divergent wills.

10.24   They must no longer say, when they experience two wills striving against each other in a single person, that there are two contrary minds—one good, one evil—contending with each other, deriving from two contrary substances and two contrary principles. For you, O truthful God, refute them; you argue against them and defeat them. Suppose both wills are bad: someone is deliberating whether to kill someone by poisoning or stabbing; whether to seize this or that part of someone else's property, when he cannot seize both; whether to spend money on pleasure in the service of lust or to save money in the service of greed; whether to go to the circus or to the theater, if both have performances on the same day—and I shall add a third: whether to go into someone else's house to rob him, if the occasion arises—even a fourth: to commit adultery, if the opportunity presents itself to do that as well at the same time. If all these things are present at a single moment of time and one desires them all equally but cannot do them all at

Ps. 85:15; Jn. 3:33; Rom. 3:14

the same time, these four—or more—mutually opposed wills tear the mind apart because it desires so many things; but the Manichees do not typically say that the mind is a great multitude of diverse substances.

Likewise in the case of good wills: suppose I ask them, Is it good to take pleasure in reading the Apostle? Is it good to take pleasure in the sober singing of a Psalm? Is it good to discuss the Gospel? To each of these they will reply, "It is good." So then what if all of them are equally appealing, and at the very same time? Will not divergent wills distend the human heart while we deliberate about which of the three we prefer to have? They are all good, and they are in conflict with one another until one is chosen and the whole will, which was divided into many, is drawn toward it. And so when someone would prefer to rise up to eternity but the pleasure of temporal goods holds him down, it is one and the same soul that does not will either with its whole will; so the soul is torn into pieces in its great distress, as long as it prefers the eternal as truth demands but will not cast away the temporal because it is easy and familiar.

11.25   In this way I was sick and in agony. I brought bitter accusations against myself, much more bitter than ever before, and I squirmed and writhed in my chains until they would be wholly broken and cast off. By now they barely held me, but they did still hold me. And in your severe mercy, O Lord, you rose up in the hidden places of my inmost self and whipped me more and more with the lash of fear and shame so that I would not give up and go back to my old ways, lest I fail to cast off the small and fragile chain that yet remained and it would grow strong again and bind me more powerfully than ever. Inwardly I was saying to myself, "Let it be now; let it be now," and by saying this I was already on the journey to where I wanted to be. I nearly did it, but I did not do it; yet I did not fall back into my former ways. Instead I stood on the threshold and caught my breath. Once again I made an effort, and I was nearly there—I was nearly there—I was touching it, I had it in my grasp. And then I was not there, not touching it, not grasping it, hesitating to die unto death and live unto life. The evil that had a firm place in me was more powerful than the good to which I was not accustomed. The closer I drew to the moment when I would be changed, the more I was struck with terror. But it did not thrust me back or turn me away; it left me hanging.

11.26   My old loves—utter trifles, the vanities of those who work vanity—held me back. They snatched at the garments of my flesh and whispered, "Are you leaving us behind? From this moment and for ever we will no longer be with you. From this moment and for ever these

Eccl. 1:2

things will no longer be permissible for you." O Lord, may your mercy turn away the soul of your servant from "these things," the things my old loves put before me. How filthy, how dishonorable they were! They were already so far from me that I did not half hear them. They did not confront me openly as I went on my way; in a stifled whisper they nagged at me from behind my back as I walked away and tried to make me look back. Yet even so they slowed me down; I hesitated to tear myself away from them, cut myself off from them, and leap ahead to the place where I was being called, while the violent power of habit asked me, "Do you really think you will be able to live without these things?" *Sir. 5:8*

11.27 But by now it was saying all this in a most half-hearted way. For from the place on which I had set my sights, and to which I was afraid to go, the chaste dignity of Continence was revealed to me. Serene, not wantonly joyful, she beckoned to me honorably to come to her and not hesitate. She held out her holy hands to me to take hold of them and embrace her, hands teeming with a host of good examples: so many boys and girls, many youths and people of every age, venerable widows and elderly women who had remained virgins. In all of them Continence herself was revealed, not as in any way sterile, but as the fertile mother of children of joy by you, O Lord, her husband. She *Ps. 112:9* laughed at me with the laughter of encouragement, as if to say, "Can you not do what these men and women did? Was it possible for these men and women to do this by their own strength, and not in the Lord their God? The Lord their God gave me to them. Why do you stand still in yourself and not stand firm? Cast yourself upon him! Fear not. He will not withdraw himself from you and let you fall: cast yourself upon him in full assurance! He will catch you and heal you." And I was deeply ashamed, because I still heard the murmur of those trifles, and I was held in suspense, lingering. Again she spoke, as if she were saying, "Close your ears against those unclean members of yours upon the earth, that they may be put to death. They tell you tales of pleasure, *Col. 3:5* but they have nothing to compare with the law of the Lord your God." *Ps. 118:85*

This debate within my heart was nothing less than a struggle of myself against myself. Alypius remained close by my side, waiting in silence for the outcome of this uncommon agitation of mine.

12.28 But as this profound self-examination dredged up all my wretchedness and brought it together in a heap before the eyes of my heart, a great storm arose and brought on a great shower of tears. And so that I could shed them freely and give voice to my sobbing, I arose and left Alypius—solitude seemed more appropriate for me to give vent to my weeping—and secluded myself in a more remote spot, so that even his presence would not be a burden to me. That is how I felt at the time, and he understood it: there was something in my voice, I think, that made it clear I was ready to break down and cry. And so I arose, and he remained where we had been sitting, thunderstruck.

I stretched out somehow or other under a fig tree[16] and gave full rein to my tears. Rivers streamed forth from my eyes, an acceptable sacrifice to you. And I said many things to you—not indeed in these words, but this was the meaning: "How long, O Lord? How long, O Lord; will you be angry for ever? Remember not our sins of old." For I felt the strength of my sins holding me back. I gave voice to cries of wretchedness: "How long—how long—will I go on saying, 'Tomorrow and tomorrow'? Why not right now? Why can my wickedness not come to an end at this very hour?"

Mt. 21:19; Jn. 1:47–48

Ps. 50:19

Ps. 6:4

Ps. 78:5 / Ps. 78:8

12.29   I said these things and wept most bitter tears in the brokenness of my heart. Then suddenly I heard a voice from next door—a boy's voice or a girl's, I do not know—singing, repeating again and again, "Pick up and read, pick up and read." At once my countenance was changed and I began to think most intently about whether there was any sort of game in which children would say something like that. I could not recall ever having heard it before, so I stopped the flow of my tears and arose, taking this to be no less than a divine voice commanding me to open a book and read whatever passage I first came upon. For I had heard how Antony happened upon the reading of the Gospel and took what he heard as an admonition, as though what was read was said directly to him: "Go, sell all that you have and give to the poor, and you will have treasures in heaven; and come, follow me." And by such a divine announcement he was turned immediately to you. And so, stirred by this voice, I returned to the place where I had been sitting with Alypius: for I had set down a book of the Apostle there when I got up and left. I snatched it up, opened it, and read in silence the passage that first caught my eye: "not in reveling and drunkenness, not

Ps. 50:19

Mt. 19:21

---

16. The fig tree is a powerful Scriptural image. In Genesis 3:7 Adam and Eve make coverings of fig leaves for themselves to cover the shame of their nakedness after their fall. Micah 4:4 prophesies that in "the latter days . . . they shall sit every man under his vine and under his fig tree, and none shall make them afraid." (See also Zechariah 3:10.) In Matthew 21:18–20 (par. Mark 11:12–13, 20–21) Jesus curses a barren fig tree, which withers. The budding of the fig tree is a sign of the coming summer in Matthew 24:32 (par. Mark 13:28). In John 1:48 Jesus sees Nathanael under a fig tree before he calls him to be a disciple. Foremost in Augustine's mind are the allusions to the cursing of the barren fig tree, which speaks of the flesh in need of grace, and the calling of Nathanael, which speaks of that very grace in the making of a disciple.

in debauchery and licentiousness, not in quarreling and jealousy, but put on the Lord Jesus Christ and make no provision for the flesh in its lusts." I had no desire to read further; there was no need. As soon as I *Rom. 13:13–14* reached the end of this sentence the light of assurance was poured into my heart and all the clouds of doubt melted away.

12.30   I closed the book, marking the place by keeping a finger there or in some other way. My face now calm and still, I told Alypius what had happened. He likewise told me what had been happening in him, which I did not know. He asked to see what I had read. I showed him, and he looked further than I had read. I did not know what came next, but it was this: "Welcome the one who is weak in faith." He applied *Rom. 14:1* these words to himself and explained this to me. Yet he took strength from this admonition, and without any turmoil of doubt he was joined to me in the wholesome resolution and purpose that was so much in harmony with his accustomed behavior, which for so long had been different from mine, and far better.

From there we went inside to my mother and told her; she was overjoyed. We told her the story of how it happened. She exulted and was triumphant and blessed you, who are able to do more than we ask or understand. For she saw that you had granted me even more than *Eph. 3:20* she had so often asked for with sorrowful and tearful cries. For you had so turned me to yourself that I would not look for a wife or for any other hope in this present world. I was standing on that rule of faith on which you had revealed me to her so many years before.[17] You had turned her sorrow into joy more abundantly even than she had desired, *Ps. 29:12* a joy much dearer and purer than she could have sought from grand-children of my flesh.

---

17. See 3.11.19.

Book Nine

Augustine abandons his career and retires to a country estate with his mother, son, and friends to enjoy unconstrained discussion and contemplation. Returning to Milan, he, Alypius, and Adeodatus are baptized, plunged into the sacramental death and rebirth that establish the central theme of this book. Augustine records the baptisms and deaths of his friends Verecundus and Nebridius; his father, Patrick; and his son, Adeodatus; but the death of Monnica receives the most attention. Augustine recounts her life, her wisdom, and her devotion to God. Shortly before her death, as they are waiting to sail back to Africa from Ostia (the port of Rome), she and Augustine discuss the eternal life of the saints; they "traverse all bodily things" and "touch [Wisdom]—just barely—with the utmost energy of [their] hearts" (9.10.24). Augustine grieves deeply over his mother's death; his reflections on the proper place of grief in human life are gentler than his conclusions in Book 4 after the death of his unnamed friend: for his love for Monnica was true friendship.

Augustine throws off his old life, including his career as a teacher of rhetoric (9.1.1–9.3.6). He goes to Cassiciacum (9.4.7–9.5.13) with his mother, son, and friends, enjoying philosophical discussions and writing dialogues (9.4.7). He is deeply moved by the Psalms (9.4.8) but baffled by Isaiah (9.5.13). He returns to Milan (9.6.14–9.7.16) for baptism. Augustine recounts the life of Monnica (9.8.17–9.9.21). In the course of a conversation together at Ostia, Monnica and Augustine have an experience of glimpsing Wisdom beyond all earthly things (9.10.23–26). A few days later, Monnica dies (9.11.27–28), and Augustine grieves (9.12.29–9.13.36). He asks that Monnica and Patrick be remembered at the altar (9.13.37).

1.1 O Lord, I am your servant; I am your servant and the child of your handmaid: you have broken my chains. I will offer to you a sacrifice of praise. Let my heart and my tongue praise you, and let all my *Ps. 115:16–17* bones say, "O Lord, who is like you?" Let them say this, and you answer *Ps. 34:10* me and say to my soul, "I am your salvation." Who am I, and what *Ps. 34:3* sort of man am I? What evil was lacking from my deeds, or if not from my deeds then from my words, or if not from my words then from my will? But you, O Lord, are gracious and merciful, and your right hand *Ex. 34:6; Ps. 85:5,* in its tender care has regard for the immense darkness of my death and *102:8* drains the bottomless pit of corruption from the depths of my heart. And this was the whole of it: not to will what I willed, and to will what you willed. But where was my free choice in all those long years? And *Mt. 26:39;* from what deep and hidden recess was it called forth in that moment *Mk.14:36; Jn. 5:30, 6:38*

139

when I bowed my neck to your easy yoke and my shoulders to your
light burden, Christ Jesus, my helper and my redeemer? How sweet it   *Mt. 11:30 / Ps.*
suddenly became for me to be without the sweetness of those trifles,   *18:15*
which I had feared to lose but now rejoiced to send away. For you cast
them away from me, you who are the true, the supreme, sweetness; you
cast them away and in their place you yourself entered into me, sweeter
than any pleasure, though not for flesh and blood; brighter than any
light, yet deeper and more intimate than any hidden recess; loftier than
any honor, but not for those who are lofty in themselves. At last my
soul was free from its gnawing cares: its ambition and greed, its obses-
sion with scratching the itch of its lusts. At last I was speaking freely
to you, my brightness, my wealth, and my salvation, O Lord my God.

2.2   And it pleased me in your sight not to make a noisy spectacle of   *Ps. 18:15*
withdrawing the service of my tongue in the marketplace of unbridled
speech, but instead to slip away quietly, so that young men who were
not meditating on your law, not meditating on your peace, but instead   *Ps. 1:2, 118:70,*
on mad falsehoods and court battles, would not purchase from my   *77, 92, 97, 174 /*
mouth the weapons of their frenzy. Fortunately it was now only a few   *Ps. 39:5*
days from the Vintage Vacation,[1] and I made up my mind to hold out
for those few days so that I could retire gracefully; now that you had
bought me for yourself, I would not go back to putting myself up for
sale. So our resolution was known to you, but not to anyone else except
for our close friends; we agreed not to share the news with just anyone. But to us who were climbing up from the valley of weeping and   *Ps. 83:7*
singing a song of degrees[2] you had sent sharp arrows and hot burning
coals against the deceitful tongue[3] that might speak against us under   *Ps. 119:3–4*
the guise of giving advice and devour us like food under the pretext of
friendship.

2.3   You had pierced our heart with the arrows of your charity, and we
carried about your words like swords that had penetrated to our inmost

---

1. 23 August to 15 October, "a time for respite from the summer heat and for bringing in the
autumn harvest" (*Codex Theodosianus* 2.8.19).
2. Each of the Psalms from 119 through 133 is labeled "a song of degrees" (*canticum graduum*). The
sense of *gradus* here is "steps upward."
3. *en. Ps.* 119.5, "The sharp arrows of the warrior are the words of God. Behold, they are shot at
the heart and transfix it; but when the heart is transfixed by the arrows of the word of God, it is
not made desolate; no, love is awakened. . . . But what are the hot burning coals? [more literally,
"the coals that lay waste"] It is no great matter to contend with words against the deceitful tongue
and sinful lips; it is no great matter to contend with words. One must contend also with examples.
Examples are the hot burning coals."

being.[4] And the examples of your servants, whom you had brought out of darkness into light and out of death into life, were brought together into the very center of our thought and burned fiercely. They burned off our heaviness, our sluggishness, so that we would not fall back into the depths; they enkindled us powerfully, so that no breath of contradiction from a deceitful tongue could put out the fire, but would only make us burn all the more brightly.

We knew, of course, that there would also be some who would praise our vow and resolution for the sake of your Name, which you have hallowed throughout the earth. So it seemed like self-aggrandizement not to wait for the holidays that were so close, but instead to make a public show of resigning my position in front of everyone so that my action would be on everyone's lips; seeing that I had decided to depart so close to the upcoming Vintage Vacation, people would have a great deal to say about how I had set my heart on making myself look terribly important. And how would it have served me for people to question and argue about my state of mind and to let our good be spoken of as evil?

Ez. 36:23; Mt. 6:9

Rom. 14:16

2.4   As it happened, that summer my lungs had begun to give way under the strain of too much work teaching. I found it difficult to breathe, and the pains in my chest betrayed the weakened state of my lungs. I could no longer speak in a full voice or for prolonged stretches of time. At first this concerned me, because my symptoms were practically forcing me to set down the burden of my teaching position, or, if I could be cured and recover, at least to take some time off. But once the wholehearted will to be still and see that you are the Lord had arisen in me and become firmly fixed—as you know, my God—I actually began to rejoice in having this honest excuse to mitigate the offense I would cause to people who for the sake of their children wanted me never to be free.[5] So, full of such joy, I put up with the delay until it had run its course—it was about twenty days, I think—though it required strength to make it through, because the greed that had once made my heavy work bearable had disappeared; had patience not taken its place, I would have been crushed under the load.

Ps. 45:11

Some of your servants, my brothers and sisters, will perhaps say that I sinned by remaining even one hour in the seat of the liar when my heart was already fully intent on serving you. I will not argue with them. But you, most merciful Lord: did you not cast this sin into

Ps. 1:1

---

4. "our inmost being": *visceribus*. On this word see 5.9.17, fn. 12.
5. There is untranslatable wordplay here: "children" is *liberos*, "free" is *liberum*.

oblivion and forgive it, along with all my other hideous and deadly sins, in the sacred water of baptism?

3.5   Verecundus was consumed with anxiety over this salutary resolution of ours, because he saw that he would lose our fellowship owing to the chains by which he was so tightly bound. He was not yet a Christian. His wife was a baptized believer, yet it was on account of her, more than anything else, that he was held back from joining us on the journey that we had undertaken. He said that he was unwilling to be a Christian in any other way than the one way he could not follow. But he very kindly offered us his hospitality as long as we wanted to stay. You will reward him, O Lord, at the resurrection of the just, *Lk. 14:14* because you have already rewarded him with his allotted place among the just. For after we had left him and gone to Rome, he was chastened *Ps. 124:3* by a bodily illness, and while he was sick he became a Christian; and having been baptized, he departed this life. In this way you had mercy not only on him but on us as well, so that we would not be tortured by the unbearable grief of remembering his outstanding generosity as our friend but being unable to count him among your flock.[6] Thanks be to you, our God! We are yours. Your encouragements and your consolations testify that we are yours. Faithful to your promise, you are rewarding Verecundus for granting us the use of his country house at Cassiciacum,[7] where we rested in you from the turmoil of this present world; you are rewarding him with the delights of your paradise, which is lush and green for ever. For you have forgiven his earthly sins on the mountain flowing with milk, your mountain, the mountain of abundance.[8] *Ps. 67:16–17 VL*

3.6   So Verecundus was distressed, but Nebridius rejoiced with us. For although he was not yet a Christian and had fallen into that most destructive pit of error, so that he believed that the flesh of the Truth, *Jn. 14:6* your Son, was a phantasm, still, he was beginning to climb up out of

---

6. Another bit of untranslatable wordplay: "outstanding" is *egregiam*, "flock" is *grege*.

7. The location of Cassiciacum is disputed.

8. "on the mountain flowing with milk": *in monte incaseato*, literally, "on the mountain where much cheese is made." Augustine comments in *en. Ps.* 67.22, "But what are we to understand as the 'mountain of God, the mountain of abundance, the mountain where much cheese is made'? What else but the Lord Christ, of whom another prophet says, 'In the last days the mountain of the Lord will be established as the highest of the mountains' (Is. 2:2)? Christ himself is the mountain where much cheese is made because he nourishes his little children with grace as with milk; he is the mountain of abundance for strengthening and enriching them with the excellence of his gifts. For milk itself, from which cheese is made, signifies grace in a wondrous way, since it flows abundantly from mothers' breasts and with a delightful mercy is poured forth for little children."

it: he was not yet initiated into any of the sacraments of your Church, but he was a most ardent seeker after truth. Not long after our conversion and regeneration through your baptism, you released him from the flesh; he was by then a baptized catholic, serving you among your people in Africa in perfect chastity and continence, and through him his entire household had become Christian. And now he lives in the bosom of Abraham. Whatever is meant by the bosom of Abraham, *Lk. 16:22* that is where my Nebridius lives, my dear friend, once a freedman but now your adoptive son, O Lord; that is where he lives.[9] For what other place could there be for such a soul? He lives in that place about which he used to ask me so many questions, insignificant and ignorant man that I am. He no longer gives his ear to my mouth but puts his spiritual mouth to your fount and drinks from it as much wisdom as he can in *Sir. 1:5, 26:15;* his great eagerness, happy without limit and without end. And I do not *Prov. 18:4* think that he is so intoxicated from this that he forgets me, since you, O Lord, whom he drinks, keep us always in remembrance.

And so this is how we were. We offered comfort to Verecundus in his sadness, assuring him that our conversion would not put an end to our friendship and encouraging him to embrace the faith appropriate to his status, that is, to married life. And we awaited the time when Nebridius would follow us. He was so close that he could easily have done it, and he was already on the verge of doing so by the time those days had at last run their course. For it did seem that those days were long and many, because we greatly desired the freedom and leisure to sing to you from our innermost being, "My heart has said to you, 'I have sought your face; your face, O Lord, I will seek.'" *Ps. 26:8*

4.7   The day came when I was set free from the profession of rhetoric in actual fact; I had already been set free from it in thought, but now it was done. You rescued my tongue from it as you had already rescued my heart, and I blessed you with joy when I arrived at the country house with all my friends. The books recording the discussions I had with my friends who were with me,[10] and the dialogue I had with

---

9. "once a freedman but now your adoptive son": *ex liberto filius*. The expression is obscure. Chadwick takes it to mean that he was "God's freedman by baptism, adopted son in paradise." But it seems unlikely that Augustine would think baptism itself falls short of making someone God's son or daughter by adoption. Another possibility, suggested by Chadwick and (perhaps) implied by Boulding, is that Nebridius had the social status of a freedman. More remote still is the possibility that *Augustine* is the freedman and Nebridius *his* adoptive son ("most unlikely," as O'Donnell rightly says). My translation is deliberately non-committal, though it excludes the last of these possibilities.
10. *Against the Academics, On the Happy Life,* and *On Order.*

myself alone in your presence,[11] bear witness that what I wrote there was indeed already in your service, though in this in-between time it still breathed too much of the school of pride.[12] My letters[13] bear witness to what I wrote to Nebridius, who was not with us.

And when will there be time enough for me to recount all your great acts of kindness toward us in those days, especially as I am hastening to things that are greater still? For my memory calls me back there, and it becomes sweet to me, O Lord, to confess to you the inward lashings by which you brought me to heel, and how you made me into level ground, bringing low the mountains and hills of my thoughts, making my crooked places straight and my rough places smooth, and how you made even Alypius, the brother of my heart, subject to the name of your Only-begotten, our Lord and Savior Jesus Christ. He had at first rejected that name as unworthy of being included in our writings, for he wanted them to carry the aroma of the cedars of higher learning, which the Lord has already brought low, rather than the life-giving herbs of your Church that ward off serpents.

Is. 40:4 qtd. Lk. 3:5

Ps. 28:5

4.8   How I lifted up my voice to you, my God, when I read the Psalms of David, those songs of faith, sounds of true religion that banish the spirit swollen with pride! I was still unformed in genuine love for you, a catechumen at leisure in a country house with Alypius, likewise a catechumen. My mother clung to us with the tenderness of a woman, the robust faith of a man, the steadfastness of age, the charity of a mother, and true Christian piety. How I lifted up my voice to you in those Psalms, and how they set me afire in you, so that I burned to recite them before the whole world, if only I could, to confound the arrogance of the human race! And yet indeed they are sung throughout all the world, and no one is hidden from your burning heat. With what passionate and bitter mortification did I despise the Manichees—and yet I pitied them too because they did not know those sacraments, those instruments of healing, and in their sickness they raged against

Ps. 18:5 / Ps. 18:7

---

11. *Soliloquies*, in which Augustine carries on a dialogue with personified Reason.

12. In their edition, Gibb and Montgomery say, "The point of the comparison seems to be that the pride of the schools was still noticeable in his style, as the loud breathing of the combatants in a gymnastic contest continues after the bout is over" (O'Donnell III:83). Perhaps, but a *pausatio* (a new word in the fourth century) need not be an ending; it can be an interruption or interval. So taken, Augustine could be saying that the school of pride was still breathing heavily through his writings like a boxer between rounds—but that would suggest an impending return to the fight, which Augustine does not envisage. So I take *pausatio* as an "in-between time," when his writing betrays a still-too-confident Platonism not yet fully disciplined by Scripture and Christian doctrine, as it will later come to be.

13. Letters 3 and 4.

the medicine that could have made them well. I could wish that they were there with me, without my knowing it, so that they could see my face and hear my voice when I read the fourth Psalm[14] in that time of leisure. They would hear how that Psalm affected me—"You answered me when I called upon you, O God of my justice; you set me free when I was in distress; have mercy on me, O Lord, and hear my prayer"— *Ps. 4:2* they would hear without my knowing that they were listening, so that they would not suppose the words I spoke in the midst of the words of the Psalm were spoken on their account. For in truth I would not have spoken them, or would not have spoken them in the same way, if I had known that they could hear me and see me; and if I had so spoken, they would not have received my words in the way that I spoke them to myself and in your presence, giving voice to the deepest devotion of my mind.

4.9   I shuddered with fear and at the same time burned with hope and exultation in your mercy, Father. And all these went forth through *Ps. 30:8* my eyes and my voice when your good Spirit turned to us and said to *Ps. 142:10* us, "Children of men, how long will your hearts be hardened? Why do you love emptiness and seek after a lie?" For truly I had loved emptiness *Ps. 4:3* and sought after a lie, and you, O Lord, had already magnified your Holy One, raising him from the dead and setting him at your right hand; and from there he sent from on high the one he had promised, *Lk. 24:49; Jn.* the Paraclete, the Spirit of truth. Your Holy One had already sent him, *15:26 / Jn.* but I did not know it. He had sent him, because he had already been *14:16–17* magnified by his rising from the dead and his ascending into heaven, whereas before that time the Spirit had not yet been given, since Jesus had not yet been glorified. And the prophecy cries out, "How long will *Jn. 7:39* your hearts be hardened? Why do you love emptiness and seek after a lie? Know that the Lord has magnified his Holy One." It cries out, *Ps. 4:3–4* "How long?"; it cries out, "Know." And for so long I did not know; for so long I loved emptiness and sought after a lie. And so I heard these words and trembled, because I remembered that I had been like those of whom these words were spoken. For I had clung to phantasms in place of the truth, and in them there was emptiness and a lie. Deep and fierce were my many groans from the pain of this memory. If only those who still love emptiness and seek after a lie could have heard them: perhaps they would have been confounded and vomited up their error. And you would hear them when they cried out to you, for the *Ps. 30:23*

---

14. 9.4.8 through 9.4.11 offer an extended reading of Psalm 4. For Augustine's text of the Psalm, see Appendix A.

one who intercedes with you for us died for us, died a true death in   Rom. 8:34 / Rom.
his flesh.   5:9

4.10   I read, "Be angry and do not sin," and oh, how this stirred me,   Ps. 4:5
my God! For I had already learned to be angry with myself for my past
sins, so that I might sin no more. And I was right to be angry, for it
was not some other nature from the race of darkness that sinned in me,
as those who are not angry with themselves say, storing up wrath for
themselves on the day of wrath, the day when your righteous judgment
will be revealed.   Rom. 2:5
   Likewise my goods were no longer outside me; they were not to be
sought by the eyes of the flesh in the light of this earthly sun. For those
who desire to rejoice in what is outside themselves easily become empty: Rom. 1:21
they are poured out into things that are seen, temporal things, and in   2 Cor. 4:18
the hunger of their thought they lick the images of those things. If only
they would grow weary of their starvation and say, "Who will show us
good things?" And let us say—and let them hear—"The light of your   Ps. 4:6
countenance has set its seal upon us, O Lord." For we ourselves are not   Ps. 4:7
the Light that enlightens every human being; no, we are enlightened   Jn. 1:9
by you, so that we who once were darkness may be light in you. If only   Eph. 5:8
they could see this inward light! I had tasted it, and because I had tasted   Ps. 33:9; 1 Pet. 2:3
it I gnashed my teeth in frustration because I had no power to show it
to them. If only they would set before me their hearts, which have their
eyes fixed on things outside you, and say to me, "Who will show us
good things?" It was there: there, in the place where I was angry, in the   Ps. 4:6
inner chamber where I felt the stings of remorse, where I had made my   Mt. 6:6
sacrifice to you, offering up my old nature and looking to you in hope   Ps. 4:5 / Eph. 4:22;
as I began to set my thoughts upon a life made new; there, where I had   Col. 3:9 / 2 Cor.
begun to taste your sweetness, where you had given me gladness in my   4:16; Col. 3:10
heart. As I read these things with my outward eyes and acknowledged   Ps. 4:7
them within me, I shouted for joy. And it was not my will that earthly
goods be multiplied for me, consuming times even as times consumed
me, for in your eternal simplicity I had other grain and wine and oil.   Ps. 4:8

4.11   At the next line I cried out from the depths of my heart, "Oh,
in peace! Oh, in the Selfsame!"[15] Oh, what does it say? "I will lie down
and fall asleep." For who will withstand us when the saying that is writ-   Ps. 4:9
ten shall come to pass: "Death is swallowed up in victory"? And you   1 Cor. 15:54
are truly the Selfsame, you who do not change, and in you is rest that   Mal. 3:6
makes us forget all our labors, for there is none besides you, and there   Gn. 41:51 / Deut.
                                                                        4:35; Is. 45:5

_____

15. See 1.6.10, fn. 7.

will be no more striving for the many things that are not what you are: no, it is in unity, O Lord, that you have established me in hope.

Ps. 4:10

I went on reading, and I was on fire, and I could find nothing to do for those who were deaf and dead, as I had been, a plague, bitterly and blindly carping against writings that are sweet with the honey of your heaven and bright with your light. But now I was sickened by the enemies of your Scriptures.

Ps. 118:103

Ps. 118:105; Jn. 1:9, 8:12 / Ps. 138:21

4.12 When will I have time to recount all the days of that vacation? But I have not forgotten them, and I will not pass over in silence the bitterness of your chastisement and the marvelous quickness of your mercy. You tormented me then with toothache, and when it grew so bad that I could no longer speak, it entered into my heart to entreat all those who were with me to pray on my behalf to you, the God of every kind of salvation.[16] I wrote this on a wax tablet and gave it to them to read. No sooner had we fallen to our knees in fervent prayer than the pain went away. But what was the pain? And how did it go away? I was filled with holy fear, I admit, my Lord, my God. I had never experienced such a thing in my life: your purposes for me had penetrated to the very depths of my being. Rejoicing in faith, I praised your Name, and that faith did not allow me to feel assurance concerning my past sins, for which I had not yet been forgiven through your baptism.

1 Cor. 2:9

Ps. 17:47, 37:23

Jn. 20:28

Ps. 144:2; Sir. 51:15

5.13 When the Vintage Vacation had come to an end, I resigned my post. The people of Milan would have to look for some other salesman of words for their students. The reasons were that I had chosen to serve you, and also that I was no longer capable of doing the job because of my difficulty breathing and the pains in my chest. And I wrote letters to your bishop Ambrose, that holy man, acknowledging my past errors and my present resolution. I asked him to advise me concerning the best way to go about reading your Scriptures, so that I could be better prepared and fitter to receive such great grace. He recommended the prophet Isaiah, I think because he foretells, more clearly than anyone else, the Gospel and the calling of the Gentiles. But when I began to read it, I could make no sense of it; and thinking the whole book would be more of the same, I decided to put off any further reading until I had become better acquainted with the Lord's way of speaking.

6.14 When the time had come for me to give in my name for baptism, we left the countryside and returned to Milan. Alypius, too,

---

16. "salvation": *salutis*, also meaning health; hence Augustine's addition of the word *omnimodae*, "every kind of," to express that God is the God of both salvation from sin and healing from illness.

desired to be reborn in you along with me. He had already put on the humility that befits your sacraments and had vigorously subdued his body, to the point that with extraordinary daring he would walk around barefoot on the cold Italian ground. We included in our company the boy Adeodatus, who had been born of the sin of my flesh. You had made him a remarkable young man. He was about fifteen years old, but he surpassed in intellectual talent many serious and learned men. I praise you for your gifts, O Lord my God, Creator of all things and wondrously powerful in bringing form to our deformities. For I had brought nothing to that boy but my sin. We gave him the nourishment of your teaching, but it was you alone, and no other, who inspired us to do so. I praise you for your gifts. My book entitled *On the Teacher* is a discussion between him and me. You know that all the words I put in the mouth of my interlocutor in that book were his own thoughts, when he was sixteen years old. And I experienced many other great things from him at other times, things more marvelous still: his brilliance dumbfounded me. Who besides you could work such miracles? It was not long before you took his life from this earth, and I call him to mind with full confidence; nothing from his boyhood or adolescence makes me afraid; indeed, I have no fear at all on his account. He was our companion as one of the same age as we were in your grace, standing in need of training in your teaching.

Rom. 13:14; Col. 3:12

And we were baptized,[17] and all anxiety over our past life vanished. In those days[18] I could not have enough of the wonderful sweetness of meditating on the depth of your plan for the salvation of the human race. How I wept as your hymns and songs were sung, cut to the quick by the voices of your Church lifted up in sweet music! Those voices flooded my ears, and your truth poured forth as a clear stream into my heart, welling up into passionate devotion; the tears flowed, and it was good for me that they did.

Rom. 11:33

Eph. 5:19

7.15 The Church in Milan had only recently begun to employ this form of comfort and encouragement; the brethren lifted up their voices

---

17. Ambrose himself baptized Augustine at the Easter Vigil during the night of 24–25 April 387. As early as the time of Charlemagne (742–814) the legend had arisen that Augustine and Ambrose improvised the *Te Deum* (which begins "We praise thee, O God; we acknowledge thee to be the Lord"—"acknowledge" being a form of the verb that gives us the noun translated "Confessions") as Augustine came up from the font. This was probably the first time that Augustine witnessed the full Eucharistic liturgy, and certainly the first time he received Communion.

18. The days from Easter through the Sunday following, when newly initiated Christians retained their white baptismal garments and were given further daily instruction in the faith. Many such Easter Week sermons from Augustine himself survive.

together with great enthusiasm. It had been a year, or not much longer, since Justina, mother of the boy-king Valentinian, was persecuting
your man Ambrose in the interest of her heresy; she had been led astray
by the Arians.[19] The devout congregation kept watch in the church,
prepared to die with their bishop, your servant. My mother, your handmaid, was there, foremost among them all in her care and watchful-
ness, fully alive with her prayers. We were still cold, untouched by the
heat of your Spirit, but we were excited by the chaos and disturbance
in the city. At that time the singing of hymns and psalms in the manner of the Eastern churches was introduced, so that the people would
not grow faint from sorrow and fatigue. The practice has been kept up
from that time until today, and many, perhaps nearly all, of your flocks
throughout the world now do likewise.

Ps. 115:16

7.16 It was at this time that you revealed to Bishop Ambrose,
through a vision, the place where the bodies of the martyrs Protasius
and Gervasius were hidden. You had concealed them, uncorrupted, for
many years in a treasury known only to you, so that at the right time
you could bring them forth to restrain the fury of a woman—albeit
a woman of the royal house. For when their tombs had been opened
and their bodies dug up, and they were brought with due honor to
the basilica of Ambrose, those who were troubled with unclean spirits
were healed, the demons themselves making their confession. And not
only that, but one citizen, quite well known in the city, who had been
blind for many years, asked what was the cause of the people's noisy
celebration. When he was told, he leapt to his feet and asked his guide
to lead him there. Upon arriving, he begged to be allowed in so that
he could touch with his handkerchief the bier on which lay the bodies of your saints, whose death is precious in your sight. When he did
this and touched the handkerchief to his eyes, immediately they were
opened. From there the story spread, your people praised you fervently,
with hearts aglow, and the mind of your enemy, though not brought
to healing faith, was at least checked in her frenzied desire to persecute.
Thanks be to you, my God!

Lk. 6:18

Ps. 115:15

From what source, and to what purpose, have you guided my recollection so that I might confess even these things to you, when I have
passed over many important things that I have forgotten? And yet at
that time, when your anointing oils spread their sweet fragrance, we

---

19. Arians denied the full divinity of Christ. Justina was the second wife of Valentinian I and the
mother of Valentinian II, who became emperor (nominally) at the age of four in 375. The events
that Augustine goes on to recount took place when Justina demanded that Ambrose make a church
available for the Arians within the city walls.

were not chasing after you. And it was for this reason that I wept so much when your hymns were sung: for so long I had been sighing for you, and now at last I had begun to breathe you in—so far as air was free to move in a house of grass.[20]

Song 1:3

2 Cor. 5:1 / Is. 40:6

8.17 You, who make those who dwell together in a house to be of one accord, brought into our fellowship Evodius, a young man from our hometown. While serving as an *agens in rebus*,[21] he had turned to you—this was before we did—and was baptized; he left the service of the world and was bound to you. We were together, and we made a holy decision that we would dwell together in the future. Seeking a place where we could be of the greatest use in your service, we made ready to return as a group to Africa. And while we were at Ostia on the Tiber,[22] my mother died.

Ps. 67:7

I am leaving out many things, for I am in great haste: accept my confessions and thanksgivings, O Lord, even for the countless things I am passing over in silence. But I will not pass over whatever my soul brings forth concerning your servant who brought me forth both in her flesh, that I might be born into this temporal light, and in her heart, that I might be born into light eternal. I will speak, not of her gifts, but of your gifts in her. For she did not make herself or bring herself up: you created her—neither her mother nor her father knew what sort of person their child would become—and the rod of your Christ, the discipline of your Only-begotten, trained her in reverence for you in a faithful household, by a good member of your Church.

Ps. 22:4

Ps. 5:8

But she did not speak as much about the careful discipline she received from her mother as she did about what she received from an elderly servant who had carried her father on her back when he was an infant, as nearly grown girls so often carry younger children. For this reason, and because of her age and excellent character, she was held in great honor by her masters in that Christian household and was entrusted with the care of the master's daughters, a task she carried out faithfully. She was stern with holy severity in correcting them when there was need, and she showed solid good sense in teaching them. For she would

---

20. 2 Corinthians 5:1 says, "We know that if the earthly house in which we dwell is destroyed, we have a building from God, a house not made with hands, eternal in the heavens." The "house" is therefore not merely the body, but the whole of our earthly life as "flesh": temporary, deficient, destined to be "further clothed, so that what is mortal may be swallowed up by life," as Paul goes on to say. Augustine adds "of grass" because of Isaiah 40:6, "All flesh is grass." Augustine comments strikingly in *en. Ps.* 102.23, "All flesh is grass, and the Word was made flesh. . . . What abides in eternity has not scorned to take upon himself grass, so that grass would not be bereft of hope."

21. For the meaning of *agens in rebus* see 8.6.15, fn. 15.

22. Cf. Virgil, *Aeneid* 1.13–14.

not let them drink water, even if they were parched with thirst, except at mealtimes, when they were nourished quite moderately at their parents' table. She was taking care that they not develop a bad habit, and she added this sound advice: "For now you drink water, because you can-not drink wine. But once you are married and take charge of the store-houses and cellars, water will not satisfy you, but the habit of drinking will overpower you." By the reasonableness of this instruction and her authoritative way of giving commands, she restrained the eager desire of a tender age and imposed an honorable limit on the girls' very thirst, so that they would not even desire what was not fitting.

2 Tim. 1:13; Tit. 2:8

8.18   It did creep up on her, though, as your servant told me, her son; drunkenness did creep up on her. It was her parents' custom to send her, as a reliable young girl, to draw the wine from the cask. She would plunge the cup through the opening at the top and then, before she poured it into the jug, she would put it to her lips for a tiny sip—no more than that, because she disliked the taste. She did not do this out of a desire to get drunk, but just from an excess of the high spir-its of youth, which often find boisterous release in playful acts of the sort that adults, with their weightier judgment, suppress in immature minds. And so by adding to that small sip a little more every day (for one who scorns small things falls little by little) she fell into a habit, and before long she was greedily drinking small cups full of wine.

Sir. 19:1

What had become then of that wise old woman and her stern pro-hibition? Did it have no power against that secret sickness unless your medicine,[23] O Lord, watched over us? Her father and mother and guardians were not there, but you were present: you who created us, who call us, who work for our good and for the salvation of our souls even through those who are placed in authority over us. What were you doing then, my God? How did you cure her? How did you restore her to health? Did you not wield the harsh and sharp outcry from another soul as a healing sword, drawn from your hidden providence, and with a single stroke cut off that rottenness? For the servant who used to accompany her to the cask was quarreling with her young mistress, as sometimes happens, and when they were alone together she threw my mother's misdeeds in her face with a bitter insult, calling her a drunk-ard. Pierced by this rebuke, she looked upon her own uncleanness and immediately condemned it and cast it off.

---

23. "your medicine" is, implicitly, Christ, as also at 7.8.12, "Through the hidden hand of your medicine, my swelling subsided, and the turbulent and clouded gaze of my mind was being healed" (and see fn. 11 there). The connection is explicit at 9.13.35, "Hear me through the Medicine for our wounds, who hung upon the tree, and now is seated at your right hand and intercedes for us."

Just as the praises of friends lead us astray, so too the rebukes of our enemies often set us back on the right path. But you repay them, not for what you do through them, but for what they themselves will. That girl in her anger wanted to antagonize her young mistress, not to heal her. That is why she spoke in private, either because the quarrel happened to break out at a time and place where they were alone, or perhaps because she was afraid she would be in trouble for taking so long to report it. You, O Lord, Ruler of things in heaven and things on earth, bend to your own purposes the depths of the torrent, the turbulent flow of the ages on which you impose your order. By the madness of one soul you healed another, so that no one who observes this will credit his own power if someone else whom he intended to correct is corrected by his words.

9.19   And so she was brought up modestly and soberly; it was you who made her obedient to her parents, rather than they who made her obedient to you. When she reached the age to be married,[24] she was given to her husband and served him as her master. She did everything she could to win him to you, speaking about you to him through her actions, by which you made her beautiful, worthy of reverent love, and wonderful in the eyes of her husband. She bore with his unjust use of the marriage bed[25] and had no quarrel with her husband on that account. For she was awaiting your mercy upon him, so that he would be made chaste through believing in you. Now in those days he was outstandingly generous but equally quick-tempered. But she knew not to oppose her husband when he was angry: not in what she did, not even in what she said. Instead she would wait for the right time, when his anger had cooled and he was calm, and then she would explain to him why she had acted as she did, in case he had perhaps reacted without giving the matter sufficient thought. Many wives with gentler husbands bore the marks of beatings on their disfigured faces, and in their friendly talks together they would complain about their husbands' conduct. But my mother, in a lighthearted tone but with utter seriousness, warned them against such talk. From the time they heard the marriage contract read out, she said, they should have regarded it as a legal document making them handmaids of their husbands; from then on they should be mindful of their status and not rise up in pride against their lords. Her friends, knowing what a foul-tempered husband she had to put up with, were astounded that no one had ever heard, or seen any

Eph. 5:22

1 Pet. 3:1–2

Ps. 85:13

1 Pet. 1:22; 1 Jn. 3:3

---

24. Cf. Virgil, *Aeneid* 7.53.
25. "unjust use of the marriage bed": *iniurias cubilis.* Most likely not "infidelities" (as some translators have it) or spousal abuse, but excessive or improperly directed passion.

indication, that Patrick beat his wife, or that they were at odds with each other over some domestic quarrel even for a day. In their friendly conversation they asked her why that was, and she taught them the approach on which she had decided, which I described earlier. Those who followed her advice discovered its value and were happy; those who ignored it were left oppressed and troubled.

9.20   She won over even her mother-in-law, who had at first been set against her by the whispers of mischievous servant girls, by her obedience and her unstinting patience and gentleness: so much so that her mother-in-law went of her own accord to her son to expose the meddling tongues of the servant girls that had shattered the domestic peace between her and her daughter-in-law, and to insist that they be punished. And so he, in obedience to his mother and out of concern for discipline within his family and harmony among those belonging to his household, subjected the girls to beatings, just as his mother had decided. She assured them that anyone who spoke ill of her daughter-in-law thinking it would please her should expect such punishment from her. No one dared to say anything more, and the mutual goodwill of their life together was remarkable for its sweetness.

9.21   And there was another great gift you had bestowed on your good servant, in whose womb you had created me, my God, my mercy: whenever she could, she offered herself as a peacemaker between souls who were at variance and quarreling. When she heard them say severe and bitter words about each other—the sort of acrimonious words that are brought up like vomit from the heaving and indigestion of strife, when the caustic speech of a present friend about her absent enemy gives vent to the glutted stomach of her hatreds—she would say nothing to either about the other except what might serve to reconcile them. I would think this only a small good were it not that I have sorrowful experience of countless hordes of people—infected by who knows what sort of plague of sins, seeping out in some utterly mysterious way—who do not merely pass on what one angry enemy said of another, but even add things that were not said at all. But it should be a matter of simple humanity to refrain from instigating or fomenting enmity by malicious speech, if not indeed to work hard to put an end to it by speaking graciously. Such a person was my mother, because you, her inmost Teacher, had taught her thus in the schoolroom of her deepest self.[26]

Ps. 58:18

---

26. As O'Donnell points out, in the first six books *magister*, "teacher," is often "schoolmaster"; here, for the first time, and from now on, the Teacher is Christ. For Christ as the sole teacher of intelligible truth, see Augustine's dialogue *On the Teacher* (*De magistro*), mentioned earlier in this Book (9.6.14).

9.22   At last she also won her husband for you near the end of his   *1 Pet. 3:1*
life in this world, and once he had been baptized she no longer had
any cause to complain of the things she had borne with before he was
baptized. And she was a servant of your servants: all of your servants
who knew her praised and honored and loved you greatly in her, for
they recognized your presence in her heart, attested by the fruits of her
holy life. For she had been the wife of one husband; she had made due   *Tob. 14:17; Mt.*
repayment to her parents; she had managed her household religiously;   *7:20; 1 Pet. 3:11 /*
1 Tim. 5:9 /
she was well attested for her good deeds. She had brought up her chil-   *1 Tim. 5:4*
dren, laboring again and again to give them birth whenever she saw   *1 Tim. 5:10 / Gal.*
they were going astray from you. Finally, Lord, in the days before she   *4:19*
fell asleep[27] in you, when we were all living together as companions
after we had received the grace of your baptism, she took such great
care of all of us, your servants—for it is by your Gift[28] that you allow us
to speak—as though she were the mother of each of us, and she served
us as though we were all her fathers.

10.23   Now when the day on which she was to depart this life was
close at hand (what day that was, you knew, but we did not), it came
to pass—and I believe that you arranged this, by the hidden working
of your providence—that she and I were standing alone together, leaning against a window that looked out on a garden within the house
where we were staying at Ostia on the Tiber, where we could be away
from the crowds after the fatigue of a long journey and rest before we
set sail. We were talking together very sweetly, just the two of us, and
forgetting what lies behind and straining forward to what lies ahead,   *Phil. 3:13*
we were asking each other, in the presence of the Truth, which you
yourself are, what the eternal life of your saints will be like, which no   *Jn. 14:6; 2 Pet.*
eye has seen, nor ear heard, nor has it entered into the human heart.   *1:12 / Is. 64:4;*
1 Cor. 2:9
But with the mouth of our heart we were panting after the heavenly
streams that flow from your fount, the fount of life, which is in your   *Ps. 35:10*
presence; we longed to be sprinkled with the water from that fount,
so far as our capacity allowed, so that we might somehow conceive so
great a thing.

10.24   And when our conversation had reached such a point that it
seemed to us that no pleasure of the senses of the flesh, however great,
in any bodily light, however splendid, was worthy to be compared
with the joy of that life—no, not worthy even to be mentioned in

---

27. "Falling asleep" is Biblical language for death in anticipation of resurrection: see, in particular,
John 11:11–12, Acts 13:36, 1 Corinthians 6:15–20, and 1 Thessalonians 4:13–15.
28. "Gift" is capitalized here because it refers to God the Holy Spirit.

the same breath—we lifted ourselves up, with affections more fiercely enkindled, to the Selfsame. Step by step we traversed all bodily things, *Ps. 4:9* and even the heavens from which the sun and moon and stars shed their light upon the earth. And we climbed higher still in our inner thoughts and speech and in wonder at your works: and we entered into *Rom. 1:20* our own minds and passed beyond them until we reached that land of unfailing plenty where you feed the flock of Israel for ever with the *Ez. 34:14; Ps. 79:2* food of truth, where life is the Wisdom by whom all things were made, *Jn. 1:3* both those that once were and those that are yet to be; but Wisdom is not made: she[29] is as she always was and always will be. Or rather, there is no "was" or "will be" in Wisdom, but only *is*: for she is eternal, and what was or will be is not eternal. And while we were speaking and gazing at her with eager longing, we touched her—just barely—with the utmost energy of our hearts.

And we sighed and left the first fruits of our spirit[30] bound there; we *Rom. 8:23* returned to the noise of our mouths, where a word has a beginning and an ending. How little like your Word, our Lord, who abides for ever in himself without growing old, and makes all things new! *Wisd. 7:27*

10.25   So we said,
   "if for someone the noise of the flesh fell silent,
         images of earth and water and air fell silent,
         the heavens fell silent,
         and the soul itself fell silent and transcended itself by thinking
            no longer of itself;
   if dreams and revelatory visions fell silent,
         every tongue, every sign, and whatever speaks only by passing
            away:
   if for someone all these things fell completely silent—
         for if someone heard them, all of them would say, 'we did not
            make ourselves; no, he who abides for ever made us'; *Sir. 18:1; Ps. 32:11,*
         if, having said these things, they ceased to speak, *116:2; Is. 40:8;*
            Jn. 12:34 / Ps.
            because they had turned our ears to the one who made *99:3*
            them—

---

29. Though "Wisdom" here refers to Christ, the Latin word (*sapientia*) is feminine, so I use feminine pronouns, as Augustine does.

30. Although Paul's use of the expression "first fruits of the spirit" is most naturally taken to mean the first workings of the Holy Spirit in the human soul, Augustine takes the "first fruits" to be an offering to God (a frequent usage in the Old Testament) of what is best and highest in the human spirit, thus "bound" as for sacrifice, a token of the complete dedication of the whole person to God in the life of the world to come.

and he spoke, not through them, but through himself,

> so that we might hear his Word, not by any bodily tongue,

Jn. 1:1

> not through the voice of an angel or a noise from the clouds,

Gn. 22:11 / Ex.
33:9; Ps. 76:18 /
Num. 12:8; 1
Cor. 13:12

> not by any riddling likeness,

> but himself, the very one whom we love in these things:

if we were to hear him apart from these things,

>> as we now strain forward and with our fleeting thought touch
>> the eternal Wisdom who abides above all things,

Phil. 3:13

>> if this could endure, and all the visions that fall so far short of this
>> could vanish away,

>> and this vision alone were to seize the one who beholds it and take
>> full possession of him and hide him away in inner joys,

>> so that the momentary knowledge that had left us sighing
>> would endure as life everlasting:

is not this what it would mean to 'enter into the joy of your Lord'?

Mt. 15:21

And when will this be?

Will it be when we all rise again, but we are not all changed?"[31]

1 Cor. 15:51

10.26   Such were the things I said, even if not in just this way or exactly these words. Yet you know, Lord, that on that day when we had this conversation, and in the midst of our words this world and all its pleasures came to seem worthless in our eyes, my mother said, "Son, as for me, I no longer have pleasure in anything in this present life. I do not know what there is left for me to do here, and why I remain here, now that everything I hoped for in this world has been fulfilled. There was but one thing for which I wanted to remain yet a little while in this present life: to see you a catholic Christian before I died. And God has granted this to me even more abundantly than I had hoped, for I see that you have even spurned earthly happiness to be his servant. What, then, am I doing here?"

11.27   How I replied to her words I do not clearly remember, for about that time—within five days, or not much longer—she took to her bed with fever. One day during her illness she lost consciousness and for a short time was unaware of what was going on around her. We ran to her, but she quickly regained consciousness. She looked at my brother and me standing there, and asked us, "Where was I?" in the way that someone who is looking for something might do. Then,

---

31. The version of 1 Corinthians 15:51 that Augustine knows ("We shall all rise again, but we shall not all be changed") differs from ours ("We shall not all sleep, but we shall all be changed"). He takes it to mean that the just and the unjust alike will all be resurrected, but only the just will be changed so as to have a spiritual body free from all weakness and pain.

seeing us thunderstruck with grief, she said, "Bury your mother here."
I was silent, holding back my tears, but my brother said something to
the effect that he hoped she would not die abroad, but in her homeland, for that would be more auspicious. When she heard this, her
distress showed on her face and her eyes rebuked him for entertaining
such thoughts; then she turned from him and looked at me and said,
"Can you believe what he is saying?" And then she said to both of us,
"Bury this body anywhere; do not worry about it at all. All I ask is that
you remember me at the altar of the Lord, wherever you may be." And
when she had made her meaning clear to us in such words as she could
manage to speak, she fell silent, in agony as her illness grew worse.

11.28   But I pondered your gifts, O invisible God, the gifts that you *Col. 1:15*
send into the hearts of your faithful people, gifts that produce such
astonishing fruits, and I rejoiced and gave thanks to you,[32] because I *Col. 1:3*
remembered what I had known so well: she had always been passionately concerned about the grave she had provided and made ready for
herself next to the body of her husband. Because they had lived together
so harmoniously, she had wanted (so small is the power of the human
mind to grasp the things of God!) to be granted the further happiness
that after her journey overseas, the husband and wife whose earthly
bodies had been joined together in life would be joined together under
the same earth, and that everyone would remember this and speak of it.
But when, by your abundant goodness, this foolishness had begun to
leave her heart, I was not aware of it; and now I rejoiced, marveling that
this change had become evident to me in this way—though during our
conversation at the window, when she asked "What am I doing here?",
she had given no indication that she longed to die in her homeland. I
heard later that when we were already at Ostia she had been talking one
day in her trusting, motherly way with some of my friends about scorn
for this life and the blessing of death. I was not there at the time. They
were astonished at such masculine resolve on the part of a woman—for
you had given it to her—and asked her whether she did not fear leaving her body so far from her own city. "Nothing," she said, "is far from
God, and there is no reason to fear that he will not know where to find *Acts 17:27*
me so that he can raise me again at the end of the age."

---

32. Both allusions to Paul's Letter to the Colossians have Christological overtones: "[Christ] is the
image of the invisible God, the firstborn of all creation" (Colossians 1:15); "We give thanks to God,
the Father of our Lord Jesus Christ" (Colossians 1:3). And since for Augustine the Holy Spirit is pre-
eminently the giver of gifts and himself the pre-eminent gift sent from God into the human heart
(see, for example, Luke 24:29, John 14:16–17 and 15:26, and Romans 5:5), this passage is firmly,
though quietly, Trinitarian.

So on the ninth day of her illness, in the fifty-sixth year of her age, in the thirty-third year of my age, that devout and pious soul was set free from the body.

12.29 I closed her eyes, and an immense sorrow welled up in the depths of my heart and was ready to flow forth in tears; yet in that moment, by a fierce command of my mind, my eyes held back the flood until it dried up, and the struggle caused me great pain. But when she breathed her last, the child Adeodatus wailed with grief; all of us restrained him and kept him quiet. And in this way something childish in myself that would have burst into tears was restrained and hushed by the more grown-up voice of my heart. For we did not judge it fitting to observe her burial rites with the tearful lamentations and cries of sorrow with which people often bewail the misery of the dying or mourn as if the dead were altogether gone. For she had not died in misery,   *1 Thess. 4:13* nor was she altogether dead. The testimony of her way of life and her unfeigned faith gave us unshakeable reasons to be confident of this.   *1 Tim. 1:5*

12.30   What was it, then, that made the grief I kept inside me such a heavy burden? Just this: we had grown accustomed to living together, such sweet and precious companionship, and its sudden ending was a fresh wound. I did take comfort in the solemn words she spoke in the final days of her illness, thanking me kindly for my help and calling me a dutiful son; she recalled with great affection that she had never heard from my lips a harsh word or an insolent expression hurled against her. But my God, who made us, how was the respect I showed her in any   *Ps. 99:3; Bar. 4:7* way similar, in any way worthy of comparison, to the service she had done for me? And so because I was now deprived of the great comfort I had from her, my soul was wounded, and the one life in which my life and hers had been joined was ripped apart.

12.31   Once the boy's tears had been checked, Evodius took up a Psalter and began to sing a Psalm. All of us in the house joined in: "I will sing of your mercy and judgment, O Lord."[33] Now when they   *Ps. 100:1* heard what was happening, many brothers and religious women gathered, and while those whose duty it was made arrangements for the funeral according to custom, I withdrew as politely as I could to a place where I could be with friends who did not think I should be left alone, and I engaged in such discussion as was suitable for the occasion, applying the truth as a balm to lighten my anguish: you knew my anguish, but they did not; they listened intently and thought I had no feeling of sorrow. But in your ears, where none of them could hear,

---

33. Augustine's text of Psalm 100 is translated in Appendix C.

I railed against the softness of my affection and dammed the flood of grief, and it did abate, though only a very little. Then it returned with renewed vehemence, and though I did not break into tears and the grief did not show on my face, I did know very well how heavy a burden lay upon my heart. And because I violently resented that these human feelings had such great power over me—though indeed they must come about in due order, because such is the condition of human life—my grief over my grief added sorrow to sorrow, and I was steeped in a twofold sadness.

12.32   When the body was borne out, we went out and returned without shedding a tear. Not even in the prayers that we poured out to you when the sacrifice of our redemption was offered for her next to her tomb, where the body had been laid before it was buried, as is the custom there—not even in those prayers did I weep. But the whole day my grief oppressed me, though no one could see it, and with a troubled mind I begged you with all my might to heal my sorrow. But you did not—meaning, I believe, to impress upon my mind by this one example that every kind of habit is bondage, even for a mind that is no longer fed by any deceitful word.

And it struck me as a good idea to go to the baths, for I had heard that the baths derived their name from the Greek word *balanion*, because they banish trouble from the mind.[34] And I confess to your mercy, O Father of orphans, that I bathed, and I was no different from what I had been before I bathed; I had not sweated out the bitterness of grief from my heart. Then I went to sleep, and when I awoke I found that my sorrow had been greatly relieved, so much so that as I sat alone on my bed, I called to mind the truthful verses of your servant Ambrose. For you are

> God, Creator of all things that are,
> ruling the firmament, and clothing
> day with robes of light,
> granting gracious sleep at night,
> to weary laborers giving rest
> that they return to work refreshed:
> calm and lighten weary minds,
> and set free those enchained by grief.[35]

Ps. 67:6

---

34. The etymology proposed here—from *ballo*, "to cast away," and *ania*, "sorrow"—is not actually correct.
35. A hymn for evening, evidently one of Augustine's favorites, because he quotes or alludes to it frequently in the *Confessions* (2.6.12, 4.10.15, 5.5.9, 6.4.5, 9.6.14, 10.34.52, 11.37.45) and elsewhere; Monnica herself quotes it in *On the Happy Life* 4.35. I have tried to translate as literally as possible while preserving something of the rhythm of the Latin, an effort in which I have been helped by the rhyming metrical translation by Charles Bigg in *The New English Hymnal* (Hymn 152).

12.33   And little by little I returned to my earlier thoughts about your handmaid, the devout life she led in you, her holy kindness and forbearance toward us. Now, all at once, I had lost her, and I found comfort in weeping in your sight, about her and for her, about myself and for myself. The tears that I had been holding in I now set free to flow as much as they would, a flood that bore up my heart so that it rested upon them. For it was your ears that heard my weeping, not the ears of any human being who would twist the meaning of my tears to suit his own pride.

And now, O Lord, I confess to you in writing: let anyone who desires read it, and let him interpret it as he desires. And if he finds sin in the tears I shed for my mother for that brief stretch of time—the mother who was, for a time, dead before my eyes, who had wept for me for so many years that I might live before your eyes—let him not mock me; no, rather, if he is great in charity, let him weep himself for my sins to you, the Father of all who are brothers and sisters of your Christ.

13.34   But now that my heart has been healed of that wound, in which I could be blamed for a too-worldly affection,[36] I pour forth to you, our God, tears of a very different kind for your servant, tears that flow from a spirit shaken by thoughts of the dangers that beset every soul that dies in Adam. Although she had been made alive in Christ, and before she was set free from the body she so lived that your Name was praised in her faith and in her conduct, yet I cannot be so bold as to say that from the time when you regenerated her through baptism no word fell from her lips contrary to your commandment. And the Truth, your Son, has said, "If anyone says to his brother, 'You fool,' he will be liable to the hell of fire." Woe betide even a praiseworthy human life if you examine it minutely and leave your mercy behind! But in truth you are not eager to search out our sins, and so we have confidence in our hope that we will find a place with you. If anyone recounts his true merits to you, what is he recounting? Nothing but your own gifts. Oh, that human

1 Cor. 15:22

Tit. 3:5

Mt. 12:36–37

Mt. 5:22

Ps. 129:3

---

36. *in quo poterat redargui carnalis affectus:* super-literally, "in which carnal affection could be charged [against me]." The phrase gives translators fits. Some want to add a concessive word like "perhaps" (Boulding: "in which I was perhaps guilty of some carnal affection"), but the Latin says flat-out that he could in fact be blamed. "Carnal" is also a difficulty; some commentators who have clearly read more Freud than Paul find something vaguely Oedipal here. Chadwick understands Augustine as speaking of an "emotion of physical kinship" and Ruden as "emotions with a mere physical basis." But "carnal" is the regular Pauline (and Augustinian) contrast term for "spiritual": it means "worldly" or "this-worldly," of "the flesh" (*caro*) in the sense of everything about human life that is destined to pass away.

beings might know that they are indeed human, and that anyone who boasts might boast in the Lord!

Ps. 9:21

1 Cor. 1:31; 2 Cor. 10:17

13.35   And so, my praise and my life, I set aside for a brief moment her good deeds, for which I praise you and give you thanks, and now I pray to you on account of my mother's sins. Hear me through the Medicine for our wounds, who hung upon the tree and now is seated at your right hand and intercedes for us. I know that she dealt mercifully with others and heartily forgave their debts. Forgive her her debts, if indeed she incurred any debts in the many years she lived after receiving the water of salvation. Forgive her, Lord; forgive her, I beseech you; do not enter into judgment with her. Let mercy be exalted above judgment,[37] because your words are true and you have promised mercy to those who are merciful. It is by your gift that they are merciful: you will have compassion on those to whom you have shown compassion, and you will show mercy to those on whom you have had mercy.

Ex. 15:2; Deut. 10:21; Ps. 21:4, 117:14; Is. 12:2; Jer. 17:14 / Jn. 14:6 / Ps. 68:14, 142:1; Jdt. 9:17 / Gal. 3:13 qtg.

Deut. 21:23 / Ps. 109:1 / Rom. 8:34 / Mt. 6:12

Ps. 142:2

Jas. 2:13

Mt. 5:7

Rom. 9:15 qtg. Ex. 33:19

13.36   And I believe that you have already done what I am asking of you; but accept, O Lord, the willing tribute of my lips. For when the day of her release was drawing near, she took no thought for having her body buried in a costly tomb or anointed with sweet-smelling spices; she desired no choice memorial and had no concern about being buried in her native land. About these things she had no instructions to give us: she asked only that we remember her at your altar, where she had served you without missing even a single day; for she knew that the sacred Victim was given there, the one who erased the handwriting of the decree that was against us, who defeated the enemy who was reckoning up our sins and looked for some fault in him but found none, in whom we are conquerors. Who is there to repay him for the shedding of his innocent blood? Who is there to restore to him the price by which he bought us and so steal us away from him? Your handmaid bound her soul by the chains of faith to the sacrament of the price of our redemption, and no one will snatch her away from the shelter of your presence. Let no lion or dragon hinder her, not by force, not by stealth.[38] For she will not say that she owes no debt, lest the crafty Accuser convict her of guilt and take possession of her; she will testify that her debts have been forgiven by the one whom no one can repay, who repaid our debts though he owed nothing.

Ps. 118:108

2 Tim. 4:6

Col. 2:14

1 Cor. 6:20, 7:23

Jn. 10:28–29

Ps. 90:13

Mt. 6:12

---

37. Not "let mercy triumph over judgment," for, Augustine says in Letter 167.9.16, mercy "is not opposed to judgment, but is exalted above it, because more people come within the scope of mercy, but only those who themselves have offered mercy."

38. *en. Ps.* s 2.9: "The lion rages openly; the dragon lies in wait stealthily. The devil has both powers."

13.37   Let her therefore be in peace with her husband, her first and only husband, whom she served, offering fruit to you by her forbear- *1 Tim. 5:9* ance, that she might also win him for you. Inspire, O my God, inspire *Lk. 8:15 / 1 Pet.* your servants, my brothers and sisters, your children, my masters, *3:1–2* whom I serve in heart and voice and words: inspire them so that all who read these things will remember your servant Monnica[39] at your altar, with Patrick, once her husband, by whose flesh you brought me into this life, though I do not know how.[40] Let them remember with devout affection my parents in this fleeting light, my brother and sister through you, Father, and our mother the catholic Church, my fellow citizens in the eternal Jerusalem, for which your pilgrim people sigh *Gal. 4:26; Rev.* with longing from their going forth until their return, so that her last *21:2 / Heb.* request of me will be fulfilled more abundantly by the prayers of many, *11:13–14* inspired by these confessions, than by my prayers alone.

---

39. This is the only place in Augustine's works where his mother is named. The manuscripts overwhelmingly give this spelling (with two *n*'s).

40. See 1.6.7. Augustine entertained three possibilities—that the soul is transmitted by the ordinary process of reproduction, that it is created by a special act of God, or that it pre-exists the body—and never found conclusive arguments for or against any of them.

Book Ten

Augustine has been testifying to what he once was; now he testifies to what he is at the time of writing his *Confessions*. He loves God, but how does he know God, and where does he find God? Following the inward-and-upward path he has traveled before, he looks for God first in creatures outside himself, then in the powers of his own soul, from least to greatest, until he comes to memory. There he finds an endlessly mystifying power, storing and retrieving images of sensible things, intelligible realities, the affections of the soul, memory itself—even, paradoxically, forgetfulness. He finds God through the universal human desire for the happy life: the happy life is joy in truth, and God is Truth. Augustine examines his present life under the headings of the lust of the flesh (taking each of the five senses in turn), the lust of the eyes, and worldly ambition, concluding with an appeal for reconciliation with God through the Mediator.

Augustine ponders the benefit of confessing what he has been and what he is now (10.1.1–10.5.7). He looks for God in creatures (10.6.8–10), in the powers of his own soul (10.7.11), and finally in memory (10.8.12–10.28.39). Examining his present life, Augustine first considers the lust of the flesh (10.30.41–10.34.53), considering the temptations of touch (10.30.41–42), taste (10.31.43–47), smell (10.32.48), hearing (10.33.49–50), and sight (10.34.51–53). He then examines the lust of the eyes (10.35.54–57) and, finally, his greatest continuing struggle, worldly ambition or pride (10.36.58–10.39.64). After giving an overview of his discussion of memory and his self-examination (10.40.65–10.41.66), Augustine concludes by invoking Christ as Mediator, priest, intercessor, and atoning sacrifice (10.42.67–10.43.70).

1.1 O you who know me: let me know you; let me know even as I am known. Strength of my soul, come into her and mold her to yourself, so that you might hold her and take her as your own, without spot or blemish. This is my hope. It is the reason I am speaking, and in that hope I rejoice, when my rejoicing is sound. But as for the other things of this life, the more we weep over them, the less they deserve our tears; and the less we weep when we are in the midst of them, the more we ought to weep. For behold, you have loved the truth, because the one who does the truth comes to the light. I am resolved to do the truth in my heart before you in my confession, and to do the truth in my writing before many witnesses.

1 Cor. 8:2–3, 13:12; Gal. 4:9

Eph. 5:27

Rom. 12:12

Ps. 50:8

Eph. 4:15; 1 Jn. 1:6 1 Jn. 3:21

2.2 And indeed, Lord, to whose eyes the depths of the human conscience are laid bare, even if I were not willing to confess to you, what

Sir. 42:18; Heb. 4:13

in me would be hidden from you? I would only hide you from myself, not myself from you. But now that my groaning testifies that I am displeased with myself, you shed your light upon me and please me; you are loved and longed for. And so I blush for myself; I throw myself away and choose you; it is from you alone that I please either you or myself.

So to you, Lord, I am fully known, known exactly as I am. I have explained what benefit I have from my confession to you, a confession I make not in bodily words and sounds, but through the words of my soul and the clamor of my thinking that have reached your ear. For when I am wicked, to confess to you means being displeased with myself; when I am righteous, to confess to you means not ascribing my righteousness to myself. For you, Lord, bless the just; but first you justify the unrighteous. And so, my God, the confession that I make in your sight is made to you both silently and not silently: my speech is silenced, but my affections cry out. For if I tell other people anything of value, it is only what you have already heard from me; and if you hear any such thing from me, it is only what you have already told me. *2 Cor. 5:11 · Ps. 5:13 · Rom. 4:5 · Ps. 95:6*

3.3 So what does it matter to me that human beings should hear my confessions—as though they were the ones to heal all my diseases? They are a race that is energetic in prying into other people's lives but lethargic about correcting their own. Why should they seek to hear from me what I am when they refuse to hear from you what they are? And from what source will they know, when they hear from me about myself, whether I am telling the truth, since no one among human beings knows what goes on inside a human being except the human spirit that is within? But if instead they hear from you about themselves, they will not be able to say, "The Lord is lying." For to hear from you about oneself is simply to know oneself. And if one knows oneself and says, "This is false," one must be lying. But since charity believes all things—at any rate among those whom it binds together into one—I too, Lord, confess to you in such a way that human beings may hear, even though I have no way of showing them that I am telling the truth; yet those whose ears are opened to me by charity believe me. *Ps. 102:3; Mt. 4:23 · 1 Cor. 2:11 · 1 Cor. 13:7 · Eph. 4:2–4*

3.4 Even so, Physician of my inmost self, I ask you to make clear to me what benefit I am to gain from doing this. For when people read and hear the confessions of my evil deeds in the past—deeds that you have forgiven and covered over so that you might make me happy in you, transforming my soul through faith and your Sacrament—their hearts are roused, so that instead of falling asleep in their despair and saying, "I cannot," they remain wakeful, in love with your mercy and *Ps. 31:1 · Song 5:2; Mt. 25:13* the sweetness of your grace, which gives power to all those who, though weak, are brought by that very grace to an awareness of their own weakness. And those who are good are pleased to hear about the past sins of those who are now free from those sins: pleased, not because they are sins, but because the sins that once were are no longer.

But, my Lord, to whom my conscience makes its confession day by day, more confident in the hope of your mercy than in its own innocence, I ask you: what benefit do I gain if, in your presence, I also confess within these pages to human beings, not who I once was, but who I am now? I have already seen and declared the benefit of confessing who I once was. But many people want to know who I am now—now, in this very moment of writing my confessions—both people who know me and people who do not know me. They have heard me, or heard something about me, but have not had their ears up against my heart, where I am whoever I am. So they want to hear as I confess what I am within myself, beyond the reach of their eye or ear or mind. Yet what they want, surely, is not something they will know, but only something they will believe. For the charity that makes them good tells them that I am not lying as I make my confession about myself, and that very charity in them believes me.

4.5   But what benefit do they want from this? Do they desire to rejoice with me when they hear how close I have come to you through your gift, and to pray for me when they hear how much I am held back from you by my own heaviness? To people like this I will disclose myself. It is indeed no meager benefit, O Lord my God, when many people give thanks to you on our behalf, and many prayers are brought before you for our sake. Let brotherly minds love in me what you teach should be loved and lament in me what you teach should be lamented. But let it be a brotherly mind that does this, not one that is estranged, not one of the foreign children whose mouth has spoken vanity and whose right hand is a right hand of iniquity, but a brotherly mind, one that rejoices when it sees good in me and is grieved when it sees something amiss in me. For whether it sees good in me or sees something amiss in me, it loves me. To people like this I will disclose myself, so that they might find relief in what is good in me and grief in what is bad. The good things in me are your works and your gifts; the bad things are my own transgressions and your judgments. Let them find relief in the good things and grief in the bad, and let brotherly hearts, your censers, raise up a hymn and a lamentation before you. But of you, Lord, who take delight in the fragrance of your holy temple, I ask that you have mercy upon me according to your great mercy, for your own Name's

2 Cor. 12:9–10

1 Cor. 13:7

2 Cor. 1:11

Ps. 143:7–8, 143:11

Rev. 8:3–4

1 Cor. 3:17

Ps. 50:3

sake, and that you by no means abandon the work you have begun in me, but complete what remains unfinished.

Mt. 10:22, 24:9; Jn. 15:21 / Phil. 1:6

4.6   This, then, is the benefit in confessing not what I once was but what I am now: that I make my confession not only before you, with a hidden rejoicing mixed with trembling and a hidden sorrow mixed with hope, but also in the ears of those among the children of men who are believers, companions in my joy and sharers in my mortality, my fellow citizens and fellow pilgrims, those who have gone before and those who will follow and those who journey with me in this life. They are your servants, my brothers and sisters; you have chosen them to be your sons and daughters and my masters. You have commanded me to serve them if what I want is to live with you and in dependence on you. And this word of yours would be of little account if it were only a spoken command, but it has also gone before me and done as you have commanded. I carry out this charge in deeds and in words; I carry it out under your wings, and the danger would be too great if my soul were not sheltered beneath your wings and my weakness were not known to you. I am no more than a little child, but my Father lives always, and my Guardian is all-sufficient. For the very one who has begotten me also guards me, and you are yourself every good thing that is mine, O Almighty; you are with me even before I am with you. So to people like these, whom you have commanded me to serve, I will disclose not who I once was, but who I am now, and who I continue to be. But neither do I judge myself. May I be heard, therefore, in just this way.

Ps. 2:11; Phil. 2:12

Jn. 13:15

Ps. 61:2 / Ps. 16:8, 35:8

Ps. 101:28 qtd. Heb. 1:12

1 Cor. 4:3

5.7   For it is you, Lord, who judge me. True, no one knows what is in human beings except the human spirit that is within; yet there is something in each of us that not even the human spirit within us knows. But you, Lord, know everything that is in us, because you made us. And as for me, though in your sight I despise myself and account myself dust and ashes, there is nonetheless something I know about you that I do not know about myself. Truly we now see in a mirror, dimly, and not yet face to face; and so as long as I am wandering away from you, I am more present to myself than to you. Yet I know that you are utterly incapable of falling into dishonor, but I do not know which temptations I will succeed in resisting and which I will not. There is hope, because you are faithful and will not allow us to be tempted beyond what we can bear; but along with temptation you make a way of escape, so that we can endure. Therefore, I will confess what I know about myself, and I will confess what I do not know about myself; for whatever I know about myself, I know it because you shine your light

1 Cor. 2:11

Gn. 18:27; Job 42:6 VL; Sir. 10:9

1 Cor. 13:12

2 Cor. 5:6

1 Cor. 10:13

upon me, and whatever I do not know about myself, I will continue
not to know it until my darkness becomes as the noonday in the light
of your countenance.

Is. 58:10

Ps. 89:8

6.8 I know within myself, unwaveringly and with full conviction,
that I love you. You pierced my heart with your word, and I fell in love
with you. Heaven and earth and all that is in them—from every direction they tell me I should love you; they do not cease to say this to all,
so that they are without excuse. But you, from on high, will be merciful
to whomever you will, and will show compassion to whomever you
will; if it were not so, heaven and earth would be singing your praises
to deaf ears.

Rom. 1:20

Rom. 9:15 qtg.
Ex. 33:19 / Ps.
68:35

But what do I love when I love you? Not physical beauty or transient grace, not the resplendence of light, so pleasing to our eyes; not
the sweet melodies of all kinds of music; not the lovely fragrance of
flowers and perfumes and spices; not manna and honey; not bodies
that we delight to embrace: these are not what I love when I love my
God. And yet I do love a certain light and sound and fragrance and
nourishment and embrace when I love my God: a light, sound, fragrance, nourishment, and embrace in my innermost self, where there is
a radiance upon my soul that no place can contain, a sound that time
does not destroy, a fragrance that no wind disperses, a taste that does
not grow stale no matter how eagerly I feed, an embrace of which I
could never tire, which I could never seek to escape. This is what I love
when I love my God.

6.9 And what is this? I asked the earth, and it said, "It is not I." And
everything that is in the earth made the same confession. I asked the
sea and the depths and the creeping things with living souls, and they
replied, "We are not your God; seek him above us." I asked the blow-
ing winds, and all the air with its inhabitants said, "Anaximenes[1] was
wrong; I am not God." I asked the sky, the sun, the moon, the stars:
"neither are we the God whom you are seeking," they said. And I said
to all these things that surround the gateways of my flesh, "Tell me
about my God—the God who you are not—tell me something about
him." And they cried out with a loud voice, "He is the one who made
us." My scrutiny of them posed the question; their beauty answered it.

Job 28:14 VL / Gn.
1:20

Ps. 99:3

Then I turned my attention toward myself. "And you: who are
you?" I asked myself; and I replied, "A human being." And indeed I
am intimately aware that there is in me a body and a soul, one of them

---

1. Anaximenes was a pre-Socratic philosopher who taught that air was the first principle of all
things.

outward and the other inward. From which of them should I have set forth to seek my God? I had already sought him through the body all the way from earth to heaven, as far as I could send my messengers, the rays from my eyes. But what is inward is better. It was, surely, to this inward part that all the messengers of the body delivered their messages; it was this inward part that oversaw and judged the answers of heaven and earth and all that is in them when they said, "We are not God" and "He is the one who made us." The inward human being came to know these things through the assistance of the outward human being. I, the inward human being, came to know them; I, the mind, came to know them through my body's senses. I questioned the vast expanse of the world about my God, and it answered me, "I am not God, but he is the one who made me."

Rom. 7:2; 2 Cor. 4:16; Eph. 3:16

6.10   Is not this beauty evident to all whose senses are intact? Then why does it not say the same thing to them all? Creatures both small and great see it, but they cannot ask it questions; for reason has not been given to them as overseer, as judge of the messages conveyed by the senses. Human beings, by contrast, can ask it questions; and thus, through the things that have been made, they can look with understanding upon the invisible things of God. Yet through love they become subject to created things, and subjects cannot pronounce judgment. These things answer questions only for those who pronounce judgment. They do not change their words—that is, their beauty—because one person merely sees whereas another sees and questions; they do not appear one way to the first and another way to the second. Instead, their beauty appears exactly the same to both; but to the first it is mute, and to the second it speaks. Or rather, it speaks to everyone, but it is understood only by those who compare the word received from outside with the truth that dwells within. It is truth, you see, that says to me, "Your God is not earth and heaven; it is not any body." Their nature says this. Do you see? Their nature is an expanse, less in any part than in the whole. Surely you are better—I am speaking to you, my soul—because you quicken the expanse of your body by giving it life, which no body offers to a body. Now your God is also the life of your life.

Ps. 103:25

Rom. 1:20

7.11   What, then, do I love when I love my God? Who is this God who is above the pinnacle of my soul? Through my soul itself I will ascend to him. I will pass through the power of mine by which I cling to a body and fill its structure with life. It is not by that power that I find my God. For if it were, horse and mule, which have no understanding, would find him; it is by that same power that their bodies,

Ps. 31:9

too, have life. But there is another power, by which I do not merely quicken my flesh but also endow it with sensation. The Lord created this power in me, commanding the eye not to hear and the ear not to see, but giving me eyes so that I might see and ears so that I might hear, *Rom. 11:8* bestowing on each of the senses in turn its proper dwelling place and its proper function. I act through them, doing various things; but I who act am one mind. I shall pass through even this power of mine—for horse and mule have it too; they, too, perceive by means of the body.

8.12   So I will pass through even this nature of mine, climbing step by step to the one who made me; and I come into the open fields and spacious mansions of memory, where there are storerooms of countless images brought in by the senses from all kinds of things. There, too, is found whatever we think by enlarging or reducing or in any way varying the things our senses have perceived, and anything else that has been brought in and stored and has not yet been swallowed up and buried by forgetfulness. When I am there, I ask for whatever I want to be brought out for me. Some things come forth right away, but for others I must search a long time, as though I had to retrieve them from some well-concealed hiding place. Still others rush forward like an army, and though I am asking for and seeking something else altogether, they intrude, saying, "perhaps we are the ones." With the hand of my heart I drive them away from the face of my recollection until the cloud is dispersed and what I want emerges from its concealment and comes into view. Other things are brought out easily and in exactly the right order, just as I have asked for them; earlier things give way to later ones, and as they give way they are put back in storage so that they can be produced again when I want them. All this takes place when I tell a story from memory.

8.13   Every single thing, by whatever path it may have made its entry, is stored there distinctly and according to its proper kind: as light and all colors and the shapes of bodies entered through the eyes, and every kind of sound through the ears; all smells made their entry through the nostrils and all tastes through the mouth; and by the sense of the whole body we detect what is hard or soft, hot or cold, smooth or rough, heavy or light, whether outside the body or inside it. The vast storehouse of memory, with its hidden and indescribable recesses that evade my knowledge, receives all these things so that when there is need they can be retrieved and thought about again. All these things enter memory by their own gateways and are stored there—though indeed it is not the things themselves that enter memory; instead, images of things sensed are on hand in memory for thought to recall them.

Who can say how these images are produced? It is clear, though, which senses captured them and stored them within us. For even when I dwell in darkness and silence, I can bring forth colors in my memory if I so choose, and I distinguish between white and black and any other colors I want to think about; sounds do not interrupt and disturb my consideration of these images drawn from the eyes, even though sounds are there too, hidden away, as it were, in their own compartments. If I feel like it, I can ask for them too, and there they are; with my tongue at rest and my throat stilled, I can sing as much as I like, and those images of colors—which are no less present in memory—do not interfere or break in when I am reexamining that other storehouse of images that came in through the ears. In the same way I recall at will other things that were brought in and collected through the other senses: I distinguish the smell of lilies from that of violets even though I am smelling nothing, and I prefer honey to sweet wine or something smooth to something rough simply by memory, without tasting or touching anything.

8.14   It is within myself that I do these things, in the remarkable chambers of my memory, where heaven and earth and sea are at hand, together with everything I have been able to perceive in them, apart from what I have forgotten. There too I encounter myself and recollect myself: I remember what I did, and when and where; I remember my state of mind when I did it. Everything I remember—whether I experienced it or believed it—is there. From this same storehouse I draw out likenesses of experiences and of things believed on the basis of what I have experienced; I weave them together with things past to envision future actions, events, and hopes, and I contemplate all these things as present.[2] In that remarkable treasure-house of my mind, full of so many images, images of so many things, I say to myself, "I shall do this and that"—and this or that follows. I say to myself, "Oh, that this or that were the case!" or "May God prevent this or that!"—and when I say these things, the images of everything I am talking about are at hand from that same storehouse of memory; and indeed I would not be able to say any of these things if those images were lacking.

8.15   This power of memory is a great power—indeed, an exceedingly great power, my God, a vast and boundless sanctuary. Who has ever penetrated to its furthest reaches? And it is a power of my own

---

2. Not "as though they were present"—there is no deception involved, no unclarity about the fact that these things are merely anticipations of the future; but "as present," meaning, with the same directness and immediacy that characterizes the perception of things that are actually present.

mind; it belongs to my nature, and I cannot contain everything that I am. Is the mind, then, too small to contain itself—so that we must ask, "Where is this part of the mind that the mind itself does not contain? Is the mind outside itself and not within itself? How does the mind not contain itself?"

Great wonder springs up in me concerning this; amazement overtakes me. People go forth to wonder at the heights of mountains, the vast waves of the sea, waterfalls of immense breadth, the expanse of the ocean, the courses of the stars—but they pay no heed to themselves. Nor do they wonder at the fact that as I was speaking of all these things, I was not seeing them with my eyes, and yet I could not have spoken of them unless I saw within myself, in my memory, the mountains and waves and rivers and stars that I have seen, and the ocean that I have believed in—and saw them in their full extent, just as if I were seeing them outwardly. Yet when I saw them with my eyes, I did not take them into myself by seeing them; it is not the things themselves, but their images, that are within me, and I know which of the body's senses impressed each image on me.

Wisd. 13:2

9.16 Yet even this does not exhaust the immense capacity of my memory. Here too, stored in some placeless place, are all the things I have learned in the liberal arts and not forgotten—and it is not their images that I possess, but the things themselves. What grammar is, what the art of disputation is, how many kinds of questions there are: any of these things that I know is in my memory, and not as though I retained an image but left the thing itself outside me. These things did not sound and then pass away like a noise impressed by my ears, leaving behind a trace by which I can recollect it as though it were still sounding, even though it sounds no longer. They are not like a smell that, as it is passing away and is scattered by the winds, affects the sense of smell and casts into memory an image of itself, which we repeat when we remember the smell; or like food that no longer has a taste in the stomach but still has a kind of taste in memory; or like something that is perceived when the body touches it and is imagined by memory even after it is separated from us. Obviously these things are not conveyed into memory; only their images are captured with amazing quickness, stored in amazing places of safekeeping (as it were), and brought forth in an amazing way for remembering.

10.17 By contrast, when I hear that there are three kinds of questions—"Does it exist?" "What is it?" "What is it like?"—I do of course retain images of the sounds of which these words were composed, and I know that those sounds rumbled through the air and passed away and are no more: but the things themselves that are signified by those sounds did not reach me by any bodily sense. I have never seen them, except in my mind; and what I have hidden away in memory is not their images, but the things themselves. Let them tell me, if they can, from what source they came into me. For I run through all the gateways of my flesh and do not find the one by which they made their entrance. The eyes say, "If they were colored, we are the ones who reported them"; the ears say, "If they made a sound, it is we who made them known"; the nostrils say, "If they had a smell, they entered through us"; the sense of taste says, "If it is not a flavor, do not ask me"; touch says, "If they were not bodily, I did not handle them; and if I did not handle them, I did not make them known." From what source, then, and by what path did these things enter my memory? I do not know how they entered. For when I learned them, I did not put my faith in someone else's heart; no, I examined them in my own heart and pronounced that they were true, and then I entrusted them to my heart, as though putting them where I could retrieve them whenever I might wish. So they were there even before I learned them, yet they were not in memory. So where were they? And how is it that when I heard about them, I recognized them and said, "That is right; that is true," unless they were already in memory, but so remote, shoved so far back in the most obscure hiding places, that if they had not been dug out by someone who drew them to my attention, I might never have been able to think about them?

11.18   So we find that learning things whose images we do not draw in through the senses, but which instead we see within us—directly, as they are, and without images—is simply a matter of taking things that memory already contained, but in a scattered and disorderly way, and gathering them together in thought, giving them our careful attention so that we have them at our fingertips, so to speak, in our memory; where formerly they were lying hidden, dispersed and unheeded, they now present themselves readily to the mind's accustomed gaze. My memory contains many such things that have already been discovered and placed at my fingertips; these are the things that we are said to have learned and to know. Yet if for even a short time I cease to recall them, they are buried once again; they are torn apart and hidden piece by piece in the most obscure places, and once again I have to think them out afresh as if for the first time, gathering them from those same places (for there is nowhere else for them to have gone) and bringing them together so that they can be known, as though gathering them from their dispersion. That is how we get the word "think" (*cogito*): for *cogito* is to *cogo* as *agito* to *ago* and *factito* to *facio*.[3] But the mind has claimed this word for itself, so that in current usage what is brought together elsewhere is not properly said to be thought (*cogitari*), but only what is brought together—that is, gathered (*cogitur*)—in the mind itself.

12.19 Memory also contains the innumerable principles and laws of numbers and dimensions, which are not impressed by any bodily sense, since they have no color or sound or smell or taste or feel. I have heard the sounds of the words by which they are signified when someone discusses them, but those sounds are not the same thing as the principles themselves. The sounds, after all, are different in Greek from what they are in Latin; but the principles are not Greek or Latin or any other kind of speech. I have seen the lines drawn by architects, as thin as can be, like spiders' silk. But these principles are something different; they are not images of things that my bodily eyes have reported to me, and anyone who knows them has recognized them inwardly, without any thought of a body of any kind. With all the bodily senses I have perceived the numbers that we count, but these are not the same as—nor are they images of—the numbers by which we count, which therefore have a mighty existence of their own. Someone who does not see those numbers may perhaps laugh at me for talking about them, and I will feel sorry for him for laughing at me.

13.20 I hold all these things in my memory; I even hold in my memory how I learned them. I have heard many utterly misguided objections raised against them, and those too I hold in my memory; the objections are false, but it is not false that I remember them. I also remember that I distinguished between the truths and the false objections raised against them, and I see that my distinguishing between them now is different from my remembering that I have often distinguished between them in the past when I thought about them, as I often did. So I remember that I have often understood these things, and I also store up in my memory the fact that I now distinguish between them and understand them, so that later I can remember that I understood them now. So I also remember that I have remembered; and later, if I should recall that I was able to remember these things now, it will surely be through the power of memory that I recall it.

---

3. "-ito" is a suffix denoting repeated or intense action. Thus, *ago* is "I act," and *agito* is "I put into motion, impel"; *facio* is "I do" and *factito* is "I do frequently/habitually." Augustine's etymology, derived from Varro, posits the same relationship between *cogo*, "I gather," and *cogito*, usually translated "I think," but originally meaning (on this account) "I gather again and again."

14.21   This same memory contains the affections of my mind—not in the way in which the soul has them when it is undergoing them, but in a very different way that is appropriate to the power of memory. For when I am not happy, I remember that I used to be happy; when I am not sad, I recall my past sadness; sometimes, though I feel no fear, I remember that I was once afraid; and without experiencing any desire I remember my former desire. Sometimes what I remember is the opposite of what I am experiencing: I am happy and remember my past sadness, or sad and remember my past happiness. Now it is not surprising that this should be true of what concerns the body. Mind and body are distinct, after all; and so if, when I am in a state of joy, I remember my past pain, there is nothing surprising about that. But the cases I have been talking about are different. For the mind is also memory itself. (Note that when we instruct someone to remember something, we say, "Be sure to keep it in mind"; and when we forget, we say, "It wasn't in my mind" or "It slipped my mind." Thus we call memory itself mind.) And given that this is so, how is it that when I am happy and remember my past sadness, my mind contains happiness and my memory contains sadness, and my mind is happy because it contains happiness, yet my memory is not sad because it contains sadness? Does memory not belong to the mind? Who would say such a thing? Undoubtedly memory is like the mind's stomach, and happiness and sadness are like sweet and bitter food: when they are entrusted to memory, they are conveyed into the stomach, where they can be stored but not tasted. It is ridiculous to think memory is like the stomach, and yet they are not completely dissimilar.

14.22   Now notice that when I say there are four disturbances of the mind—desire, happiness, fear, sadness[4]—I bring this forth from my memory. And that is where I find anything that I can say in explaining them, classifying each in terms of genus and species, stating their definitions; I bring it all forth from my memory. And yet when I call these disturbances to mind by remembering them, I am not disturbed by any of them. And they were already there before I recalled and reconsidered them; that is precisely why I was able to retrieve them from there. So perhaps when we remember these things, they are brought forth from memory in something like the way food is brought forth from the stomach when an animal chews its cud. Why, then, does someone who discusses these things—and thus remembers them—not taste the sweetness of happiness or the bitterness of sorrow in the mouth

---

4. Augustine takes this list from Cicero, who gets it from the Stoics.

of thought? Is this where the analogy—for it is merely an analogy—fails? Who, after all, would be willing to talk about such things if every time we spoke of sadness or fear we could not help experiencing sorrow or terror? And yet we could not talk about them unless we found in our memory not merely the sounds of the words (in the form of images impressed by our bodily senses) but the notions of the things themselves. And we did not receive those notions through any gateway of the flesh: the mind itself perceived these passions by experiencing them, and then it entrusted them to memory—or else memory simply retained them even though they were not entrusted to it.

15.23   But does this happen by means of images or not? It would be hard for anyone to say. I speak of a stone or the sun when the things themselves are not present to my senses, but of course their images are on hand in my memory. I speak of physical pain when no such pain is present and nothing is hurting me; yet if no image of pain were present in my memory, I would not know what I was saying, and I would not be able to give an account distinguishing pain from pleasure. I speak of physical health when I am physically healthy; then, certainly, the thing itself is present to me. But if its image were not also present in my memory, I would have no way of remembering what the sound of the word "health" means; and sick people, hearing the word "health," would not understand what was being said if they did not hold that same image in the power of memory, though the thing itself is absent from their body. I speak of the numbers by which we count; the numbers themselves, not their images, are present in my memory. I speak of the image of the sun, and that image is present in my memory; after all, I do not recall an image of that image, but the image itself, which is on hand when I remember. I speak of memory and I recognize what I am speaking of. And where do I recognize it? Precisely in memory itself. And surely memory is not present to itself through an image of itself, rather than through itself.

16.24   I speak of forgetfulness and in just the same way as before I recognize what I am speaking of. How would I recognize it unless I remembered it? (I do not mean the sound of the word; I mean the thing it signifies. If I had forgotten the thing, I would of course have no way of recognizing the meaning of the sound.) Now when I remember memory, memory itself is present to itself through itself. So when I remember forgetfulness, both memory and forgetfulness are present: memory, by which I remember, and forgetfulness, which I remember. But what is forgetfulness other than a privation of memory? So how is forgetfulness present so that I can remember it, when its presence means that I cannot remember? Moreover, if we did not remember forgetfulness, we would in no way be able to recognize the thing that is signified by that word; but what we remember, we hold in our memory—which means that we hold forgetfulness in our memory. Therefore, the very thing that, when present, makes us forget is present so that we do not forget. Are we to understand from this that when we remember forgetfulness, it is present in memory not through itself but through its image, because if forgetfulness were present through itself, it would cause us to forget rather than remember? Who can search this out and fully grasp how this can be?

16.25   Certainly, Lord, this is a struggle for me, a struggle within myself. I have become for myself a stretch of ground to be worked with difficulty and much sweat. We are not now exploring the expanses of the sky or measuring the distances of stars or inquiring after the weight of the earth. I am the one whom I remember: I, the mind. It is no great surprise if what I am not is far from me: but what is closer to me than I myself? And yet I do not fully grasp the power of my own memory, even though apart from my memory I could not so much as speak of myself. What am I to say, then, when I am certain that I remember forgetfulness? Shall I say that what I remember is not in my memory? Shall I say that forgetfulness is present in my memory in order that I might not forget? Both possibilities are utterly ridiculous.

Gn. 3:17, 3:19

Job 28:25 VL

And what of the third possibility? Can I somehow say that when I remember forgetfulness, what is held in my memory is not forgetfulness itself, but an image of forgetfulness? How can I say that? For when an image of something is impressed on memory, the thing itself must first be present as the source of the image. That is how I remember Carthage, how I remember all the places I have been, the faces of the people I have seen, and the things reported by the other senses; it is how I remember the health or suffering of the body. When these things were present, memory captured images from them, images that I could behold as present and consider again in my mind when I recalled the things themselves, now absent. So if forgetfulness is held in memory through an image rather than through itself, it must at least have been present at some point, so that its image could be captured. But when it was present, how did it inscribe its image in memory, since its presence erases from memory whatever has already been marked down there? And yet somehow—how, exactly, is incomprehensible and inexplicable—I am certain that I remember the very forgetfulness that wipes out what we once remembered.

17.26 The power of memory is great indeed, something terrifying, my God, a deep and boundless multiplicity. And this is the mind; it is I myself. What am I, then, my God? What nature am I? A various, manifold, and powerfully vast life. Behold the countless fields and caves and chasms of my memory, uncountably full of countless kinds of things: whether by means of images, as with all bodies, or through the presence of the things themselves, as with the liberal arts, or through some sort of notions or notings, as with the affections of the mind (for the memory retains these even when the mind is not experiencing them, and whatever is in memory is in the mind). I hasten through all these things, I fly here and there; I make what progress I can, but I never come to the end of it. So great is the power of memory, so great is the power of life in human beings who live only to die.

What, then, shall I do, my God, you who are my true life? I will pass beyond even this power of mine that is called memory; I will pass beyond it so that I can progress toward you, O sweet Light. What are you saying to me? See, I am making my ascent through my soul to you, who abide above me; I will pass beyond even this power of mind that is called memory, eager to touch you in whatever way you can be touched, to embrace you in whatever way you can be embraced. For even beasts and birds have memory. Otherwise they would not find their way back to their dens or nests, or do the many other things that they are accustomed to doing; indeed, without memory they could not become accustomed to doing anything at all. So I will pass beyond even memory and reach the One who has separated me from four-footed beasts and made me wiser than the birds of the air. I will pass beyond even memory so that I might find you—where? Where will I find you, my true good, my sure sweetness? If I find you outside my memory, I have no memory of you. And how will I find you if I have no memory of you?

Jn. 14:6

Eccl. 11:7

Job 35:11 VL

18.27 A woman had lost a coin, and she looked for it by the light of a lamp.[5] If she had not remembered the coin, she would not have been able to find it. For once it was found, how would she know whether that was indeed it, unless she remembered it? I remember many times that I have looked for, and found, things that I had lost. From those occasions I know that when I was looking for something, if someone said to me, "Might this be it?" "Might that be it?" I would keep saying no until the thing I was looking for was produced. If I had not remem-

Lk. 15:8

---

5. The Parable of the Lost Coin (one of ten coins) immediately follows the Parable of the Lost Sheep (one of a hundred) and immediately precedes the Parable of the Prodigal Son (one of two).

bered that thing, whatever it was, I would not have found it even if it had been produced for me, because I would not have recognized it. Such is always the case when we look for and find something we have lost. Now if something—some visible body—is lost to the eyes, not to memory, an image of that thing is retained within us, and the search continues until the thing is brought back into view; once it has been found, it is recognized through that image within us. We do not say that we have found something that had been lost if we do not recognize the thing, and we cannot recognize it if we do not remember it. But it was lost only to the eyes; it was retained in memory.

19.28   Yet suppose memory itself loses something, as happens when we forget and we seek to remember. Where do we seek, if not in memory itself? And if things other than what we are seeking should be produced there, we keep rejecting them until what we are looking for turns up. And when it does, we say, "This is it"—which we would not say if we did not recognize it, and we would not recognize it if we did not remember it. Surely, though, we had forgotten it. Did it perhaps not fall out of memory entirely, so that we used the part we retained in order to seek the other part, because memory was aware that it was not holding together what it had been used to holding together, and so, limping along, maimed by the loss of something to which it had been accustomed, it urgently demanded the restoration of what was missing? It is like when we catch a glimpse of someone we know, or think about him, but we have forgotten his name and are trying to recall it. If a name occurs to us that is not his, we do not connect it to him, because memory is not in the habit of thinking of him along with that name. And so each wrong name is rejected until the right name comes along; then our accustomed knowledge comes into alignment and is stable and at rest. And from where does the right name come along, if not from memory itself? Even if we remember it because someone else has reminded us, the name still emerges from memory: we do not believe what we are told, as though it were something new. Instead, we remember it and therefore affirm that what we are told is true—whereas if the name is completely erased from the mind, we do not remember it even if someone reminds us. For if we remember even the fact that we have forgotten, we have not entirely forgotten. We cannot seek what we have lost if we have forgotten it entirely.

20.29   How, then, do I seek you, Lord? For when I seek you, my God, I seek the happy life. I will seek you so that my soul may live. *Ps. 68:33* My body lives by my soul, and my soul lives by you. How, then, do I seek the happy life? The happy life is not mine until I can say, "This is sufficient; the happy life is here." It is incumbent on me to say how I seek it. Do I seek it by way of remembrance, as though I have forgotten it but still remember that I have forgotten it? Or do I seek it by way of a desire to learn something unknown, either something I have never known or something I have so thoroughly forgotten that I do not even remember that I have forgotten it? Is not this the happy life that all people want, that absolutely no one fails to want? Where did they come to know it, so that they could want it? Where did they see it, so that they could love it? Surely we have this happy life—but in what way we have it, I do not know. There is another way of having it; in that way, anyone who has it is thereby happy. There are also those who are happy through hope; they have the happy life in a way that is inferior to those who are already in fact happy, yet they are better than those who are happy neither in fact nor through hope. Yet even these last have the happy life in some way, for if they did not, they would not will to be happy, as in fact they most certainly do. I do not know how they have come to know the happy life and therefore have it—in some way that escapes me—in their knowledge.

I am struggling to determine whether this knowledge is in their memory. If it is there, we were happy at some time: whether each of us individually, or in the human being who first sinned, in whom we all died and from whom we are all born into unhappiness, I am not now asking. But I am asking whether the happy life is in memory. After all, we would not love it if we did not know it. We hear the words "happy life" and we all acknowledge that we desire the thing itself. It is not, of course, the sound that we find appealing. If a Greek speaker hears the words in Latin, he will find nothing appealing, because he will not know what is being said; but we find it appealing, just as he would if he heard the words in Greek, because the thing itself is neither Greek nor Latin, and speakers of Greek and Latin and other languages all long to attain it. It is therefore known to all of them, and if they could be asked in one voice, "Do you want to be happy?", without hesitation they would respond that they do. And that would not happen unless the thing itself, which these words express, were retained in their memory.

1 Cor. 15:22

21.30   Is it retained in the same way that someone who has seen Carthage remembers Carthage? No. The happy life is not seen with the eyes, since it is not a body. Is it retained in the same way that we remember numbers? No. Someone who knows numbers does not still seek to attain them, whereas we know the happy life and for that very reason love it and still seek to attain it, so that we might be happy. Is it retained in the way that we remember eloquence? No. Granted, the cases are similar in certain respects: when people hear the word "eloquence" they remember the thing itself, even if they are not yet eloquent themselves; and many people do long to be eloquent (and from that fact it is evident that they know eloquence). But through the bodily senses they have observed other people who are eloquent, and they took pleasure in this and want to be eloquent themselves—though their pleasure in eloquence depends on some inward knowledge, and apart from that pleasure they would not want to be eloquent—whereas we do not experience the happy life in others through any bodily sense. Is it retained in the same way that we remember joy? Perhaps so. For though I am unhappy I remember the happy life, in the same way that I remember my own joy even when I am sad, and I never saw or heard or smelled or tasted or touched my joy by any bodily sense; rather, I experienced it in my mind when I was joyful, and the knowledge of that joy stuck to my memory so that I would be able to recall it, sometimes with contempt, sometimes with longing, in keeping with the variety of things I remember enjoying. For I have been flooded with a kind of joy even in disgraceful things, a joy that I detest and abhor as I recall it now; but sometimes I have rejoiced in good and noble things, and I recall that joy with longing, even if perhaps those good and noble things are absent and so I grieve when I recall my former joy.

21.31   So where and when did I experience this happy life of mine, so that I remember and love and desire it? And it is not just I, or I and a few others: truly, we all want to be happy. Now if we did not have some reliable knowledge of the happy life, we would not will it so reliably. But how can that be? Suppose two people are asked whether they want to join the military. It could certainly turn out that one of them says yes and the other says no. But if they are asked whether they want to be happy, both will say straightaway and without hesitation that they desire happiness—and one of them wants to join the military, and the other one does not, for no other reason than to be happy. Could it perhaps be the case that one person finds joy in one thing and another person in something else? In that way all people agree that they want to be happy, since they would all agree, if asked, that they want joy, and that very joy is what they call a happy life. So even if different people attain such joy from different things, there is still just one thing— joy—that everyone is seeking to acquire. And no one can claim never to have experienced joy, so when we hear the words "happy life," we find joy in our memory and recognize it.

22.32   Far be it, Lord, far be it from the heart of your servant who is making his confession to you, far be it that I should think I am happy

for experiencing just any joy. For there is a joy that is not granted to
the unrighteous, but only to those who worship you without looking
for any reward, because you are yourself their joy. To rejoice for you,
in you, about you: this is itself the happy life, this alone, and no other.
Those who think there is some other happy life are pursuing a joy that
is no true joy, though their wills have not turned away altogether from
some shadowy image of joy.

Is. 48:22

23.33 Therefore it is not certain that everyone wants to be happy,
since not everyone wants to rejoice in you, which is the only happy
life. So indeed not everyone wants the happy life. Or is it that all do
want this, but because the flesh so lusts against the spirit and the spirit
against the flesh that they do not do what they want, they sink down
into the kind of life they have the strength to lead and are content with
that, because their will for the life that they lack the strength to lead is
not great enough to empower them to lead it? For I would ask them all,
"Would you rather rejoice in truth than in falsehood?" And as unhesitatingly as they had answered that they want to be happy, they would
now answer that they would rather rejoice in truth. The happy life, in
fact, is joy in truth: and that means joy in you, who are Truth, O God
my light, the health of my countenance, my God.

Gal. 5:17

1 Cor. 13:6

Jn. 14:6

*Ps. 26:1 / Ps. 41:6,
41:12, 42:5*

All want this happy life; all want this life, which alone is happy; all
want joy in truth. I have known many people who want to deceive,
but not one who wanted to be deceived. Where, then, did they come
to know this happy life? Surely it was where they also came to know
truth. For they do love truth, since they do not want to be deceived;
and because they love the happy life, which is nothing other than joy in
truth, they must of course love truth as well. And they would not love
truth if there were no knowledge of truth in their memory. Why, then,
do they not rejoice in truth? Why are they not happy? It is because they
devote more energy to things that make them wretched than to the one
hazily remembered thing that would make them happy. For there does
remain a little light in human beings. Let them walk, let them walk, so
that the darkness does not overcome them.

Jn. 12:35

23.34 How is it, then, that truth breeds hate,[6] that your man became
their enemy by preaching the truth? How is this so, given that people
love the happy life, which is nothing other than joy in truth? It must
be that this is how they love the truth: they want what they love, whatever that might be, to be the truth; and because they do not want to
be deceived, they do not want their mistakes to be exposed as such. So

Gal. 4:16

---

6. Terence, *Andria* 68: "For in these days flattery wins friends but truth breeds hate."

they hate truth for the sake of the thing that they love as truth. They   *Jn. 3:20*
love truth when it puts them in a good light; they hate truth when it
exposes their error. For because they do not want to be deceived—but
they do want to deceive—they love truth when it reveals itself but hate
truth when it reveals them. And this will be their reward: those who
do not want the light of truth to show them for what they are will be
exposed by the truth against their wills, but truth itself will refuse to
show itself to them. This, even this, is the state of the human mind:
blind and listless, so foul and unsightly that it wants to stay hidden,
but unwilling that anything should be hidden from it. And how is it
repaid? With the very opposite of what it wants: it cannot hide from
truth, but truth is hidden from it. And yet even in this state, wretched
though it is, it would rather have joy in true things than in false. So it
will be happy if it rejoices without hindrance and without interruption
in the one and only Truth by which all true things are true.

24.35   Look how widely I have ranged in my memory looking for
you, Lord, and I have not found you outside it. For I have found nothing of you that I did not remember, since the time that I learned about
you; for since the time I learned about you, I have not forgotten you.
Yes: where I found truth, that is where I found my God, Truth Itself,
which I have not forgotten from the time I learned it. And so, beginning with the time I first learned about you, you abide in my memory;
and when I remember you, that is where I find you and delight in you.   *Ps. 36:4*
These are my sacred delights, which you in your mercy have given me,
looking with favor on me in my poverty.   *Ps. 10:5; Lk. 1:48*

25.36   But where do you abide in my memory, Lord? Where do
you abide there? What sort of dwelling place have you fashioned for
yourself? What kind of sanctuary have you built for yourself? You have
conferred upon my memory the dignity of abiding in it, but in what
part of it do you abide? That is what I am seeking to understand. For
in remembering you I have passed beyond the parts of memory that
even the beasts have, because I did not find you there, among images
of bodily things. Then I went to the parts of memory to which I have
entrusted the affections of my mind, and neither did I find you there.
Then I entered the residence of the mind itself, where the mind dwells
in my memory—for the mind also remembers itself—and you were
not there, because just as you are not an image of something bodily
or an affection of something living, as when we rejoice, grieve, desire,
fear, remember, forget, and so on, so also you are not the mind itself,
because you are the Lord and God of the mind. And all these things
undergo change, but you abide unchangeably above them; and from

the time that I first learned about you, you have seen fit to dwell in my memory. And what do I mean by asking in what place you dwell, as though there were really places in memory? Certainly you dwell in my memory, because from the time I first learned about you I have remembered you; and when I recall you, I find you in my memory.

26.37   So where did I find you so that I could learn you? For you were not already in my memory before I learned you. So where did I find you so that I could learn you, if not in yourself, above me? It is nowhere, this "place"; and though we approach it and draw back from it, it is nowhere, a place that is no place. You, Truth, preside everywhere, and to all who seek to learn from you, however varied their questions, you give an answer, all in a single moment. You give your answer clearly, though not all of them hear it clearly. They all ask you about what they want to learn, but they do not always hear what they want to hear. Those who serve you best are not so much intent on hearing from you whatever they already want, but instead on wanting whatever they hear from you.

27.38   Late have I loved you, beauty so ancient and so new!
  Late have I loved you!
  And behold, you were within, but I was outside and looked
    for you there, and in my ugliness I seized upon these beau-
    tiful things that you have made.
  You were with me, but I was not with you.
  Those things held me far away from you—
    things that would not even exist if they were not in you.
  You called, you shouted, and you broke through my deafness;
    you flashed, you shone, and you dispersed my blindness;
    you breathed perfume, and I drew in my breath and pant
      for you;
    I tasted, and I hunger and thirst;   *Ps. 33:9; 1 Pet. 2:3 /*
    you touched me, and I was set on fire for your peace.   *Mt. 5:6; 1 Cor.*
                                                                          4:11 / Ps. 4:9

28.39   When at last I cling to you with all that I am,
    there will be no place in me for pain and struggle;   *Ps. 89:10*
    my life will be wholly alive, filled wholly with you.
  But as things stand now, I am a burden to myself,
    because I am not filled with you—
    for you uphold those whom you fill.
  The joys that I ought to bewail do battle with the sorrows in
    which I ought to rejoice, and which side will prevail I do
    not know.

My evil sorrows do battle with my good joys, and which side
will prevail I do not know.

How wretched I am!

Lord, have mercy on me!   *Ps. 30:10*

How wretched I am!

Look: I do not conceal my wounds.

You are the Physician, I am ill;

you are merciful, I am miserable.

Is not human life on this earth a trial?   *Job 7:1 VL*

Who would want to encounter its troubles and difficulties?

You command us to endure them, not to love them.

People do not love what they endure, even if they love
enduring.

Though they are glad that they endure, they would prefer
that there be nothing to endure.

In times of adversity, I long for good fortune;

in times of good fortune, I fear adversity.

What is the middle ground between these two, the place
where human life is not a trial?

Cursed is the good fortune of this world, and doubly cursed,
by the fear of adversity and the destruction of happiness.

Cursed are the adversities of this world, doubly and triply
cursed, by the longing for good fortune and the hardness
of adversity and the anxiety that adversity will break down
our endurance.

Is not human life on this earth an unrelenting trial?

29.40 All my hope is in your abundantly great mercy.

Grant what you command, and command what you will. You
enjoin continence on us. As a certain writer says, "When I knew that
no one can be continent unless God grants it, the knowledge of who
grants continence was itself an element of wisdom."[7] Through conti-   *Wisd. 8:21*
nence we are gathered together and brought back to the One, whom
we abandoned by dispersing ourselves amongst the many. For those
who love anything alongside you, unless they love it for your sake, love

---

7. Augustine does not finish the quotation: "I went to God and implored him." That Augustine
leaves off the conclusion—therefore I prayed for continence—recalls his earlier failure to ask for
God to give him continence (6.11.20). But why leave it off here? Perhaps because the first two
sentences of the paragraph (which will be repeated, in reverse order and with some variation of
vocabulary, at the end of the paragraph) have already implicitly stated that prayer; perhaps because
at this point Augustine is not interested in his past prayer ("I went . . . and implored") but in what
continues to need prayer.

you too little. O Love, ever-burning and never extinguished, Charity, my God: enkindle me! You command continence: grant what you command, and command what you will.

30.41   Certainly you command that I restrain myself from the lust of the flesh, the lust of the eyes, and worldly ambition. You com-   *1 Jn. 2:16* manded me not to sleep with my mistress, and concerning marriage you encouraged me to take a better path than the one you left open for   *1 Cor. 7:38* me. And because you granted it, it was done, even before I became a steward of your Sacrament. Yet even now the images of such things are   *1 Cor. 4:1* alive in my memory, about which I have spoken at such great length. The kind of life to which I was once accustomed impressed those images firmly on my memory, and they intrude upon my thoughts. They have no power when I am awake, but when I am asleep they lure me not merely into pleasure but even into consent and something very much like action. The deceitful image in my soul has such power in my flesh that false visions induce me to do in my sleep what true visions cannot when I am awake. Am I not myself when I am asleep, O Lord my God? Yet there is such a difference between myself and myself in that moment in which I pass from wakefulness to sleep or return from sleep to wakefulness! When I am asleep, where is reason? For when I am awake, it is by reason that I resist such suggestions and remain unshaken even if the things themselves are presented to me. Is reason shut down when I shut my eyes? Does reason fall asleep along with the bodily senses? And how does it come about that even in dreams we often resist such suggestions, remaining mindful of our resolve and persevering in it with perfect chastity, and give no assent to such enticements? And yet there is a great difference. For if it turns out otherwise, upon waking we return to a conscience that is at ease; that very difference between waking and sleeping shows us that what grieves us was not something we did, but something that was in some sense done in us.

30.42   Is not your hand mighty enough, Almighty God, to heal all   *Num. 11:23* the infirmities of my soul and, by your even more abundant grace,   *Ps. 102:3* to still these lustful stirrings in my sleep? Lord, you will increase your gifts in me more and more, rescuing my soul from the honey-trap of concupiscence so that it will follow me to you and not be in conflict with itself: so that not even in its dreams will it carry out—or even consent to—the disgusting corruptions that arise from bestial images and pollute the flesh. To you, Almighty, who can do more than we ask, more than we understand, it is no great task to ensure that no such   *Eph. 3:20* thing, even so slight an inclination that the merest nod would check it, troubles the chaste mind of a sleeper, not merely at some point in this life but even at my present age.

But now I have told my good Lord what I am even now, in this aspect of the evil of my life; I have told it to you rejoicing with trembling in what you have given me, grieving that I am still unfinished, hoping that you will complete your mercies in me until I reach that perfect peace that my inward and outward self will have in your presence when death has been swallowed up in victory. *Ps. 2:11*

1 Cor. 15:54

31.43 There is another evil of the day—would that it were sufficient for it! For we repair the daily devastations of the body by eating and drinking, until you destroy food and the stomach, killing insatiable desire with a marvelous satisfaction, and clothing this corruptible body with everlasting incorruption. But for now, this neediness is sweet to me. I fight against this sweetness so that I will not be overcome by it. I wage daily war in fasting, bringing my body into submission again and again, and my sufferings are driven out by pleasure—for hunger and thirst are indeed sufferings of a sort; they burn, they destroy us like a fever, unless the medicine of food and drink brings us relief. That medicine is always at hand, thanks to the consolation of your gifts, in which land and water and sky minister to our weakness; and so our distress is called delight. *Mt. 6:34* *1 Cor. 6:13* *1 Cor. 15:53* *1 Cor. 9:26–27* *2 Cor. 11:27*

31.44 You have taught me that I should take food and drink in the same way that I take medicine. But as I am passing from the discomfort of craving to the satisfaction of fullness, a snare is set for me, hidden in that very movement. It is the snare of concupiscence. For that movement is a pleasure, and there is no other way to pass through it; there is only the path along which necessity compels us. And although we eat and drink for the sake of health, there is a dangerous pleasure that attends eating and drinking like a servant—and often this servant tries to lead the way, so that I do for the sake of pleasure what I say I do, or intend to do, for the sake of health. Nor is there the same measure for both: what is enough for health is too little for pleasure, and it is often hard to tell whether a genuine need of the body still requires provision or a deceptive pleasure of greed is demanding indulgence. A wretched soul is thrilled with such uncertainty and uses it to provide a pretext and an excuse, delighted that what is enough for the modest requirements of health is difficult to judge, so that it can disguise its preoccupation with pleasure as a concern for health. I try every day to resist these temptations, and I call upon your right hand; I bring my uncertainties to you, for in this matter I have not yet found a stable resolution. *Ps. 79:18*

31.45   I hear the voice of my God commanding me, "Do not let your hearts be weighed down with overindulgence and drunkenness." *Lk. 21:34* Drunkenness is far from me: you will have mercy, so that it does not come near me. But overindulgence does sometimes sneak up on your servant: you will have mercy, so that it stays far from me. For no one can be continent unless you grant it. You give us many things in *Wisd. 8:21* answer to our prayers, and whatever good things we received before we prayed, we received from you; and the fact that we realize afterward that we received them from you, that too we received from you. I have never been a drunkard, but I have known drunkards whom you have made sober. So it is your doing that some have never been drunkards; it is your doing that others who once were drunkards did not always remain so; and it is your doing that both of these know that this is your doing.

I have heard another voice from you: "Do not run after your desires; turn away from your pleasure." This voice, too, I have heard through *Sir. 18:30* your Gift, and I have loved it dearly: "Neither if we eat will we abound, nor if we do not eat will we lack anything"; that is to say, the one will not *1 Cor. 8:8* enrich me and the other will not distress me. And I have heard another: "I have learned, you see, to be satisfied in whatever condition I am in. I know how to abound, and I know how to endure poverty. I can do all things through him who gives me strength." So speaks a soldier of *Phil. 4:11–13* the heavenly hosts, not dust, such as we are. Yet remember, Lord, that *Ps. 102:14* we are dust, and you have made man[8] from the dust of the earth; he was lost, but now he has been found. He had no strength in himself, *Lk. 15:24, 15:32* for he was that same dust—dust into which you breathed your inspiration, so that he said these words that have kindled my love for him: "I can do all things," he says, "through him who gives me strength." Give *Phil. 4:13* me strength, so that I may be able to do all things. Grant what you command, and command what you will. This man confesses that he has received, that when he boasts, he boasts in the Lord. I have heard *1 Cor 1:31; 2 Cor.* another praying in such a way that he deserves to receive: "Take from *10:17* me," he says, "the desires of the belly." Thus, my holy God, it is evident *Sir. 23:6* that when what you command to be done is done, it is because you grant it.

31.46   You have taught me, good Father, that to the pure all things are pure, but it is bad for the person whose eating causes another to *Tit. 1:15*

---

8. Whenever possible I translate *homo* as "human being(s)" rather than "man" in order to avoid unnecessarily gendered language, but the masculine singular pronoun is important here, since Augustine is speaking of Paul as a kind of everyman; the masculine singular also allows the echo from the Prodigal Son story (at the end of this sentence) to be heard properly.

stumble; that every creature of yours is good, and nothing is to be   *Rom. 14:20–21*
rejected that is received with thanksgiving; that food does not com-   *1 Tim. 4:4*
mend us to God, and no one should judge us in matters of food or   *1 Cor. 8:8*
drink; that one who eats should not look down on one who does not   *Col. 2:16*
eat, and one who does not eat should not judge one who eats. These   *Rom. 14:3*
things I have learned: thanks and praise be to you, my Teacher, who
knock on my ears and shine on my heart. Rescue me from all temp-   *Rev. 3:20*
tation. It is not impurity in my food that I fear, but the impurity of   *Ps. 17:30*
ravenous desire. I know that Noah was permitted to partake of every
kind of meat that is good for food, that Elijah was fed with meat,   *Gn. 9:3 / 1 Kgs.*
that John, with his wondrous gift of abstinence, was not polluted by   *17:6*
animals but had locusts as his food. I know too that Esau was tricked   *Mt. 3:4*
through his desire for lentils, that David reproached himself for his   *Gn. 25:34*
desire for water, and that our King was tempted not with meat but   *2 Sam. 23:15–17*
with bread. It was not because the people in the wilderness desired   *Mt. 4:3*
meat that they earned condemnation, but because in their desire for
food they murmured against the Lord.   *Num. 11:1–20*

31.47   So, surrounded as I am by these temptations, I struggle every
day against concupiscence in eating and drinking—for this is not
something I can decide once and for all to give up and never touch
again, as I was able to do with sex. I must keep a temperate hand on
the bridle of my throat, the reins neither too firm nor too slack. Is
there anyone, Lord, who is not pulled a little too far, past the boundary
marker, which is need? Whoever he is, he is a great man: let him proclaim the greatness of your Name. I am not the one, for I am a sinful   *Ps. 68:31; Lk.*
man. Yet I too proclaim the greatness of your Name, and the One who   *1:46; Rev. 15:4 /*
                                                                                Lk. 5:8
has overcome the world intercedes with you on account of my sins,   *Jn. 16:33 / Rom.*
counting me among the weak members of his Body. For your eyes have   *8:34*
                                                                          Rom. 12:5; 1 Cor.
looked upon what is yet unfinished in his Body, and everyone will be   *12:12, 12:22*
inscribed in your book.   *Ps. 138:16*

32.48   As for the enticements of smells, I am not overly concerned
about them. I do not seek them out if they are absent; I do not spurn
them if they are present; I am always ready to do without them. Or so
it seems to me—perhaps I am mistaken about this. There is a lamentable darkness in me that obscures what I am really capable of, so that
when my mind interrogates itself about its powers, it realizes that it can
scarcely trust its own answer. For there is so much in the mind that is
largely hidden unless it comes to light in experience; and in this life,
which is described as temptation from start to finish, those who have   *Job 7:1 VL*
been able to rise from worse to better dare not be confident that they

will not fall from better to worse. There is one hope, one assurance, one steadfast promise: your mercy.

33.49   The pleasures of the ears had entangled me and enslaved me with great ferocity, but you loosed me and set me free. Now, I admit, I do take some pleasure in the sounds to which your words[9] give life, when they are sung with a sweet and well-trained voice—but not so much pleasure that I am strongly attached to them; no, I can arise and depart when I wish. Nevertheless, these sounds claim a place of some dignity in my heart alongside the meanings they convey, by which they are alive and gain admittance into me, and I scarcely know what sort of place is fitting for them. Sometimes I think I honor them more than is right, when I consider that our hearts are enkindled with the flame of piety more devoutly and more intensely by the very same holy words when they are sung than if they were not sung, and that all the affections of our spirit, in all their variety, are aroused—each in its own way—by voice and song, through some hidden kinship that I do not profess to understand. My mind ought not to be given over to the pleasure of the flesh, lest it grow weak; but such pleasure often leads me astray: sense ought to accompany reason patiently, as its follower, for sense deserves admittance only for reason's sake; but instead sense tries to go first and lead the way. Thus I sin in these matters without being aware of it; only later do I realize it.

33.50   Yet sometimes I go too far in avoiding this danger and make the mistake of being too strict. In such a frame of mind I would banish from my own ears, and from the ears of the Church, every sweet melody to which the Psalms of David are sung; it seems safer to me to follow the words of Athanasius, bishop of Alexandria, of which I have so often been reminded. He instructed the reader of the Psalm to use so little inflection in his voice that it was closer to reading than to singing. Yet when I remember the tears I shed over the Church's song in those earliest days when I had recovered my faith—and even now, whenever[10] I am moved not by the singing but by the things sung, when

---

9. "your words": *eloquia tua,* an expression frequent in Psalm 118, where it often has the sense "your promises" (thus, "word" as in "I give you my word").

10. "whenever": *cum.* Alternatively, "because," which O'Donnell (III:219) describes as "on balance the more likely reading" and which is adopted by several translators. But Augustine has already told us that he does not *always* have (what he takes to be) the right kind of pleasure in church music, so "because" seems to go too far. Rather, he recognizes the utility of church music *when* he takes the right kind of pleasure in it—the kind of pleasure he had in his earliest days as a Christian.

they are sung by a serene voice and with the most suitable melody—I acknowledge again the great usefulness of this practice.

Thus I waver between the danger of pleasure and the experience of something wholesome. Though I offer no definitive opinion, I am more inclined to approve the custom of singing in church, so that through the pleasures of the ears a weaker mind may arise to the fervor of devotion. But when it happens to me that the singing moves me more than the things sung, I confess my sin and my need for chastisement; and in such a case I would prefer not to hear the singer. Look at my state! Weep with me—weep for me—any of you who are stirred by something good within you from which good acts spring forth. For if you are not stirred, these things will not move you. But you, O Lord my God, hear me: look with favor upon me and behold me, have mercy upon me and heal me. For in your eyes I have become a question to myself, and this is my infirmity. *Ps. 12:4, 79:15* *Ps. 6:3, 9:14, 24:16* *Ps. 102:3; Mt. 4:23*

34.51   If we are to complete this account of the temptations of the lust of the flesh that continue to assail me as I groan, longing to put on my heavenly dwelling, there remains yet the pleasure of the eyes *2 Cor. 5:2* of this flesh, which I confess in the hearing of the ears of your temple, brotherly and devout ears. My eyes love beautiful forms in all *1 Cor. 3:16, 6:19; 2 Cor. 6:16* their variety, bright and pleasant colors. Let these things not hold my soul in their power; no, let God, who made them all very good, take *Gn. 1:31* possession of my soul; he is my good, and not these things. Every day they impress themselves upon me throughout my waking hours, and I have no respite from them as I have from the sounds of singing—sometimes, in silence, from all sounds. For wherever I might be during the daytime, the very queen of colors, the light that floods everything we perceive, furtively makes its way to me and caresses me while I am doing something else and paying no heed to it. Yet it imposes its presence with such great force that if it is suddenly taken away, we seek it with longing; and if it is absent for a long time, the mind is grieved.

34.52   O Light that Tobit saw, though the eyes of his flesh were blind, *Tob. 4:2ff.* when he taught his son the way of life and walked before him on the feet of charity, never going astray. O Light that Isaac saw, though the *Gn. 27:1–40* lights of this bodily world were dimmed and obscured by age, when he blessed his sons without recognizing them, and in blessing them earned the gift of recognizing them aright. O Light that Jacob saw, though his eyes too were weak because of his great age, when his heart shone with radiant light as he blessed his sons and prophesied the peoples who would one day come forth from them, and with mystical insight *Gn. 49* crossed his hands and laid them upon the heads of his grandsons by Joseph, acting not as Joseph admonished him outwardly, but as he himself discerned inwardly.[11] This is itself the one Light, and all who see and love it are likewise one.

Gn. 48:10–20

Jn. 17:22

But this bodily light of which I was speaking has an alluring and dangerous sweetness by which it fashions a worldly life for those who are blind in their love for it. But when they learn to praise you for it, O God, Creator of all things,[12] it no longer lulls them asleep; instead they take it up in a hymn to you—and this is what I long to do. I fight against the enticements of the eyes, lest the feet by which I walk in your way become entrapped; and I lift unseen eyes to you, that you might free my feet from the snare. And again and again you set them free, for they do indeed become ensnared. You do not cease to set them free, even though I so often yield to the temptations that beset me on every side, for you who keep watch over Israel will neither slumber nor sleep.

Ps. 24:15

Ps. 120:4

34.53 And human beings have added so many things, countless things, to the temptations of the eyes: the products of various trades and artisans, clothing, footwear, pottery and all sorts of craftworks, even paintings and various images, far beyond what is needed for use, restrained within reasonable bounds, and expressive of some devout meaning. They run after the outward things that they make and depart inwardly from the One by whom they themselves are made and banish from their minds what they were made to be.

But even for these things, O my God, my Beauty, I will sing a hymn to you and offer a sacrifice of praise to the One who offered himself as a sacrifice for me, because the beautiful things that are brought forth from our souls by skilled hands come from the Beauty that is above all souls, the Beauty for which my soul sighs day and night. It is from that Beauty that those who craft beautiful things and those who run after them derive the standard by which they acclaim such beauty, but they fail to take from there the standard of right use. It is there, but they do not see it, and so they depart further from you; they do not entrust their strength to your safekeeping but disperse it in delights that can only make them weary.

Ps. 115:17

Ps. 58:10

But I who say these things and recognize their truth still get my feet entangled by these beautiful things: yet you set them free, O Lord, you

---

11. Joseph brought his sons before Jacob in such a way that the firstborn, Manasseh, would be at Jacob's right and the second son, Ephraim, at his left. But Jacob, over Joseph's objections, laid his right hand on Ephraim and his left on Manasseh, prophesying that Ephraim would be greater than Manasseh.

12. From Ambrose's evening hymn: see 9.12.32.

set them free, because your mercy is before my eyes. For I am held cap-   Ps. 24:15 / Ps. 25:3
tive in misery, but you in mercy set me free: sometimes when I am not
even aware of it, because I have stumbled only slightly, but sometimes
with suffering, because I have already become stuck.

35.54   There is yet another kind of temptation, one that is far more
dangerous. For besides the lust of the flesh, which concerns the enjoyment of all the senses and of pleasures—ruinous to those whom it
enslaves, who take themselves far away from you—there is in the soul a   Ps. 72:27
certain empty and inquisitive[13] passion, not for enjoyment *in* the flesh,
but for experience *through* the flesh, through the same bodily senses,
a passion that disguises itself under the name of understanding and
knowledge. Now because this passion is a desire to know, and the eyes
are foremost among the senses as sources of knowledge, the language
of Scripture calls it "the lust of the eyes." Strictly speaking, seeing is the   1 Jn. 2:16
function of the eyes, but we use the verb "to see" of the other senses
as well when we make use of them to know something. We do not say
"hear how it glows red" or "smell how bright it is" or "taste how shiny it
is" or "feel how it gleams"—but we do speak of seeing all these things.
For we say not only "See how bright it is" (something only the eyes can
perceive) but also "See how it sounds," "See what it smells like," "See
how it tastes," "See how hard it is." And so, as I have said, the endeavor
to gain knowledge through any of the senses is called "the lust of the
eyes," because the other senses claim for themselves by analogy the
function of seeing, which belongs to the eyes first of all, whenever they
seek any kind of knowledge.

35.55   From this we recognize more clearly what is done through
the senses for the sake of pleasure and what is done out of curiosity.
Pleasure attends things that are beautiful, harmonious, sweet-smelling,
tasty, and gentle to the touch; but curiosity will seek out even their
opposites simply to give them a try, not in order to suffer harm, but
from a lust for experience and knowledge. For what pleasure is there in
looking at a mangled corpse? It horrifies you. And yet people go running to wherever it lies, just so that they can feel gloomy and grow pale.
They fear seeing such a thing in a nightmare, as if someone had forced
them to look at it when they were awake or some report of its beauty
had convinced them to seek it out. The same holds true for the other
senses, though it would be tedious to name them one by one.

This disease of curiosity is the reason that stupendous sights are
presented in shows. It is the reason that people pry into the mysteries

---

13. "inquisitive": *curiosa*, but "curious" could be misread here as bearing the sense "peculiar, odd."

of the nature that is outside us, which it does no good for us to know—
yet people have a passion to know them simply for the sake of knowing
them. It is also the reason that some seek perverse knowledge through
the practice of magic. Even in religion, it is the reason that some put
God to the test, demanding signs and wonders not for the sake of salvation, but out of the sheer desire for experience.

Mt. 4:1, 4:7 qtg.
Deut. 6:16; Lk.
11:16; Jn. 4:48;
1 Cor. 1:22

35.56   In this vast thicket full of snares and dangers, see how many
things I have cut off and driven away from my heart, as you have
granted me the grace to do, O God of my salvation. Yet when do I dare
to say—for all around us, every day of our lives, many things of this
kind clamor for our attention—when do I dare to say that I am not
drawn to gaze upon any such thing and captivated by some interest
that amounts to nothing? Certainly the theater no longer has a grip
on me; I have no interest in the courses of the stars; my soul has never
sought answers from the shades of the departed; I detest all sacrilegious
rites. The enemy has used so many tricks and insinuations to induce
me to seek some sign from you, O Lord my God, before whom I ought
to be a humble and guileless servant! But I beg you through our King
and through Jerusalem our homeland, guileless and pure, that as consent is far from me now, so may it be always far from me, and ever
further. But when I pray to you for someone's salvation, my attention
has a very different aim. You grant me, and you will continue to grant
me, the grace to follow you gladly, whatever you choose to do with me.

Ps. 17:47, 37:23,
50:16

35.57   Yet who can recount the many utterly trivial and contemptible
things by which our curiosity is tempted every day, and how often we
fall? We begin by indulging people who speak of worthless things—not
wanting to offend those who are weak—but very soon we are gladly
paying attention. I no longer watch a dog chasing a rabbit when it happens in the circus; but in the country, if I happen to encounter it, the
pursuit might divert me from some important thought and turn me to
the hunt itself. It is not the body of the animal I am riding, but the inclination of my own heart, that compels me. And unless you make my
weakness evident to me and swiftly remind me either to rise above that
sight by turning my thoughts to you or else to scorn the whole thing
and pass on by it, I linger there like a fool. And why is it that when I am
sitting at home, a lizard catching flies or a spider trapping the insects
that get entangled in its webs so often captures my attention? Does the
fact that the animals are small make any difference? I quickly move on
from there to praising you, the wondrous Creator and Orderer of all
things, but that is not what first drew my attention. It is one thing to
get up quickly, quite another not to fall in the first place.

My life is full of such distractions, and there is only one hope for me: your abundantly great mercy. For when our hearts become a repository for such things and carry the heavy weight of throngs of idle thoughts, our prayers are often interrupted and thrown into disorder; and in your presence, as we are directing the voice of our hearts to your ears, trivial thoughts rush in from who knows where and abruptly put an end to an act of such great importance.

Ps. 85:13

36.48   Are we to regard this as a fault too small to be worth worrying about? Surely not. And is there anything that can restore our hope besides your mercy, which we have come to know because you have begun to change us? You know how much you have changed me. First you healed me from my passion for self-justification, so that you might also forgive all my other sins and heal all my infirmities, that you might redeem my life from corruption and crown me with mercy and loving-kindness, that you might satisfy my desire with good things. You have curbed my pride through fear of you, and you have bowed my neck in submission under your yoke. Now I bear that yoke, and it is easy upon me, just as you promised, just as you made it. And indeed it was always so, but I did not know this when I was afraid to take it upon me.

Ps. 102:3–5

Mt. 11:30

36.59   But you, O Lord, you alone exercise lordship without arrogance, for you alone are the true Lord, and no one is lord over you. I ask you: has the third kind of temptation[14] ever ceased to trouble me? Can it ever, over the course of my whole life, cease to trouble me? I mean the desire to be feared and loved by other people, for no other reason than that it brings a joy that is no true joy. It is a miserable life and revolting ostentation, the foremost reason that we fail to love you and to fear you with a holy fear; and so you resist the proud and give grace to the humble; you thunder against worldly ambitions, and the foundations of the hills quake. The enemy of our true happiness aggressively sets traps for those of us who must be loved and feared by others for the sake of our duties in human society,[15] scattering cries of "Well done! Well done, indeed!" everywhere we turn, so that when we eagerly receive such acclaim we are captured without even realizing it; we cease to find our joy in your truth but find it instead in human deceit. We enjoy being loved and feared, not on account of you, but instead of you. In this way the enemy—who resolved to establish his

Is. 37:20

Ps. 18:10

Jas. 4:6, 1 Pet. 5:5 / Ps. 17:14, 28:3 / Ps. 17:8

---

14. That is, *ambitio saeculi*, worldly ambition, the third of the three temptations listed in 1 John 2:16.

15. Augustine particularly has in mind himself and his role as bishop, but he speaks here in the first-person plural.

throne in the north, so that those who dwell in darkness and cold *Is. 14:13*
would be slaves to him as he imitates you in his perverse and distorted
way—makes us like himself, not in the charity that binds all together
in harmony, but as sharers in his punishment.

But we, O Lord, are your little flock; hold us in your safekeeping. *Lk. 12:32 / Is.*
Stretch forth your wings, and let us flee for refuge beneath them. Be *26:13 VL*
our glory: let us be loved for your sake; let it be your word that people
fear in us. Those who desire human praise and disparage you will find
no one to defend them from your judgment, and you will not spare
them from your condemnation. Even when praise is not being given
to those who are sinners in the desires of their heart, or blessing to
those who work iniquity, but instead people are being praised for some *Ps. 9:24*
gift that you have given them, those who have greater joy in receiving
praise than in having the gift for which they are praised are disparaging
you in accepting such praise, and then the one who offers praise is better than the one who receives it. For the one who offers praise delights
in God's gift, but the one who receives it has more delight in the praise
he receives from human beings than in the gift he has from God.

37.60   We are tested by these temptations every day, O Lord; we
are endlessly tempted. Our daily furnace[16] is the human tongue. You *Prov. 27:21; Wisd.*
demand continence of us in this domain as well: grant what you com- *3:6*
mand, and command what you will. You know the groaning of my
heart and the streams of tears from my eyes in this matter. For it is not *Ps. 37:9*
easy for me to know how far my cleansing from this plague has come,
and I fear the hidden depths of my heart, which your eyes see clearly *Ps. 18:13–14 / Sir.*
but mine do not. I have some sort of capacity to examine myself con- *15:20*
cerning the other temptations, but concerning this one I have almost
none. I can see how far I have come with regard to the pleasures of the
flesh and needless curiosity for knowledge by my power to hold my
mind in check when I do without those things, either by choice or
because they are not at hand: for I ask myself how much it disturbs me
not to have them. Moreover, people seek wealth in order to give themselves over to one of these three passions, or to two, or to all of them;
if the mind cannot perceive clearly whether it scorns to have wealth,
one can simply give it away in order to put oneself to the test. But how
can we do without praise, and how can we know by experience that we
can do so? Surely we are not to lead bad lives, so abandoned and savage

16. The image of the furnace in which gold is purified is frequent in the wisdom literature of Scripture as a simile for testing and temptation. See, for example, Proverbs 27:21, "As the crucible is for
silver, and the furnace is for gold, so a man is tested by the mouth of one who praises him"; Wisdom
3:6, "Like gold in a furnace he tested them."

that all who know us loathe us. Could anything more insane than that be said or thought? But if praise ordinarily does and should accompany a good life and good deeds, it is no more right to avoid such praise than to avoid the good life itself. Yet it is only when I must do without something that I perceive whether its absence pains me, or whether I bear it with a mind undisturbed.

37.61　What, then, do I confess to you, Lord, concerning this third kind of temptation? That I love praise? But I love truth even more than praise. For if someone asked me whether I would rather be a madman or completely astray in all things but praised by everyone, or else steadfast and utterly resolute in the truth but disparaged by everyone, it is clear to me what I would choose. Yet I would not want someone else's words of approval to increase my joy in any good of mine. But it does, I admit; and more than that: disparagement dampens my joy. When this wretchedness troubles me, I fall into making excuses for myself; you know, O God, how far my self-exoneration is justified, but it perplexes me.

For you have demanded of us not only continence but also justice: continence in restraining our love for certain things, and justice in bestowing our love on others. You have willed that we love not only you but also our neighbor. It does often seem to me that when I take *Mt. 22:37–39* pleasure in the praise of someone with good discernment, I am taking pleasure in the progress or hope of my neighbor, or that when I hear my neighbor disparage something he does not understand or something that is good, I am pained by what is bad in him. For I am also sometimes pained by praise that I receive, when I am praised for things in me that displease me, or even when lesser, inconsequential goods receive greater approval than they deserve. But once again, how can I know whether I react in this way because I do not want the person praising me to contradict my own opinion of myself, not because I care about what is beneficial for him, but because the good things in me that give me pleasure are more enjoyable to me when they also please someone else? In a way I am not really being praised if the praise does not conform to my own judgment about myself, when qualities that I dislike receive praise or qualities that I like less receive greater praise. Am I not right, then, in saying that in this matter I am unsure of myself?

37.62　Behold, in you, O Truth, I see that I ought to be moved by *Jn. 14:6* praise not for my own sake, but for the sake of what is beneficial for my neighbor. But whether I am indeed moved for that reason, I do not know. In this matter I know myself less well than I know you. I beg you, my God: show me myself, so that I may confess to my brothers and sisters, who will pray for me, the wound that I discover in myself.

Let me question myself again, and this time more sharply. If what moves me when I am praised is my neighbor's benefit, why am I less moved if someone else is unjustly criticized than if I am? Why does an insult hurled at me sting more than one hurled at someone else in my presence when both insults are equally unfair? Do I really not know the answer? Is there any explanation left but this: I deceive myself, and in your presence I do not do what is true in my heart and with my tongue? O Lord, put this madness far from me, lest my own words provide the oil of the sinful to swell my head.

Gal. 6:3

Jn. 3:21; Eph. 4:15; 1 Jn. 1:6 / Prov. 30:8

Ps. 140:5

38.63 I am poor and needy, but I am better for the lamentation that is hidden deep within me, better for being discontented with myself and seeking your mercy until what is lacking in me is made whole again and brought to perfection so that I attain that peace that the eye of the arrogant cannot know. Yet the words that fall from our lips, and the deeds that draw attention from other people, present an exceedingly dangerous temptation because of our love for praise, a love that begs for applause and treasures every bit of it to inflate one's sense of personal superiority. It is a temptation for me even when I condemn it in myself, precisely because I condemn it in myself—my contempt for empty pride becomes a source of pride that is emptier still, and so I am not really proud of my contempt for empty pride, for one does not really have contempt for what one is proud of.[17]

Ps. 39:18, 108:22

39.64 And within us, deep within us, is another evil that belongs to this same kind of temptation: those who are pleased with themselves, though they do not please others or even displease them and care nothing about pleasing others, grow worthless. But those who please themselves are greatly displeasing to you, not only by taking what is not good in them to be good, but even by taking the genuinely good things they have from you to be their own accomplishments; or even if they recognize that those good things are from you, they act as if they received them because they deserved them; or if they acknowledge that they have those good things by your grace, they do not share their joy in a spirit of fellowship, but grudge their gifts to others.

You see how my heart trembles in the face of all these temptations and struggles, and many others like them. It is not that I no longer suffer these wounds—this I know—but rather that again and again you heal me.

---

17. "Proud" and "pride" here translate various forms of the noun *gloria* and the verb *glorior*, which I usually translate as "boast/boasting." Clearly in the background here is the Scriptural injunction, "Let the one who boasts (*gloriatur*), boast in the Lord" (1 Corinthians 1:31, 2 Corinthians 10:17).

40.65   Where, O Truth, have you not walked with me, teaching me
what I should avoid and what I should seek, whenever I have brought
before you what I have been able to see here below and sought to learn
from you? I have observed the world by my outward senses to the best
of my ability, and turned my thoughts to myself, to the life of my body
and to my senses themselves. From there I entered into the recesses of
my memory, intricate expanses wondrously full of uncountable treasures, and I examined them and was filled with dread. Apart from you   *Hab. 3:2*
I could not have recognized any of them, and I found that not one of
them was you. Nor was I you: I who found them, who passed through
all of them and tried to distinguish them all and evaluate the worth of
each. Some I received from the reports of my senses, and I questioned
them. Others—the very senses that reported those things to me—were,
I realized, part of myself; I distinguished them and named them one by
one. Still others were found in the broad expanses of memory: some I
examined thoroughly, some I put away, some I drew out into the open.
But I, when I was doing all this, was not you, nor was the power by
which I was doing it—that power also was not you. For you are the
Light that abides for ever, the Light from which I sought to learn about   *Jn. 1:9, 8:12, 9:5,*
all these things—whether they exist, what they are, how much they are   *12:46; 1 Jn. 1:5*
to be valued—and I heard you teaching and commanding.

   And I return to you in this way often. It gives me great delight, and
whenever I can have a respite from pressing duties, I take refuge in this
pleasure. And in all the things through which I pass when I seek to
learn from you, I find no safe place for my soul except in you, in whom
the scattered fragments of myself are bound together, and no part of
me will depart from you. And sometimes you lead me into a state of
feeling quite unlike anything I ordinarily experience, a sweetness I cannot describe; if it should ever be brought to fullness in me, my life will
be far different, though I cannot conceive what it will be like. But I fall
back into ordinary things under the weight of my troubles; my usual
affairs engross me again and hold me in their grip. My grief is powerful, but their grip on me is also powerful. How great is the burden of
habit! I have strength to be here, where I do not want to be; I want
to be elsewhere but lack the strength to go there; and for both these
reasons I am wretched.

41.66   And so I have examined the infirmities of my sins according
to this threefold lust,[18] and I have called upon your right hand[19] for my

---

18. That is, under the general headings of the three sins named in 1 John 2:16: the lust of the
flesh (10.30.41–10.34.53), the lust of the eyes (10.35.54–10.35.57), and worldly ambition
(10.36.58–10.39.64).
19. "your right hand": Christ. See 11.29.39.

salvation. For I have looked upon your glory with a wounded heart, and I reeled back and said, "Who can approach you?" I have been cast away from the sight of your eyes. You are the Truth that presides over all things, and I in my greed did not want to lose you, but I wanted to possess you alongside a lie, just as no one wants to say what is false in such a way that he loses his grip on what is true. And so I lost you, because you would not stoop to be possessed in company with a lie. *Ps. 30:23 / Jn. 14:6*

42.67 Was there anyone I could find to reconcile me with you? Was I to solicit help from angels? By what prayer? By what rites? Many who seek to return to you but lack the strength to do so by themselves have tried these things—so I hear—and they have fallen into a desire to pry into visions that do not concern them;[20] they have been justly rewarded with delusions.[21] For they sought you in pride, puffing out their chests in the arrogance of their teaching instead of beating their breasts,[22] and they drew to themselves the powers of this air, whose *Eph. 2:2* hearts were like their own, as co-conspirators and companions in their pride. These powers deceived them through magic: they looked for a mediator through whom they could be made pure, but there was none to be found. For it was the devil, transforming himself into an angel of light. How great an enticement it was for proud flesh that the devil *2 Cor. 11:14* had no fleshly body! For they were mortal and sinful; but you, O Lord, with whom in their pride they sought to be reconciled, are immortal and sinless.

Now a mediator between God and humanity must have some like- *1 Tim. 2:5* ness to God and some likeness to humanity: if he were like humanity in both respects, he would be far from God, and if he were like God in both respects, he would be far from humanity, and so he would not be a mediator. That is why the false mediator by whom their pride was deservedly deceived, according to your hidden judgments, has something in common with humanity, namely, sin, and wants to appear to have something in common with God: he presents himself as

---

20. "desire to pry into visions that do not concern them": *desiderium curiosarum visionum*, that is, the desire for visions that are objects of the vice of curiosity.

21. Augustine is speaking of the neo-Platonic practice of theurgy, religious ritual aimed at self-purification and union with the One.

22. An outward sign of repentance, still seen in Christian liturgy. (It is prescribed, for example, at certain points in the Roman Rite, and many Anglicans make the gesture at the words "And although we are unworthy, through our manifold sins, to offer unto thee any sacrifice" in Cranmer's Eucharistic Prayer.) The gesture calls to mind the Parable of the Pharisee and the Tax Collector in Luke 18:9–14, in which the tax collector, "standing far off, would not even lift up his eyes to heaven, but beat his breast, saying, 'God, be merciful to me, a sinner.'" Augustine comments in Sermon 67.1.1, "What is it to beat one's breast? Just this: to disclose what is in one's breast (*pectus*) and to chastise one's own hidden sin by an outwardly visible blow."

being immortal because he is not clothed in the mortality of flesh. But because the wages of sin is death, what he has in common with human beings means that he, like them, is condemned to die.   *Rom. 6:23*

43.68   But by your hidden mercy you have given conclusive testimony to the true Mediator and sent him to human beings so that by his example they might learn humility. The Mediator between God and humanity, the man Christ Jesus, has appeared, standing in between   *1 Tim. 2:5* mortal sinners and the immortal Righteous One: mortal like human beings, righteous like God. And so, because the wages of righteousness is life and peace, by the righteousness he shared with God he emptied   *Rom. 8:6* death of its power for the wicked whom he made righteous, whose   *2 Tim. 1:10 / Rom.* death he chose to share. The saints of old received conclusive testimony   *4:5* of him so that by faith in his future suffering they might be saved, just   *Rom. 4:5; 1 Tim.* as we have been saved by faith in his past suffering. He is Mediator   *2:4* insofar as he is human; but insofar as he is the Word, he is not intermediate: no, he is equal to God, God with God, and at once one God.   *Phil. 2:6 / Jn. 1:1*

43.69   How much you have loved us, good Father, who did not spare
            your only Son, but gave him up for us, the ungodly!   *Rom. 8:32 / Rom.*
            How much you have loved us!   *5:6*
        It was for our sake that he, who did not regard equality with
            you as something to be exploited,[23] became obedient even   *Phil. 2:6*
            unto death on a cross.   *Phil. 2:8*
        He alone among the dead was free,   *Ps. 87:6*
            because he had the power to lay down his life and he had
            the power to take it up again.   *Jn. 10:18*
        It was for our sake that he was victor and victim before you:
            victor precisely because he was victim.
        It was for our sake that he was priest and sacrifice before you:
            priest precisely because he was sacrifice.   *Heb. 7:27*
        By being born of you to be our servant, he made us no longer
            servants, but sons and daughters.   *Gal. 4:7*
        My hope in him is strong, and rightly so,
            for you will heal all my infirmities through him who sits at   *Ps. 102:3*
            your right hand and intercedes with you for us.   *Rom. 8:34*

---

23. "who did not regard equality with you as something to be exploited": *non rapinam arbitratus esse aequalis tibi.* The reading of the Authorized Version, "thought it not robbery to be equal with [you]," gives a literal translation of the Latin text, but its sense is obscure to a contemporary reader.

Otherwise I would be in despair,
    for many and great are my infirmities,
    many and great;
    but your medicine is yet more abundant.
We could have thought that your Word is far from any fellowship
    with human beings and so have fallen into despair,
    had he not become flesh and dwelt among us.   *Jn. 1:14*

43.70   Terrified by my sins and by the burden of my wretchedness,
    I was greatly troubled at heart,
    and I had a mind to flee into solitude;
    but you prevented me.
You gave me strength, saying, "Christ died for all,
    so that they might live no longer for themselves,
    but for him who died for them."   *2 Cor. 5:15*
Behold, O Lord, I cast my care upon you that I may live,   *Ps. 54:23; 1 Pet. 5:7*
    and I will meditate on the wonders of your law.   *Ps. 118:18*
You know my ignorance and weakness: *Ps. 24:5, 142:10*
    teach me and heal me.   *Ps. 6:3, 102:3*
Your only Son, in whom are hidden all the treasures
    of wisdom and knowledge,   *Col. 2:3*
    has redeemed me by his blood.   *Rev. 5:9*
Let not the proud deride me,   *Ps. 118:22*
    for I think upon the price that has been paid for me,   *1 Cor. 6:20, 7:23*
    and I eat it and drink it and give it away;   *Jn. 6:54, 55, 57;*
    poor man that I am,   *1 Cor. 10:31,*
                                                          11:29
    I long to have my fill of it   *Lk. 16:20–21*
    among those who eat and are satisfied.
And those who seek the Lord praise him.   *Ps. 21:27*

Book Eleven

Augustine turns from the story of his own life to the story of the world in which he seeks God, the world he knows as God's own creation. This story too has a beginning: "In the beginning God created heaven and earth." But the beginning in which God created was not a temporal beginning: it is the Beginning, the coeternal divine Word by whom God speaks all of creation into existence. Time itself is a creature, a mysterious creature that resists understanding, one that exists only insofar as it is hastening toward non-being. Only in the mind, which can be stretched out or "distended" to encompass many times that cannot all exist at once, can we measure times and hold them together. In this way we have a glimpse of eternity, in which there is no before and after, no coming into being and passing away, but instead an all-encompassing stability and permanence.

Acknowledging that God already knows anything Augustine can say to him (11.1.1), Augustine asks for the power to look into Scripture and confess both what he understands and what remains a mystery to him (11.2.2–4). He begins with the opening words of Genesis, arguing that God created heaven and earth in his coeternal Word (11.3.5–11.9.11). Because God is eternal, there is no sense to be made of the question, "What was God doing before he made heaven and earth?" (11.10.12–11.13.16). God created time, which is both familiar and baffling (11.14.17–11.22.28). Time does not consist in the motion of the heavenly bodies (11.23.29–11.25.32); we measure it by the distention of our minds (11.26.33–11.28.38). Time and eternity are irreducibly different (11.29.39–11.31.41).

1.1 O Lord, eternity is yours, so surely you know all the things I am telling you; you do not see at a time what takes place in time. Why then am I assembling so many stories for you? It is certainly not so that you will learn about them from me. No, I am kindling my affections, and the affections of those who are reading these things, so that we will all say, "Great is the Lord and highly to be praised." As I have said before, I will say again: "It is for the love of your love that I do this."[1] *Ps. 47:2, 95:4, 144:3* For we do pray, and yet Truth tells us, "Your Father knows your needs *Jn. 14:6* before you ask him." So to you we lay open our affections, confessing *Mt. 6:8* to you our own miseries and your mercies toward us so that you might *Ps. 32:22* make us wholly free—for you have begun to free us; so that we might

---

1. 2.1.1.

cease to be miserable in ourselves and become happy in you—for you have called us; so that we might be poor in spirit, meek, mourning, hungering and thirsting after righteousness, merciful, pure in heart, and peacemakers. Truly, then, I have told you these many things, so far as I had the power and the will to tell them, because you first willed that I confess to you, O Lord my God, because you are good, because your mercy endures for ever.

Mt. 5:3–9

Ps. 117:1

2.2 But when will I have sufficient skill with my pen, my tongue, to tell of all your encouragements and all your terrors, the consolations and guidance by which you have led me to preach your word and administer your Sacrament to your people? And even if I do have the skill to tell all these things in order, the drops of time are precious to me, and for a long time I have been desiring to meditate on your law and to confess to you my knowledge and my ignorance, the first glimmers of your illumination and the darkness that remains in me, until weakness is engulfed by strength. I do not want to waste on any other matter the few hours in which I find myself free from the demands of restoring the body and the mind's attention, and from the service that we owe to others, or that we do not owe but give anyway.

Ps. 44:2

1 Cor. 4:1

Ps. 1:2

Ps. 17:29

2.3 O Lord my God, give heed to my prayer, and by your mercy hearken to my desire, for it does not burn for myself alone but is eager to be of use in brotherly love. You see in my heart that it is so. Let me sacrifice to you the service of my thought and my tongue; grant what I would offer to you. For I am destitute and poor; you are generous to all who call upon you. And though nothing can threaten your tranquility, you make our cares your business. Circumcise both my inward and my outward lips from all rashness and all deceit. Let your Scriptures be my chaste delights; do not let me fall into error in them or lead others into error by them. Give heed, O Lord; have mercy, O Lord my God, Light of the blind and Strength of the weak—Light, too, of those who see and Strength of those who are strong—give heed to my soul and hear its cry out of the depths. For unless your ears are present even in the depths, where will we go? To whom will we cry?

Ps. 60:2

Ps. 9:38

Ps. 39:18, 85:1

Rom. 10:12

Ex. 6:12

Ps. 26:7, 85:3; Jer. 18:19

Ps. 129:1–2

Ps. 138:7

Yours is the day, yours also the night. At your command the moments fly away. Generously make room in them for our meditations on the hidden things of your law, and do not close your law against us when we knock. For it was not in vain that you willed the writing of so many pages of dark secrets, and those woods do not lack for your stags, which shelter there and are refreshed, ranging and feeding, lying down and chewing the cud. O Lord, perfect me and reveal them to

Ps. 73:16

Mt. 7:7–8 par. Lk. 11:9–10

Ps. 28:9

me.² Behold, your voice is my joy; your voice surpasses an abundance
of pleasures. Grant what I love—for I do love it, and it is you who have
granted me this love. Do not abandon your gifts; do not despise the
ground that thirsts for you. Let me confess to you whatever I find in
your books; let me hear the voice of praise and quench my thirst with   *Ps. 25:7*
you and ponder the wonders of your law all the way from the begin-   *Ps. 118:18*
ning, in which you made heaven and earth, to the everlasting kingdom   *Gn. 1:1*
we will share with you in your holy city.   *Rev. 21:2, 21:10*

2.4   O Lord, have mercy on me and hearken to my desire. It is not,   *Ps. 9:38, 26:7*
I feel sure, an earthly desire, a desire for gold and silver and precious
stones, for fine clothing, for honor and influence, for physical pleasures, or for the needs of the body and of this present wayfaring life;
we who seek your kingdom and your righteousness are given all those
things as well. You see, my God, the source of my desire. The wicked   *Mt. 6:33*
have told me of pleasures, but they are not like the pleasures of your
law, O Lord: behold, then, the source of my desire. See it, Father: *Ps. 118:85*
look upon it and see it and give your approval. May it be pleasing
in the eyes of your mercy that I find favor in your sight, so that the   *Ps. 18:15 / Ex. 33:13*
inner chambers of your words may be opened to me when I knock. I   *Mt. 7:7–8 par. Lk.*
beseech you through our Lord Jesus Christ your Son, the man of your   *11:9–10*
right hand, the Son of Man, whom you have established for your-   *Ps. 79:18 / Mt.*
self as Mediator between you and us, through whom you sought us   *8:20; Mk. 2:10;*
                                                                               etc. / 1 Tim. 2:5
who did not seek you—sought us, indeed, that we might seek you—   *Is. 65:1; Rom.*
your Word, through whom you made all things, me among them;   *10:20 / Jn.*
                                                                               1:1, 1:3
your Only-begotten, through whom you have called into adoption   *Gal. 4:4–5*
the company of believers, to which I belong: I beseech you through
him, who is seated at your right hand and intercedes with you for us,   *Rom. 8:34*
in whom are hidden all the treasures of wisdom and knowledge, the   *Col. 2:3*
treasures that I seek in your books. Moses wrote of him: he says so;   *Jn. 5:46*
Truth says so.³   *Jn. 14:6*

3.5   I would like to hear and understand how in the beginning you
made heaven and earth. Moses wrote these words. He wrote them and   *Gn. 1:1*
departed; he passed over from here, from you to you, and he is not now
before me. If he were, I could get hold of him and ask him and implore
him, for your sake, to explain them to me. And I would open my ears to

---

2. Grammatically, "them" could refer to either "pages" or "woods"; since the woods are an image
for the pages, the meaning is the same either way. The strange imagery of these two sentences derives
from Augustine's text of Psalm 28:9 (29:5): "The voice of the Lord perfects the stags and has revealed
the woods; and in his temple all cry, 'Glory.'" Note, then, that Augustine is asking to be one of the
stags who are at home in, and nourished by, the mysterious dark woods of Scripture.
3. John 5:46 (Jesus speaking): "If you believed Moses, you would believe me, for he wrote of me."

the sounds that would emerge from his mouth. If he spoke in Hebrew, he would strike against my sense in vain, and nothing of what he said would touch my mind; but if he spoke in Latin, I would know what he was saying. But from what source would I know whether it was true? And if I did know this, I would surely not know it from him, would I? No, indeed: the inward Truth, within me in the dwelling place of my thought, would say to me—not in Hebrew or Greek or Latin or any barbarous language, without any organ of mouth or tongue, without any rattling of syllables—"What he says is true." And I with certainty and confidence would immediately say to him, "What you say is true." So, since I cannot question Moses, I ask you, God; it was by being filled with you, who are Truth, that Moses said true things. I ask you, God: have mercy on my sins, and as you empowered your servant to say these things, empower me to understand them.

Jn. 14:6

Ps. 118:34, 118:73, 118:144

4.6   Consider: heaven and earth exist. They cry out that they were made, for they undergo change and variation. By contrast, if anything was not made and yet exists, there is nothing in it that was not in it before—which is what it is to undergo change and variation. They also cry out that they did not make themselves: "We exist because we were made. So before we existed, we were not anything, so as to be able to make ourselves." And it is by their manifest character that they say these things. Therefore, you, O Lord, made them: you who are beautiful, for they are beautiful; who are good, for they are good; who have being, for they have being. And they are not as beautiful or as good as you, their Creator, nor do they have being as you have being; in comparison with you they have neither goodness nor beauty nor being. We know these things, thanks to you; and our knowledge, in comparison with yours, is but ignorance.

5.7   But how did you make heaven and earth? What was the mechanism by which you carried out so great a work of yours? A human craftsman decides to shape a material thing, and the soul that makes this decision has the power, somehow, to impose on that material thing a form that it perceives within itself by its inward eye. But this is not how you form material things—and indeed how would a human craftsman have the power to do this, except because you made his mind? Further, he imposes a form on something that already exists and has being, such as earth or stone or wood or gold or something of that sort. And how would any of those things exist unless you had established them? You made the craftsman's body. You made the soul that commands his bodily members. You made the matter out of which he makes something. You made the talent by which he grasps his art and sees within himself what he will make outside himself. You made the bodily sense by which he translates his work from mind into matter and then reports back to the mind what he has made, so that he may take counsel with the truth that presides within him to see whether the work has been well made.

All these things praise you, the Creator of them all. But how did you make them? How, God, did you make heaven and earth? It was not *in* heaven and earth that you made heaven and earth; nor was it in the air or in the waters, for they too belong to heaven and earth. Nor did you make the whole world in the whole world, since before it was made, there was no place in which it could be made so that it might exist. Nor did you hold in your hand something from which you would make heaven and earth, for where would this thing have come from—this thing that you did not make—from which you would make something? What, indeed, exists at all, except because you exist? Therefore, you spoke and they were made; and in your word you made them.

Ps. 32:9, 148:5

Ps. 32:6

6.8   But how did you speak? Was it in the same way in which a voice came from the cloud, saying, "This is my beloved Son"? That voice went forth and was completed; it had a beginning and an ending. Its syllables sounded and passed away: the second after the first, the third after the second, and the rest in order, until the last syllable sounded after all the rest, and after the last was silence. From this it is clear and evident that the movement of a creature pronounced that voice; it was a temporal thing serving your eternal will. These words of yours, made in accordance with time, were conveyed by the outward ear to the understanding mind whose inward ear is attuned to your eternal Word. Then the mind compared these words that sounded in time with your eternal Word in his silence, and it said, "They are far different. They are far different. These temporal words are far beneath me; nor do they really have being, since they flee and pass away. But the Word of my God is above me, and he abides for ever." So if it was by words that sounded and then passed away that you spoke, so that heaven and earth might be made, and in that way you made heaven and earth, then there was already some bodily creature before you made heaven and earth, and by the temporal movements of that creature your utterance was extended through time. But there was no body before heaven and earth—or if there was, you had certainly made it without any transitory speech, so that from it you would make the transitory speech by which you would say, "Let heaven and earth be made." For whatever that might have been, by which such a speech would be made, it would

Mt. 3:17, 17:5

Is. 40:8

not have existed at all unless you had made it. By what word, then, did you make the body by which those words would be made?

7.9   And so you call us into understanding the Word, God with you, O God: the Word who is uttered eternally and by whom all things are   *Jn 1:1* uttered eternally. It is not that one word is completed and then another word is spoken, so that all things may be uttered; all are uttered at once and eternally. Otherwise there would already be time and change, not true eternity and true immortality. I know this, my God, and I give you thanks. I know this and I confess to you, Lord; and everyone who   *Mt. 11:25 par. Lk.* is thankful for assured truth joins me in knowing it and in blessing   *10:21* you. We know this, Lord; we know this because insofar as anything is not what it once was, and is what it once was not, it passes away and comes to be. Therefore, nothing of your Word gives place to another or follows another, since he is truly immortal and eternal. And so it is by the Word, coeternal with you, that you all at once and eternally utter all the things you utter; and it is by him that whatever you speak into existence is made. You make these things precisely by speaking them, and yet the things that you make by speaking are not made all at once, and they are not made to be eternal.

8.10   Why is this, I ask you, O Lord my God? I do see it, in a way, but I do not know how to express it, unless it is because all that begins to be and ceases to be begins and ceases at the right time as it is known in the eternal reason where nothing either begins or ceases. This is your eternal Word, who is also the Beginning, because he speaks to us.[4] In   *Jn. 8:25* this way he speaks to us in the Gospel through the flesh; he proclaimed it outwardly to human ears so that the word might be believed and sought within and found in that eternal Truth where the good Teacher,   *Mk. 10:17 par.* the only Teacher, teaches all his students. In that eternal Truth, O Lord,   *Lk. 18:18 / Mt.* I hear your voice, the voice of one who is speaking to me. For anyone   *23:8* who teaches us speaks to us, whereas one who does not teach us does not speak to us, even if he does speak. And indeed what teaches us, besides unwavering Truth? For even when we are admonished by a changeable creature, we are led to unwavering Truth; that is where we truly learn when we stand and listen to him and exult with joy because of the bridegroom's voice, giving ourselves back to him from whom we   *Jn. 3:29* have our being. And this is why he is the Beginning: for if he did not abide when we went astray, there would be nowhere for us to return.

---

4. John 8:24–25 in Augustine's version reads, "[Jesus said,] 'Unless you believe that I am he, you will die in your sins.' So they said to him, 'Who are you?' Jesus said to them, 'the beginning, because I am also speaking with you.'"

Now when we return from error, it is of course by knowing that we return; and in order that we might know, he teaches us, because he is the Beginning and speaks to us.

9.11   In this Beginning, God, you made heaven and earth in your Word, your Son, your Power, your Wisdom, your Truth, uttering them *1 Cor. 1:24* in a wondrous way, and in a wondrous way making them. Who can grasp this? Who can set it forth in words? What is this that shines through me and buffets my heart without injury? I shudder and I am alight: I shudder insofar as I am unlike him; I am alight insofar as I am like him. It is Wisdom, Wisdom herself,[5] who shines through me and pierces the clouds that surround me. But when I fall away from Wisdom because of that gloom and the burden of my punishments, the clouds envelop me again. For in my neediness my strength has wasted away, so that I cannot sustain even what is good in me until you, Lord, *Ps. 30:11 / Ps. 64:8* who have forgiven all my sins, also heal all my infirmities; for you will also redeem my life from corruption and crown me with mercy and loving-kindness; and you will satisfy my desire with good things, since my youth will be renewed like an eagle's. For in hope we have been *Ps. 102:3–5* saved, and through patience we look for your promises. *Rom. 8:24–25*

Let those who are able hear you speaking within. I will cry out confidently in words you have provided: "How magnificent are your works, O Lord! In Wisdom you have made them all." And that Wisdom is the *Ps. 103:24* Beginning, and in that Beginning you made heaven and earth.

10.12   Those who say to us, "What was God doing before he made heaven and earth?" are undoubtedly full of their old carnal nature. "For if he was idle," they say, "and was not doing anything, why did he not always stay that way from then on, just as up to that point he had always refrained from action? After all, if some new motion and new will arose in God, so that he created something he had never created before, how will that be a true eternity in which a will comes into being that once did not exist? For God's will is not a creature; it is before any creature, since nothing would be created unless the Creator's will came first. Therefore, God's will belongs to his very substance. And if something came into being in God's substance that had not existed before, his substance cannot with truth be called eternal. Yet if God's will that creation should exist is eternal, why is creation not also eternal?"

11.13   Those who say these things do not yet understand you, O Wisdom of God, Light of Minds; they do not yet understand how

---

5. See 9.10.24, fn. 29.

those things are made that are made by you and in you. Such people
strive to be wise concerning what is eternal, but their heart is still foolish, still flitting about in past and future movements of things. Who
will catch hold of their heart and pin it down so that it will be still for
just a little while and seize, for just a little while, the glory of an eternity
that remains ever steadfast and set it beside times⁶ that never remain
steadfast and see that eternity is in no way comparable to them? Then
their heart would see that a time can become long only through many
movements that pass away and cannot be stretched out all at once, but
that in eternity nothing passes away, but the whole is present—whereas
no time is present as a whole. And their heart would see that everything
past is thrust back from the future and everything future follows upon
the past, and everything past and future is created and set in motion
by the One who is always present. Who will catch hold of the human
heart so that it will be still and see how eternity, which stands still and
so has neither past nor future, decrees both future and past times? Does
my hand have the strength to do this? Does the hand of my mouth
accomplish so great a deed by the power of its speech?

12.14   Look, I shall answer the one who asks, "What was God doing
before he made heaven and earth?" I do not give the answer that one
fellow is reported to have given, making a joke to evade the force of the
question: "He was preparing hell for people who pry into deep matters." Ridiculing a question is quite different from seeing the answer,
so that is not how I will respond. I would much more willingly say,
"What I don't know, I don't know" than offer a response that mocks
someone who has asked about deep matters and wins me praise for a
false answer. Rather, I say that you, our God, are the Creator of every
creature; and if by "heaven and earth" is meant every creature, then I
confidently say, "Before God made heaven and earth, he was not making or doing anything." After all, if he was making something, what
would he have been making other than some creature? If only I knew
everything that I desire to know for my own benefit with as much clarity as I know that no creature was made before any creature was made!

13.15   But if some flighty mind wanders through images of times gone
by and marvels that you, Almighty and All-creating and All-sustaining

6. Throughout Books 11 and 12 Augustine typically speaks of "times" in the plural (*tempora*)
rather than "time" in the singular (*tempus*). "Times" is not altogether natural in English, at least
without a modifier ("ancient times," "good times"), so translators generally prefer the singular. But
the plural carries meaning: it expresses the multiplicity, dispersion, and evanescence of the temporal
order as contrasted with the perfect unity and steadfastness of divine eternity. I have accordingly
retained the plural wherever Augustine uses it.

God, Maker of heaven and earth, should have refrained for countless ages from so great a work until at last you carried it out, he needs to wake up and pay attention, because he is marveling at falsehoods. How could countless ages pass that you had not made? For you are the Author and Creator of all the ages. And what were these times that you had not created? How could they have passed if they never existed? Since, therefore, all times are your work, what sense does it make to say that you refrained from any work if in fact there was some time before you made heaven and earth? That time itself was something you had made; times could not pass before you made times. But if there was no time before you made heaven and earth, what sense is there in asking what you were doing then? There was no "then," for there was no time.

Gn. 2:3

Heb. 1:2

13.16   It is not in time that you precede times, since otherwise you would not precede all times. No, it is by the loftiness of ever-present eternity that you precede all past things, and you surpass all future things because they are future, and once they have come, they will be past. But you are the Selfsame, and your years will not fail. Your years do not come and go. Our years come and go, so that they all may come; your years stand all at once because they stand still, and those that go do not give way to those that come, for your years do not pass away. Our years will be completed only when they will all no longer exist. Your years are one day, and your day is not day-after-day but today, because your today does not give way to any tomorrow or follow after any yesterday. Your today is eternity. And so it was one coeternal with yourself whom you begot, to whom you said, "Today have I begotten you." You made all times, and before all times, you are. Nor was there any time at which there was no time.

Ps. 101:28; Heb. 1:12

Ps. 89:4; 2 Pet. 3:8

Ps. 2:7 qtd. Acts 13:3; Heb. 1:5, 5:5

14.17   Therefore, there was no time at which you had not made anything, because you made time itself. And no times are coeternal with you, since you persist, whereas they would not be times if they persisted. What, after all, is time? Is there any short and simple answer to that question? Can anyone even wrap his mind around time so as to express it in words? Is there anything we talk about more familiarly, more knowingly, than time? And surely we understand it when we talk about it; we even understand it when we hear someone else talking about it.

So what is time? If no one asks me, I know; if I want to explain it to someone who asks me, I do not know. Yet I say with confidence that I know that if nothing passed away, there would be no past time, and if nothing were approaching, there would be no future time, and if nothing existed, there would be no present time. So how do those two times, the past and the future, exist when the past no longer exists and the future does not yet exist? But if the present were always present and did not flow away into the past, it would no longer be time, but eternity. So if, in order to be time, the present comes into being precisely by flowing into the past, how can we say that the present exists, given that it exists only because it will not exist? In other words, if time did not tend toward non-existence, we could not truly say that it exists at all.

15.18   And yet we speak of "a long time" and "a short time," and we say this only of the past or the future. For example, we call a hundred years ago a long time in the past and a hundred years from now a long time in the future; but we call, say, ten days ago a short time in the past and ten days from now a short time in the future. But how is something that does not exist either long or short? The past, after all, no longer exists, and the future does not yet exist. So let us not say, "It is long," but instead let us say of the past, "It *was* long," and of the future, "It *will be* long."

Even so, my Lord and my Light, will not your Truth scoff at human beings? This past time that was long: was it long when it was already past or when it was still present? It could be long only when it existed so that it could be long. But once it was past, it did not exist anymore; hence, it also could not be long, since it was not anything at all. Therefore, let us not say, "The past time was long," for we will not even be able to find the thing that was long—by the very fact that it is past, it does not exist—but instead let us say, "That present time was long," since when it was present, it was long. For at that point it had not yet passed away into non-existence, and therefore there was something that could be long; after it had become past, however, that which ceased to be also, at that very same time, ceased to be long.

Mic. 7:8; 1 Jn. 1:5 / Ps. 58:9

15.19   Let us see, then, O human soul, whether a present time can be long—for you have been given the power to perceive duration and to measure it. What answer will you give me? Are one hundred present years a long time? Examine first whether one hundred years can *be* present. If the first of those years is in progress, then it is present, but the other ninety-nine are future and therefore do not yet exist. If, however, the second year is in progress, then one year is already past, another year is present, and the rest are future. And so it is if we assume that any one of the years in the middle of the hundred is present: there will be past years before it and future years after it. Accordingly, one hundred years cannot be present.

Now examine whether that one year, at any rate, can be present as it is in progress. If its first month is in progress, the other months are future. If the second month is in progress, the first month has already passed and the remaining months do not yet exist. So not even the whole year that is in progress is present. And if the whole is not present, the year is not present. For a year is twelve months, and when any one of those months is present, the others are either past or future.

For that matter, not even the month that is in progress is present, but only one day. If the first day of the month is present, the rest are future; if the last, the rest are past; if one in the middle, it is between past days and future days.

15.20   Look! The present time, which we found to be the only time that can be called "long," has shrunk to the size of barely one day. But let us break up even that: for not even one whole day is present. It comprises twenty-four hours of day and night. The first of these hours has other hours future to it, the last has others past, and any of the hours in between has some past hours before it and some future hours after it. And that one hour passes by in small, fleeting pieces. Any part of it that has flown away is past, and any part that remains is future. If any part of time can be conceived that cannot be further divided into even the tiniest parts of moments, that alone is what should be called "present." Yet that present flies away from the future into the past with such speed that it has no extension, no expanse of time at all. For if it is extended, it is divided into past and future; but the present has no duration.

Where, then, is a time that we can call "long"? Is it in the future? Then we do not in fact say, "It is long," because the thing that would be long does not yet exist; but instead we say, "It will be long." So when will it be long? If even then it is still future, it will not be long, because the thing that would be long does not yet exist. Suppose instead that it will be long when, out of the future that does not yet exist, it begins to exist and becomes present and thus exists so that it can be long. In that case, the present time cries out, in the words already spoken, that it cannot be long.

16.21   And yet, Lord, we experience intervals of time and compare them with each other. We say that some are longer, others shorter. We even measure how much longer or shorter one time is than another; we determine that one is twice as long or three times as long as another, or that two are equally long. But when we measure times by experiencing them, we are measuring things that are passing away. And who can measure past things, which no longer exist, or future things, which do not yet exist? Surely no one will be so brazen as to say that what does not exist can be measured. So while time is passing, it can be experienced and measured; but once it has passed, it cannot, because it does not exist.

17.22   I am inquiring, Father, not making assertions. My God, guide me and govern me. We learned as children, and we have taught children, that there are three times: past, present, and future. Will someone tell me that this is not so: that there are not three times, but only one, the present, because the other two do not exist? Or do they perhaps exist after all, but time comes forth from some secret place when the future becomes present, and recedes into some secret place when the present becomes past? Where did those who prophesied future events see them, if future things do not yet exist? After all, what does not yet exist cannot be seen. And those who tell stories of the past would certainly not be telling the truth if they did not perceive those past things in their mind; and if no past things existed, they could not in any way be perceived. It follows, then, that both future and past things exist.

Ps. 22:1, 27:9, 47:15

18.23   Permit me to inquire further, O Lord, my hope; do not let my attention be distracted. If indeed future and past things exist, I want to know where they are. If I do not yet have the strength to know where they are, I do at least know that wherever they are, they are not future or past there, but present. For if they are future there, they do not yet exist there; and if they are past there, they no longer exist there. So wherever they are, whatever they are, they must be present. Yet when a true story is told about past things, it is not the things themselves that are brought forth out of memory—for the things themselves have passed away—but words conceived from images of the things. These images are like imprints that the things themselves, as they were passing away, stamped on the soul through the senses. My boyhood, for example, which no longer exists, is in past time, which no longer exists. But when I recall it and tell stories about it, I see an image of it in the present time, since it still exists in my memory.

Ps. 70:5

Whether there is a similar explanation for foretellings of the future—that already-existing images of things that do not yet exist are made present—I must confess, my God, I do not know. This much I do know: we often deliberate about our future actions, and that deliberation is present, although the action we are deliberating about does not yet exist, because it is future. Once we undertake the action we were deliberating about and begin to do it, the action will exist, because then it will be present, not future.

18.24   Whatever else is true of the mysterious presentiment of future things, it is not possible for something to be seen that does not exist. Further, what already exists is present, not future. So when we say that future things are seen, it is not the things themselves that are seen—for they do not yet exist; they are in the future—but perhaps their causes or signs, which do already exist. So the things conceived by the mind, on the basis of which future things are predicted, are present to those who see them, rather than future. Again, these conceptions already exist, and those who foretell future things look upon these present conceptions within themselves.

There is such a great multitude of these things, but just one can serve me as an example. I see the dawn and I foretell that the sun is going to rise. What I see is present; what I foretell is future. The *sun* is not future—it already exists—but its rising, which does not yet exist, is future. Still, I would not be able to predict the sunrise unless I were imagining it in my mind, in the way I am doing now as I speak. Now the dawn that I see in the sky is not the sunrise, although it does precede the sunrise; nor is that image in my mind the sunrise. Perceiving these two present things is what allows me to speak beforehand of the future thing. So future things do not yet exist; and if they do not exist *yet*, they do not exist; and if they do not exist, they cannot in any way be seen, though they can be predicted on the basis of present things that already exist and are seen.

19.25   And you, Sovereign of your creation, how do you teach souls those things that are future? Certainly you have taught your prophets. How do you, to whom nothing is future, teach future things? Or do you instead teach present things concerning future things? For what does not exist cannot even be taught. The way in which you do this is far beyond my power of vision; it is too much for me. In my own strength I cannot attain to it. But in the strength that comes from you, sweet Light of my hidden eyes, I will be able to attain to it, when you have granted me your help.

Ps. 138:6

Ps. 37:11; Eccl. 11:7

20.26   It is now clear and evident that neither future things nor past things exist. Nor is it strictly correct to say, "There are three times: past, present, and future." Instead, it would perhaps be correct to say, "There are three times: the present of things past, the present of things present, and the present of things future." These are certainly three things in the soul (and I do not see them anywhere else): the present of things past is memory, the present of things present is attention, and the present of things future is expectation. If we are allowed to use such language, I see three times, and I acknowledge that they are three. And let people go ahead and say, "There are three times: past, present, and future," as ordinary language inaptly puts it; let them go ahead and say that. I do not mind; I do not object or find fault, provided that one understands what is being said, and that neither the future nor the past now exists. There are few things that our ordinary language expresses correctly, and many things that it does not; but it is clear what we mean.

21.27   I said a bit earlier[7] that we measure passing times, so that we can say this time is twice as long as that one, or this time is exactly as long as that one, and whatever else we can say by way of measuring the parts of time. So, as I was saying, we measure passing times; and if anyone asks me, "How do you know this?" I will answer, "I know because we measure them, and we cannot measure what does not exist, and past and future things do not exist." But how do we measure present time, which has no duration? It must be measured as it passes, since once it has passed, it is not measured—for then there is no longer anything there to be measured.

But when it is measured, where does it come from, by what path does it go, and to where does it pass? There are no answers but these: it comes from the future, goes through the present, and passes into the past. So it comes from what does not yet exist, goes through what has no duration, and passes into what no longer exists. Yet our measurements of time are always in terms of some duration. We say that a time is one unit long, or that one time is twice as long or three times as long or equally long as another; and all such statements, and others like them, are in terms of some duration. So in what duration do we measure passing time? In the future, from which it comes? We do not measure what does not yet exist. In the present, through which it goes? We do not measure what has no duration. In the past, into which it passes? We do not measure what no longer exists.

22.28   My mind is on fire to solve this most perplexing mystery. O Lord my God, good Father, I implore you in the name of Christ: do not hide these things, so familiar and yet so secret, from my longing; let me break through to them until they begin to shine by the light of your mercy, O Lord. From whom shall I earnestly seek answers to these questions? To whom shall I more profitably confess my ignorance than to you? For you are not displeased by the raging fire of my zeal to understand your Scriptures. Grant what I love—for I do love it, and even that love is your gift. Grant it, Father, who truly know how to give good gifts to your children; grant it, because I have set out to   *Mt. 7:11*

---

7. 11.16.21.

understand these things but the labor is too great for me, until you *Ps. 72:16*
open the door. I implore you in the name of Christ, in the name of him *Mt. 7:7–8 par. Lk.*
who is the Holy of Holies, let no one hinder me. I have believed, and *11:9–10*
therefore I speak. This is my hope, and for this I live, that I might gaze *Ps. 115:10*
upon the delight of the Lord. Behold, you have made my days old; and *Ps. 26:4 / Ps. 38:6*
they pass away, I know not how.

We speak of time and time, of times and times: "How long ago did
he say that?" and "How long ago did he do that?" and "For how long
a time have I not seen that?" and "This syllable takes twice the time
of that short, simple syllable." We say these things and hear them; we
are understood and we understand. They are utterly obvious, utterly
familiar—and yet they are desperately obscure, a fresh discovery.

23.29   A certain learned person once said to me that the movements
of the sun and moon and stars are times, but I did not agree. Why not
rather say that the movements of *all* bodies are times? If the heavenly
lights stood still but a potter's wheel moved, would there not be time
by which we would measure its revolutions and say that they were
of equal periods—or, if the wheel moved at an unsteady speed, that
some revolutions took less time and others more? And as we said these
things, would not we ourselves be speaking in time? Would not some
syllables in our speech be long and others short—and that only because
the longer syllables sounded for a longer time and the shorter syllables
for a shorter time? God, grant human beings the power to see in small
things the common principles of things both small and great. Stars and
heavenly lights are for signs and times and days and years. That is cer- *Gn. 1:14*
tainly true. But I would not say that the rotation of that little wooden
wheel is a day; and that learned man should not say that if the heavenly
bodies stood still, there would be no time.

23.30   I desire to know the power and nature of the time by which
we measure the movements of bodies and say that (for example) this
movement takes twice as long as that one. Here is my question: "day"
is used not only for the period in which the sun is over the earth—this
is the sense in which day is distinguished from night—but also for the
whole of its circuit from east to east. In this latter sense we say "So-and-
so many days have passed" (the number of days here includes nights as
well; the periods of night are not regarded as extra). So since a day is
completed along with the movement and circuit of the sun from east to
east, I ask whether a day is this motion itself, or instead the amount of
time that elapses while that motion takes place, or both. If the motion
itself were a day, then even if the sun completed its course in an interval
of time equal to one hour, that would be a day. If a day is the amount

of time, then if the interval between one sunrise and the next were as short as one hour, that would not constitute a day; the sun would have to complete twenty-four revolutions for one day to pass. If both the motion and the amount of time are a day, then it would not be called a day if the sun completed its revolution in the space of one hour; nor would it be called a day if the sun stood still but the amount of time passed in which the sun ordinarily makes its circuit from one morning to the next.

And so I will not ask now what it is that is called a day. Instead I will ask this: what is the time by which we measure the sun's circuit, so that if it were completed in the span of time in which twelve hours elapse, we would say that it was completed in half the time it ordinarily takes; and, comparing the two times, we would say that one is a single period and the other double, even if the sun completed its circuit from sunrise to sunrise sometimes in the single period and sometimes in the double? So let no one say to me that times are the movements of the heavenly bodies. For once, in answer to someone's prayer, the sun stood still so that he might fight a battle to victory; the sun stood still, but time passed. Indeed, the fighting was carried out and completed over a span of time that was sufficient for it. *Josh. 10:13–14*

I see, therefore, that time is a kind of distention. But do I see this, or do I merely think I see it? You, Light and Truth, will show me. *Jn. 1:9 / Jn. 14:6*

24.31 Do you command me to agree when someone says that time is the movement of a body? You do not. For I hear that no body moves except in time; you say this. But I do not hear that the movement of a body is itself time; you do not say that. For when a body moves, I measure in time how long its movement takes, from when it begins to move until it stops. If I did not see when it began to move, and it continues to move and I do not see when it stops, I cannot measure—except perhaps from when I begin to see it until I stop paying attention. If I watch it for a good while, I can report only that it was a long time, but not how long, since when we say how long something lasts, we do so by means of a comparison: for example, "This is as long as that" or "This is twice as long as that" or something of that sort. But if we can mark off the spans of the places from which and to which a moving body goes—or its parts, if it is moved as on a lathe—we can say how long a time it takes for that body (or its parts) to move from this place to that.

And so the body's movement and that by which we measure it are two distinct things. That being so, does anyone not realize which of these two is more properly called "time"? If a body sometimes moves and sometimes is at rest, we measure not only its motion but also its rest in time. We say, "It was at rest as long as it was in motion" or "It was at rest twice as long, or three times as long, as it was in motion" or whatever else our measurement might be, whether we have determined it exactly or merely estimated ("more or less," as we say). So time is not the movement of a body.

25.32   I confess to you, Lord, that even now I do not know what time is. And again I confess to you, Lord, that I know I am saying these things in time, and that I have already been speaking for a long while about time, and that this long while is long only as a period of time. How, then, do I know all this when I do not know what time is? Do I perhaps not know how to express what I do know? Woe is me: I do not even know what it is I do not know! Behold, my God, before you I do not lie. As I am speaking, so is my heart. You, O Lord, will light my lamp; my God, you will make my darkness bright.

Ps. 9:2; Mt. 11:25 par. Lk. 10:21

Gal. 1:20

Ps. 17:29

26.33   Does not my soul confess to you in a true confession that I measure times? So I measure, my God, and I do not know what it is I am measuring. By time I measure the movement of a body. Do I not likewise measure time itself? Could I, in fact, measure the movement of a body—how long it is, and how long it takes in going from here to there—without measuring the time in which it moves? How, then, do I measure that time itself? Do we measure a longer time by a shorter time in the way that we measure the length of a crossbeam by a yardstick? That would seem to be how we measure the length of a long syllable by that of a short syllable and say that the former is double the latter. It is how we measure the length of poems by the length of their lines, and the length of lines by the length of their feet, and the length of feet by the length of their syllables, and the length of long syllables by the length of short syllables: not in pages (that is a way for us to measure places, not times), but as the sounds pass by in being pronounced. And we say, "The poem is long because it contains so many lines; the lines are long because they consist of so many feet; the feet are long because they stretch out for so many syllables; the syllable is long because it is double a short syllable." But even this does not establish a reliable measure of time, because a shorter line, if recited very deliberately, might sound for a greater length of time than a longer line spoken hastily. And the same goes for poems, feet, and syllables.

Hence it appears to me that time is nothing other than distention— but a distention of *what* I do not know. I should be surprised if it were not a distention of the mind itself. I implore you, God: what, then, am I measuring when I say, indefinitely, "This time is longer than that one," or even, definitely, "This time is twice as long as that"? I am measuring time—so much I know. But I am not measuring the future, which does not yet exist; I am not measuring the present, which is not extended for any duration; I am not measuring the past, because it no longer exists. What, then, am I measuring? Not *past* times, but *passing* times? So I said earlier.[8]

27.34 Be still, my mind; be vigorous in your attention. God is our helper; it is he who has made us, and not we ourselves. Give your atten- *Ps. 61:9 / Ps. 99:3*
tion where the truth is beginning to dawn. A bodily voice, let us say, begins to sound; it sounds and keeps sounding. Then it stops. Now there is silence, and the voice is past and is no longer a voice. Before it sounded, it was future; and it could not be measured, because it did not yet exist. And it cannot be measured now, because it no longer exists. So it could be measured while it was sounding, because that was when a voice existed that could be measured. But even then it was not standing still; it was moving and passing away. Or was that all the more reason it *could* be measured? For in passing away it was extended through some span of time that could be measured, since the present has no duration.

So let us assume that it could be measured then, and imagine another voice. It begins to sound and keeps sounding uniformly and without interruption. Let us measure it while it is sounding. After all, once it has stopped sounding, it will already be past and there will be nothing to measure. Let us measure it with precision and say how great it is. But it is still sounding, and it can be measured only from its beginning, when it starts to sound, to its end, when it stops. (What we measure is, of course, the interval between a beginning and an end.) So a voice that is not yet finished cannot be measured so that one can say how long or short it is, or that it is equal to another, or that in relation to another it is single or double or anything else. But once it has been completed, it will no longer exist. How, then, will anyone be able to measure it? And yet we do measure times: but not those that do not yet exist, nor those that no longer exist, nor those that are not extended for any duration, nor those that have no ending point. It follows that we do not measure future times, or past times, or present times, or passing times. And yet we do measure times.

27.35 *Deus Creator omnium.*[9] This eight-syllable line alternates between short and long syllables. The four short syllables (the first,

---

8. 11.16.21, 11.21.27.
9. "O God, Creator of all," the opening line of a hymn for evening composed by Ambrose: see 9.12.32.

third, fifth, and seventh) are single in comparison with the four long syllables (the second, fourth, sixth, and eighth): each long syllable takes twice as much time as each short syllable. I recite the line and report this; and it is true, so far as I experience it with clear perception. So far as my perception is clear, I measure the long syllable by the short one and perceive that it is exactly twice as long. But since one sounds after the other—the short one first, and then the long—how will I retain the short one and set it against the long one to measure it so that I find it to be exactly twice as long? For the long syllable does not begin to sound until the short one stops sounding. Do I measure the long syllable when it is still present? Surely not, since I do not measure it until it is complete. But once it is complete, it is in the past: so then what am I measuring? Where is the short syllable by which I measure it? And where is the long syllable that I measure? Both have sounded. They have fled and passed away. They no longer exist. But I do measure, and I answer with all the confidence that one can repose in finely honed perception, that the short syllable is single and the long one double, in terms of the time they take. I cannot do this unless they have passed away and are complete. So I am not measuring the syllables themselves, which no longer exist; I measure something in my memory that stays imprinted there.

27.36   It is in you, my mind, that I measure times. Do not hinder me—that is, do not let the tumult of your impressions hinder you. In you, I say, I measure times. I measure the impression that passing things make on you, an impression that remains after the things have passed away. I measure the impression, which is present, not the things that made the impression by passing away. It is the impression that I measure when I measure times. So either these impressions are times, or else I do not measure times.

And when we measure a silence and say that this silence lasted for just as long a time as that voice, do we not distend our thought to measure the voice as if it were sounding, so that we can report something about the duration of the silences within a span of time? With voice and lips stilled, in our thought we run through poems and lines and speeches; and we report on the measure of their movements, and the time one takes in relation to another, just as we would if we said them aloud. Suppose someone wanted to make a rather long sound, and he settled beforehand how long it was going to be. He has of course thought through that span of time in silence, and committing it to his memory, he begins to make the sound, which sounds until it is brought to the ending point that he had in view. Or rather, it has sounded and will sound: for whatever part of it is already finished has sounded, whereas whatever remains will sound. And thus the sound is being completed as long as present intention propels the future into the past; as the part of the sound that is future shrinks, its past grows, until its future is completely used up and the whole sound is past.

28.37   But how does the future, which does not yet exist, shrink or get used up? How does the past, which no longer exists, grow? It can only be because these three exist in the mind, which accomplishes this. For the mind looks ahead, it attends, and it remembers, so that what it looks ahead to passes through what it attends to and into what it remembers. Who, then, denies that future things do not yet exist? But even so, in the mind there is already an expectation of future things. And who denies that past things no longer exist? But even so, in the mind there is still a memory of past things. And who denies that the present time lacks duration, since it passes away in an instant? But even so, attention endures; and that which will be passes through attention on its way to being no more. So future time, which does not exist, is not long; a long future is a long expectation of the future. And past time, which does not exist, is not long; a long past is a long memory of the past.

28.38   I am about to sing a song I know. Before I begin, my expectation is stretched out through the whole song. But once I have begun, my memory too is stretched out, over as much as I have gathered from my expectation and stored in the past. And the life of this action of mine is distended into memory because of what I have already sung and into expectation because of what I am going to sing. But my attention is present and exists now, and what was future passes through my attention so it becomes past. As more and more of the action is completed, expectation grows shorter and memory longer, until all of the expectation is used up and the whole, completed action has passed into memory. And what is true of the whole song is true of each of its stanzas and of every one of its syllables. It is true of a longer action, of which perhaps the song is a small part. It is true of a whole human life, whose parts are all of a person's actions. It is true of the whole age of the children of men, whose parts are all human lives.

Ps. 30:20

29.39   Yet because your mercy is better than lives, behold, my life is a distention, and your right hand has lifted me up in my Lord, the Son of Man, the Mediator between you, who are one, and us, who are many—with many distractions about many things—so that through him I might grasp the one who also has me in his grasp, and from the

Ps. 62:4

1 Tim. 2:5

fragments of days past be gathered up to follow the One, forgetting
those things that are past, and not stretched out through distention but
straining forward in intention to the things that lie ahead (not to future
things that are but fleeting), I press on toward the prize of the upward
call, where I will hear the voice of praise and gaze upon your delight,
which neither comes to be nor passes away.

Phil. 3:12–14 / Ps. 25:7 / Ps. 26:4

But for now my years are wasted with sighing, and you are my comfort, O Lord; you are my eternal Father. But I am scattered through
times whose order I do not know, and my thoughts, the inmost
entrails of my soul, are torn to shreds by turbulent changes, until the
time comes when I flow into you, purified and melted by the fire of
your love.

Ps. 30:11

30.40   And I will stand firm and become whole in you, in my form,[10]
your Truth—and I will not put up with questions from people who, for
their punishment, are sick with a disease that makes them drink more
than they can hold, who ask, "What was God doing before he made
heaven and earth?" or "Why did it occur to him to make something
when he had never made anything before?" Grant, O Lord, that they
might think clearly about what they are saying and realize that where
there is no time, it makes no sense to use the word "never." So to say
that God had "never" made anything is simply to say that he had not
made anything at any time. Let them see, then, that there can be no
time apart from some creature, and let them stop talking nonsense. Let
them, too, strain forward to the things that lie ahead; let them understand that you are before all times, the eternal Creator of all times, and
that no times are coeternal with you, nor is any creature, even if there
is some creature that is above times.

Phil. 4:1; 1 Thess. 3:8 / Jn. 14:6

Ps. 143:8

Phil. 3:13

31.41   O Lord my God, where are your deep mysteries concealed,
and how far from there have I been driven by the consequences of my
sins? Heal my eyes, and I will rejoice with you in your light. Surely if
there is a mind endowed with such great knowledge and foreknowl-
edge as to know all past and future things—in the way that I know an
utterly familiar song—that mind is altogether wonderful and terrify-
ingly astonishing. Whatever has already been done, and whatever ages
are yet to come, lie open before that mind, just as when I sing a song,

---

10. This sentence continues the metallurgical metaphor of the previous sentence, so "become whole
in you, in my form" (*solidabor in te, in forma mea*) could be translated "become set in you, in my
mold." I have kept with the translation "form" because of its importance in the triad measure/form/
order—note that Augustine here identifies his form with Truth, by which he means (as always) God
the Son.

I know what and how much of it has gone by since its beginning, and what and how much remains until I reach its end. But far be it from you, Creator of the universe, Creator of souls and bodies, far be it from you to know all past and future things in this way. Your knowledge is far different from this, far more wonderful and far more mysterious. When someone sings or hears a song he knows, his feelings are changed and his perception distended by the expectation of sounds yet to come and the memory of sounds already past. But it is not so with you: nothing happens to you, the unchangeably Eternal, that is, the truly eternal Creator of minds. Therefore, just as in the Beginning you knew heaven and earth without any variation in your knowledge, so too in the Beginning you made heaven and earth without any distention in your action.

Gn. 1:1

Let anyone who understands this confess to you; let anyone who does not understand it confess to you. How lofty you are, and you make your home in those who are humble of heart! For you lift up those who are bowed down, and those who have you as their lofty dwelling place do not fall.

Ps. 137:6

Dan. 3:87; Is. 57:15 / Ps. 144:14, 145:8

Book Twelve

Augustine interprets "In the beginning God created heaven and earth" to mean "In his coeternal Word God created the heaven of heaven"—an intellectual creature that unfailingly clings to God—"and unformed matter." But other interpretations are possible, and so long as those interpretations say true things, Augustine will not reject them. There is no point in arguing about what the Scriptural author meant, for we cannot know that. We cannot know another person's mind, but we can know the truth through the Inner Teacher. Attachment to one's own interpretation is a form of pride; truth is common property, and we should rejoice in it no matter who discovers it.

After introducing the theme of multiplicity in the search for understanding (12.1.1), Augustine returns to his exegesis of the opening words of Genesis. He interprets "heaven" as the "heaven of heaven" and "earth" as unformed matter (12.2.2–12.8.8, 12.12.15–12.13.16); neither of these undergoes change, and so there is no mention of "days" in the story of their creation (12.9.9–12.11.14). Augustine entertains alternative interpretations and concedes their truth (12.14.17–12.23.32). What we cannot know with certainty is which interpretation expresses what Moses had in mind (12.24.33–12.25.35). A variety of interpretations is not only possible but desirable; the purpose of exegesis is not unanimity but charity (12.26.36–12.32.43).

1.1   My heart is preoccupied with many things, O Lord, in the neediness of my life, because the words of your Holy Scripture knock at my heart. The poverty of human understanding so often makes for an abundance of speech, for seeking says more than finding, asking takes longer than obtaining, and the hand that knocks has more to do than the hand that is open to receive. We have your promise, and no one can cause it to fail. If God is for us, who can be against us? "Ask, and you will receive; seek, and you will find; knock, and it will be opened to you. For everyone who asks, receives; those who seek will find; and to those who knock, it will be opened." These are your promises, and how can anyone fear deception when Truth himself makes the promises?

2.2   The humility of my tongue confesses before your loftiness that you made heaven and earth; the heaven that I see, and the earth on which I tread, from which comes this earth that I carry about: all this you made. But where, O Lord, is the heaven of heaven, of which we hear in the words of the Psalm: "The heaven of heaven is for the Lord, but the earth he gave to the children of men"? Where is this heaven we

Lk. 10:40–42

Rom. 8:31

Mt. 7:7–8 par. Lk. 11:9–10 / Jn. 14:6

Gn. 1:1

Ps. 113:24

do not see, to which all we do see is but earth? This whole bodily realm, which does not exist as a whole in every place,[1] has received beautiful form even in the very lowest things, and its bottom-most place is our earth; but by comparison with that heaven of heaven, even the heaven of our earth is earth. Both of these vast bodies are rightly called earth by comparison with the heaven of heaven, whatever exactly it might be like, which is for the Lord and not for the children of men.

3.3   Truly this earth was invisible and unorganized, and there was an unfathomably deep abyss over which there was no light, because *Gn. 1:2* it had no form.[2] And for that reason you commanded it to be written that darkness was over the abyss. What else is darkness but the *Gn. 1:2* absence of light? For where would light be, if it existed, unless it were above, shedding its light from on high? So where there was as yet no light, what could it mean for darkness to be present? Simply that light was absent. And so there was darkness over the abyss because there was no light over it, just as there is silence wherever there is no sound. For there to be silence somewhere is simply for there to be no sound there, nothing more. Have not you, O Lord, taught this soul what it *Ps. 70:17* confesses to you? Have not you, O Lord, taught me that before you formed this unformed matter and fashioned it into distinct things, it *Wisd. 18:11 VL* was not anything: not color, not shape, not body, not spirit? Yet it was not altogether nothing: it was an undifferentiated something without any form.

4.4   What, then, should we call this? And how can the meaning of such a thing be conveyed somehow or other to those whose minds are sluggish? We must resort to some word in common use: and what can be found in any part of the world that is closer to being completely undifferentiated than earth and the abyss? For they, being at the lowest level, are less formed than all other things, higher things that are resplendent and full of light. Why, then, should I not conclude that the undifferentiatedness of matter, which you made without form so that from it you could form the world, is fitly made known to us by being called "earth invisible and unorganized"?   5.5   Thus, when thought seeks some way to make sense of this earth, and says, "It is not an intelligible form like life or justice, because it is the matter of bodies;

---

1. "which does not exist as a whole in every place": *non ubique totum*. Compare the description of God as *ubique totus*, "everywhere as a whole," at the end of 1.3.3.

2. "form" consistently translates *species*, which is that aspect of being by which a thing is a particular kind of thing. By its *species* a thing approximates more or less to the perfect idea of it in the Word and makes its impression on the human mind both as an object of thought (*species* as appearance) and as an object of wonder (*species* as beauty).

nor is it a sensible form, because there is nothing to be seen or sensed in what is invisible and unorganized"—in saying these things to itself, let human thought attempt to know it by being ignorant of it or to be ignorant of it by knowing it.

6.6   But, O Lord, if I am to confess to you by my mouth and my pen the whole of what you have taught me about this matter, I must acknowledge that I formerly heard the word and did not understand it, for those who told me about it likewise did not understand it. I thought of matter as having countless and varied forms, and so I was not thinking of it at all. My mind envisioned a disorderly range of loathsome and terrifying forms. What I called "unformed" was not what lacked form, but what had such a form that, if it appeared, my sense would turn away from it as something bizarre and unseemly, and human weakness would reel back from it in distress. But in fact what I was thinking of was not unformed in the sense of being deprived of all form, but unformed only by comparison with things that were beautifully formed; true reason exhorted me to remove every remnant of form whatsoever if I wanted to conceive what was altogether unformed, but I could not. For I would more readily think that what was deprived of all form did not exist at all, rather than conceiving something intermediate between form and nothing, neither formed nor nothing, something unformed and nearly nothing.

And my mind gave up on questioning this spirit of mine, which was full of images of formed bodies, and changed and varied those images as it pleased. I trained my attention on those very bodies, and I looked more deeply into their changeableness, by which they cease to be what they once were and begin to be what they were not before. I began to have an inkling that this passage from one form to another took place through something unformed, not through nothing at all. But I longed to know, not merely to have an inkling. And if I were to confess to you by my mouth and pen the whole story of how you freed me from this question, who among my readers would have the patience to take it all in? Yet my heart will not therefore cease to give you honor and to sing a song of praise for these things that it has no room to speak of here.

The very changeableness of changeable things is what is capable of receiving all the forms into which changeable things are changed. And what is this capacity for change? Not a mind, surely; not a body, surely; not, surely, a form of a mind or a body. If one could say, "It is a nothing-something," "It is a what-is-not," that is what I would say of it. And yet in some way or other it was, so that it could take on these visible and organized forms.

7.7   And how could it be in any way at all except by being from you, from whom all things exist, insofar as they exist? But the further they are from you, the more unlike you they are: and their distance from you is not a matter of place. And so you, O Lord, who are not one thing at one time and something else at another, but are the Selfsame and the Selfsame and the Selfsame,³ holy, holy, holy, Lord God Almighty: in the Beginning, who is from you, in your Wisdom, who is born from your substance, you made something, and you made it from nothing. For you made heaven and earth, and you did not make them from yourself. If you had, they would have been equal to your Only-begotten, and thereby equal also to you, and it would have by no means been right for what was not from you to be equal to you. And there was nothing besides you from which you might make them, O God, one Trinity and threefold Unity, and so it was from nothing that you made heaven and earth, something great and something lowly, because you are almighty and good and so make all things good, the great heaven and the lowly earth, two things, one close to you, one close to nothing; to one, you alone would be superior; to one, only nothingness would be inferior.

Rom. 11:36; 1 Cor. 8:6

Ps. 4:9, 33:4, 121:3 / Is. 6:3; Rev. 4:8

8.8   But that heaven of heaven is for you, O Lord, whereas the earth, which you gave to the children of men to perceive and touch, was not then like the earth that we now perceive and touch. For it was invisible and unorganized, and there was an abyss over which there was no light; rather, darkness was over the abyss, that is, the darkness was even greater than in the abyss. In fact this abyss of waters, now visible, has even in its greatest depths a light suited to its own form, one that can somehow be sensed by the living things that dwell at its bottom, the fish and creeping things. But that whole was nearly nothing, for it was still altogether unformed, though it was already something that could be formed. For you, O Lord, made the world from unformed matter, and you made this unformed matter, which was so nearly nothing, from nothing. From unformed matter you made the great things that the children of men behold in wonder.

Ps. 113:24

Gn. 1:2

Gn. 1:20, 1:26

Wisd. 11:18 VL

For this bodily heaven is truly wondrous, this heaven that is the firmament between water and water. On the second day, after the creation of the light, you said, "let it be made," and thus it was made. You called this firmament heaven: but it was the heaven of this earth and sea, which you made on the third day by giving visible form to the unformed matter that you made before there was any day. For there

Gn. 1:6–8

Gn. 1:9–10, 13

---

3. See 1.6.10, fn. 7.

was another heaven that you had already made before there was any day: the heaven of this heaven. For in the Beginning you made heaven and earth. Now the earth that you had made was unformed matter, because it was invisible and unorganized, and darkness was over the abyss. From this invisible and unorganized matter, from this undiffer-   *Gn. 1:2* entiatedness, from this almost-nothing, you would make all the things by which this changeable world stands firm without ever standing still. That it is changeable is evident from the fact that times[4] can be experienced and distinguished in it, for times come about through the changes in things as their forms are varied and altered. And the matter of these things is the invisible earth of which I have been speaking.

9.9   And that is why the Spirit, the teacher of your servant,[5] says nothing about times, not a word about days, when he recounts that in the Beginning you made heaven and earth. For surely the heaven of heaven, which you made in the Beginning, is some sort of intellectual creature. Although it is in no way coeternal with you, O Trinity, it nonetheless has a share in your eternity. By the sweetness of its utterly blessed contemplation of you it keeps its own changeableness firmly in check; it does not fall away from the state in which it was created, but instead, by clinging to you, it escapes all the swiftly rolling changes of times. Moreover, that undifferentiatedness, earth invisible and unorganized, is likewise not counted in the number of days. For where there is no form, there is no order; nothing comes to be, and nothing passes away. And where nothing comes to be or passes away, there are no days; there is no change over any spans of time.

10.10   O Truth, Light of my heart, do not let my darkness speak to me!
      I have descended into these things and been enveloped by shadows;
          yet here too, even here, I have fallen in love with you.
      I went astray, but then I remembered you.   *Ps. 118:176; Jonah*
      I heard your voice calling after me, beckoning me to return to you,   *2:8 / Ez. 3:12; Is.*
          but I could scarcely hear you over the clamor of those who hate   *30:21*
      peace.
      And now, behold, I return to you,
          my heart enkindled with desire for you,
          athirst for the spring of water that wells up from you.   *Jn. 4:14*

---

4. For the significance of the plural "times" throughout Books 11 and 12, see 11.11.13, fn. 6.

5. "your servant": *famuli tui*, meaning Moses. O'Donnell rightly comments that *famulus* is "[v]irtually a proper title for [Moses], even in scripture"; for that reason it is perhaps especially significant that the only other person described in the *Confessions* as "your [= God's] servant" is Monnica (9.8.17). (The word used of Paul in 12.15.20 is *servus* rather than *famulus*.)

Let no one hinder me:
  let me drink from this spring,
  and let me draw life from it.
Let me not be my own life:
  how badly I lived when I lived from myself!
I was death to myself;
  in you I come back to life.
Speak words of comfort to me;
  enter into conversation with me.
I have put my faith in your Scriptures,
  and their words are full of hidden treasures.

11.11 You, O Lord, have already said to me, with a strong voice in my inward ear, that you are eternal, that you alone have immortality, *1 Tim. 6:16* because you are not changed by any form or motion and your will is not altered with the passing of times: for a will that is now one way, now another, is not immortal. This truth shines brightly for me in your sight, and I pray that it will shine ever more brightly, and that I will remain steadfast and circumspect beneath your wings as I behold its unveiling.

O Lord, you have also said to me, with a strong voice in my inward ear, that you made all natures and substances that are not what you are, but nonetheless are. What is not from you? Only what is not, and the movement of the will away from you, who are, toward what is less, for such a movement is wrongdoing and sin. You have said to me also that no one's sin harms you or upsets the order of your kingdom—not at its highest point, not even in its depths. This truth shines brightly for me in your sight, and I pray that it will shine ever more brightly, and that I will remain steadfast and circumspect beneath your wings as I behold its unveiling.

11.12 You have also said to me, with a strong voice in my inward ear, that not even the creature whose delight is in you alone is coeternal with you. It drinks deeply from you with utterly steadfast fidelity; it is not subject to change in any place or at any time. It holds on to you with all its strength, and because you are always present to it, it has no future that it awaits, nor does it consign to the past what it remembers. It is not altered by any change or distended by any time. O blessed creature, if there is any such creature: blessed by clinging to your blessedness, blessed because you dwell within it for ever and shed your light upon it! I can think of no name that I would more gladly give to "the heaven of heaven, which is for the Lord" than your House, *Ps. 113:24* which meditates on your delights and never falls away, never departs *Ps. 26:4*

from you, this pure mind that enjoys perfect harmony and unity on the
foundation of peace with the spirits of the saints, the citizens of your
city in the heavens that are above these heavens.   *Eph. 2:19, 4:3*

11.13   How is the soul, whose journey has taken it to a far-off place,   *Lk. 15:13*
to discern whether it indeed thirsts for you, whether its tears have
become its food, while day after day people say to it, "Where is your
God?"—whether there is one thing it asks of you, one thing it seeks: *Ps. 41:2–4, 41:11*
to dwell in the house of the Lord all the days of its life? What is its life   *Ps. 26:4*
but you? And what are your days but your eternity—and likewise your
years, which do not fail—because you are the Selfsame? Therefore, let   *Ps. 101:28*
the soul that is capable discern from this how far above all times you
are eternal, because your House, which has not journeyed to a far-off
place, unceasingly and unfailingly clings to you and so undergoes no
change through time, though it is not coeternal with you. This truth
shines brightly for me in your sight, and I pray that it will shine ever
more brightly, and that I will remain steadfast and circumspect beneath
your wings as I behold its unveiling.

11.14   In the changes that befall the last and lowest things there is
something undifferentiated that I cannot quite describe. Would anyone try to tell me that when all form has been removed and destroyed,
and there remains only the undifferentiatedness by which a thing is
changed and altered from one form to another, it can manifest the
changes that happen in times? Only someone who is completely astray
and adrift among the images churned up by the emptiness of his heart
could suggest such a thing. No, it is in no way possible: for without
variation in motions there are no times, and where there is no form,
there is no variation.

12.15   Reflecting on these things as far as you give me the capacity, my God—as far as you rouse me to knock and open the door to
my knocking—I find two things you made that lack times, though   *Mt. 7:7 par. Lk.*
neither is coeternal with you. One was formed in such a way that   *11:9*
it has perfect enjoyment of your eternity and immutability, without
ever ceasing its contemplation, without any space of time in which it
undergoes change; though it is changeable, it does not change. The
other was unformed in such a way that there was nothing in it by
which it could be changed from one form to another, whether by
moving or by being at rest, and so it was not subject to time. But you
did not leave this unformed, because in the Beginning, before any
day, you made heaven and earth: these two things of which I have
been speaking. "Now the earth was invisible and unorganized, and

darkness was over the abyss": those who cannot imagine a complete   *Gn. 1:2*
privation of all form that does not collapse into nothingness receive
from these words a kind of hint by which they can be rescued little
by little from their confusion; the words express the formlessness out
of which another heaven and earth, visible and organized, would be
made, along with the beautifully formed waters and whatever else is
recounted in the story of the days in which this world was created.
For in all those things the changes of times take place because of the
orderly variation of motions and forms.

13.16   This, for now, is how I understand what I hear when your
Scriptures say, "In the Beginning God created heaven and earth. But
the earth was invisible and unorganized, and darkness was over the
abyss," and they do not recount any day on which you made these   *Gn. 1:1–2*
things. So, for now, I understand "heaven" to mean the heaven of
heaven, the intellectual heaven, where the intellect knows all at once—
not in part, not dimly, as if in a mirror, but in full, openly, and face
to face; it does not know now one thing, now another, but as I have   *1 Cor. 13:12*
said, whatever it knows, it knows all at once, with no change over the
course of times. And by "earth invisible and unorganized" I understand   *Gn. 1:2*
something that likewise does not change over the course of times; it is
not first this and then that, because where there is no form, there is no
this or that.

So I understand these two things—one perfectly formed from the
very beginning, the other completely unformed: the first is heaven, but
the heaven of heaven, and the second is earth, but earth invisible and
unorganized—and my interpretation, for now, is that because of what
these two things are, there is no mention of any day when Scripture
says, "In the Beginning God made heaven and earth." Indeed, Scripture goes on immediately to specify what it means by "earth," and the
fact that it recounts that God made the firmament on the second day
and called it "heaven" suggests which heaven it was talking about ear-   *Gn. 1:7–8*
lier when it mentioned the creation of heaven without saying anything
about days.

14.17   O wondrous depth of your words!
   Behold, their surface is open before us and invites us little ones,
      but wondrous is their depth, my God:
      how wondrous is their depth!
   It is terrifying to look into it:
      a terror of reverence,
      a trembling with love.

I have a violent hatred for the enemies[6] of your word: *Ps. 138:21–22*
   if only you would slay them with a two-edged sword,   *Ps. 149:6*
   that they might be its enemies no longer.
For what I love is that they should die to themselves
   so that they might live for you.

Now there are others—people who do not reject the Book of Gen-esis, but in fact praise it—who will say this: "The Spirit of God, who wrote these words through his servant Moses, did not mean for them to be understood as you say, but in some other way, as we interpret them." To them I reply as follows, presenting my account before you, O God of us all, as Judge.

15.18   You[7] will surely not say that what Truth says to me with a strong voice in my inward ear about the true eternity of the Creator— that his substance undergoes no change through times, and that his will is nothing apart from his substance—is false. Hence, he does not will first one thing and then another: no, whatever he wills, he wills once and for all and always, not again and again, not one thing at one time and another thing at another; nor does he will later what he had previously not willed, or cease to will what he had previously willed. For such a will is changeable, and whatever is changeable is not eternal: but our God is eternal. Truth also says to me in my inward ear that the   *Ps. 47:15* expectation of things yet to come becomes vision when those things are present, and such vision becomes memory when they have passed away. Certainly any thought that varies in this way is changeable: but our God is eternal.   *Ps. 47:15*

I gather these thoughts and join them together and find that my God, the eternal God, did not make creation by any new will, and that in his knowledge there is nothing fleeting.

15.19   What, then, will you say, you objectors? Are these claims false? "No," they reply. What, then? Surely it is not false that every formed nature, and all formable matter, has its being from the One who is supremely good because he supremely is. "We do not dispute that either," they say. Then what? Do you deny that there is a certain lofty created being that clings with such pure love to the true, and truly eternal, God that although it is not coeternal with God, it neverthe-less does not untether itself from God and slip into the succession and

---

6. Augustine has in mind the Manichees. In the next paragraph he turns to other objectors who (unlike the Manichees) accept the Genesis account of creation but reject Augustine's interpretation of that account.
7. Now second-person plural, addressing his objectors.

change of times, but instead rests in its perfectly truthful contemplation of God alone? For to those who love you as you command, O
God, you show yourself, and they are satisfied; and so this being does   *Jn. 14:8*
not turn away from you or toward itself. This is the house of God: not   *Gn. 28:17; Ps. 26:4*
an earthly house, not even a heavenly house made of bodily matter,
but a spiritual house, one that has a share in your eternity because it
is eternally unblemished. For you have made it stand fast for ever and
ever; you have given it a command, and it shall not pass away. Yet it is   *Ps. 148:6*
not coeternal with you, because it had a beginning: for you made it.

15.20   True, we find no time before it. Indeed, wisdom was created
before all things: not, of course, the Wisdom who is clearly coeternal   *Sir. 1:1–5*
with you and equal to you, our God, his Father, the Wisdom through   *Phil. 2:6*
whom all things were created, the Beginning in whom you made   *Col. 1:16*
heaven and earth, but rather the wisdom that was created, an intellectual nature that is a light because it contemplates Light. For this too
is called wisdom, even though it was created: but as great as the gulf
is between the Light that gives light and a light that receives light, so
great also is the gulf between the Wisdom that creates and the wisdom
that was created, as great as the gulf between the Justice that justifies
and the justice that is brought about by justification. (For we ourselves
are said to be your justice: as your servant says, "so that in Christ we
might be the justice of God.") So before all other things there was cre-   *2 Cor. 5:21*
ated a certain wisdom, a rational and intellectual mind belonging to
your pure city, our mother, which is above and free and eternal in the   *Gal. 4:26*
heavens—and what heavens are those? Surely the heavens of heavens   *2 Cor. 5:1*
that praise you, for this is also the heaven of heaven that is for the Lord.   *Ps. 148:4 / Ps.*
Therefore, even though we find no time before this creature—for what   *113:24*
was created before all other things precedes time, since time itself is a
creature—there was, before it, the eternity of the Creator by whom
it was made and from whom it had its beginning: not a beginning in
time, for as yet there was no time, but a beginning of its creation.

15.21   Hence, it is from you, our God, in such a way that it is clearly
distinct from you and not the Selfsame. True, not only do we find
no time before it, we also find no time within it. For it is fitting that
it should always see your face and never turn aside from it, and so it   *Mt. 18:10*
undergoes no change. Yet even so, it is capable of change; hence its
light would grow dim and its ardor cold if it did not cling to you with
great love, so that by you its light is always as the noonday and its love   *Is. 58:10*
enkindled as with fire. O House full of light and splendid in form,
I have loved your beauty and the place where the glory of my Lord
abides, my Lord who has fashioned you and holds you in his grasp! On   *Ps. 25:8*

this pilgrimage of mine may I sigh with longing for you. And I ask the one who made me to hold me also in his grasp in you, for he made me also. I have strayed like a lost sheep, but I have hope that my Shepherd, *Ps. 118:176* your Builder, will carry me back to you on his shoulders. *Lk. 15:5*

15.22   What are you saying to me, you objectors whom I was addressing, objectors who nevertheless believe that Moses was a faithful servant of God and that his books are declarations of the Holy Spirit? Is not this the House of God, which is not coeternal with God and yet is, in its way, eternal in the heavens, where you look for the changes of *2 Cor. 5:1* times, but in vain, because you find none there? It transcends all distention; it transcends every stretch of time in which there can be variation; its good is to cling to God always. "This is true," they say. *Ps. 72:28*

Then what is it—out of all the things that my heart has cried out before my God when I heard the voice of his praise in my inward *Ps. 25:7* ear—what is it that you still contend is false? That there was unformed matter, where there was no order because there was no form? But where there was no order, there could be no succession of times; and yet this almost-nothing, precisely because it was not altogether nothing, surely had its being from him from whom whatever exists, whatever is in any way something, has being. "This too," they say, "we do not deny." *Rom. 11:36; 1 Cor. 8:6*

16.23   For I want to engage in a bit of discussion in your presence, my God, with those who grant that these things your Truth says to me inwardly, in my mind, are in fact true. As for those who deny these things, let them bark as much as they will and so drown themselves out: I will try to persuade them to be still and to allow your Word to make its way to them. If they should refuse and drive me away, I beg you, my God, not to grow silent toward me. Speak truthfully in my *Ps. 27:1* heart; you alone speak truthfully. And I will leave outside those who *Ps. 14:3* breathe into the dust and stir up a cloud of earth into their own eyes; I will go into my room and sing love songs to you, sighing on my *Mt. 6:6* pilgrimage with sighs too deep for words, and remembering Jerusa- *Rom. 8:26* lem, straining forward with my heart lifted up[8] to her—Jerusalem, my *Ps. 136:1, 136:5–6* homeland, Jerusalem, my mother—and above her to you, her Ruler, *Phil. 3:13 / Gal. 4:26* Light, Father, Guardian, Husband, her pure and strong delights, her unshakeable joy, and all good things that surpass description, all of them at once, for you are the one, supreme, and true Good. And I will not turn aside until you bind together all that I am from its dispersion and deformity and impose form upon it and give it strength for *Is. 11:12*

---

8. "Lift up your hearts" was (and remains) a phrase used in the Eucharistic liturgy by which the celebrant bids the faithful to attend to things on high.

eternity, my God, my mercy; I will not turn aside until you bind it all together into her peace, the peace of our dearest mother. In her are the first fruits of my spirit,[9] and so I have firm confidence in these things. *Ps. 58:18* *Rom. 8:23*

But to those who do not say that all these truths are false, who honor your Holy Scripture set forth by holy Moses and, with us, hold it up on high as an authority to be followed, and yet object to some of what I have said, here is my reply—O our God, be the Judge between my confessions and their objections.

17.24   For they say, "Although these things are true, Moses did not have those two creatures in mind when, by the revelation of the Holy Spirit, he said, 'In the beginning God made heaven and earth.' By the word 'heaven' he did not signify that spiritual or intellectual creature who always contemplates the face of God, and by 'earth' he did not signify unformed matter." *Gn. 1:1*

What, then?

"He meant what we say," they reply, "and that is what he expressed by those words."

And what is that?

"By 'heaven and earth' he intended to signify this whole visible world all together in a few words, and then, in his account of the days, he would go on to divide up all the things that it pleased the Holy Spirit to speak of in this way, and to treat them individually. For the people to whom Moses was speaking were so ignorant and unspiritual that he determined he could speak only of visible things in bringing the works of God before their minds."

They agree, however, that it makes perfect sense to interpret "earth invisible and unorganized" and "the dark abyss"—from which, as Moses goes on to show, all the visible things that are familiar to everyone were made and put in order over the course of the days—as unformed matter.

17.25   Someone else might say that the phrase "heaven and earth" gives an early intimation of precisely that unformed and disorderly matter, because this visible world with all the natures that appear so clearly in it, which is often called "heaven and earth," was created and completed from that matter.

Yet another person might say that both invisible and visible nature are fittingly called "heaven and earth," and so those words encompass the whole creation that God made in Wisdom, that is, in the Beginning. But because all things were made, not from the substance of God, but from nothing—because they are not the Selfsame as God—there *Ps. 103:24*

---

9. For Augustine's use of this expression, see 9.10.24, fn. 30.

is a certain capacity for change in them all, whether they abide, like the eternal House of God, or change, like the human soul and body. The words "earth invisible and unorganized" and "darkness over the abyss" therefore express the as-yet unformed, but certainly formable, matter that is common to all invisible and visible things, the matter from which heaven and earth—that is, both invisible and visible creation, fully formed—were to be made. But there is a distinction: "earth invisible and unorganized" means bodily matter before it received any characteristic from a form, whereas "darkness over the abyss" means spiritual matter before its excess and instability were restrained and it was illuminated by Wisdom.

17.26 There is still another reading that someone might put forward should he so choose, namely, that when we read "in the beginning God made heaven and earth," the words "heaven and earth" do not signify the invisible and visible natures of heaven and earth that are already completed and formed, but rather the as-yet unformed matter that is the incipient state of things that can be formed and created. Those things existed in unformed matter in an indistinct way, not yet distinguished by their characteristics and forms; now that they have been disposed in their separate orders, they are called "heaven and earth": "heaven" meaning the spiritual creation and "earth" the physical.

18.27 Having heard and considered all these things, I do not wish to dispute about words, which does no good, but only ruins the hearers. *2 Tim. 2:14* But the law, if anyone uses it lawfully, is good for building up, for its *1 Tim. 1:8 / Eph.* end is charity that issues from a pure heart and a good conscience and *4:29* unfeigned faith; and I know on what two commandments our Teacher *1 Tim. 1:5 / Mt.* made all the law and the prophets depend.[10] My God, Light of my *23:10 / Mt.* eyes in the darkness, I passionately acknowledge all these truths in my *22:40* confession to you—so what harm does it do me if these words can be *Ps. 37:11* understood to bear other meanings, all of which are true? What harm does it do me if what I think the writer of those words meant is different from what someone else thinks he meant? Certainly all of us who read try to investigate and understand what the author we are reading meant to say; and when we believe that the author was truthful, we do

---

10. Matthew 22:35–40: "And one of [the Pharisees], a lawyer, asked [Jesus] a question, to test him. 'Teacher, which is the great commandment in the law?' And he said to them, 'You shall the love the Lord your God with all your heart, and with all your soul, and with all your mind. This is the great and first commandment. And a second is like it: you shall love your neighbor as yourself. On these two commandments depend all the law and the prophets.'" For love of God and love of neighbor as the only proper goals of Scriptural exegesis, see Augustine's *On Christian Teaching* (*De doctrina christiana*).

not dare suppose that he said anything we know or think is false. So as long as each of us is trying to discover in the Holy Scriptures what their author meant, how is it objectionable if someone interprets them as meaning something that you, the Light of all truthful minds, show to be true, even though that is not what the author meant—when what the author meant was also true, just not that particular truth?

19.28   It is true, Lord, that you made heaven and earth. It is true that the Beginning is your Wisdom, in whom you made all things. It is true that this visible world comprises those spacious regions, heaven and earth, and by that short phrase, "heaven and earth," we mean all made and created natures. It is true that anything changeable suggests to our awareness a certain formlessness in which it receives form, or by which it changes and alters. It is true that what clings to the Unchangeable Form in such a way that it never changes, even though it is changeable, has no experience of times. It is true that formlessness, which is almost nothing, cannot undergo the successions of times. It is true that the source from which something is made can, in a certain way of speaking, have the name of that which is made from it: hence, the formlessness from which heaven and earth were made could itself be called "heaven and earth." It is true that of all formed things, nothing is closer to formlessness than earth and the abyss. It is true that you, from whom all things exist, made not only what is created and formed but also whatever is creatable or formable. It is true that whatever is formed from what is formless is first formless and then formed.

Ps. 103:24

Rom. 11:36; 1 Cor. 8:6

20.29   Those whom you have granted the power to see these truths by their inward eye have no doubt that they are true, and they believe with unshakeable assurance that your servant Moses spoke by the Spirit of Truth. From all these truths one interpreter selects one for himself and says, "'In the Beginning God made heaven and earth' means that in his coeternal Word God made the intelligible and the sensible creation, that is to say, the spiritual and the bodily creation."

Jn. 14:17

Another says, "'In the Beginning God made heaven and earth' means that in his coeternal Word God made the whole mass of this bodily world, with all the evident and familiar natures that it contains."

Another says, "'In the Beginning God made heaven and earth' means that in his coeternal Word he made the unformed matter of the spiritual and the bodily creation."

Another says, "'In the Beginning God made heaven and earth' means that in his coeternal Word God made the unformed matter of the bodily creation, in which heaven and earth, which we now perceive as distinct and formed in the mass of this world, were still in disorder."

Another says, "'In the beginning God made heaven and earth' means that when God first began to make his works, he made unformed matter, which contained heaven and earth in a disorderly state; now that heaven and earth have been formed, along with all that is in them, they stand out clearly and are manifest."

21.30   Likewise, as for the interpretation of the words that follow, from all those truths one interpreter selects one for himself and says, "'But the earth was invisible and unorganized, and darkness was over the abyss' means that the bodily creation that God made was as yet the unformed matter of bodily things, without order, without light."

Another says, "'But the earth was invisible and unorganized, and darkness was over the abyss' means that the totality that is called heaven and earth was as yet dark and unformed matter from which the bodily heaven and bodily earth, along with everything in them that is known by the bodily senses, would be made."

Another says, "'But the earth was invisible and unorganized, and darkness was over the abyss' means that the totality that is called heaven and earth was as yet dark and unformed matter from which the intelligible heaven (which is elsewhere called the heaven of heaven) and the earth (which is to say, every bodily nature—and thus the word 'earth' includes this bodily heaven as well) would be made; in other words, it was the matter from which the whole invisible and visible creation would be made."

Another interprets "But the earth was invisible and unorganized, and darkness was over the abyss" in this way: Scripture, he says, did not call that formlessness "heaven and earth"; rather, the formlessness that Scripture calls "earth invisible and unorganized" and "the dark abyss" already existed, and from that formlessness God (as had already been said) made heaven and earth, that is, the spiritual and the bodily creation.

Another says, "'But the earth was invisible and unorganized, and darkness was over the abyss' means that there was a certain formlessness: the matter from which (as Scripture already said) God made heaven and earth, which is to say, the whole bodily mass of the world divided into two most spacious regions, a higher and a lower, along with all the well-known and familiar creatures that are in them."

22.31   To these last two interpretations one might well be tempted to object, "If you do not understand 'heaven and earth' to signify the formlessness of matter, it follows that there was something God had not made, from which he made heaven and earth. For unless we understand 'heaven and earth' (or just the word 'earth' by itself) to signify matter, it will turn out that Scripture did not indicate that God made this matter when it said, 'In the Beginning God created heaven and earth.' Thus, in the words that follow, 'But the earth was invisible and unorganized,' although this was how he chose to describe unformed matter, we are to understand that matter as nothing other than what God is said to have made in what was written before: 'God made heaven and earth.'"

When those who put forward either of the two interpretations we put last hear these objections, they will reply, "Of course we do not deny that that unformed matter was made by God, from whom all things exist and are very good. We say, after all, that what has been created and formed has greater goodness, and we acknowledge that what was made capable of being created and formed is less good, but good nonetheless. But we say that Scripture does not explicitly record that God made this formlessness, just as there are many other things that Scripture does not explicitly say God made: cherubim and seraphim, and the creatures of whom the Apostle speaks one by one, 'thrones, dominions, principalities, powers.' Yet it is perfectly clear that God made them all. Or if 'he made heaven and earth' includes everything, what are we to say about the waters over which the Spirit of God was borne? For if we understand the waters to be included in what is called 'earth,' how can we interpret the word 'earth' as meaning unformed matter when we see that the waters are beautifully formed? Or if we do understand 'earth' in that way, why is it written that the firmament was made from that very formlessness and called heaven, but not written that the waters were made? For the waters that we perceive flowing in their lovely form are no longer unformed or unseen. Perhaps you will say that they received their form when God said, 'Let the water that is beneath the firmament be gathered together': its being gathered together is precisely its being formed. But then what will you say about the waters that are above the firmament? For it was not as unformed that they were fit for such an honorable dwelling place, and yet there is no mention of any word by which they were formed. Hence, just as neither sound faith nor reliable understanding doubts for a moment that God made something even if Genesis does not mention that he made it, so too no sensible teaching will dare to say that these waters are coeternal with God on the grounds that we hear them mentioned in the Book of Genesis but are not told anywhere that they were made. Why, then, should we not understand, with Truth as our Teacher, that the formless matter that this passage of Scripture calls 'earth invisible and unorganized' and 'the dark abyss' was made from nothing by God and is therefore not

Rom. 11:36; 1 Cor. 8:6 / Gn. 1:31

Col. 1:16

Gn. 1:2

Gn. 1:9

Gn. 1:7

coeternal with God, even though this account nowhere explicitly says that it was made?"

23.32   So, having heard these things and fully looked into them as far as I can in my weakness, which I confess to you, my God, who already know it, I see two kinds of disagreement that can arise when something is articulated through signs by truthful messengers: one concerns the truth of the matter, the other is disagreement about what the speaker meant. For it is one thing when we ask what is true concerning the creation of your works, and another thing when we ask what Moses, that outstanding member of the household of your faith, wanted his readers and hearers to understand by his words. Let all those who think they know things that in fact are false—the first kind of disagreement—depart from me. Let all those who think the things Moses said are false—the second kind of disagreement—depart from me. But let me be joined in companionship with those who feed on your truth in the breadth of charity; let me be joined in companionship with them in *Eph. 3:18–19* you, O Lord, and delight in you in their company; and let us approach the words of your book together and seek your meaning through the meaning[11] of your servant, by whose pen you set these things forth.

24.33   But who among us will find your meaning among so many truths that present themselves to those who seek your meaning and understand these words in various ways—find it in such a way that one can say confidently that *this* is what Moses meant, *this* is how he wanted his account to be understood, as confidently as we say that, whatever he meant, it was true? For behold, my God, I, your servant,[12] who have vowed to make a sacrifice of confession to you in these writings *Ps. 115:16–17* of mine and pray that by your mercy I make good my vow to you:[13] *Ps. 21:26, 115:18* behold how confidently I affirm that you made all things, invisible and visible, in your unchangeable Word. But surely I cannot be as confi- *Col. 1:16*

---

11. "meaning" in both instances translates *voluntas*, which is usually "will" but in this context has been "meaning" or "what [Moses] wanted" his readers to understand. There is perhaps an echo here of John 5:30: (Jesus speaking) "For I do not seek my will, but the will of him who sent me."
12. Psalm 115:16–17 reads, "O Lord, I am your servant; I am your servant and the son of your handmaid. You have broken my bonds. I will offer you a sacrifice of praise." So by this brief quotation Augustine manages to express his gratitude for divine liberation, his intention to praise God (one of the meanings of *confessio*), and even his gratitude for his mother, God's handmaid (*ancilla*, the same word the Virgin Mary uses in her reply to the angelic salutation, "Behold the handmaid of the Lord; be it unto me according to your word").
13. O'Donnell (III:331) rightly points out that in his commentary on the two Psalms in which the phrase "I will make good my vow [to the Lord]" appears, Augustine reads the words Eucharistically. Here, however, nothing more seems intended than a prayer that he will carry out faithfully his vow to make his confession to God.

dent in affirming that this, and only this, is what Moses had in mind when he wrote, "In the Beginning God made heaven and earth." For though I see in your Truth that this is certain, I do not see into Moses' mind so that I can know that this is what he was thinking when he wrote those words. When he wrote, "in the beginning," he could have been thinking "at the outset of God's works." By "heaven and earth" he could have meant, not any formed and completed nature, whether spiritual or bodily, but both in their incipient and as-yet unformed state. Certainly I see that he could have spoken truly, whichever of these things he said; but I do not in the same way see which of them he was thinking of when he wrote those words. Nevertheless, whatever that great man had in mind when he uttered these words—whether it was one of the meanings I have mentioned or some other that has not occurred to me—I have no doubt that what he saw was true and that he expressed it appropriately.

25.34   Let no one trouble me any longer by saying to me, "Moses did not have in mind what you say; he had in mind what I say." For if someone were to ask me, "How do you know that Moses had in mind the meaning that you take from his words?" it would be right for me to be unperturbed, and perhaps I would give the same answer that I gave earlier—or a somewhat fuller version of it, if my objector should prove particularly stubborn. But when he says, "Moses did not have in mind what you say, but what I say," yet does not deny that what each of us says is true, O Life of the poor, my God, in whose embrace there is no disputing, rain down your showers of comfort upon my heart so that I might be patient in bearing with such people. They do not say these things because they have superhuman insight and are speaking of what they have seen in the heart of your servant; no, they say these things because they are proud. It is not that they know what Moses thought, but that they love what they themselves think, not because it is true, but because it is theirs. Otherwise they would equally love any other true view, just as I love what they say when they say something true, not because the view is theirs, but because it is true: indeed, it is not theirs, precisely because it is true. If they love it because it is true, it is both theirs and mine, because it is the common property of all who love the truth.

As for their contention that Moses did not have in mind what I say, but rather what they say, I want nothing to do with it; I have no love for such talk. Even if they are right, their foolhardy confidence is not a matter of knowledge but of presumptuousness, born not of vision but of arrogance. And so we ought to stand trembling before your

Gal. 6:17

judgments, O Lord, because your truth is neither mine nor anyone else's; it belongs to all of us whom you call publicly into the common property that is your truth, enjoining us with fearful solemnity that we are not to desire any truth as our own private possession, lest we be deprived of it. For anyone who claims for himself what you offer for all to enjoy, anyone who wants to possess exclusively what belongs to all, is driven away from what is common property to what belongs only to himself: that is, he is driven away from the truth to a lie. For someone who speaks a lie speaks what belongs only to himself. *Jn. 8:44*

1 Tim. 6:5

25.35   Give heed, most worthy Judge, God, Truth Itself: give heed to what I say to this objector; give heed. I say it before you and before my brothers and sisters, who use the law lawfully, with charity as their aim. Give heed and see whether what I say to him is pleasing to you. I speak to him in a brotherly way, meaning to make peace: "If we both see that what you say is true, and we both see that what I say is true, where, I ask, do we see this? I do not see it in you, nor do you see it in me. No, we both see it in the unchangeable Truth that is above our minds. Why, then, since we do not dispute about the light of the Lord our God, do we dispute about the thoughts of our neighbor, which we cannot see in the way that we see the unchangeable Truth? Even if Moses himself were to appear to us and say, 'This is what I thought,' we would not see that he was telling the truth: we would merely believe him. Let no one go beyond what is written so as to be puffed up in favor of one against another. Let us love the Lord our God with all our heart, with all our soul, and with all our mind, and let us love our neighbor as ourselves.[14] Unless we believe that Moses meant to follow those commandments of charity, whatever he meant by the words in those books, we make the Lord a liar, because in our judgment of the mind of our fellow servant we reject what the Lord has taught us. There are so many true meanings that can be drawn from those words: see, then, how foolish it is to state with confidence which of them Moses had in mind most of all, and by such pernicious quarreling to offend against the very charity for the sake of which he said all the things we are trying to expound."

1 Tim. 1:8
1 Tim. 1:5

1 Cor. 4:6

Deut. 6:5; Mt. 22:37–39 par. Mk. 12:30–31; Lk. 10:27 / 1 Jn. 1:10, 5:10

26.36   And yet, my God, who exalt my lowliness and give me rest from all my labors, who hear my confessions and forgive my sins, because you command me to love my neighbor as myself, I cannot believe that your gifts to your most faithful servant Moses were any less than the gifts I would hope and long for if I had been born in his day and you

Mt. 6:15

---

14. See 12.18.27, fn. 10.

had appointed me to his place, to set forth, by the service of my heart and my tongue, the writings that would afterward be proclaimed to all the peoples and occupy such a pinnacle of authority throughout the whole world that they would vanquish the words of all false and proud teachings. If I were Moses—for we all come from the same lump, and what are human beings unless you are mindful of them?—if I were what he was, and you had directed me to write the Book of Genesis, I would want you to give me such facility in speaking and such a way of weaving language that not even those who cannot yet understand how God creates would reject my words as being beyond their capacity; and those who are already capable of such understanding would find that every truth their thought had grasped was contained in the few words of your servant; and if someone else had seen some other truth in the Light of Truth, that too would be present in the meaning of those same words.

Rom. 9:21

Ps. 8:5

27.37 A spring confined in a small space wells up more abundantly, and flows in more streams and over a wider expanse, than any single stream that is drawn from the same source and flows through many places. In the same way the steward of your message expressed it in a very few words, but it was to bubble up into many great discourses, gushing forth as a flood of limpid truth. From this flood each reader would draw out for himself whatever truth he could find concerning these matters—one reader finding this truth, another that—and carry it along the winding channels of a longer discourse.

Now when some people read or hear these words, they think of God as if he were a human being, or as some sort of massive body endowed with immense power, who all of a sudden decided to make heaven and earth outside himself, as if at some distance: two vast bodies, one above and one below, containing all things. And when they hear "God said, 'Let it be made,' and it was made," they think of words that had a beginning and an end, words that sounded through times and then passed away; and after these words were finished, what God had commanded came immediately into being. And perhaps they hold other views along these lines, views that derive from their close acquaintance with the flesh. They are still children, unspiritual; but as long as they allow themselves to be embraced in their weakness by this most lowly kind of language as children are held in their mother's arms, their faith is being built up for their health and salvation; by that faith they hold with certainty that God made all the natures that their senses observe, in all their wondrous variety. If any of them should scorn the plainness of these words and try, with proud feebleness, to leave the nest in which

1 Cor. 2:14, 3:1–3

they have been raised, beware! They will fall, wretched. Have mercy on
them, Lord God; do not let the unfledged chicks get trampled by those
who walk along the path; send your angel to restore them to the nest,
so that they may live until they are able to fly.

28.38   There are others for whom these words are no longer a nest,
but a shady grove. They see the fruits hidden there and fly to them
with delight; they seek them out, chirping, and pluck them. For when
they read or hear these words of yours, eternal God, they see that your
steadfast abiding exceeds all past and future times, and yet there is no
time-bound creature that you did not make. They see that the will by
which you made all things was in no way changed, and that no new
will arose in you that had not been present before, for your will is you
yourself. They see that you did not make all things from yourself—you
did not make them your Likeness,[15] who gives form to all things—but
rather you made all things from nothing; you made them an unformed
unlikeness, which would be formed by your Likeness so as to return
to you, the One, according to the order you imposed on each thing,
the capacity you gave every single thing according to its kind. They see
that all things would be made very good, whether they abide close to
you or recede from you step by step through times and places, causing
and undergoing changes of great beauty. All of this they see, and they
rejoice in the light of your Truth, in whatever limited way they can in
this present life.

28.39   One of them gives attention to the words "In the beginning
God made" and sees Wisdom, the Beginning, because he also speaks to
us.[16] Another likewise gives attention to these same words and understands "beginning" as the outset of creation; thus he understands "in
the beginning God made" as meaning "God first made."
     And among those who understand "the Beginning" as the Wisdom
in whom you made heaven and earth, one takes "heaven and earth"
to express the matter out of which heaven and earth could be created; another takes it to mean natures that are already formed and distinguished; another understands "heaven" to mean a formed spiritual
nature and "earth" to mean unformed bodily nature.
     Now those who understand "heaven and earth" as meaning the as-
yet unformed matter out of which heaven and earth would be formed

Ps. 55:2

*Mal. 3:1; 2 Macc.
15:23; Mt.
11:10 qtg. Ex.
23:20*

Gn. 1:11–25

Gn. 1:31

Jn. 8:25

---

15. Although "likeness" suggests an echo of Genesis 1:26 ("Let us make the human being in our
own image and likeness"), the context requires that the likeness in question here be understood as
God the Word, who gives form to all things (and was "begotten, not made").
16. See 11.8.10.

are not all of one mind in how they understand this: some understand it as the matter out of which both the intelligible and the sensible creation would be brought to completion, others as only the matter for this sensible bodily mass that enfolds in its wide embrace all the natures that are evident and manifest to the senses.

And even those who take "heaven and earth" in this passage to mean creatures that have been differentiated and set in order are not all of one mind: some think this means both the invisible and the visible creation, whereas others think it means only the visible creation in which we behold the luminous heaven and the dark earth and everything that is in them.

29.40   But those who understand "In the beginning God made" as meaning "God first made" cannot offer a truthful interpretation of "heaven and earth" unless they understand it as meaning the matter of heaven and earth, that is, the matter of the whole creation, both intelligible and bodily. For if they interpret "heaven and earth" as meaning the whole creation as already formed, one could rightly ask them, "If God first made the whole creation, what did he make after that?" They will find nothing that could have been made after the whole of creation, and so they will be mortified[17] when they hear us ask, "How was that first if there was nothing afterward?" If, however, they say that God first made unformed matter and then formed it, there is no absurdity, so long as they make suitable distinctions about the ways in which one thing can precede another: in eternity, in time, in choice, and in origin. One thing precedes another in eternity as God precedes all things; in time, as the flower precedes the fruit; in choice, as the fruit precedes the flower; in origin, as sound precedes song.

Of these four, the first and last I mentioned are quite difficult to understand; the second and third are quite easy. It is a rare and extraordinarily demanding insight for us to contemplate your eternity, O Lord, which unchangeably makes all changeable things and is in that way prior to them. And who has such a keen mind that he can discern without great effort how sound is prior to song, precisely because song is formed sound? Certainly it is possible for something unformed to exist, but what does not exist cannot be formed. It is in this way that matter is prior to what is made out of it. Matter is not prior in the sense that it makes the thing—on the contrary, matter is what is made into the thing—nor is it prior by some interval of time. It is not that we first produce unformed sounds without song and then afterward

---

17. A bit of untranslatable wordplay: "find" is *inveniet*, "mortified" is *invitus*.

shape or fashion those sounds into a song, as we do with the wood out
of which someone makes a chest or the silver out of which someone
makes a vase. Those materials are indeed temporally prior to the forms
of things that are made from them, but that is not the case with song.
When someone sings, one hears his sound. He does not first produce
unformed sound and then form it into a song. For whatever the first
sound he makes might be, it passes away, so you will not find any part
of it left for you to shape into a song by means of your musical skill. So
a song depends upon its sound, for its sound is its matter, the very matter that is formed so as to be a song. And this is the sense in which, as I
was saying, the matter of sound is prior to the form of a song. Sound is
not prior to song in the sense that it is the power to make song: sound
is not the artisan that crafts song; rather, sound is subject to the soul of
the singer in virtue of the body out of which he makes sound. Nor is
sound prior in time, since sound is produced simultaneously with song.
Nor is it prior in choice: sound is not more important than song, since
song is not just sound, but sound given a beautiful form. It is, however,
prior in origin, since song is not formed in order that there might be
sound, but rather sound is formed in order that there might be song.

For anyone who is capable of understanding, let this example serve
to explain the sense in which the matter of things was made first, and
called "heaven and earth" because heaven and earth were made from
it. Matter was not made first in time, for it is the forms of things that
give rise to times, whereas matter was formless; and now that there are
times, matter and form are perceived simultaneously. Yet we cannot
help speaking of matter as if it were temporally prior. Even so, it is
the least valuable thing, since formed things are obviously better than
unformed things, and it is preceded by the eternity of the Creator, who
made it from nothing so that from it everything could be made.

30.41   In this diversity of true interpretations, let Truth itself bring
forth harmony,[18] and may our God have mercy on us, that we may
use the law lawfully, for the sake of the aim of the commandment,
which is pure charity. Accordingly, if anyone asks me which of these
meanings your servant Moses had in mind, I would not be speaking
the language of my confessions if I did not confess to you that I do not
know. This much, however, I do know: those interpretations are true
(leaving aside those unspiritual people about whom I believe I have
said enough—still, they are children of great promise, and they are

Ps. 66:2

1 Tim. 1:8

1 Tim. 1:5

---

18. Again drawing on the line from Terence quoted at 10.23.34 (see fn. 6), but reversing its meaning. Instead of breeding hate, truth is to bring forth harmony. (The Latin verb is the same in both
places: *parit*, literally, "give birth to.")

not frightened by the words of your book, which express lofty things in a humble way, and in few words convey an abundance of meaning). But as for all those who, I acknowledge, discern and state truths expressed by those words, let us love one another; and together let us love you, our God, the Fount of Truth, so long as we thirst for truth and not for trifles. And let us so honor your servant, the steward of this Scripture, filled with your Spirit, that we believe that when he wrote these words by your revelation, his mind was firmly fixed on whatever meaning was most resplendent with the light of truth and most useful for the believer.

31.42 So when one person says, "He meant what I say," and another says, "No, he meant what I say," I think it would be more pious for me to say, "Why not both, if both are true?" And if someone should see in his words a third truth, or a fourth, or indeed any other truth, why not believe that Moses saw all these truths? For by Moses the one God attuned the Holy Scriptures to the minds of many people, who would see different things in those words, all of them true.

As for me, I say this with certainty and proclaim it boldly from my heart: if I were to write something at this pinnacle of authority, I would prefer to write in such a way that my words would resound with every truth that anyone could grasp through them, rather than stating a single true view so explicitly that I ruled out other views that could not offend me by their falsity. And so I do not want to be so thoughtless as to suppose that this great man did not deserve such favor from you, my God. When he wrote these words, he had in mind and considered absolutely every truth that we have been able to find in them, every truth that we have not been able to find, and every truth that we have not yet found but that remains for us to find in them.

32.43 Finally, Lord, you who are God and not flesh and blood, even if one who was merely a human being did not see all that was to be seen, did not your good Spirit, who will lead me into the land of uprightness, know everything that you would reveal through these words to later readers, even if the one who uttered them was perhaps thinking of only one of the many true meanings? If so, let us suppose he was thinking of whatever meaning is most exalted. O Lord, show us that meaning; or if you please, show us some other true meaning. In this way, whether you show us just what you showed your servant, or something else that emerges from the same words, we will in any event be fed by you, not mocked by error.

O Lord my God, I pray you, look how much we have written on so few words! Look how much we have written! How much energy

Mt. 16:17; 1 Cor.
15:50

Ps. 142:10

it would take, how much time, to comment in this way on all your books. And so allow me to speak more briefly in my confession to you, and to choose just one thing that you have inspired in me—one thing, true, certain, and good—even if many meanings come to mind where many meanings are possible. I make my confession in the confidence that if I have said what your steward meant, I have spoken correctly, indeed as well as possible (for that is what I must try to do); but if I have not succeeded in that effort, let me at least say what your Truth wants me to say through the words of Moses, to whom that same Truth also said what he wanted Moses to say.

Book Thirteen

God is complete and perfect within himself; he has no need of creation. And creation could have no claim on God to exist, for what does not exist has no claim on anything. Yet God creates from the abundance of his goodness. In that act of creation we see the Trinity: we can try to understand the Trinity through the triad of being, knowing, and willing in ourselves, but ultimately the Trinity eludes our grasp. Augustine reads the six days of creation as an allegory for the work of the Holy Spirit in restoring human beings to fellowship with God through Scripture, the Church, sacraments, and the spiritual gifts. On the seventh day God rested: a sign of the perfect peace that will come when this created order has passed away and human beings will at last know the rest in God for which their hearts long.

God has no need of creation, and no creature has any claim on God (13.1.1–13.3.4). Nonetheless, the Spirit of God is borne over the waters, bringing to perfection the creatures God makes out of the abundance of his goodness (13.4.5). With the mention of the Holy Spirit, Scripture has now introduced the Trinity, which we must try to understand, though it is beyond our comprehension (13.5.6–13.11.12). On the first day of creation God separates light, the spiritual members of the Church, from darkness, the carnal members (13.12.13–13.14.15). On the second day he creates the firmament: the solid authority of Scripture (13.15.16–13.16.19). On the third day he separates the sea, the bitter wills of the wicked, from the dry land, souls who thirst for God (13.17.20–21). On the fourth day he creates lights in the sky: the spiritual gifts (13.18.22–13.19.25). On the fifth day he creates sea creatures: signs, wonders, and sacraments (13.20.26–28). On the sixth day he creates animals, living souls (13.21.29–31), and human beings, who discern God's will for themselves (13.22.32–13.23.34); he gives the command to be fruitful and multiply (13.24.35–37) and allots to each creature its proper food (13.25.38–13.27.42). God sees that the whole of creation is very good (13.28.43–13.31.46). Augustine summarizes both his literal (13.32.47) and his allegorical exegesis (13.33.48) and then turns to God's rest, and our rest with God, on the seventh day (13.35.50–13.38.53).

1.1   I call upon you,[1] my God, my mercy, who made me and did   *Ps. 58:18*
not forget me when I forgot you. I call you into my soul, which you
are making ready to receive you through the longing that you have
inspired in it. Do not abandon me now as I call upon you. Even before

---

1. Here, as he begins the last book of the *Confessions*, Augustine returns to the language of invocation with which he began the work. See 1.1.1–1.2.2, including fn. 2.

I called upon you, you went before me and urged me on by a chorus of voices of all sorts, so that I might hear you from afar and turn to you and call upon you who call me. For you, O Lord, have wiped out all my sins; you will not repay the works of my hands, by which I fell away from you; and you have gone before me in every good deed of mine, so that you might repay the works of your own hands, the hands by which you made me. For before I was, you were; I was nothing at all, nothing even to which you could grant being. And yet here I am: your goodness went before me, and by it I am everything you have made me, everything from which you have made me. You had no need of me; I am not such a good thing that I can be of help to you, my Lord and my God, as if I could spare you from weariness by serving you, as if your power would be diminished without my obedience. Nor did you mean for me to cultivate you as someone cultivates land, as if you would be neglected if I failed to attend to you; no, I was to serve you and worship you so that it might be well with me because of you, who gave me being so that I might have well-being.[2]

Ps. 58:11

Ps. 17:21

Ps. 118:73

Jn. 20:28

2.2 Truly your creation stands firm because of your abundant goodness: for in your goodness you did not want this good thing to fail to exist, this good thing that could be of no use to you, and was not from you and equal to you, but could nevertheless be made by you. What claim on you did heaven and earth have, which you made in the Beginning? Let the spiritual and bodily nature that you made in your Wisdom say what claim they had on you. Even in their incipient and unformed state, all spiritual and bodily things according to their kind depended on your Wisdom, though they went forth into excess, into a land of unlikeness far from you. The unformed spiritual creation was more excellent than if it were a formed body, but even the unformed bodily creation was more excellent than if it were nothing at all. And so unformed things would have depended on your Word even if that very Word had not called them back into your unity and formed them, so that the whole of creation would be from you, the One Highest Good, and would itself be very good. So what claim did they have on you that they should exist, even as unformed, since it was only from you that they existed at all?

Phil. 2:6

Ps. 103:24

Lk. 15:3

Gn. 1:31

2.3 What claim did bodily matter have on you, even to be invisible and unorganized? For it would not have been even that had you not made it, and so, precisely because it did not exist, it could not have had

---

2. "cultivate," "attend to," and "worship" all translate *colere*, which means both to cultivate land and to worship a deity; "neglected" translates *incultus*, literally "uncultivated" (or "unworshiped").

any claim on you to exist. Or what claim did the spiritual creation in its incipient state have on you, even to waver in a darkness like the abyss, and unlike you? Only the Word by whom it was made could turn it to that same Word, and shed his light upon it so that it might be light, and be conformed, though not made equal, to the Form that is equal to *Rom. 8:29* you. For a body, to be is not the same as to be beautiful (for otherwise *Phil. 2:6* no body could be ugly); and in the same way, for a created spirit, to live is not the same as to live wisely: otherwise it would be unchangeably wise. But it is good for it to cling to you always, lest by turning *Ps. 72:28* from you it lose the light it received by being turned toward you, and fall back into a life of darkness like the abyss. For we ourselves, who in virtue of our souls are a spiritual creation, were turned away from you, our Light; in that life we once were darkness, and we struggle still in *Eph. 5:8* the shadows that remain, until we become your righteousness in your only Son, righteousness like the mountains of God, where once we *2 Cor. 5:21* were your judgments, like the great abyss.[3] *Ps. 35:7*

3.4 Now among the first acts of creation you said, "Let light be made," and light was made. I am right, I think, to interpret this as *Gn. 1:3* referring to the spiritual creation, since it was already a kind of life on which you could shed your light. But just as it had no claim on you to exist as the sort of life on which you could shed your light, it also had no claim on you, once it existed, to receive light from you. Its formlessness would not be pleasing to you unless it were made light, not simply by existing, but by gazing upon your Light and clinging to it; thus it would owe not merely its being alive at all, but its living happily, entirely to your grace, which changed it for the better by turning it toward what cannot be changed either for the better or for the worse: you yourself. For you alone simply are; it is not one thing for you to live and another for you to live happily, because you are your own happiness.

---

3. Psalm 35:7: "Your righteousness is like the mountains of God, your judgments like the great abyss." As the abyss is dark until it is illuminated by the Word, human beings turned away from God dwell in the dark abyss of his judgments until they are turned toward the Word and become, as Paul says (2 Corinthians 5:21), the righteousness of God. This analogy between the formation of creatures and the re-formation of sinful humanity is the key to Augustine's exegesis in Book 13. I translate *conversio* (and its cognates) as "turning toward" rather than "conversion," first because that's what it means, and second because "conversion" has overtones of a once-for-all decision, rather than a continuing process. As for the mountains of God, in his commentary on this Psalm Augustine says that they represent the apostles: as the light of the rising sun falls first on the mountains and then spreads down into the valleys, so the light of Christ shone first on the apostles, the great preachers, and then spread into the valley. Here, however, the hope is clearly that all Christians might become the lofty mountains of God's righteousness.

4.5   What, then, would be lacking from the Good that you yourself are, even if these things did not exist at all or remained unformed, these things that you made, not from any need, but out of the abundance of your goodness? You impose restraint on them and turn them toward form, but not as though your joy will be made complete through them. Their imperfection is displeasing to you, who are perfect, and so it pleases you to bring them to perfection: not, however, as though you were imperfect and needed their perfection to become perfect yourself. For your good Spirit was borne over the waters; he was not held aloft *Gn. 1:2* by them as if he were resting on them. No, your Spirit is said to rest on those whom he brings to rest in himself. Instead, your incorruptible *Num. 11:25; Is.* and unchangeable Will, sufficient in himself, was borne over the life *11:2, 66:2 VL; 1 Pet. 4:14* that you had made. For that life, to live was not the same as to live happily, since it was alive even in its wavering and darkness. It still needed to be turned toward him by whom it had been made, and to live more and more from the Fount of Life, and in his Light to see light: to be *Ps. 35:10* made perfect and full of light and happy.

5.6   Here I see a dim and shadowy image of the Trinity that you are, *1 Cor. 13:12* my God. For you, Father, made heaven and earth in the Beginning of our wisdom, the Beginning who is your Wisdom, born of you, equal to you and coeternal with you: that is, in your Son. And we have spoken *Phil. 2:16* at length of the heaven of heaven, of earth invisible and unorganized, and of the dark abyss—dark in the churning flux of its spiritual formlessness, unless it should be turned to him who had made it a kind of life, so that by his Light it might be made a life beautifully formed, the heaven of the heaven he made afterward and placed in the midst of the waters. By the word "God" I already understood you, O Father, who *Gn. 1:6* made these things; by the word "Beginning" I already understood the Son, in whom you made these things. And believing that my God is a Trinity, I looked further into his sacred writings, and there it was: I found your Spirit borne over the waters. Behold the Trinity, my God: Father, Son, and Holy Spirit, Creator of the whole of creation.

6.7   But why was it—O truth-telling Light, I bring my heart before you, lest it teach me delusions and follies. Dispel the darkness of my heart and tell me, I beg you through Charity our Mother,[4] why was it

---

4. "Charity our Mother" is the Holy Spirit; the identification of charity with the Holy Spirit appears in Augustine as early as *De moribus ecclesiae catholicae et de moribus manichaeorum* (388) and is especially prominent in *On the Trinity* (399–422/6). For charity as mother, see *De catechizandis rudibus* (399): "Although the same charity is owed to all, the same remedy is not to be applied to all. One and the same charity gives birth to some, is made weak with others; some it works hard to build up,

that your Scripture did not name your Spirit until after it had named heaven, and earth invisible and unformed, and the darkness over the abyss? Was it that the right way to bring the Spirit before our minds was to speak of him as being "borne over" the waters? And he could not be spoken of in that way unless there was first a mention of that over which your Spirit could be understood to be borne. He was not borne over the Father or the Son, and he could not rightly be said to be "borne over" unless he was borne over something. So that over which he was borne had to be mentioned first, and only then could he be mentioned, for it was fitting for him to be described in exactly that way, as "being borne" over the waters. But then why was it not fitting for him to be brought before our minds in any other way, but only as being "borne over" the waters?

7.8   Now let anyone who is capable of understanding follow your Apostle as he says that your charity has been poured into our hearts through the Holy Spirit who has been given to us, as he teaches us *Rom. 5:5* about spiritual matters and shows us the surpassingly excellent way of *1 Cor. 12:1* charity, as he bows his knees to you on our behalf so that we might *1 Cor. 12:31 / Eph.* have the surpassingly excellent knowledge of the charity of Christ. And *3:14 / Eph. 3:19* so the Spirit, surpassingly excellent from the beginning, was borne over the waters.

To whom shall I speak, and how shall I speak, of the weight of cupidity that drags us into the abyss, of how we are lifted up by charity through your Spirit, who was borne over the waters? To whom shall I speak of this? How shall I express it? These are not places where we sink down and rise up. What could be more like places, and yet what could be more unlike? They are affections; they are loves: the uncleanness of our spirit drags us down by our love for our anxious concerns; the holiness of your Spirit raises us up by our love for a peace free from all anxiety, so that we might have our hearts lifted up to you,[5] where your Spirit is borne over the waters, and so that we might come to that surpassingly excellent rest after our soul has passed over the waters that have no substance.[6] *Ps. 123:5*

---

others it fears to offend; it stoops to some, stands upright for others; it is gentle to some, stern with others. To no one is it an enemy; to all it is a mother."

5. See 12.16.23, fn. 8. Here Augustine combines the priest's bidding, "Lift up your hearts" (*sursum corda*), with the congregation's response, "We lift them up to the Lord" (*habemus ad Dominum*).

6. *en. Ps.* 123.9: "What is the water that has no substance? It is the water of sins, which have no substance. For sins have no substance. They have emptiness, not substance. They have poverty, not substance. In that water without substance the younger son [the prodigal] lost all his substance."

8.9   The angel fell; the human soul fell; they showed that the abyss
would have held the whole spiritual creation in its deep darkness had
you not said from the outset, "Let light be made," and light was made,
and had not every obedient intelligence in your heavenly city clung to
you and rested in your Spirit, who is borne unchangeably over every
changeable thing. Otherwise even the heaven of heaven would have
been a dark abyss in itself; but now it is light in the Lord. For even in   *Eph. 5:8*
the wretched disquiet of fallen spirits who bear witness to the darkness
that is theirs when they are stripped of the garment of your light, you
show how great you made rational creatures: nothing less than you is
enough for them to enjoy the happiness of perfect rest, and for that
very reason no rational creature is adequate to make itself happy. For
you, O Lord, will make our darkness bright. Our garments of light   *Ps. 17:29*
have their sunrise from you, and our darkness will be as the noonday.   *Is. 58:10*

Give me yourself, O my God; restore yourself to me. Truly I do
love you, and if my love is too feeble, let me love you more powerfully.
I cannot measure myself so that I know how far short I fall of loving
you enough that my life runs to meet your embrace, and does not turn
aside until it is hidden in the secret hiding place of your countenance.   *Col. 3:3 / Ps. 30:21*
All I know is this: apart from you, everything goes ill for me, not only
outside me, but within my very self; and any wealth I have that is not
my God is poverty.

9.10   Was the Father or the Son not borne over the waters? If we
mean as a body is borne over a place, then neither was the Holy Spirit
borne over the waters. If we mean the Godhead's unchangeable excellence surpassing all that is changeable, then the Father and the Son
and the Holy Spirit were all borne over the waters. Why, then, is this
said only of the Holy Spirit? Why is he alone spoken of as if he were in
a place, when he is not in a place? Why is this said only of him, who
alone is called your Gift?   *Acts 2:38*

In your Gift we find rest; there we enjoy you. Our rest is our place.
Love raises us up to that place, and your good Spirit lifts up our lowli-   *Ps. 142:10*
ness from the gates of death. There is peace for us in a good will.[7] By its   *Ps. 9:14–15 / Lk.*
weight a body seeks its own place. Weight does not move a body only   *2:14*
to the lowest point; no, it moves a body to its own place. Fire tends
upward, a stone downward. They are put in motion by their weights;
by their weights they seek their proper places. Oil poured over water

---

7. "in a good will": meaning here, as again in the last sentence of this paragraph, both in our own
good will (from the angels' song to the shepherds, "And on earth peace among human beings of good
will") and in God's good Will, the Holy Spirit. The expression includes both meanings without distinction, since for Augustine our own good will is precisely the work of the Holy Spirit (Romans 5:5).

rises above the water; water poured over oil sinks beneath the oil. They are put in motion by their weights; by their weights they seek their proper place. Things that are not fully ordered are restless; they are put in order and find rest. My weight is my love: by it I am carried wherever I am carried. By your Gift we are set on fire and carried upward; we are kindled and go forth. In our heart we climb the upward path, *Ps. 83:6* and we sing a song of degrees.[8] By your Fire, by your good Fire, we are kindled and go forth: we are journeying above toward the peace of Jerusalem. For I was glad among those who said to me, "We will go into the house of the Lord." By a good will we shall find our place *Ps. 121:1* there, so that we want nothing but to abide there for ever. *Ps. 60:8*

10.11 O happy creature that has known no other state! Yet it would have been different had it not been raised up by your Gift, who is borne over every changeable thing—raised up as soon as it was made, with no lapse of time after you called it by saying, "Let light be made," and light was made. For us there is a difference in time: once we were darkness, but then we are made light. But that creature is described as what it *Eph. 5:8* would have been had it not received light; it is described as though it had first been wavering and dark, so that the cause that made it otherwise can be clearly seen: it was light by being turned to the Light that does not fail. Let those who can, understand this; let them ask you for *Sir. 24:6* understanding. Why should they trouble me, as though I were the one *Gal. 6:17* to enlighten any human being who comes into this world? *Jn. 1:9*

11.12 Who can understand the almighty Trinity? Yet everyone speaks of the Trinity, if indeed it is the Trinity of whom we speak. It is a remarkable soul that knows what it is saying when it speaks of the Trinity. People quarrel and struggle, and only those who are at peace behold that vision.

I would urge people to consider these three things in themselves— these three things are very different from that Trinity, but I offer them as a means by which people can put their minds to work and test their thoughts and perceive how great a difference there is. These are the three things of which I am speaking: being, knowing, and willing. For I am, and I know, and I will; I am something that knows and wills, and I know that I am and that I will, and I will to be and to know. So let those who can, see the inseparable life that consists in these three—one life, one mind, one being—a distinction that permits no separation, but a distinction nonetheless. Unquestionably these three are within them; let them look within themselves and see them and tell me.

---

8. See 9.2.2, fn. 2.

But when they discover something in these three and tell me, let them not suppose that they have discovered the Unchangeable, which surpasses all these things, which unchangeably is and unchangeably knows and unchangeably wills. Is it because of these three that there is a Trinity also in the Unchangeable, or are these three in Each, so that Each is threefold? Or are both of these true in some wondrous way, and the Unchangeable is both one and many, bounded by itself, unbounded in itself, so that in the immense riches of its unity it is, and is known to itself, and is sufficient for itself, unchangeably the Selfsame?[9] Who can easily grasp this? Who can in any way express it? Who would be so rash as to make any definitive statement about it?

12.13   Go further, my faith, in your confession. Say to the Lord your God, "Holy, holy, holy, O Lord my God; we have been baptized in *Is. 6:3; Rev. 4:8* your Name, O Father, Son, and Holy Spirit; we baptize in your Name, O Father, Son, and Holy Spirit." For God in his Christ has made in *Mt. 28:19* us too a heaven and earth, the spiritual and the carnal members of his Church. And our earth, before it received form from teaching, *1 Cor. 3:1* was invisible and unorganized; we were enshrouded by the darkness *Gn. 1:2* of ignorance, for you chastened human beings because of their sin, *Ps. 54:6 / Ps. 38:12* and your judgments are like a great abyss. But because your Spirit was *Ps. 35:7* borne over the water, your mercy did not abandon us to our wretchedness. You said, "Let light be made"; "Repent, for the kingdom of *Gn. 1:3* heaven has drawn near." "Repent"; "Let light be made."[10] And because *Mt. 3:2, 4:17* our soul was disquieted within us, we remembered you, O Lord, from *Ps. 41:6* the land of Jordan and from the Mountain that is equal to you but *Phil. 2:16* became small for our sake.[11] Our darkness became hateful to us, and *Ps. 41:7* we were turned to you, and light was made. And behold, once we were darkness, but now we are light in the Lord. *Eph. 5:8*

---

9.   For "the Selfsame" see 1.6.10, fn. 7. Augustine's language here deliberately stretches the bounds of intelligibility, precisely to convey the difficulty of conceiving the Trinity, and English translators do Augustine no favors by supplying technical vocabulary (such as "Person") or otherwise tidying up the language to offer the superficial appearance of the very clarity that he is at pains to deny.

10.   Developing the parallel between the forming of unformed creation and the re-forming of fallen humanity, Augustine juxtaposes the first words of God in Genesis, "Let light be made," with the first words of John the Baptist urging people to be baptized (Matthew 3:2) and the first words of Jesus inaugurating his public mission after his baptism (Matthew 4:17).

11.   From here through 13.14.15 Augustine frequently echoes Psalm 41, which was sung by baptismal candidates in procession to the baptistery. Appendix B offers a translation of Augustine's text of this Psalm.

13.14   And yet still by faith, not by sight.[12] For in hope we have been   2 Cor. 5:7
saved. Now hope that is seen is not hope. Deep still calls to deep, but   Rom. 8:24
now in the voice of your waterfalls.[13] And still the one who says, "I   Ps. 41:8
could not speak to you as spiritual people, but as carnal," even he does   1 Cor. 3:1
not yet consider that he has laid hold of it; forgetting what lies behind,
he strains forward to what lies ahead and groans under the weight of   Phil. 3:13
his burden. His soul thirsts for God as deer thirst for the water-brooks,   2 Cor. 5:4
and he says, "When shall I come?" He longs to put on his heavenly   Ps. 41:2–3
dwelling, and he calls to the lower deep, "Do not be conformed to   2 Cor. 5:2
this world, but be transformed by the renewal of your mind," and   Rom. 12:2
"Do not be children in your thinking, but be babes in evil, that you
may be mature in your thinking," and "O foolish Galatians, who has   1 Cor. 14:20
bewitched you?" But he speaks no longer in his own voice; he speaks in   Gal. 3:1
your voice. For you sent your Spirit from the highest heaven through   Wisd. 9:17
him who ascended on high and opened the floodgates of your gifts, so   Ps. 67:19 qtd. Eph.
that the flowing stream might gladden your city.   4:8 / Gn. 7:11;
Mal. 3:10 / Ps.

The friend of the Bridegroom sighs for him.   45:5 / Jn. 3:29

Already he has the first fruits of his spirit[14] in the Bridegroom's
 safekeeping,
  but still he groans inwardly as he waits for his adoption,
  the redemption of his body.   Rom. 8:23
He sighs for the Bridegroom,
  for he is a member of the Bride;   1 Cor. 12:27
he is eager for the Bridegroom,
  for he is a friend of the Bridegroom.
He is not eager for himself:
  it is not in his own voice,
  but in the voice of your waterfalls,
  that he calls to the other deep that he eagerly loves,
  fearing that, as the serpent deceived Eve by his cunning,

---

12. "We walk by faith, not by sight," Paul says in 2 Corinthians 5:7. The word for "sight" is *species*, the same word Augustine uses for "form" in his description of the forming of creation, and so the Scriptural text is especially apt for Augustine to continue his parallel between the forming of creation and the ongoing re-forming (*conversio*) of the human soul. "Vision" in the last sentence of this paragraph is likewise *species*.

13. Augustine explains in *en. Ps.* 41.13 that "one deep calls to another" means that "the holy preachers of the word of God" call out to others to teach them "something of faith, something of truth, for the sake of eternal life." Even these great preachers (his example there is Peter, whereas here it is Paul) are a deep (*abyssus*) because "a depth (*profunditas*) of weakness was hidden" in them, though it was "bare before the eyes of God."

14. For the meaning of this expression, see 9.10.24, fn. 30.

their thoughts will be led astray from their fidelity to
   our Bridegroom, your only Son.   *2 Cor. 11:3*
What is the light of that vision,
   when we shall see him as he is,   *1 Jn. 3:2*
   and he will wipe away the tears that have been my food day and night,
   while day after day they say to me,
      "Where is your God?"?   *Ps. 41:4*

14.15   I too say, "Where are you, my God?" And behold, you are
here. For a little while I draw breath in you as I pour out my soul over
me with a noise of exultation and thanksgiving, of the sound of one
celebrating a festival. And still my soul is sorrowful, for it falls again   *Ps. 41:5*
and becomes a great deep, or rather, it realizes that it is still a great deep.
   My faith, which you have enkindled in the night to guide my feet,
says to my soul, "Why are you sorrowful, my soul, and why do you disquiet me? Hope in the Lord. His word is a lantern to your feet." Hope   *Ps. 41:6, 41:12,*
and persevere until the night, the mother of the wicked, passes away,   *42:5 / Ps.*
                                                                          118:105
until the wrath of the Lord passes away. We too were once children   *Is. 26:20*
of his wrath, we too were once darkness, and we carry the remnants   *Eph. 2:3/ Eph. 5:8*
of that darkness in our body, which is dead because of sin. Hope and   *Rom. 8:10*
persevere until the day dawns and the shadows are dispelled. Hope in   *Song 2:17 VL*
the Lord.
   In the morning I will stand before him and gaze upon him; I will   *Ps. 5:5*
give thanks to him always. In the morning I will stand before him and
see the health of my countenance, my God, who will give life even to   *Ps. 41:6, 41:12,*
our mortal bodies through the Spirit who dwells in us, because in his   *42:5 / Rom. 8:11*
mercy he is borne over the dark and turbulent deep within us. In the
midst of our journey we have received from him this pledge that we   *2 Cor. 1:22, 5:5 /*
are already light. As yet we have been saved in hope, but even now we   *Eph. 5:8 / Rom.*
                                                                          8:24
are children of light and children of God, not children of night or of
darkness, as we once were. You alone, who test our hearts and call the *1 Thess. 5:5 / Eph.*
light "day" and the darkness "night," you alone distinguish between   *5:8 / Ps. 16:3;*
                                                                          1 Thess. 2:4 /
them and us, for there is as yet no certainty in our human knowledge.   *Gn. 1:5*
Who can set us apart? Only you. And what do we have that we have
not received from you, who from the same lump make some vessels for   *1 Cor. 4:7*
honor and others for dishonor?   *Rom. 9:21*

15.16   And who made for us the firmament of authority that is over
us in your divine Scripture? Only you, our God. For the sky shall be
rolled up like a scroll, but for now it is stretched over us like a skin:[15]   *Is. 34:4 / Ps. 103:2*
that is, your divine Scripture has an even higher authority now that

---

15. "like a skin": that is, like a tent (for tents were made of skins).

the mortals by whom you imparted it to us have encountered death. And you know, Lord, you know how you clothed human beings with garments of skin when by their sin they became mortal. So you have *Gn. 3:21* stretched out like a skin the firmament of your book, your harmonious words, which you have set in authority over us through the ministry of mortals. For by their very death the unwavering authority of your words, which they declared to us, is stretched out high above all that is beneath; when they were still alive, it had not yet been stretched out in so lofty a way. You had not yet stretched out the sky like a skin; you had not yet spread the glory of their death throughout all the world.

15.17 O Lord, may we see the heavens, the works of your fingers; *Ps. 8:4* clear away from our eyes the cloud by which you have veiled them. In them is your testimony, which gives wisdom to little children. My *Ps. 18:8* God, perfect your praise from the mouths of infants, of babies at their mothers' breast. We have known no other books like these, books that *Ps. 8:3* destroy pride, that destroy the enemy and the defender who resists *Ez. 30:6 / Ps. 8:3* your reconciliation by defending his own sins. O Lord, I have known no other words like these, pure words that call on me to make my *Ps. 11:7* confession, that unstiffen my neck to receive your yoke, that summon *Mt. 11:29–30* me to worship you with no thought of reward. No, I have known no other words like these. I submit to them: grant to me, good Father, that I may understand them, for you have established their unwavering authority over those who submit to them.

15.18 There are other waters above the firmament, I believe: immor- *Gn. 1:7* tal waters set apart from all earthly corruption. Let them praise your Name; let the host of your angels above the heavens praise you. They *Ps. 148:3–5* have no need to look upon your firmament, to know your word by reading. For they always see your face, and they read there, not in syl- *Mt. 18:10* lables dispersed through times, what you eternally will. They read, they choose, and they love. They always read, and what they read never passes away. For it is by choosing and loving that they read the unchangeable nature of your purpose. Their book is not closed; their scroll is not rolled up. For you are their book; you are their scroll; and *Is. 34:4* you are eternal. You set them in their place above the strong firmament *Ps. 47:15* that you established over the weakness of the peoples below, so that they could look upon it and know your mercy, which unfolds in time to proclaim you, who made times. For your mercy, Lord, reaches to the heavens, and your faithfulness to the clouds. The clouds pass away, *Ps. 35:6 / Ps. 17:13* but the heavens remain. The preachers of your word pass away from this life into another life, but your Scripture is stretched out over the peoples to the end of the age. Heaven and earth too will pass away, but

your words will not pass away. For the skin will be rolled up, and the   *Mt. 24:35*
grass over which it was stretched will fade away with all its beauty; but   *Is. 40:6–8*
your Word endures for ever. Now we see him dimly, through clouds
and in the mirror of the sky, and not as he is; for although we are   *1 Cor. 13:12*
beloved by your Son, what we shall be has not yet appeared. He gazed   *1 Jn. 3:2*
at us through the windows of the flesh; he caressed us and enkindled   *Song 2:9 VL*
us, and we run after his fragrance. But when he appears, we shall be like   *Song 1:3*
him, for we shall see him as he is. Then our seeing will be a seeing-as-   *1 Jn. 3:2*
he-is, but that vision is not yet ours.

16.19   For you alone, who are unchangeably and know unchangeably
and will unchangeably, have full and perfect knowledge. Your being
knows and wills unchangeably, and your knowledge is and knows
unchangeably, and your will is and knows unchangeably. And it does
not seem right in your eyes that what receives light and is subject to
change should know the Unchangeable Light as it knows itself. And so
my soul gasps to you like a thirsty land, because it cannot give light to   *Ps. 142:6*
itself any more than it can satisfy itself. For with you is the well of life,
and so in your Light we will see light.   *Ps. 35:10*

17.20   Who gathered into one society those who do bitter deeds?   *Ps. 65:7, 77:8*
They all have the same end, temporal and earthly happiness; whatever
they do, they do for the sake of that end, though they waver amidst a
countless variety of anxious cares. Was it not you, O Lord, who commanded the waters to be gathered together into one place and the dry
ground, thirsting for you, to appear? For even the sea is yours, and you   *Gn. 1:9*
made it, and your hands molded the dry land. It is not the bitterness   *Ps. 94:5*
of wills, but rather the gathering of the waters, that is called the sea.
For you restrain even the evil desires of souls; you set the limits beyond
which the waters cannot go, so that their waves may break upon them-
selves. And thus by the order of your command, which is above all   *Job 38:10–11*
things, you make them a sea.

17.21   But there are souls kept apart from the fellowship of the sea
because they have a different end, souls that thirst for you and appear
before you, and you water them by a sweet and hidden spring so that   *Ps. 41:3, 62:2*
the earth brings forth its fruit. It brings forth its fruit and by your com-   *Gn. 1:12; Ps. 84:13*
mand, O Lord its God, our soul puts forth works of mercy according
to its kind: loving our neighbors by relieving their bodily needs. By   *Gn. 1:11–12*
our likeness to them[16] we have in ourselves the seed of such works:

---

16. "By our likeness to them": *secundum similitudinem*. Augustine's text of Genesis 1:12 has *secundum speciem* ("according to [their] species") here, whereas elsewhere the expression is *secundum genus* ("according to [their] kind"). Species and likeness are closely connected for Augustine, but likeness is

our own weakness moves us with compassion to help those in need as
we would want to be helped if we were in the same need—not only   *Mt. 7:12*
in easy matters, like plants yielding seed, but in matters that call for
strong and determined help, like a tree bearing fruit, that is, in the   *Gn. 1:11–12*
generous work of rescuing one who suffers injustice from the hand
of the powerful and offering a safe refuge in the mighty strength of
righteous judgment.

18.22   This, O Lord, this is my prayer to you: as you create, as you
grant cheerfulness and ability, let truth spring up from the earth and
righteousness look down from heaven,[17] and let there be lights in the   *Ps. 84:12*
firmament. Let us share our bread with the hungry and bring the   *Gn. 1:14*
homeless poor into our house; let us clothe the naked and not despise
those of our own kindred who dwell with us. When these fruits come   *Is. 58:7*
up from the earth, see that it is good. Then, when the right time has
come, let our light break forth: passing beyond this lower fruit, action,   *Is. 58:8*
to the delights of contemplation, and holding fast the higher word of
life, may we shine as lights in the world, clinging to the firmament of   *Phil. 2:15–16*
your Scripture. For there you teach us to separate intelligible things   *Is. 1:18*
from sensible things, like separating day from night, and to separate   *Gn. 1:4*
souls devoted to intelligible things from souls devoted to sensible
things. Before the firmament was made, it was you alone who separated light from darkness by the hidden depths of your judgment; but
now that you have placed your spiritual ones in that same firmament
and set them apart by your grace, which is manifest throughout the
world, they shine upon the earth, and they too separate the day from
the night. They are signs for times, signs that the old has passed away   *Gn. 1:14–18*
and, behold, the new has come; that our salvation is nearer than when   *2 Cor. 5:17*
we first believed, that the night is far gone and the day is at hand; that   *Rom. 13:11–12*
you bless the crown of your year, sending laborers into your harvest,   *Ps. 64:12 / Mt. 9:38*
for which others worked by sowing the seed; you send them also into   *Jn. 4:38*
another sowing, whose harvest is at the end of the age. You grant the   *Mt. 13:39*
prayers of those who call upon you and bless the years of the righteous;   *Ps. 64:12*

---

his preferred expression here because we understand the needs of others not merely because we share
the same species or form, but because we are like others in our weakness and need.
17. *en. Ps.* 84.13–14: "'Truth has sprung up from the earth': Christ was born of a woman. 'Truth has
sprung up from the earth': the Son of God came forth from flesh. What is truth? The Son of God.
What is earth? Flesh. . . . In order that righteousness might look down from heaven—that is, in
order that human beings might be made righteous by divine grace—Truth was born of the Virgin
Mary, so that he could offer sacrifice for those who needed to be made righteous: the sacrifice of his
suffering, the sacrifice of the Cross. . . . We can offer another interpretation of these words. 'Truth
has sprung up from the earth': confession has sprung up from human beings. . . . Confess your sins,
and truth will spring up from you."

but you are the Selfsame, and in your years, which do not fail, you   *Ps. 101:28*
make ready a storehouse for years that pass away.

By your eternal plan you shower heavenly gifts upon the earth at
their proper times.

18.23   For to one is given through the Spirit the utterance of wisdom
as a greater light for those who delight in the splendor of truth as in the
dawn; to another the utterance of knowledge as a lesser light according
to the same Spirit. To another is given faith; to another, gifts of healing;
to another, the working of miracles; to another, prophecy; to another,
the ability to distinguish between spirits; to another, various kinds of
tongues; and all these are like stars. For one and the same Spirit is at   *2 Cor. 12:8–10*
work in them all; he distributes these gifts to each as he wills and causes   *2 Cor. 12:11*
stars to appear, to give their light for the benefit of all.

Now the utterance of knowledge, which contains all mysteries that   *1 Cor. 13:2*
vary through times like the moon, and the other gifts listed after it,
which are like stars, fall far short of the brightness of wisdom in which
the day of which I have spoken[18] rejoices; they are suited only to rule
the night. They are necessary for those to whom your most discerning   *Ps. 135:7–9*
servant could not speak as spiritual people, but as carnal; among the   *1 Cor. 2:6*
mature he speaks wisdom. The unspiritual are like infants in Christ,   *1 Cor. 2:6*
still drinking milk. Until they acquire the strength for solid food and   *1 Cor. 3:1–2 / Heb.*
they can fix their gaze on the sun, may their night not be utterly dark;   *5:12–14*
but let them be content with the light of the moon and the stars.

These things you teach us most wisely, our God, in your book,   *Is. 1:18*
your firmament, so that we might discern all things in a wondrous
contemplation, though as yet we see them only by signs and in times
and days and years.   *Gn. 1:14*

19.24   "But first, be washed, be clean; remove the wickedness from
your souls and from before my eyes, so that the dry land may appear.   *Is. 1:16 / Gn. 1:9*
Learn to do good; defend the fatherless and plead for the widow, so   *Is. 1:17*
that the earth might put forth vegetation for food and trees bearing
fruit. And come, let us reason together," says the Lord, "that lights may   *Gn. 1:11–12 /*
be made in the firmament of the heaven, and let them give light upon   *Is. 1:18*
the earth."   *Gn. 1:15, 1:17*

That rich man asked the good Teacher what he must do to attain
eternal life. He thought the Teacher was a human being and nothing   *Mt. 19:16*
more: but he is good because he is God. Let the good Teacher tell him   *Mt. 19:17*
that if he desires to enter into life, he must keep the commandments;
he must put aside from himself the bitterness of evil and wickedness.

---

18. "the day of which I have spoken": that is, the day that is "at hand" (13.18.22).

He must not kill, he must not commit adultery, he must not steal, he must not bear false witness, so that the dry land may appear and bring forth the fruit of honoring his mother and father and loving his neighbor. "All these things I have done," he says. But then where do such great thorns come from, if the earth is fruitful? Uproot the tangled thickets of greed: sell what you have and be filled with fruits by giving to the poor, and you will have treasure in heaven; and follow the Lord if you would be perfect. He knows what belongs to the day and what belongs to the night, and if you join the company of those among whom he speaks wisdom, you too will know this, and lights in the firmament will be made for you. But this will not happen unless your heart is there; and your heart will not be there unless your treasure is there, as you have heard from the good Teacher. But the barren ground was sorrowful, and thorns choked the word.

Mt. 19:18 qtg.
Ex. 20:13–16 / Mt. 19:19 qtg. Ex. 20:12 / Mt. 19:19 / Mt. 19:20 / Mt. 13:7, 13:22

Mt. 19:21

1 Cor. 2:6

Mt. 6:21

Lk. 18:23 / Mt. 13:7, 13:22

19.25 But you are a chosen race, the weak things of the world, who left everything behind to follow the Lord. Run after him and shame the strong; run after him, beautiful feet, and shine in the firmament, that the heavens may declare his glory, separating the light of those who are mature but not yet like the angels from the darkness of those little ones who are nonetheless not without hope. Shine upon the whole earth: the day radiant with sunlight will speak to the day the utterance of wisdom, and the night bathed in moonlight will impart to the night the utterance of knowledge. Moon and stars give light to the night, and the night does not engulf them in darkness; for they make the darkness light so far as their power allows. It is as if God says, "Let lights be made in the firmament," and suddenly a sound came from heaven, like the rush of a mighty wind, and there appeared to them divided tongues as of fire, which rested upon each of them, and they were made lights in the firmament of heaven, having the word of life. Run everywhere, holy fires, fires of beauty. For you are the light of the world; do not hide under a bushel basket. The one whom you dearly love has been exalted, and he will exalt you. Run, therefore, and make this known to all the nations.

1 Pet. 2:9 / 1 Cor. 1:27 / Mt. 19:27 par. Mk. 10:28; Lk. 18:28 / 1 Cor. 1:27 / Is. 52:7 qtd. Rom. 10:15 / Gn. 1:17 / Ps. 18:2 / Mt. 23:30 par. Mk. 12:25 / Gn. 1:14–18 / Ps. 18:8 / Ps. 18:3

Gn. 1:14

Acts 2:2–3

Phil. 2:15–16; 1 Jn. 1:1

Mt. 5:14–15

Phil. 2:9

Mt. 28:19

20.26 Let the sea also conceive and give birth to your[19] works; let the waters produce creeping things with living souls. For by separating what is precious from what is worthless, you have become the mouth of God, by which he said, "Let the waters produce" not the living soul, which the earth produces, but "creeping things with living souls,

Gn. 1:20–22

Jer. 15:19

---

19. "Your" is second-personal plural, continuing Augustine's address from the previous paragraph to those who are the "light of the world."

and birds flying above the earth." For your sacraments, O God, crept   *Gn. 1:21–25*
through the works of your saints in the midst of the waves of temptation in this life to mark the peoples with your Name by plunging them
in the waters of your baptism. And in the midst of these, mighty works
and wonders were done, like great sea monsters, and the voices of your   *Ps. 105:21; Acts*
messengers flew above the earth, close to the firmament of your book,   *2:11*
which was placed in authority over them; wherever they went, they
flew beneath it. For there are no words or languages in which their
voices are not heard, when their sound has gone out into all the land
and their message to the ends of the earth. For you, O Lord, have given   *Ps. 18:4–5*
them your blessing, and so you have multiplied them.   *Gn. 1:22*

20.27   Surely I am not lying. Surely I am not confusing one thing
with another and failing to distinguish the clear knowledge of these
things in the firmament of heaven with the bodily works in the turbulent sea and beneath the firmament of heaven. For the conceptions
of these things are steadfast and well defined, like lights of wisdom
and knowledge; they do not grow as one generation succeeds another.
But the bodily works of those same things are manifold and various,
and as one grows from another, they are multiplied by your blessing,   *Gn. 1:22*
O God. You have dealt gently with the restlessness of mortal senses:
something that is one in the understanding of our mind is repre-
sented and expressed in many ways through bodily movements. The
waters have produced these things, but at your command. The needs
of peoples estranged from the eternity of your truth have produced
these things, but in your Gospel. For these very waters, whose bitter
illness was the reason these things came forth in your word, have cast
them forth.

20.28   All these things are beautiful, for you are their Maker; and
yet behold, you who made them are inexpressibly more beautiful than
they. If Adam had not fallen away from you, the salty sea of the human
race—bottomless in their curiosity, stormy in their pride, unsteady
in their wavering—would not have flowed forth from his womb.[20]
And so there would have been no need for your stewards to perform
their mystical deeds and words in many waters, in bodily and sensible ways—for those works, it now seems to me, are what is meant
by creeping things and flying birds. Human beings subject to bodily
sacraments, surrounded by such works and initiated into them, do not

---

20. Augustine held that if Adam had not sinned, the human race would have been propagated
spiritually rather than physically. "Womb" indicates that "Adam" is being used as a shorthand way
of referring to our first parents.

progress further unless their soul comes to live spiritually on a higher level, leaving behind the elementary doctrine of Christ and looking ahead to maturity.

Heb. 6:1

21.29   And thus by your command it was not the depth of the sea, but the earth, separated from the bitterness of the waters, that brought forth not creeping things with living souls and birds of the air, but a living soul. This soul no longer stands in need of baptism, which the nations need, as it had once needed baptism when it was yet covered by the waters. For there is no other way to enter the kingdom of heaven besides the one you have established. And the soul does not look for mighty works and wonders to awaken faith; it does not insist on seeing signs and wonders or else refuse to believe. For the believing earth has now been separated from the waters of the sea, which are bitter with unbelief; and tongues are a sign not for believers but for unbelievers.

Gn. 1:24

Jn. 3:5

Jn. 4:48; 1 Cor. 1:22

1 Cor. 14:22

Nor does the earth, which you founded upon the waters, have any need of the birds that the waters produced at your command. Send out your command to the earth through your messengers. For we tell of their works, but it is you who work in them so that their works bring forth a living soul. Earth brings it forth, because earth is what causes them to act on the soul, just as the sea caused them to act on the creeping things with living souls and the birds beneath the firmament of heaven, which the earth no longer needs, though at the table you have prepared for those who believe in you it feeds on the Fish brought up from the depths of the sea; for he was brought up from the depths of the sea that he might nourish the dry land.[21]

Ps. 135:6

Gn. 1:20–22

Ps. 147:15

Phil. 2:12–13

Ps. 22:5

Birds too are the offspring of the sea, but they are multiplied on the earth. Human unbelief was the reason that the first preachers of the Gospel spoke, but believers too are encouraged and blessed by them day by day. The living soul, however, has its beginning on the earth: only for those who are already believers is it advantageous to restrain themselves from the love of this world, so that their soul may live for you. Their soul was once dead because it lived in pleasures—deadly pleasures, O Lord. For you are the life-giving pleasures of a pure heart.

Gn. 1:22

Ps. 95:2

Jas. 1:27

2 Cor. 5:15 / 1 Tim. 5:6 / 2 Tim. 2:22

21.30   So let your ministers now work on the earth, not as they worked on the waters of unbelief by preaching and speaking through miracles and mysteries and mystical words, where ignorance, the mother of wonder, would gaze in awe on those mysterious signs. For that is the entrance into faith for children of Adam who have forgotten

---

21. The Fish is Christ, and believers feed on him in the Eucharist.

you, who hide from your face and become an abyss. Rather, let your ministers work also on the dry ground that has been set apart from the raging of the abyss; let them be an example for believers by living among them and arousing them to imitation.

Believers hear these words, not merely to hear them, but to do as they say: "Seek God and your soul will live, that the earth may bring forth a living soul; do not be conformed to this world; keep yourselves from it." The soul lives by shunning what it dies by desiring. Keep yourselves from the monstrous ferocity of pride, from the idle pleasure of lust, and from the deception of what is falsely called knowledge, that the wild beasts may be tamed, the cattle subdued, and the serpents rendered harmless. For these are an allegory for the movements of the soul. But the insolence of pride, the pleasure of inordinate desire, and the poison of curiosity are movements of a dead soul. For a dead soul does not lack movement altogether: when it departs from the Fount of Life, it dies, and so it is carried away by the passing age and is conformed to it.

21.31   But your Word, O God, is the fount of eternal life, and he does not pass away. And so our departure is restrained by your Word when we are told, "Do not be conformed to this world," that the earth may bring forth a living soul in the Fount of Life; by your word through your Evangelists it brings forth a soul that restrains itself by imitating those who imitate your Christ. This is what "according to its kind" means: it is the emulation of a man by his friend. "Be like me," he says, "for I am like you." Thus in the living soul there will be good beasts because of the gentleness[22] of their behavior—for you commanded, "Carry out your works in gentleness, and you will be loved by all"— good cattle who are not rich if they eat and not poor if they do not, and good serpents who are not dangerous and harmful, but shrewd in their wariness, investigating temporal natures just enough so that through understanding created things they can look upon eternity. For these animals serve reason when they are restrained from their deadly rampage; then they are alive and are good.

22.32   For truly, O Lord our God, our Creator, when our affections, in which we once were dead because we were living wickedly, have been restrained from the love of the world, and there begins to be a living soul because it is living rightly, then your word spoken through your Apostle will come to pass: "Do not be conformed to this

Margin references:
Gn. 3:8

1 Thess. 1:6–7

Mt. 7:24, 26 / Ps. 68:33 / Gn. 1:24 / Rom. 12:2

1 Tim. 6:20
Gn. 1:24–28

Jer. 2:13

Jn. 1:1 / Jer. 2:13; Jn. 4:14 / Mt. 24:35
Rom. 12:12

1 Cor. 1:11 / Gn. 1:21 / Eccl. 4:4 VL
Gal. 4:12

Sir. 3:19
1 Cor. 8:8

Gn. 3:1; Mt. 10:16 / Rom. 1:20

1 Jn. 2:16

---

22. The word here translated "gentleness" has the same root as the word translated "tame" in 13.21.30.

world." And what you went on to say next will follow as well: "But
be transformed by the renewal of your mind." No longer will this be
"according to its kind," as though we were imitating a neighbor who
went before us or living by the authority of a better person. For you
did not say, "Let human beings be made according to their kind."
No, you said, "Let us make human beings in our image and likeness,"
that we might prove what is your will. Your steward who became our
father through the Gospel did not mean for us always to be little children drinking milk, whom he would care for like a nurse: and that is
why he said, "Be transformed by the renewal of your mind, that you
might prove what is the will of God, what is good and acceptable and
perfect." And so you do not say, "Let human beings be made"; you
say, "Let us make human beings." Nor do you say, "according to their
kind," but "in our image and likeness." Certainly those whose minds
are renewed, who look upon your truth and understand it, have no
need of any other human being to show it to them so that they can
imitate him according to his kind; no, you show it to them, and they
themselves prove what is your will, what is good and acceptable and
perfect. And you teach them—for now they have the capacity—to
see the Trinity in Unity and the Unity in Trinity. And that is why an
expression in the plural, "Let us make human beings," is nonetheless
followed by an expression in the singular, "and God made human
beings"; and the plural "according to our image" is followed by the
singular "in the image of God." Thus human beings are renewed by
the knowledge of God according to the image of the one who made
them, and those who have been made spiritual judge all things (all
things, of course, that stand in need of judgment), but they themselves are judged by no one.

23.33   That they judge all things means that they have power over
the fish of the sea and the birds of the air, over the cattle and the wild
beasts, over all the earth, and over every creeping thing that creeps
on the earth. This they do through the understanding of their mind,
through which they discern the things of the Spirit of God. Otherwise,
though placed in a position of honor, they had no understanding; they
were joined with irrational animals and became like them. Therefore,
in your Church, our God, according to your grace, which you have
given her, because we are your workmanship, created for good works,
your spiritual ones all judge spiritually: not only those who exercise
spiritual authority but also those who are spiritually subject to those
who exercise authority. For this is the way in which you made human
beings male and female in your grace, where there is neither male nor

Rom. 12:2
Gn. 1:21; Sir. 17:1

Gn. 1:26
Rom. 12:2
1 Cor. 4:15
1 Cor. 3:1 / 1 Thess. 2:7

Rom. 12:2

Rom. 1:20

Gn. 1:26–27

Col. 3:10

1 Cor. 2:15

Gn. 1:26
1 Cor. 2:14

Ps. 48:13

1 Cor. 3:10 / Eph. 2:10 / 1 Cor. 2:15

Gn. 1:27

female in terms of bodily sex; for there is neither Jew nor Greek, neither slave nor free.[23]   *Gal. 3:28*

So your spiritual ones, whether they are in authority or are subject
to authority, judge spiritually. They do not judge the spiritual under-
standings that shine in the firmament: it is not for them to judge such   *Gn. 1:15*
a lofty authority. They do not judge your book, even if something in
it does not shine forth clearly, because we submit our understanding
to it and affirm with certainty that even what is closed to our sight is
said correctly and truly (for this is how human beings, even those who
are already spiritual and renewed in the knowledge of God according   *Col. 3:9–10*
to the image of the one who created them, should be doers of the law,
not judges). They do not judge the distinction between spiritual and   *Jas. 4:11*
carnal human beings, who are known to your eyes, our God. No works
of theirs have yet become evident to us so that we can know them by
their fruits. But you, Lord, know them already; you separated them   *Mt. 7:20*
and called them in secret before the firmament was made. Nor do they,
spiritual though they are, judge the tempestuous peoples of this world.
For what have they to do with judging outsiders? They do not know   *1 Cor. 5:12*
who will one day come into the sweetness of your grace and who will
remain in the endless bitterness of impiety.

23.34   And so human beings, whom you made in your image, did   *Gn. 1:26*
not receive power over the lights in the sky or over the hidden sky
itself, or over day and night, which you called into being before the
creation of the sky, or over the gathered waters, which are the sea. No,
they received power over the fish of the sea and the birds of the air,
over all cattle, over all the earth, and over every creeping thing that
creeps on the earth. They judge: they approve what they find to be   *Gn. 1:26*
right and disapprove what they find to be amiss, whether in the solemn
celebration of the sacraments of initiation for those whom your mercy
seeks out in many waters, or in the rite in which the Fish drawn out
of the deep is offered and devout earth feeds upon it, or in the signs
and sounds of words subject to the authority of your book, like birds
flying beneath the firmament—in interpreting, expounding, discussing, instructing, in blessing and calling upon you, they must exercise
judgment concerning the signs that emerge from their mouths and

---

23. That is, in the account of creation read literally, God's making male and female refers to the
creation of physically distinct sexes. But in the account of creation read as an allegory for the life of
grace, it must mean something different, because Paul tells us that there is no distinction between
male and female, Jew and Greek, slave and free in the life of grace. So Augustine interprets it to mean
that God gives some spiritual authority over others, though all who are spiritual—whether possess-
ing authority or subject to it—judge spiritually.

are spoken aloud, so that the people can respond, "Amen." All these
words must be audibly spoken because of the abyss of this age and the
blindness of the flesh, which cannot see thoughts, and so they must be
conveyed to the ears. Thus, though birds are multiplied on the earth,
they have their beginning in the waters.

The spiritual also judge the deeds and behavior of the faithful,
approving what is right and disapproving what is amiss: their alms-
giving, like the fruitful earth; their living soul, which is alive in the
taming of its affections, in chastity, in fasting, in devout reflection on
things perceived by the bodily senses. I am speaking now of judgment
concerning matters in which one also has the authority to discipline.

24.35   But what is this, and what sort of mystery is it? Behold, you
bless human beings, O Lord, that they may be fruitful and multiply
and fill the earth. Do you not intend to convey some further meaning
by these words? Why did you not likewise bless the light, which you
called day, nor the firmament of the heaven, nor the lights, nor the
stars, nor the earth, nor the sea? I would say, O our God, who created
us in your image, that you wanted to bestow this blessing only on
human beings, except that you also blessed the fish and the creatures of
the sea in the same way, that they might be fruitful and multiply and
fill the waters of the sea, and that the birds might be multiplied on the
earth. If I found this blessing pronounced on plants and fruit trees and
on the beasts of the earth, I would likewise say that it was meant for
every kind of creature that is propagated by reproduction. But in fact
"Be fruitful and multiply" was not said to plants and trees or to beasts
and serpents, even though all these things increase and preserve their
kind by reproduction, just as fish and birds and human beings do.

24.36   Then what shall I say, O Truth, my Light? That this means
nothing, that it is just empty words? By no means, Father of piety; far
be it from a servant of your word to say such a thing. And even if I do
not understand what you mean by this expression, let better interpreters, more intelligent than I am, make better use of these words, according to the wisdom that you have given to each of them. But let my
confession also be pleasing in your eyes, as I confess to you, O Lord,
my belief that you did not speak these words in vain; and I will not
refrain from saying what my reading of this passage suggests to me. For
it is true, and I see nothing to prevent my understanding the figurative
expressions in your books in this way. I have known something signified in many ways through bodies that is understood in only one way
by the mind, and I have known something understood in many ways
by the mind that is signified in only one way by a body. Love of God

Deut. 27:15

Gn. 1:21–22

1 Cor. 2:15

2 Cor. 6:5–6

Gn. 1:28

Gn. 1:26; Sir. 17:1

Gn. 1:22

*Gn. 1:11–12,
1:24–25*

*Rom. 12:3; 1 Cor.
3:5 / Ps. 78:10;
Is. 49:16*

and neighbor is one and simple, yet it is signified by bodies through so many sacraments and in countless languages, and by countless expressions in each language. This is the sense in which the offspring of the seas are fruitful and multiply.

Take note again, anyone who is reading these words: Scripture has only one way of saying, "In the Beginning God made heaven and earth," and only one voice resounds with those words. Yet are there not many ways of understanding them—not deceptive and mistaken ways, but all kinds of true interpretations? In this way the offspring of human beings are fruitful and multiply. *Gn. 1:1*

24.37   And so if we consider the natures of things not allegorically, but on their own terms, the words "be fruitful and multiply" apply to all things that develop from seeds. But if we treat these words figuratively (which is what I prefer to think Scripture intended, because surely it is not utterly meaningless that Scripture attributes this blessing only to the offspring of sea creatures and human beings), we find multitudes in spiritual and bodily creatures, as in heaven and earth; in righteous and sinful souls, as in light and darkness; in holy authors by whom the law was set forth, as in the firmament established between water and water; in the fellowship of those who do bitter deeds, as in the sea; in the zeal of devout souls, as on the dry land; in works of mercy in this present life, as in seed-bearing plants and fruit trees; in spiritual gifts made manifest for the common good, as in the lights of the sky; and in affections formed for temperance, as in a living soul. *Gn. 1:22, 1:28*

1 Cor. 12:7

In all these we find multitudes and fruitfulness and increase. But it is only in signs expressed bodily and things considered intelligibly that we find something that is fruitful and multiplies in this way: one thing uttered in many ways and one utterance understood in many ways. We understand signs expressed bodily as the creatures generated from the waters, necessary because the flesh goes so deep; whereas we understand things considered intelligibly as the offspring of human beings, because of the fecundity of reason. We believe that this is why you, O Lord, said to these two kinds of creature, "Be fruitful and multiply." By this blessing, as I understand it, you granted us the skill and the power to express in many ways what we understand in only one way, and to understand in many ways a single obscure expression that we have read. In this way the waters of the sea are filled, for they are moved only by various significations; in this way too human offspring fill the earth, whose dryness is evident in their longing, and over which reason has dominion.

25.38   O Lord my God, I also want to say what the passage of Scripture that follows conveys to me; I shall speak and not be afraid, for by your inspiration I will say the true things that you wanted me to say in interpreting those words. I am confident that it is by your inspiration, and no one else's, that I speak the truth: for you are Truth, but every human being is a liar, and so those who lie say what comes from themselves alone. So in order to speak the truth, I must speak what comes from you.

Jn. 14:6

Ps. 115:11; Rom. 3:4 / Jn. 8:44

Behold, you have given us for food every plant yielding seed that is upon all the earth, and every tree with seed in its fruit. And not to us alone, but also to all the birds of the air and beasts of the earth and serpents; but you did not give these things to the fish or to the great sea monsters. For, as we have said, the fruits of the earth signify and allegorically represent works of mercy, which spring up from the fruitful earth to meet the needs of this present life. Devout Onesiphorus was such earth; you granted mercy to his household because he often brought comfort to your Paul and was not ashamed of his chains. The brothers from Macedonia who supplied his needs did this as well, and they bore this same kind of fruit. But how greatly he grieved over the trees that did not bear the fruit they owed him! He says, "At my first defense, no one stood by me; everyone deserted me. May it not be charged against them." For food is owed to those who provide instruction addressed to our reason through their own understanding of the divine mysteries; it is owed to them as human beings. But food is also owed to those who offer themselves to be imitated in every kind of self-restraint;[24] and to them it is owed as living souls. It is likewise owed to them as birds of the air because of their blessings, which are multiplied on the earth, because their sound has gone out into all the earth.

Gn. 1:29

Gn. 1:30

2 Tim. 1:16

2 Cor. 11:9

2 Tim. 4:16

Gn. 1:22 / Ps. 18:5

26.39   Those who rejoice in these foods are nourished by them; but those whose god is their belly have no joy in them. And even in those who offer these foods, the fruit is not what they give, but the spirit in which they give it. And so I see clearly why the one who served God and not his belly rejoiced; I see it, and I share heartily in his joy. For he received from the Philippians what they had sent by Epaphroditus; but I see why he rejoiced. And the reason for his joy is also the source of his nourishment. He speaks truly when he says, "I rejoiced greatly in the Lord that at last you have come to have a taste for me again as

Phil. 3:19

Rom. 16:18

Phil. 4:18

---

24. "in every kind of self-restraint": *in omni continentia.* Here *continentia* is not exclusively sexual abstinence, as in Book 8, but any sort of temperance or self-restraint with regard to love of, and pleasure in, creatures.

you once did; you had grown weary of me."²⁵ For a long time they had   *Phil. 4:10*
been faint with weariness, barren of the fruit of good works; and he
rejoices for them, because they have grown fruitful again, not for himself, because they have met his needs. That is why he goes on to say, "I
do not say that I lack anything. For I have learned, in whatever state I
am, to be content. I know how to have little, and I know how to have
an abundance. In any and all circumstances I have learned how to face
plenty and hunger, abundance and want. I can do all things through
him who gives me strength."   *Phil. 4:11–13*

26.40   Why, then, do you rejoice, great Paul? Why do you rejoice,
and on what do you feed? You are a human being renewed in the
knowledge of God according to the image of the one who created you,   *Col. 3:10*
a soul alive in its great self-restraint, and a bird taking flight in uttering mysteries. This food is surely owed to such living beings. What is   *1 Cor. 14:2*
it that feeds you? Joy. I shall hear what comes next: "Yet you did well
by sharing in my trouble." This is why he rejoiced; this was his food: *Phil. 4:14*
that they acted well toward him, not that his distress was relieved. He
says to you, "You set me free when I was in trouble," for he knows   *Ps. 4:2*
how to face abundance and want in you who give him strength. "You   *Phil. 4:12–13*
Philippians also know," he says, "that in the beginning of the Gospel,
when I left Macedonia, no church shared with me in giving and receiving except you alone; for even at Thessalonica you sent help for my
needs not once, but twice." Now he rejoices that they have returned to   *Phil. 4:15–16*
these good works, and he is glad that they are bearing fruit again, like
a field coming back to life and fertility.

26.41   Surely it was not because of his needs that he said, "You sent
help for my needs." Surely that was not why he rejoiced. No, that was   *Phil. 4:16*
not why. And how do we know this? Because he goes on to say, "Not
because I seek the gift, but because I look for fruit." I have learned   *Phil. 4:17*
from you, my God, to distinguish between gift and fruit. A gift is the
thing given by the person who bestows what we need, such as money,
food, drink, clothing, shelter, assistance, whereas the fruit is the good
and upright will of the giver. For the good Teacher does not merely say,
"Whoever receives a prophet"; he adds, "because he is a prophet." He
does not merely say, "Whoever receives a righteous person"; he adds,
"because he is a righteous person." It is in this way that the first receives
the reward of a prophet, and the second the reward of the righteous.

---

25. Augustine modifies his text of Philippians 4:10, which has Paul saying that the Philippians *feel*
for him, so that Paul instead says they *have a taste* for him. The change in vocabulary fits the theme
of food, fruit, and nourishment in this paragraph.

And he does not merely say, "Whoever gives one of the least of my disciples a cup of cold water to drink"; he adds, "because he is a disciple." And he goes on: "Truly I tell you, he will not lose his reward." The gift *Mt. 10:41–42* is receiving a prophet, receiving a righteous person, offering a cup of cold water to a disciple; the fruit is doing so because he is a prophet, because he is a righteous person, because he is a disciple. Elijah was fed by fruit from the widow who knew that she was feeding a man of God and fed him for that very reason; by the raven he was fed only by a gift. *1 Kgs. 17:1–16* And it was not the inner Elijah but the outward Elijah who was being fed, for the outward Elijah could have died for lack of such food.

27.42   And so in your presence, O Lord, I will say something that is true. Outsiders and unbelievers require the sacraments of initiation *1 Cor. 14:22–23* and great signs and miracles to be initiated and won for you; these works, as we have said, are signified by the words "fish and sea monsters." When such people receive your children to give them bodily refreshment or to help them in some need of this present life, they do not know why they should do this or what purpose they should have in mind; and for that reason they do not feed your children, and your children are not fed by them. For such people do not perform these deeds from a holy and upright will, and your children do not rejoice in their gifts because they see no fruit, and of course a mind is fed by what gives it joy. And so fish and sea monsters do not eat foods that grow only on land that has been separated and marked off from the bitterness of the turbulent seas.

28.43   O God, you saw all the things you made, and behold, they are very good; we too see them, and behold, they are very good. When *Gn. 1:31* you commanded that each of your works be made, and it was made, you saw each of them, one by one, and you saw that it is good. I have counted seven times that this is written: you saw that what you made is good.²⁶ This eighth time it is written that you saw all the things you made, and behold, they are not merely good, but indeed very good, all of them taken together. Each of them individually was merely good, but all of them together are good and indeed very good. Every beautiful body proclaims this truth. For a body whose parts are all beautiful is far more beautiful than the parts of which it consists, which come together in a perfectly ordered way to compose the whole, though each of the parts individually is also beautiful.

---

26. Once so far on each of the six days of creation (Genesis 1:4, 8, 10, 18, 21, 25), with a second such statement on the third day (Genesis 1:12). The eighth statement, to which Augustine turns next, is the second instance on the sixth day (Genesis 1:31).

29.44   I paid careful attention so that I might discover whether it was seven or eight times that you saw your works are good, because they were pleasing to you. And in your seeing I found no times by which I could count how often you saw what you made. And I said, "O Lord, is not this Scripture of yours true, since you, who are truthful and Truth, *Jn. 3:33 / Jn. 14:6* set it forth? Why then do you tell me there are no times in your seeing, and your Scripture tells me that on each day you saw that the things you made were good, and when I counted, I discovered how many times you said this?"

To this you reply, because you are my God, and you speak to your *Ps. 42:2, 142:10* servant with a strong voice in my inward ear, shattering my deafness and crying out to me, "O mortal, have no doubt that what my Scripture says is what I say. And yet Scripture speaks in terms of time, but my Word is untouched by time, because he stands fast in eternity equal with me. What you see through my Spirit, I see; and in the same way, what you say through my Spirit, I say. When you see these things in time, I do not see them in time; and in the same way, when you say these things in time, I do not say them in time."

30.45   I heard you, O Lord my God, and I sucked a drop of sweetness from your truth. And I understood that there are some who are displeased with your works. They say that you were compelled by necessity to make many of them, such as the fabric of the heavens and the arrangements of the stars. And you did not create all this from your own resources, they say; instead, when you fortified the ramparts of the world against your defeated enemies, you assembled and joined and wove together what had already been created elsewhere, from some other source, so that this fortress would prevent your vanquished foes from rebelling against you once more. Still other things, they say, you do not make or in any way put together: all flesh, the tiniest living creatures, and everything rooted in the earth; a hostile mind, another nature not created by you and opposed to you, brought these things into being and formed them in the lowest places of the world. Those who say these things are out of their minds, for they do not see your works through your Spirit or recognize you in them. *Rom. 1:20*

31.46   But you see through the eyes of those who see your works through your Spirit. So when they see that your works are good, you see that they are good; whatever pleases them for your sake pleases you in them; and what pleases us through your Spirit is pleasing to you in us. For who among human beings knows what is in a human being but the human spirit within? So too no one knows the things of God but the Spirit of God. "But we," he says, "have not received the spirit of this world, but the Spirit that is from God, so that we might know what gifts have been given us by God." I am stirred up to proclaim, "Truly no one knows the things of God but the Spirit of God. How then do we too know what gifts have been given us by God?" I receive the answer: "What we know through the Spirit of God, no one knows but the Spirit of God. To those who speak in the Spirit of God, it is rightly said, 'It is not you who speak'; and likewise to those who know in the Spirit of God, it is rightly said, 'It is not you who know.'" Thus, if by the Spirit of God they see that something is good, it is not they but God who sees that it is good.

It is one thing for someone to think that what is good is bad, like those people I described earlier. It is another thing for someone to see that what is good is good, in the way that many people are pleased with your creation because it is good, but are not pleased with you in it, and so they would rather enjoy your creation than enjoy you. It is yet another thing when someone sees that it is good because God in him sees that it is good, so that God is loved in what he made: and God would not be loved except through the Spirit whom he has given, because the charity of God has been poured into our hearts through the Holy Spirit who has been given to us. Through the Spirit we see that whatever in any way has being is good, for it is from him who does not have being in just any way, but is he who is.

32.47 Thanks be to you, O Lord! We see heaven and earth: that is, either the higher and lower parts of the bodily creation, or the spiritual and the bodily creation. And for the adornment of these parts, in which either the whole mass of the universe or the whole creation altogether consists, we see light made and separated from darkness. We see the firmament of heaven, either the fundamental body of the earth, which is between the higher spiritual waters and the lower bodily waters,[27] or the domain of air, which is also called heaven, through which the birds of the air fly, which lies between the waters that are borne above them as cloud and drop dew in the calm of the night and the heavy waters that flow on the earth. We see the beauty of the waters gathered in the fields of the sea, and we see the dry land, whether bare or formed so as to be visible and organized, the matter of plants and trees. We see lights shining from on high, the sun sufficient for the day, the moon and stars giving cheer to the night, all of them marking and signifying times. We see the watery nature all around us, made fertile for fish and beasts and

1 Cor. 2:11

1 Cor. 2:12

Mt. 10:20

Rom. 5:5

Ex. 3:14

---

27. Augustine criticizes this statement in *Reconsiderations* 2.6.2 (see Appendix D).

flying creatures, because the density of air, which supports the flight of birds, is increased by the evaporation of the waters. We see the face of the earth adorned with land animals, and we see human beings made in your image and likeness and set over all irrational creatures by your image and likeness, that is, by the power of reason and understanding. And as in the human soul there is one part that exercises control by taking thought, and another that is subject to it and ought to obey it, so also in the realm of the body woman has been made subject to man. To be sure, with regard to the mind, women are equal to men in their power of rational understanding; but in terms of the body they are to be subject to the male sex in the same way that the desire for action is subject to the rational mind's careful consideration of how to act rightly.

We see these things, and each of them is good, and all of them together are very good.

33.48   Your works praise you that we may love you, and we love you that your works may praise you. They have a beginning and an end in time, a rising and a falling, growth and decay, form and privation. As a consequence they have a morning and an evening, partly hidden and partly manifest. For they were made from nothing by you, not from you, not from anything that was not yours or that existed beforehand, but from matter that was co-created—that is to say, created at the same time—by you. For you imposed form on its formlessness without any lapse of time. The matter of heaven and earth is one thing, the form of heaven and earth is another; you made matter from nothing at all, but the form of the world from unformed matter. Yet you made both at the same time, so that form would come upon matter without delay or interruption.

Gen. 1:5, 1:8, 1:13, 1:19, 1:23, 1:31

34.49   We also looked into the figurative meaning of the fact that you willed these things to be made in a particular order or written about in a particular order, and we found that each of them is good, and all of them together are very good, in your Word, in your Only-begotten: heaven and earth, the Head and body of the Church, in a predestination that is before all times and knows no morning and evening. But when you began to carry out in time the things you had predestined, revealing what was hidden and setting in order what was amiss in us— for our sins were upon us and we had wandered away from you into deep darkness, and your good Spirit was borne over us to bring us help when the time was right—you justified the ungodly and separated them from sinners and established the firm authority of your book between those above, who would readily receive your teaching, and those below, who would be subject to your book. And you gathered

1 Cor. 12:27; Col. 1:16–18

Ps. 50:8

Ez. 33:10

Ps. 142:10 / Gn. 1:2 / Ps. 31:6 / Prov. 17:15; Rom. 4:5

together the fellowship of unbelievers into a single conspiracy so that
the zeal of believers might appear and they might give birth to works *Gn. 1:10*
of mercy for your sake, giving earthly riches to the poor for the sake of
wealth in heaven.

Then you kindled lights in the firmament: your saints who have the
word of life and shine with preeminent authority by the excellence of *Jn. 6:68; Phil. 2:16*
their spiritual gifts. Then from bodily matter you brought forth sac- *1 Cor. 12:7*
raments, visible miracles, and audible words to instruct unbelieving
peoples in accordance with the firmament, your book; believers too are
blessed by these things. Next you formed the living soul of believers
through well-ordered affections by the strength of self-restraint. And
then you renewed their minds, subject only to you and needing no *Rom. 12:2; Col.*
human authority to imitate, in your own image and likeness. You gave *3:10*
superiority to their intellect and subjected their reason-governed action
to it as you subjected woman to man. And you willed that believers
should meet the temporal needs of all your ministers who are necessary
to bring believers to perfection in this life, thus performing deeds that
would bear fruit for the life to come.

We see all these things, and they are very good. For it is you who see *Gn. 1:31*
these things through our eyes: you who gave us the Spirit by whom we
see them, the Spirit by whom we love you in them.

35.50   O Lord God, grant us peace—for you have bestowed all things *Num. 6:26; Is.*
on us—the peace of rest, the peace of the sabbath, the peace on which *26:12; 2 Thess.*
no night ever falls. For when all these very good things have run their *3:16*
course, this whole supremely beautiful order will pass away. Truly both
morning and evening were made in them.

36.51   But the seventh day has no evening and no nightfall, for you
have sanctified it to abide for ever. The words of your book tell us that
you rested on the seventh day from all your very good works (though
you were at rest when you made them), thus foretelling that we too *Gn. 2:2–3*
will rest in you from our works, which are very good because you have
given them to us, in the sabbath of eternal life.

37.52   And then you too will rest in us, just as now you are at work in
us; and so your rest will be through us, just as your works are through
us. But you, O Lord, are always at work and always at rest. You do not
see at a time or move at a time or rest at a time, and yet you make the
visions that are seen in time, you make times themselves, and you make
the rest that comes when time shall be no more.

38.53   And so we see the things you have made because they are, but
they are because you see them. We see outwardly that they are and

inwardly that they are good; but you see the things that have been made in the same place where you see that it is right for them to be made. At one time we were moved to do what is good, after our heart conceived by your Spirit; yet at an earlier time we were moved to do evil, abandoning you. But you, God, One and Good, have never ceased to do what is good. By your Gift we have certain good works, but they are not everlasting; we hope to have rest after those works in your mighty sanctification. But you are a good that lacks nothing good; you are always at rest, because you yourself are your own rest. What human being can grant another human being an understanding of this? What angel can grant it to an angel? What angel can grant it to a human being? We must ask it of you, seek it from you, knock at your door: only in this way will we receive, only in this way will we find, only in this way will the door be opened to us.

Mt. 7:7 par.
Lk. 11:9

Appendix A
Psalm 4

1 A song of David
2 You answered me when I called upon you, O God of my justice;
you set me free when I was in distress;
have mercy on me, O Lord, and hear my prayer.
3 Children of men, how long will your hearts be hardened?
Why do you love emptiness and seek after a lie?
4 Know that the Lord has magnified his holy one.
The Lord will hear me when I cry out to him.
5 Be angry and do not sin;
speak these words in your hearts,
and feel the stings of remorse in your inner chambers.
6 Offer a sacrifice of justice,
and put your hope in the Lord.
Many are saying, "Who will show us good things?"
7 The light of your countenance has set its seal upon us, O Lord;
you have given me gladness in my heart.
8 In time, its grain and wine and oil are multiplied.
9 In peace, I will lie down in the Selfsame and fall asleep.
10 For in unity, Lord, you have established me in hope.

Appendix B
Psalm 41

2 As a deer longs for the water-brooks, so longs my soul for you, O God.

3 My soul has thirsted for the living God. When shall I come and appear before the face of God?

4 My tears have been my food day and night, while day after day people say to me, "Where is your God?"

5 I have pondered these things, and I have poured out my soul over me. For I will go into the place of your wonderful temple, even to the house of God. With a noise of exultation and thanksgiving [*confessionis*], of the sound of one celebrating a festival.

6 Why are you sorrowful, my soul, and why do you disquiet me? Hope in God, for I will give thanks to him, the health of my countenance,

7 my God. My soul is disquieted within me. Therefore I have remembered you, O Lord, from the land of Jordan and Hermon, from the small mountain.

8 Deep calls to deep in the voice of your waterfalls. All your rapids and floods have gone over me.

9 The Lord has sent his mercy in the daytime and has declared it in the night. With me is a prayer to the God of my life.

10 I will say to God, you are my protector. Why have you forgotten me? Why have you rejected me, and why do I go about in sorrow while my enemy oppresses me?

11 He shatters my bones; those who trouble me reproach me, as day after day they say to me, "Where is your God?"

12 Why are you sorrowful, my soul, and why do you disquiet me? Hope in God, for I will yet give thanks to him, the health of my countenance, and my God.

Appendix C
Psalm 100

1 I will sing of your mercy and judgment, O Lord.
2 I will sing praises, and I will discern in a blameless course:
when will you come to me?
I walked in the innocence of my heart, in the midst of my house.
3 I set no evil thing before my eyes;
I hated those who deal in lies; they have not remained with me.
4 When a crooked heart fled from me, I did not know the wicked one.
5 I pursued the one who secretly slandered his neighbor;
I did not break bread with one who had a haughty eye and a greedy heart.
6 My eyes are upon the faithful in the land, that they may dwell with me;
the one who walked in a blameless course was my servant.
7 The one who acts proudly has not dwelt in my house;
the one who has spoken wickedness has not made his way in the sight of my eyes.
8 In the morning I destroyed all the sinners of the land,
that I might banish all the workers of iniquity from the city of the Lord.

Appendix D
Reconsiderations, Book 2, Chapter 6

Near the end of his career, Augustine undertook to review all his works, establish their chronology, and reexamine them in the light of his views at the time. He called this survey *Retractationes,* from the Latin *retractare,* to rehandle or take up again. It is a mistake to call them *Retractions,* since often Augustine is perfectly satisfied with what he finds in his earlier writings. A better English title would be *Reconsiderations.*

Augustine treats the *Confessions* only briefly in his *Reconsiderations.* I translate the full text here.

6.1   My thirteen books of *Confessions* praise God, who is just and good, concerning both the bad and the good things in my life, and they lift the human mind and heart to God. At least, that is the effect they had on me when I wrote them, and that is the effect they have when I read them now. Others will have to see for themselves what they think of them, though I know that many of my brothers and sisters have enjoyed them and still do enjoy them. Books 1 through 10 are about me. The remaining three books are about Holy Scripture, from the words "In the Beginning God created heaven and earth" through God's sabbath rest.

6.2   In Book 4, when I confessed the wretchedness of my mind over the death of my friend, I spoke of how from two souls we had become, in a way, one soul. "And perhaps I feared death," I said, "because I did not want the one I had loved so much to die altogether." That strikes me as a frivolous declaration rather than a serious confession, though this silliness is mitigated somewhat by the fact that I added "perhaps." In Book 13 I said that the firmament was established between the higher spiritual waters and the lower bodily waters. That was said without sufficient thought; the subject is, however, quite obscure.

This work begins with the words, "Great are you, Lord."

Topical Index

abyss, 225, 227–28, 231, 235–39,
251–54, 256, 266, 269
actors, 30–31, 54–55
Adam, ix–x, 9, 71, 114n16, 133, 134,
137n16, 160, 264, 265
Adeodatus, 96, 139, 148, 158
adolescence, xii, 11, 19, 21, 94, 98,
148
Aeneas, 12–13
Alypius, xi, 78, 86–91, 93–94, 96, 115,
119, 127–28, 131–32, 136–39, 144,
147–48
ambition, xii, 1, 25, 29, 32n3, 39n7,
43–44, 56n9, 78, 85, 140, 163, 185,
194, 198n18. *See also* pride
Ambrose, viii n3, xi, xiii, 2n1, 51n6,
61, 76–82, 92, 101n6, 121, 129,
147–49, 159, 191n12, 219n9
Anaximenes, 167
angels, 101–2, 156, 199, 244, 254, 278
Antony of Egypt, 119, 128–29, 137
Apostles' Creed, 123n9
Aristotle, xiii, 43, 58, 59n11
arrogance, xiii, 29, 32, 34, 44, 108,
118, 133, 144, 194, 197, 199, 241
ascent, xiii–xv, 109–14, 167–83. *See also*
Ostia, vision at
Aslan, 9n11
astrology, 43, 45–46, 98, 104–6

baptism, ix, xi, xii, xiv–xv, 1, 10n13,
11, 47, 65n4, 70n10, 71, 95, 122,
123n9, 139, 142–43, 147–48, 150,
154, 160, 256, 264–65
beating, 9–10, 12, 15–16, 32, 90,
152–53; the breast, 199
beauty, 20, 43, 54–57, 120, 152, 191,
192, 225n2, 244, 246, 252, 263;

false, 33; in married life, 94; of
created things, 7, 24, 25, 34, 51,
62, 167–68, 205, 260, 264, 277; of
God, 3, 7, 25, 28, 34, 58, 113, 183,
191, 205, 264; of intelligible things,
25, 97, 233; of language, 67, 77; of
material things, 23–24, 25, 58, 113,
167, 190, 225, 226, 231, 239, 251,
273, 275; of modesty, 68
beggar, 85–86
belief (contrasted with knowledge), x,
xiii, 5–6, 8, 35, 40, 54, 64, 82–84,
105, 164–65, 170, 171, 178, 242
blindness, 17, 22, 70, 82, 87, 97, 149,
182, 190–91, 203
Book of Common Prayer, xxi, xxiv
books, 49, 50, 54–55, 68, 91, 92,
143; of eloquence, 32; of secular
wisdom, 64, 66; of Seneca, 67; of the
astrologers, 45, 104; of the liberal
arts, 58–59, 128; of the Manichees,
34, 42, 67, 68, 73; of the Platonists,
xvi, xxxii, 98, 108–109, 116–18, 121
bosom of Abraham, xxxi, 84n7, 143
boyhood, 1, 8–18, 46, 148, 213

Carthage, ix, xii, 13, 21, 29, 43, 50, 58,
61, 62, 68–70, 75, 86, 89, 91, 100,
176, 179
Cassiciacum, 139, 142
catechumen, 10n13, 22, 77, 144
charity, xxxi, 31, 54, 59, 116, 124, 127,
140, 144, 160, 190, 195, 236, 240,
242; believes all things, xv, 164–65;
God's, 25, 185; our mother, 66, 252;
poured into our hearts, 47, 253, 275;
purpose of exegesis, 224. *See also*
Holy Spirit

Church, vii, ix, xiv, xvi, xxxi, 11, 42, 59,
    73, 76–77, 81–82, 90, 98, 103, 106,
    115, 122, 123n9, 128, 143, 144,
    148, 150, 162, 189, 249, 259, 267,
    276; Body of Christ, xxxi, 82, 188,
    276; Bride of Christ, 117, 257
Cicero, xii, 15n19, 29, 32–33, 67,
    96n18, 130, 174n4
circuses/gladiatorial shows, 39, 86–88,
    129, 134, 193
conscience, 17, 51, 67, 131, 163, 165,
    185, 236
continence/chastity, 21–22, 26, 46, 81,
    88, 93–94, 120n1, 131, 136, 143,
    184–85, 187, 195, 196, 269
Cranmer, Thomas, 199n22

death, xii, 4, 12, 26, 32, 35, 51, 53,
    57, 63, 71–72, 85, 92–93, 94,
    96–97, 104, 117, 124, 127, 131,
    135, 136, 139, 141, 149, 154n27,
    200, 229, 254, 259; life after, 106;
    of Adeodatus, 148; of Monnica,
    156–58; of Nebridius, 143; of
    Patrick, 33, 154; of unnamed friend,
    xi, 43, 46–50; of Verecundus, 142;
    sacramental (see baptism); swallowed
    up in victory, 146, 186; wages of sin,
    200. See also Jesus Christ, atoning
    death of
deception, 4, 17, 19, 33, 72, 181–82
demons, 16, 31, 32, 45, 122, 149
Deus Creator omnium, 51, 159, 191, 219
devil, ix, 34, 62, 101, 118n24, 122,
    125–26, 161n38, 199
Dido, 12–13
Donatism, viii–ix
dreams, 34, 41, 95, 155, 185
drunkenness/intoxication, literal,
    79–80, 85–86, 124, 137, 151–52,
    187; metaphorical, 3, 15, 21, 76,
    78, 143

eating. See food
eclipses, 63–64, 66
Elijah, 188, 273
Elpidius, xi, 75
eternal life, 10, 79, 119, 139, 150, 154,
    262, 266, 277
eternity, xvi, 60, 110, 112, 113, 124,
    135, 146, 155, 202, 206–11,
    222–23, 228–30, 232–35, 245–46,
    259, 262, 266, 274
Eucharist, xiv, xv, 72, 80, 87, 117n23,
    148n17, 161, 164, 185, 199n22,
    201, 203, 234n8, 240n13, 265n21
Eve, 9n11, 14, 71, 114n16, 137n16, 257
evil, origin of, xii–xiii, 36, 74, 98,
    101–3, 106; privation of good, 36,
    56, 74, 98, 111

Faustus, xiii, 61–63, 66–69, 76, 92
firmament, xxxi, 58, 102, 159, 227,
    231, 239, 249, 258–59, 261–65,
    268–70, 275, 277, 282
food, 7, 23, 34, 43, 67, 80, 91, 96,
    110, 124, 171, 174, 186, 188, 262,
    271–73
forgetting, 175–79; what lies behind,
    154, 257
fornication, 15, 20, 22, 26, 45, 75
fragmentation, xi–xvi, 2, 19, 59,
    133–34, 169, 172, 184, 191, 198,
    209n6, 221–22, 234, 259
Freud, Sigmund, 160n36
friendship, 18, 19, 24, 27, 29–30,
    32, 46–51, 69, 73, 85–86, 88, 91,
    93, 94–96, 104–6, 122, 124, 128,
    129–30, 139–40, 142–43, 152–53,
    158; with the world, 13

God the Father, xii, 7n8, 34, 73n15,
    84n7, 108, 117n21, 123, 145,
    157n32, 159, 160, 162, 166, 187,
    200, 202, 204, 213, 215, 222, 233,

234, 254, 256, 259, 269. *See also* Jesus Christ, Holy Spirit

Gospel, 135, 137, 147, 207, 264, 265, 267, 272

grammar, 12, 16–17, 128, 171

Greek, 12–14, 33, 54, 108, 159, 173, 179, 205

happiness, xv, 24, 31, 43, 53, 58, 64–65, 70, 78, 85–86, 91, 93, 97, 100, 126, 130, 143, 156, 163, 164, 174, 178–82, 184, 194, 203, 251, 252, 254–55, 260

heaven of heaven, 224–25, 227–33, 238, 252, 254

heavenly city, 117, 204, 230, 233, 254. *See also* Jerusalem

Hebrew, 205

hell, 2, 19, 30, 35, 71, 102, 125, 160, 209

Hierius, xii, 43, 54

Hippo Regius, viii, x

Holy Spirit, xii, xiii, xiv, xvi, xxiii, 7n8, 33, 40, 54, 65–66, 84, 115n19, 116, 117, 123n9, 145, 149, 155n30, 157n32, 228, 232, 234, 235, 237, 239, 247, 249, 252–54, 256–58, 262, 267, 274–78; Charity, xxxii, 185, 252; Fire, 255; Gift, xxxii, 154, 254–55, 187, 278

Homer, 13–14

Horace, 49n3, 91n14

image of God, 29, 36, 82, 107, 109, 267–68, 269, 272, 276–77

immutability of God, 3, 56, 57, 58, 98–99, 101, 106, 109, 113, 229, 237, 240, 242, 252, 254, 256, 259, 260

Incarnation, xvi, 2n1, 33, 43, 53, 74, 98, 107n11, 108, 114–15, 150n20, 261

incorruptibility of God, 98–100, 102, 119, 252

infancy, ix, x, 1, 4–8, 14, 44, 66, 82, 114, 150, 259, 262

innocence, 7–8, 18, 22, 26, 28, 44, 89, 90, 161, 165, 280

Jerusalem, 162, 193, 234, 255. *See also* heavenly city

Jesus Christ, xiv, xxi, 4n4, 11, 34, 106, 108, 116, 122, 123n9, 127, 137n16, 138, 140, 142, 145, 157n32, 233, 256; alive in, 160; ascension of, 53, 123n9, 145, 257; atoning death of, 53, 108–9, 117, 146, 200, 201; Beginning, xxi, 207–8, 223, 227–42, 245, 250, 252, 270; blood of, 107n11, 117n23, 161, 201; brothers and sisters of, 160; Bridegroom, 53, 57, 207, 257–58; charity of, 253; coeternal with the Father, 108, 117, 202, 207, 210, 224, 233, 237, 252; Cross of, 10, 15, 71, 108, 122, 261n17; divinity of, 6n7, 33; easy yoke of, 122, 125, 140, 194, 259; faith in, 1–2, 11, 83, 103–4, 200; Fish, 265, 268; God's right hand, 96, 120, 139, 186, 198, 204, 221; Head of the Church, 117n21, 276; heresies concerning, 70n9, 114, 115n17, 115n18, 115n19, 149n19; Holy of Holies, 216; Humble One, 114; humility of, xvi, 10, 43, 107n11, 108, 109, 116, 118, 121, 122, 200, 223; imitation of, 80, 266; infants in, 262; intercedes at the Father's right hand, 146, 151n23, 161, 188, 200, 204; Life, xv, 53, 104; maturity in, 66, 74, 257, 262, 263, 265; Mediator, 98, 114, 163, 200, 204, 221; Medicine, 151n23, 161; name of, 33–34, 77, 82, 144, 215, 216; Only-begotten, 64, 74, 144, 150, 204, 227, 276; resurrection

Jesus Christ (*Continued*)
of, 123n9, 145; Shepherd, 234;
sinlessness of, 114n16; Son, xii, xx,
xxxii, 2, 7n8, 33, 82, 84n7, 106,
108, 109, 117n21, 123n9, 142, 160,
200, 201, 204, 206, 208, 222n10,
251–54, 256, 258, 260, 261n17; Son
of Man, 204, 221; Teacher, 153, 188,
207, 224, 236, 239, 262, 263, 272;
Truth, xv, xxxii, 4, 13, 25, 34, 48, 52,
53, 57, 64, 91, 112, 114, 115, 120,
142, 160, 202, 204, 205, 207, 208,
217, 222, 224, 228, 234, 239, 241,
248, 261n17, 271, 274; Way, xv,
xxxii, 64, 98, 116–19, 120; Wisdom,
xii, xxxii, 104, 109, 114, 117n21,
139, 155, 156, 208, 227, 233,
235–37, 244, 250, 252; Word, xvi,
xx–xxi, xxxii, 2n1, 52, 64, 107n11,
108, 114–15, 117n21, 120–23, 126,
150n20, 155–56, 200–201, 202,
204, 206–208, 225n2, 234, 237, 240,
244n15, 250–51, 260, 266, 274, 276.
See also Incarnation; Passion
joy in truth, xv, 163, 181–82

Latin, 12, 14, 54, 67, 108, 121, 173,
179, 205
liberal arts, 43, 58–59, 63, 67, 104,
105, 121, 171, 177
lies, 4, 50, 64, 85–86, 109, 115, 145,
164–65, 199, 218, 242, 264, 271,
279. *See also* deception
literature, 9n10, 12–13, 17, 21, 67, 91,
126, 128
lust of the eyes, xii, xiii, 1, 3n3, 10, 25,
29, 31, 39n7, 56n9, 88, 94, 104–5,
163, 185, 192–94, 195, 198n18,
199n20, 264, 266
lust of the flesh, xii, 1, 19–20, 29, 39n7,
56n9, 163, 185–92, 198n18

Madaura, 21
magic, 44, 193, 199
Manichees, xii, xiii, 3n3, 29, 40, 42,
43, 61–68, 73–79, 83, 88, 99n4,
134–35, 144, 232n6
marriage, 20–21, 23, 44, 78, 84, 93–96,
120, 124, 143, 151–52
matter, 103, 205–6, 233, 250, 275,
277; spiritual, 236, 245; unformed,
224–28, 234–39, 244–46, 276
memory, xv, xxi, 5, 8, 18, 19, 25, 26,
44, 46, 67, 89, 113, 114, 116, 128,
144, 145, 163, 169–83, 185, 198,
213, 214, 220–21, 223, 232
Milan, 61, 76, 78, 85, 90, 91, 119, 128,
129, 139, 147, 148
milk, 4, 7, 33, 44n1, 114, 142, 262, 267
mockery, 4, 5–6, 26, 32, 39, 40, 44, 46,
47, 71, 74, 77, 84, 87, 96, 160, 173,
209, 211, 247
Monnica, viii, xii, xiii–xiv, 4, 5, 8, 10–11,
22–23, 33, 40–42, 47, 69–72, 78–80,
95, 119, 138–39, 144, 149–62, 228
Moses, 36, 204–205, 228, 232, 234–35,
237, 240–43, 247–48; intention
unknowable, 224, 240–42, 246

Nebridius, xi, 46, 78, 86, 91, 96, 100,
104, 128, 139, 142–44
Nicene Creed, vii, 73n1

Ostia, vision at, xiii–xiv, xvi, 139,
154–56

Passion, 80, 107n11
Patrick, viii, 5, 11, 21–23, 33, 139,
152–53, 162
Paul, xiv, xxiii, 98, 116, 119, 125, 128,
150n20, 155n30, 157n32, 160,
187, 228n5, 233, 251n3, 257n12,
257n13, 267, 268n23, 271–72

peace, ix, xvii, 49, 56, 70, 75, 118,
140, 146, 153, 162, 183, 186, 197,
200, 203, 228, 230, 235, 242, 249,
253–55, 277, 279
Pelagianism, ix–x
philosophy, xii–xiv, 32–33. *See also*
wisdom
Platonists, xii–xiv, xvi, xxxii, 98, 108–9,
113n13, 116, 121, 144n12, 199n21
Ponticianus, 119, 128–31
praise, love of human, xvi, 9, 16, 17,
22, 32, 54–55, 152, 194–97, 209
present, eternal, xvi, 6, 209–10;
temporal, 52, 210–15, 219, 221
pride, xii, xiii, 10, 20, 25, 32–34, 39, 43,
45, 55, 57, 58, 63, 65, 73, 78, 107,
114, 122, 125, 144, 152, 160, 163,
194–97, 199, 224, 241, 259, 264,
266. *See also* ambition; arrogance
punishment, 10, 12, 14, 17, 18, 20, 23,
32, 37–40, 51, 52, 57, 62, 69, 71,
93, 94, 101, 113n13, 116, 127, 132,
134, 153, 195, 208, 222. *See also*
beating

rest/restlessness, xvi–xvii, 1, 3, 13, 20,
25, 28, 48–53, 61, 62, 97, 107, 109,
112, 142, 146, 159, 233, 242, 249,
252, 253, 254–55, 264, 277–78, 282
rhetoric, viii, 21, 29, 32, 43, 44, 46,
75–76, 86, 123, 126, 128, 139,
143, 243
Romanianus, xi, 95
Rome, ix, x, 54, 61, 69–73, 75–76, 88,
90, 121–23, 142

sacraments, viii, xiv, xvi, 122, 134, 143,
144, 148, 249, 264, 268, 270, 273,
277. *See also* baptism; Eucharist
Sallust, 24n3, 24n4
Sayers, Dorothy, xxvii–xix

Scripture, xvii–xxiv, 16, 33–34, 42,
74–75, 115–16, 122, 128, 147, 192,
203, 215, 224, 231, 235, 237–39,
247, 249, 253, 261, 270–71, 273,
282; authority of, 83–84, 106,
258–59; faith in, 229; figurative
interpretation of, 82–84, 92;
Manichee criticisms of, 36, 147
Selfsame, 6, 146, 155, 210, 227, 230,
233, 235, 256, 262, 279
shows. *See* spectacles, theatrical
Simplicianus, 119–23, 126
singing, xvi, 7, 35, 62, 135, 137, 140,
143, 158, 167, 170, 191, 221–23,
226, 234, 246, 255, 280; in church,
xxxii n5, 149–50, 189–90
spectacles, theatrical, xii, 10, 18, 29, 30,
43, 86, 88, 192–93
stars, 25, 45–46, 63–65, 68, 102, 105,
111, 155, 167, 171, 176, 193, 216,
262–63, 269, 274, 275. *See also*
astrology

Te Deum laudamus, vii, 148
Terence, 9n9, 15, 92n15, 181n6,
246n18
Thagaste, viii, 21, 46n2, 47, 50, 57n10,
86, 95, 150
theft of the pears, 19, 23–28
time, xvi, 36–37, 50, 64, 103, 112,
202–3, 206–7, 209–23, 228–37,
243–46, 259, 261, 262, 274–77
Trinity, xii, 29, 227, 228, 249, 252,
255–56, 267
Truth. *See* Jesus Christ

unity, xvi, 18, 38, 56, 147, 209n6, 227,
230, 250, 256, 267, 279

Verecundus, 128, 139, 142–43
Victorinus, Marius, 119, 121–26

Virgil, 13n15, 13n16, 14, 16n21,
31n1, 78n1, 99n2, 107n10, 121n5,
124n10, 125n11, 150n22, 152n24
Virgin Mary, 53, 74, 114, 123n9,
240n12, 261n17
vomit, 100, 145, 153

weight, 55, 57, 65, 75, 113, 194, 198,
253–55
will, xiii, xxx, 21, 23, 31, 85, 98, 101,
112, 115, 117, 119, 126–27, 129–35,
139, 141, 152, 181–82, 203, 240n11,
249, 254–55, 260, 272–73; God's, 10,

18, 95, 102, 103, 108, 109, 116, 139,
184–85, 187, 195, 196, 203, 206,
208, 229, 232, 244, 252, 254–56,
259, 260, 262, 267, 276–77
wisdom, xxxii, 29, 32–33, 54, 64,
65, 67, 78, 91–94, 98, 121, 128,
130, 143, 184, 201, 204, 233, 259,
262–64. *See also* philosophy
words, xvi, 1, 8, 14–16, 34, 67,
147, 164, 168, 171, 173, 175,
197, 206–7, 213, 231, 234, 236,
243, 259–60, 264–66, 268–69,
277

Scriptural Index

Books of the Bible are listed in their canonical order. Citations to the Psalms are given first according to the numbering Augustine knew, and then, in parentheses, to the numbering found in most English translations.

Genesis

1:1	2, 24, 51, 204, 223, 224, 235, 270	1:26	36, 82, 227, 267, 268, 269
1:1–2	231	1:26–27	267
1:2	225, 227, 228, 231, 239, 252, 256, 276	1:27	267
		1:28	269, 270
		1:29	271
		1:30	271
1:3	251, 256	1:31	111, 190, 239, 244, 250, 273, 277
1:4	261		
1:5	258		
1:6	252	2:2–3	277
1:6–8	227	2:3	210
1:7	239, 259	2:7	114
1:7–8	231	3:1	94, 266
1:9	239, 260, 262	3:6	23
1:9–10, 13	227	3:8	266
1:10	277	3:16	9, 71,
1:11–12	260, 261, 262, 269	3:17	176
		3:17–18	20,
1:11–25	244	3:18–19	58,
1:12	260	3:19	13, 176
1:14	216, 261, 262, 263	3:20	14,
		3:21	114, 259
1:14–18	261, 263	6:6–7	3
1:15	262, 268	7:11	257
1:17	262, 263	9:3	188
1:20	167, 227	9:6	82
1:20–22	263, 265	18:27	4, 166
1:21	266, 267	19:5ff.	38
1:21–22	269	22:11	156
1:21–25	264	25:33	109
1:22	264, 265, 269, 270, 271	25:33–34	109
		25:34	188
1:24	265, 266	27:1–40	190
1:24–25	269	28:17	233
1:24–28	266	41:51	146

48:10–20	191
49	190

Exodus

3:14	110, 275
3:22	109
4:14	3
6:12	203
13:14	6
15:2	161
20:5	3
20:12	263
20:13–16	263
20:15	23
23:20	244
32:1–6	109
33:9	156
33:13	204
33:19	161, 167
33:23	4
34:6	139
34:14	3

Leviticus

16:30	11

Numbers

6:26	277
11:1–20	188
11:23	185
11:25	252
12:8	156

Deuteronomy

1:17	125
4:24	63
4:35	146
5:19	23
6:5	242
6:13	133
6:16	193
9:3	63
9:20	3
10:21	161

16:19	125
27:15	269
31:17	4
32:20	4
32:39	20
33:1	76

Joshua

1:18	34
10:13–14	217

1 Samuel

9:7	76

2 Samuel

23:15–17	188

1 Kings

8:47	117
13:4	76
15:35	3
17:1–16	273
17:6	188

2 Kings

1:9	3
17:13	14

2 Chronicles

2:12	119
7:14	14
8:14	76

Tobit

3:2	117
4:2ff.	190
4:16	17
14:17	154

Judith

6:15	88
8:22	129
9:17	161

2 Maccabees

15:23	244

Job

1:9	126
7:1	184, 188
7:2	26
9:5	3
10:15	27
12:13	33
12:16	33
14:4–5	6
15:26	107
28:14	167
28:25	176
28:28	65, 121
38:10–11	260
35:11	78, 177
38:11	52
39:26	59
42:6	4, 107, 166

Psalms

1:1	141
1:2	140, 203
2:7	210
2:9	30
2:11	18, 117, 166, 186
4:2 (4:1)	145, 272
4:3 (4:2)	44, 53, 145
4:3–4 (4:2–3)	145
4:5 (4:4)	146
4:6	146
4:7	146
4:7–8 (4:7)	76
4:8 (4:7)	146
4:9 (4:8)	6, 146, 155, 183, 227
4:10 (4:8)	147
5:3 (5:2)	14
5:5 (5:3)	258
5:8 (5:7)	150
5:13 (5:12)	164
6:3 (6:2)	61, 190, 201

6:4 (6:3)	137
6:6 (6:5)	102
6:11 (6:10)	82
8:2 (8:1)	119
8:3 (8:2)	126, 259
8:4 (8:3)	259
8:5 (8:4)	243
8:8–9 (8:7–8)	63
8:10 (8:9)	119
9:2 (9:1)	218
9:14 (9:13)	190
9:14–15 (9:13)	254
9:21 (9:20)	161
9:22 (10:1)	78
9:24 (10:3)	195
9:38 (10:17)	203, 204
10:5 (11:4)	182
11:7 (12:6)	116, 259
12:4 (13:3)	190
14:3 (15:2)	234
15:2 (16:2)	110
15:8 (16:7)	120
15:10 (16:11)	14
15:11 (16:11)	80
16:3 (17:3)	258
16:8 (17:8)	59, 83, 166
17:3 (18:2)	106, 109
17:6 (18:5)	69
17:13 (18:12)	259
17:14 (18:13)	194
17:21 (18:20)	250
17:29 (18:28)	57, 79, 100, 203, 218, 254
17:30 (18:29)	14, 188
17:32 (18:31)	3
17:47 (18:46)	147, 193
18:2 (19:1)	263
18:3 (19:2)	263
18:4–5	(19:3–4) 264
18:5 (19:4)	144, 271
18:6–7	(19:5) 53
18:7 (19:6)	62, 144
18:8 (19:7)	259, 263
18:10 (19:9)	194
18:13 (19:12)	27

18:13–14 (19:12–13)   4, 195
18:15 (19:14)   106, 107, 109,
                         127, 140, 204
21:4 (22:3)   161
21:26 (22:25)   240
21:27 (22:26)   1, 201
21:28 (22:27)   85
22:1 (23:1)   213
22:4 (23:4)   85, 150
22:5 (23:5)   265
24:5 (25:5)   201
24:7 (25:7)   33
24:9 (25:9)   109
24:15 (25:15)   49, 191, 192
24:16 (25:16)   190
24:16–18 (25:16–18)   10
24:18 (25:18)   109
25:3 (26:3)   192
25:7 (26:7)   204, 222, 234
25:8 (26:8)   120, 233
26:1 (27:1)   181
26:4 (27:4)   216, 222, 229,
                         230, 233
26:6 (27:6)   44
26:7 (27:7)   203, 204
26:8 (27:8)   16, 143
26:10 (27:10)   110
26:12 (27:12)   4, 39
27:1 (28:1)   234
27:9 (28:9)   213
28:3 (29:3)   194
28:5 (29:5)   122, 144
28:9 (29:9)   203
29:11 (30:10)   106, 109
29:12 (30:11)   138
30:3 (31:2)   79
30:6 (31:5)   64
30:8 (31:7)   145
30:10 (31:9)   184
30:11 (31:10)   208, 222
30:20 (31:19)   221
30:21 (31:20)   254
30:23 (31:22)   17, 145, 199
31:1 (32:1)   164
31:3 (32:3)   3

31:4 (32:4)   117
31:5 (32:5)   4
31:6 (32:6)   276
31:8 (32:8)   97
31:9 (32:9)   168
32:2 (33:2)   39
32:6 (33:6)   206
32:9 (33:9)   206
32:11 (33:11)   96, 155
32:22 (33:22)   119, 202
33:4 (34:3)   227
33:6 (34:5)   125, 133
33:9 (34:8)   146, 183
33:19 (34:18)   63
34:3 (35:3)   4, 11, 139
34:6 (35:6)   78
34:10 (35:10)   61, 119, 132, 139
35:3 (36:2)   130
35:6 (36:5)   259
35:7 (36:6)   47, 106, 251, 256
35:8 (36:7)   59, 166
35:10 (36:9)   122, 154, 252,
                        260
36:4 (37:4)   182
36:13 (37:13)   6
36:23 (37:23)   69
37:4 (38:3)   112
37:7 (37:6)   14
37:9 (38:8)   93, 195
37:9–11 (38:8–10)   107
37:11 (38:10)   214, 236
37:23 (38:22)   79, 147, 193
38:6 (39:5)   216
38:12 (39:11)   110, 256
39:5 (40:4)   92, 123, 140
39:16 (40:15)   13
39:18 (39:17)   53, 197, 203
40:5 (41:4)   45, 53, 73
41:2–3 (42:1–2)   257
41:2–4 (42:1–3)   230
41:3 (42:2)   260
41:3–4 (42:2–3)   16
41:4 (42:3)   258
41:5 (42:4)   258
41:6 (42:5)   48, 181, 256, 258

41:7 (42:6)	256	63:11 (64:10)	24
41:8 (42:7)	257	64:8 (65:7)	208
41:11 (42:9–10)	85, 230	64:12 (65:11)	261
41:12 (42:11)	48, 181, 258	65:7 (66:6)	260
42:2 (43:2)	57, 274	66:2 (67:1)	246
42:5 (43:5)	48, 181, 258	67:3 (68:2)	133
43:5 (44:4)	14	67:6 (68:5)	159
44:2 (45:1)	203	67:7 (68:6)	150
45:5 (46:4)	257	67:16–17 (68:15–16)	142
45:11 (46:10	141	67:17 (68:16)	14
47:2 (48:1)	1, 63, 202	67:19 (68:18)	257
47:15 (48:14)	213, 232, 259	67:23 (68:22)	78
48:13 (49:12)	267	68:3 (69:2)	41
49:21 (50:21)	130	68:14 (69:13)	161
50:3 (51:10	165	68:31 (69:30)	188
50:7 (51:5)	8	68:33 (69:33)	178, 266
50:8 (51:6)	163, 276	68:35 (69:34)	167
50:10 (51:8)	58	69:2 (70:1)	79
50:15 (51:13)	26, 85	70:3 (71:3)	23
50:16 (51:14)	193	70:5 (71:5)	78, 213
50:19 (51:17)	45, 72, 117, 137	70:17 (71:17)	225
53:8 (54:6)	26, 59, 61, 127	70:20 (71:20)	4
54:2 (55:1)	6, 14	71:18 (72:18)	56, 62
54:6 (55:5)	256	71:18–19 (72:18–19)	119
54:7 (55:6)	131	72:7 (73:7)	23
54:23 (55:22)	93, 201	72:8–9 (73:8–9)	53
55:2 (56:2)	244	72:16 (73:16)	216
56:2 (57:1)	59	72:26 (73:26)	45, 78
56:7 (57:6)	81	72:27 (73:27)	26, 45, 62, 75,
58:9 (59:8)	211		192
58:10 (59:9)	59, 191	72:27–28 (73:27–28)	12
58:11 (59:10)	250	72:28 (73:28)	85, 110, 234, 251
58:18 (59:17)	30, 32, 106, 109,	73:16 (74:16)	203
	153, 235, 249	74:5 (75:5)	39
60:2 (61:1)	203	75:2 (76:1)	119
60:5 (61:4)	59	75:8 (76:7)	14
60:8 (61:7)	255	76:18 (77:17)	156
61:2 (62:1)	166	77:8 (78:8)	260
61:2–3 (62:1–2)	118	77:39 (78:39)	12, 39, 57
61:3 (62:2)	45	78:1 (79:1)	109
61:9 (62:8)	219	78:5 (79:5)	137
62:2 (63:1)	16, 260	78:8 (79:8)	137
62:4 (63:3)	221	78:9 (79:9)	10, 39
62:7 (63:6)	127	78:10 (79:10)	19, 269
62:8 (63:7)	59, 106, 109	79:2 (80:1)	155

79:8 (80:7)	51	102:3 (103:3)	52, 93, 164, 185,
79:15 (80:140	190		190, 200, 201
79:18 (80:17)	186, 204	102:3–5 (103:3–5)	194, 208
80:17 (81:16)	76	102:8 (103:8)	16, 139
83:3 (84:2)	14	102:9 (103:9)	107
83:4 (84:3)	59	102:14 (103:14)	187
83:6 (84:5)	255	103:2 (104:2)	258
83:7 (84:6)	53, 140	103:24 (104:24)	208, 235, 237,
84:6 (85:5)	107		250
84:12 (85:11)	261	103:25 (104:25)	168
84:13 (85:12)	260	103:27 (103:27)	91
85:1 (86:1)	203	104:1 (105:1)	1
85:3 (86:3)	203	105:2 (106:2)	47
85:5 (86:5)	139	105:20 (106:20)	109
85:11 (86:11)	97	105:21 (106:21)	264
85:13 (86:13)	16, 40, 119,	106:8 (107:8)	3, 59, 62, 74, 104
	152, 194	106:15 (107:15)	3
85:15 (86:15)	16, 134	106:21 (107:15)	3
85:16 (86:16)	72	106:31 (107:31)	3
87:3 (88:2)	41	108:22 (109:22)	197
87:6 (88:5)	200	109:1 (110:1)	161
88:11 (89:10)	107	111:10 (112:10)	123
88:53 (89:52)	119	112:9 (113:9)	136
89:4 (90:4)	210	113:24 (115:16)	224, 227, 229,
89:8 (90:8)	167		233
89:10 (90:10)	183	115:10 (116:18)	4, 216
90:4 (91:4)	59	115:11 (116:11)	271
90:13 (91:13)	118, 161	115:12 (116:12)	26
91:2 (92:1)	7, 45, 94	115:15 (116:15)	149
93:1 (94:1)	47	115:16 (116:16)	8, 22, 72, 149
93:20 (94:20)	20	115:16–17 (116:16–17)	139, 240
93:22 (94:22)	9	115:17 (116:17)	119, 191
94:5 (95:5)	260	115:18 (116:18)	240
95:2 (96:2)	265	116:2 (117:2)	83, 155
95:4 (96:4)	1, 63, 202	117:1 (118:1)	72, 203
95:6 (96:6)	164	117:14 (118:14)	161
99:3 (100:3)	53, 63, 110,	118:18 (119:18)	201, 204
	155, 158, 167,	118:22 (119:22)	201
	219	118:34 (119:34)	205
100:1 (101:1)	158	118:37 (119:37)	112
101:13 (102:12)	52, 107	118:70 119:70)	140
101:28 (102:27)	6, 116, 117, 124,	118:73 (119:73)	205, 250
	166, 210, 230,	118:77 (119:77)	140
	262	118:85 (119:85)	136, 204
101:29 (102:29)	39	118:92 (119:92)	140

118:97 (119:97)	140	143:2 (144:2)	32
118:101 (119:101)	13	143:5 (144:5)	122
118:103 (119:103)	147	143:7 (144:7)	40
118:105 (119:105)	147, 258	143:7–8 (144:7–8)	165
118:108 (119:108)	161	143:8 (144:8)	222
118:137 (119:137)	101, 117	143:9 (144:9)	39
118:142 (119:142)	51	143:11 (144:11)	165
118:144 (119:144)	205	144:2 (145:2)	147
118:155 (119:155)	76	144:3 (145:3)	1, 63, 202
118:174 (119:174)	140	144:14 (145:14)	223
118:176 (119:176)	28, 228, 234	144:15 (145:15)	9
119:3–4 (120:3–4)	140	144:15–16 (145:15–16)	96
120:4 (121:4)	191	145:2 (146:1)	51, 62
121:1 (122:1)	255	145:6 (146:6)	51
121:3 (122:3)	227	145:8 (146:8)	2, 223
123:5 (124:5)	253	146:5 (147:5)	1, 64
124:3 (125:3)	142	147:14	76
127:1 (128:1)	120	147:15	265
129:1 (130:1)	21	148:1–5	111
129:1–2 (130:1–2)	203	148:3–5	159
129:3 (130:3)	4, 160	148:4	233
134:6 (135:6)	119	148:5	206
135:4 (136:3)	56, 62	148:6	233
135:6 (136:6)	265	148:7–10	111
135:7–9 (136:7–9)	262	148:11–12	111
136:1, 5–6 (137:1, 5–6)	234	149:6	232
137:6 (138:6)	63, 223		
138:6 (139:6)	214	**Proverbs**	
138:7 (139:7)	51, 203	3:5	89
138:7–8 (139:7–8)	62	3:7	121
138:8 (139:8)	2, 97	3:34	1
138:11 (139:11)	48	6:23	80
138:16 (139:16)	188	6:26	88
138:21 (139:21)	147	8:22	117
138:21–22 (139:21–22)	232	9:1	114
138:22 (139:22)	75	9:8	87
139:11 (140:10)	87	9:18	35
140:3–4 (141:3–4)	73	10:4	45
140:5 (141:5)	197	10:17	80
141:6 (142:5)	70	15:10	80
142:1 (143:1)	161	17:6	65
142:2 (143:2)	161	17:15	276
142:6 (143:6)	260	18:4	143
142:10 (143:10)	145, 201, 247, 254, 274, 276	18:21	61
		19:21	96

| 27:21 | 195 |
| 30:8 | 197 |

Ecclesiastes

1:2	135
4:4	266
11:7	177, 214

Song of Solomon

1:3	150, 260
2:9	260
2:17	258
4:14	22
5:2	164

Wisdom

1:6	89
1:16	94
3:6	195
5:7	53, 62
7:27	3, 48, 109, 110, 155
8:21	93, 184, 187
9:15	113
9:17	257
10:21	126
11:18	227
11:21	65
11:25	62
13:1	120
13:2	171
13:8–9	63
15:9	37
18:11	225
39:26	106

Sirach

1:1–5	233
1:5	143
2:10	27
2:16	131
3:17	26
3:19	266
3:27	94

5:8	93, 131, 136
6:18	59
7:5	121
10:9	166
10:10	112
15:20	195
17:1	36, 82, 267, 269
17:31	107
18:1	155
18:30	187
19:1	151
19:4	84
23:3	96
23:6	187
24:6	255
24:14	22
26:15	143
39:21	111
39:26	6
40:1	9
42:1	125
42:18	47, 163
51:15	147
51:34	122

Isaiah

1:4	6
1:16	262
1:17	262
1:18	261, 262
6:3	227, 256
6:10	85
9:2	53
11:2	252
11:12	234
12:2	161
14:4	122
14:12	122
14:12–13	64
14:13	122, 195
25:8	62
26:12	277
26:13	195
26:20	258
30:21	228

33:5	17	38:22	22
34:4	258, 259	51:6	22
34:9	30		
37:20	194	**Lamentations**	
40:4	144	2:18	99
40:6	150	5:17	47
40:6–8	260		
40:8	155, 206	**Baruch**	
44:3	2		
45:5	146	4:7	158
46:4	59, 97		
46:8	53	**Ezekiel**	
48:22	181		
49:16	269	3:12	228
49:20	4	14:7	112
50:10	78	30:6	259
52:7	263	33:10	276
57:13	89	34:14	155
57:15	223	36:10	4
58:7	261	36:33	4, 141
58:8	261		
58:10	167, 233, 254	**Daniel**	
63:7	119	3:27	117
64:4	154	3:29	117
65:1	204	3:52	30
66:2	252	3:87	223
		4:32	83
Jeremiah			
2:13	266	**Joel**	
2:27	22, 130	2:18	3
2:29	4	2:28–29	2
12:1	117		
12:15	4	**Jonah**	
15:19	263		
17:14	161	2:8	228
18:11	13		
18:19	203	**Micah**	
23:24	2, 51	2:9	21
27:12	122	7:8	211
29:23	89		
30:9	133	**Habakkuk**	
31:15	110		
32:19	3	2:3	53
36:3	14	2:4	21
36:7	14	3:2	118, 198

Zechariah

1:14	3
8:2	3

Malachi

1:10	61
3:1	244
3:6	146
3:10	257

Matthew

3:2	256
3:4	188
3:17	206
4:1	193
4:3	188
4:7	193
4:10	133
4:16	53
4:17	256
4:23	52, 93, 164, 190
5:3	129
5:3–9	203
5:6	183
5:7	161
5:14–15	263
5:17	116
5:22	160
6:6	131, 146, 234
6:8	202
6:9	141
6:12	72, 161
6:13	14
6:15	242
6:21	263
6:33	204
6:34	186
7:6	23
7:7	1, 82, 92, 93, 230, 278
7:7–8	203, 204, 216, 224
7:11	215
7:12	17, 116, 261
7:13	84
7:13–14	84, 96
7:14	119
7:20	154, 268
7:24	266
7:26	266
8:20	204
9:35	77
9:38	261
10:16	266
10:20	275
10:22	166
10:30	12, 55
10:41–42	273
11:10	244
11:25	6, 57, 73, 109, 118, 121, 207, 218
11:28	118
11:28–29	109
11:29	109, 118
11:29–30	122, 125, 259
11:30	140, 194
12:26	73
12:29	126
12:36–37	160
13:7	263
13:15	85, 99
13:22	263
13:39	261
13:45–46	121
15:14	81
15:21	156
16:17	45, 247
17:5	206
17:24–27	64
18:10	233, 259
18:32	72
19:12	20, 120
19:14	18
19:16	262
19:17	262
19:18	263
19:19	263

19:20	263	9:12	130
19:21	137, 263	9:33	56
19:24	84	10:21	6, 57, 73,
19:27	130, 263		118, 121,
21:16	126		207, 218
21:19	137	10:27	38, 242
22:37–39	196, 242	10:35	3
22:37–40	38	10:40–42	224
22:40	236	11:9	1, 82, 93, 278
23:8	207	11:9–10	203, 204, 216,
23:10	236		224
23:30	263	11:16	193
24:9	166	12:8	122
24:31	125	12:32	195
24:35	260, 266	14:14	142
25:13	164	14:28–33	130
25:21	28	15:3	250
25:27	3	15:4–6	123
25:41	71	15:5	234
26:39	139	15:7	123
28:19	256, 263	15:8	177
		15:8–10	124
Mark		15:12–13	59
		15:13	230
2:10	204	15:13–14	28
8:38	122	15:15	23
10:17	207	15:16	35
10:28	263	15:18–20	33
12:25	263	15:24	124, 187
12:30–31	242	15:30	59
12:33	38	15:32	124, 187
14:36	139	16:10	91
		16:11–12	91
Luke		16:16	116
1:46	188	16:20	29
1:48	182	16:20–21	201
2:14	254	16:22	143
3:5	144	18:13	39
5:8	188	18:18	207
5:11	85, 130	18:23	263
5:28	85, 130	18:28	263
6:18	149	21:34	187
6:31	17	24:29	130
7:12–15	79	24:49	145
8:15	162	24:52	53

John

1:1	120, 156, 200, 204, 266
1:1–3	64
1:1–5	108
1:3	114, 120, 155, 204
1:8	108
1:9	12, 57, 108, 125, 133, 146, 147, 198, 217, 255
1:10	108
1:10–11	53
1:11–12	108
1:12	125
1:13	108
1:14	108, 201
1:16	57, 109
1:47–48	137
3:3	152
3:5	265
3:13	53
3:19–21	12
3:20	182
3:21	163, 197
3:29	57, 207, 257
3:33	134, 274
4:14	79, 122, 228, 266
4:24	36
4:38	261
4:48	193, 265
5:14	45
5:30	139
5:46	204
6:33	53
6:35	12
6:38	139
6:54	201
6:55	201
6:57	201
6:68	277
7:39	145
8:12	147, 198
8:25	207, 244
8:44	117, 242, 271

9:5	198
10:10	53
10:18	200
10:28–29	161
11:25	3
11:33	132
12:34	155
12:35	181
12:46	198
13:15	166
14:6	3, 4, 34, 48, 51, 53, 64, 114, 119, 142, 154, 161, 177, 181, 196, 199, 202, 204, 205, 217, 222, 224, 271, 274
14:7	110
14:8	233
14:16	65
14:16–17	145
14:17	237
14:23	52
14:26	34
14:30	117
15:21	166
15:26	145
16:33	188
17:3	98
17:22	191
20:28	11, 147, 250

Acts

1:9	53
2:2–3	263
2:11	264
2:17	2
2:18	2
2:25	120
2:28	80
2:38	254
7:39	109
10:34	125
13:3	210
17:27	53, 157

17:28	109	8:29	251
18:25	80	8:31	224
26:14	39	8:32	109, 200
28:27	99	8:34	146, 161, 188, 200, 204

Romans

		8:35	26
1:17	21	9:5	85, 114
1:20	110, 113, 116,	9:12	109
	120, 155, 167,	9:15	161, 167
	168, 266, 267,	9:21	243, 258
	274	10:12	203
1:21	64, 65, 120, 146	10:13–14	1
1:21–22	109	10:15	263
1:22	121	10:20	204
1:23	109	11:7–11	62
1:25	21, 109	11:8	169
1:26	28	11:33	3, 47, 148
1:29	101	11:36	2, 6, 53, 56, 116, 227, 234, 237, 239
2:5	146		
2:6	45	12:2	257, 266, 267, 277
2:11	125		
2:14–15	23	12:3	269
2:15	17	12:5	188
3:4	271	12:11	80
3:14	134	12:12	163, 266
4:5	164, 200, 276	12:19	25
5:5	47, 253, 275	13:1	38
5:6	84, 109, 200	13:11–12	261
5:9	146	13:13–14	138
6:21	27	13:14	148
6:23	200	14:1	138
7:2	168	14:3	188
7:14	126	14:16	141
7:17	134	14:20–21	188
7:20	134	16:18	271
7:22–23	117, 127		
7:24	117	**1 Corinthians**	
7:24–25	127		
8:6	200	1:8	14
8:10	258	1:11	266
8:11	258	1:22	193, 265
8:23	155, 235, 257	1:24	208
8:24	257, 258	1:25	114
8:24–25	208	1:27	263
8:26	234	1:27–28	125

1:30	64	11:29	201
1:31	161	12:1	253
2:6	262, 263	12:7	270, 277
2:9	147, 154	12:12	188
2:11	164, 166, 275	12:22	188
2:12	275	12:27	257, 276
2:14	243, 267	12:31	253
2:15	267, 269	13:2	262
3:1	57, 256, 257, 267	13:4	116
3:1–2	262	13:6	181
3:1–3	243	13:7	164, 165
3:5	269	13:12	82, 119, 156,
3:10	267		163, 166, 231,
3:11	116		252, 260
3:16	190	14:2	272
3:16–17	22	14:20	257
3:17	165	14:22	265
4:1	185, 203	14:22–23	273
4:3	36, 166	15:9	118, 125
4:6	242	15:22	71, 160, 179
4:7	3, 117, 258	15:50	131, 247
4:11	183	15:51	156
4:15	267	15:52	99
5:8	119	15:53	186
5:12	268	15:54	146, 186
6:13	186		
6:19	190	**2 Corinthians**	
6:20	161, 201	1:3	72
7:1	20	1:11	165
7:7	120	1:22	117, 258
7:23	161, 201	2:16	31
7:28	20	3:6	82
7:32–33	20	4:13	4
7:38	185	4:16	146, 168
8:1	116	4:18	146
8:2–3	163	5:1	150, 233, 234
8:6	2, 53, 56, 116,	5:2	190, 257
	227, 234, 237,	5:4	257
	239	5:5	117, 258
8:8	187, 188, 266	5:6	35, 166
9:24	97	5:7	257
9:26–27	186	5:11	164
10:13	166	5:15	201, 265
10:31	201	5:17	261
11:19	115	5:21	233, 251

6:5–6	269
6:10	65
6:16	112, 190
9:15	18
10:17	161, 187
11:3	258
11:9	271
11:14	199
11:27	186
12:8–10	262
12:9–10	165
12:10	35
12:11	262

Galatians

1:20	218
2:6	125
3:1	257
3:11	21
3:13	161
3:28	268
4:4–5	204
4:7	200
4:9	163
4:12	266
4:16	181
4:19	72, 154
4:26	11, 162, 233, 234
5:5	40
5:17	126, 181
6:3	197
6:17	241, 255

Ephesians

1:6	121
1:18	27
2:2	128, 199
2:3	258
2:10	267
2:14–16	71
2:19	230
3:14	253
3:16	168
3:18–19	240
3:19	253
3:20	138, 185
4:2–4	164
4:3	230
4:8	257
4:8–9	53
4:9–10	53
4:13–14	66
4:14	55
4:15	163, 197
4:22	126, 146
4:24	66, 126
4:29	236
5:8	133, 146, 251, 254, 255, 256, 258
5:14	127
5:19	148
5:22	152
5:27	163
6:9	125

Philippians

1:6	166
2:6	200, 233, 250, 251
2:6–11	108
2:8	10, 200, 263
2:12	166
2:12–13	265
2:15–16	261, 263
2:16	252, 256, 277
3:12–14	222
3:13	154, 156, 222, 234, 257
3:18–19	70
3:19	271
4:1	222
4:10	272
4:11–13	187, 272
4:12–13	272
4:13	187
4:14	272
4:15–16	272
4:16	272

4:17	272	2:4	200
4:18	271	2:5	114, 199, 200,
			204, 221
Colossians		3:7	34, 62
1:3	157	4:4	188
1:15	157	5:4	154
1:16	73, 114, 233,	5:6	265
	239, 240	5:9	154, 162
1:16–18	276	5:9–10	80
1:18	82	5:10	72, 154
1:24	82	6:5	242
2:3	201, 204	6:9	62
2:8	121	6:16	229
2:8–9	33	6:20	266
2:14	72, 161	7:18	80
2:14–15	117		
2:16	188	**2 Timothy**	
3:3	254	1:10	53, 200
3:4	53	1:13	151
3:5	136	1:16	271
3:9	146	2:14	236
3:9–10	126, 268	2:15	81
3:10	146, 267, 272,	2:21	126
	277	2:22	265
3:12	148	2:26	34, 62
3:25	125	3:3–4	50
		4:3	115
1 Thessalonians		4:3–4	10
1:6–7	266	4:6	161
2:4	258	4:16	271
2:7	267		
3:8	222	**Titus**	
4:13	158	1:4	116
5:5	258	1:7	75, 90
5:17	72	1:9	115
		1:10	133
2 Thessalonians		1:15	187
3:16	277	2:1	115
		2:8	151
1 Timothy		2:12	8
1:5	158, 236, 242,	3:5	11, 160
	246		
1:8	236, 242, 246	**Hebrews**	
1:10	115	1:2	210
1:15	53	1:5	210

1:11	52	4:14	252
1:12	116, 117, 124,	5:2	75
	166, 210	5:5	1, 45, 108, 194
2:14	117	5:7	201
4:13	163		
5:5	210	**2 Peter**	
5:12–14	262	1:12	154
6:1	265	2:20	103
7:27	200	3:8	210
10:38	21, 53		
11:13–14	162	**1 John**	
12:15	101		
12:29	63	1:1	263
13:5	95	1:5	12, 198, 211
13:16	94	1:6	163, 197
		1:10	242
James		2:16	20, 185, 192, 266
		3:2	258, 260
1:17	34, 57	3:3	152
1:27	265	5:10	242
2:1	125		
2:9	125	**Revelation**	
2:13	161		
2:23	129	2:11	72
4:4	13	3:20	188
4:6	1, 45, 57, 108,	4:8	227, 256
	194	5:9	201
4:11	268	7:17	62
		8:3–4	165
		15:4	188
1 Peter		17:5	22, 122
1:17	125	18:2	122
1:22	152	20:6	72
1:23–25	52	20:14	72
2:3	146, 183	21:2	117, 162, 204
2:9	263	21:4	62
3:1	154	21:6	122
3:1–2	152	21:8	72
3:11	154	21:10	204